ATM
FOUNDATION
FOR BROADBAND
NETWORKS

Other Books by Uyless Black:

Computer Networks: Protocols, Standards, and Interfaces, 2/E, © 1993, 450 pp., cloth, ISBN: 1-13-175605-2

OSI: A Model for Computer Communications Standards, © 1991, 640 pp., cloth, ISBN: 0-13-637133-7

Data Networks: Concepts, Theory, and Practice, © 1989, 877 pp., cloth, ISBN: 0-13-198466-7

Data Communications and Distributed Networks, 3/E, © 1993, 448 pp., cloth, ISBN: 0-13-203464-6

Data Link Protocols, © 1993, 271 pp., cloth, ISBN: 0-13-204918-X

Emerging Communications Technologies, © 1994, 428 pp., cloth, ISBN: 0-13-051500-0

Prentice Hall Series in Advanced Communications Technologies

Emerging Communications Technologies, *Uyless Black*
ATM: Foundation for Broadband Networks, *Uyless Black*

ATM
FOUNDATION
FOR BROADBAND
NETWORKS

UYLESS BLACK

Prentice Hall PTR
Englewood Cliffs, New Jersey 07632

Library of Congress Cataloging-in-Publication Data

Black, Uyless D.
   ATM—foundation for broadband networks / Uyless Black.
     p. cm.
   Includes bibliographical references and index.
   ISBN 0-13-297178-X
   1. Asynchronous transfer mode. 2. Broadband communication
systems. I. Title.
TK5105.35.B53   1995
621.382—dc20   95-5961
                                                CIP

Acquisitions editor: Mary Franz
Cover design: Bruce Kenselaar
Manufacturing buyer: Alexis R. Heydt
Compositor/Production services: Pine Tree Composition

© 1995 by Prentice Hall PTR
Prentice-Hall, Inc.
A Simon & Schuster Company
Englewood Cliffs, New Jersey 07632

The publisher offers discounts on this book when ordered
in bulk quantities.

For more information, contact:
        Corporate Sales Department
        Prentice Hall PTR
        113 Sylvan Avenue
        Englewood Cliffs, NJ 07632

        Phone: 800–382–3419 or 201–592–2498
        FAX: 201–592–2249
        email: dan_rush@prenhall.com

Printed in the United States of America

10 9 8 7 6 5 4 3 2 1

ISBN: 0-13-297178-X

Prentice-Hall International (UK) Limited, *London*
Prentice-Hall of Australia Pty. Limited, *Sydney*
Prentice-Hall Canada, Inc., *Toronto*
Prentice-Hall Hispanoamericana, S.A., *Mexico*
Prentice-Hall of India Private Limited, *New Delhi*
Prentice-Hall of Japan, Inc., *Tokyo*
Simon & Schuster Asia Pte. Ltd., *Singapore*
Editora Prentice-Hall do Brasil, Ltda., *Rio de Janeiro*

I am told by one of my friends that a fictional creature in a novel was discussing the speed of the flight of birds and proclaimed that: perfect speed is being there.

While I do not know about the other thoughts of this creature, I have thought about this one idea many times. Aside from its physical and philosophical implications, it is appropriate to bring to mind that many of the emerging technologies (such as ATM) are attempting to close the gap (the latency) between being in one place, and then another. In this book, the issue is not the flight of birds but the movement of messages of information through a communications network.

Of course, with our current knowledge, we cannot achieve the bird's goal, due to the delay inherent in the physical aspects of travel. So, until we know about (and conquer) other dimensions (if we ever will), we are restricted to interpreting "being there" as the bird's physical flight from one point to another and its quest to make that flight of a shorter duration.

This goal has been an important aspect of communications networks since their inception, and the speed and efficiency of modern networks has surely had a profound effect on our personal and professional lives.

So, this book is dedicated to all of those in our industry who are striving to send the message faster.

At the same time, it is instructive to remember that a faster message does not necessarily make it any better.

Contents

**CHAPTER 3   Layered Protocols, the Architecture
for ATM and SONET Networks   40**

CHAPTER 8   ATM Switching Operations   181

CHAPTER 9   Traffic Management   203

CHAPTER 12   Synchronous Optical Network (SONET)   311

**CHAPTER 13   Signaling: Operations, Administration,
and Maintenance (OAM)   343**

Preface

Recently, one of my clients, who is a systems engineer for a large tele-communications firm, told me that one of her major problems is staying abreast of the technologies that are embedded into her company's products. I hear this statement often. Like many others in our industry, this person does not have the time to read the technical specifications published by the standards organizations and the user forums. She must spend her professional time performing the day-to-day tasks of the job, essentially taking care of her clients and her accounts.

The common lament is that many professionals are barely ahead of their customers in their knowledge and ability to field their questions about not just the company products, but how they fit into an overall telecommunications architecture. Increasingly, this systems engineer has been forced to know about many diverse protocols, standards, and architectures. Her clients query her on topics such as the relationship of ATM and Frame Relay, why Novell uses IPX and not IP, why NetBIOS is not routable, etc.

It is to this person that this series is devoted (indeed, most of my books are so focused). It is my hope that I have provided a series that will meet this engineer's needs in the field.

This book is the second book of Prentice Hall's *Advanced Communications Technologies,* which serves as a complement to the flagship book, *Emerging Communications Technologies.*

I have included a chapter on existing technologies, titled "Emerged Technologies". This chapter is a summary of a chapter of the same title from the flagship book for this series. I have added a section in this chapter on why functions and services of several of these technologies (for data networks) have been reduced or eliminated in an ATM network. I suggest the reader review this chapter for two reasons: (a) to make certain the ISDN, X.25, SS7, and T1/E1 systems are understood, and (b) to understand why ATM operations do not include many functions that are an integral part of current data networks.

The ATM story is far from complete. As of this writing, ATM systems are now being deployed, but some of the ATM standards are still being written. One cannot wait to write a book on emerging technologies until they have "emerged," else there would be no book to write. So, this book represents the state of ATM as of the date of submittal of my work to my publisher.

Notes for the reader:

1. In revised specifications, the ATM Forum is now using the phrase "traffic descriptor" for "user cell rate." Where appropriate, this book uses the former phrase.

2. The ITU-T is in the process of revising its ATM signaling and control procedures Recommendation (switched virtual calls/connections on demand). It is available in draft form as Q.2931. The ATM Forum's specification differs slightly from Q.2931, and this book reflects the ATM Forum's specification. The reader can refer to Appendix E of the ATM Forum UNI 3.1 specification for a comparison of the two specifications.

Introduction

INTRODUCTION

This chapter discusses the current telecommunications technologies in place today. It explains why the telecommunications industry is implementing new communications technologies to overcome the deficiencies of current systems. An analysis is made of the communications requirements of upcoming user applications.

As a prelude to subsequent chapters, a general overview is provided of the asynchronous transfer mode (ATM) and the synchronous optical network (SONET)/synchronous digital hierarchy (SDH) that are being developed to meet the needs of these applications.

THE PRESENT TELECOMMUNICATIONS INFRASTRUCTURE

Scores of books have been written about the impact of the computer on our society, and the flagship book for this series (*Emerging Communications Technologies*) examines this subject. Studies are cited as well about the role of telecommunications, and the recent growth of cordless telephony, optical fiber, cable television, and video-on-demand systems will surely have a profound effect on our professional and personal lives. This book shall not reiterate the thoughts cited in these books, but shall concentrate on the technical underpinnings that must be in place for these technologies to flourish.

Before introducing the asynchronous transfer mode (ATM), a brief review is provided of the current communications infrastructure.

Present Technologies for Voice, Video, and Data Networks

The present communications infrastructure supporting voice, video, and data networks is founded on technology that is over 25 years old. In spite of their age, these networks have served the industry well, even in recent times, for they have provided a cohesive foundation on which to build the modem telecommunications infrastructure.[1] Yet when we consider that the modern commercial computer is only about 35 years of age, and the personal computer came into being in the early 1980s, a 25-year-old technology seems like a technical dinosaur.

In 1962 the U.S. Bell System (as it was known in the pre-divestiture days) installed the first commercial digital voice system in Chicago, Illinois. The system was known as T1, and carried 24 voice channels over copper wire between Bell's telephone offices. As technology improved, T1 was deployed in higher capacity systems. Shortly thereafter, T3 became a common carrier system for users who needed greater capacity than the T1 offerings. The T3 system can transport 28 T1 signals, which means one T3 link can support 672 voice calls.

T1 and T3 have become the foundations for the majority of voice networks systems provided by the telephone companies.[2] While these systems were designed originally for voice systems, they now can be configured to support data and video applications as well.

In the early 1970s, another technology was deployed to support data

---

[1]As of this writing, the favored term for this infrastructure is the "information highway," apparently coined (or made popular) by Al Gore. With all due respect to the Vice President of the United States (and I support his attention to this important aspect of our society), the information highway is being paved already, and is becoming a "highway" with or without the support of a political apparatus. Mr. Gore can certainly aid the process: (1) by helping to dismantle the archaic set of regulations in the telecommunications industry that have existed since divestiture, (2) by encouraging the use of standards among the different vendors, and (3) by supporting additional certification and conformance testing operations (as part of 2). Given that support, the marketplace will take care of the highway.

[2]T1 and T3 are often used synonymously with DS1, and DS3. While DS1 and DS3 are systems that actually use the T1 and T3 carriers, this book will use them interchangeably, in deference to common industry practice.

networks. This technology is called packet switching. Unlike the T1 and T3 networks, packet switching was designed for data applications, and packet switching networks have become the foundation for the majority of data networks.

At about the same time that packet switching networks were being deployed, the International Telecommunications Union-Telecommunication Standardization Sector (ITU-T, formerly the CCITT) published the X.25 specification. As the reader may know, X.25 defines the procedures for user computers to communicate with network machines (packet switches), and to transport data to another user computer. X.25 has become a widely used industry standard and has facilitated the building of standardized communications interfaces among different vendors' machines.

These communications technologies were designed to support fairly modest requirements for voice and data transmissions, at least when compared to modern applications needs. For example, the T1 systems support a transfer rate of 1.544 Mbit/s, and the T3 system operates at approximately 45 Mbit/s. These bit transfer rates may seem high to the reader, but remember that a 45 Mbit/s transport system like T3 only supports 672 voice calls—a lot of T3s have to be in operation to support the public telephone network.

Likewise, X.25 was designed for data systems that operate at only a few bit/s or a few hundred bit/s—typically 600 to 9600 bit/s. Although X.25 can be placed on very high-speed media and can operate quite efficiently at high speeds, a substantial amount of subscriber equipment and software has been designed for modest transfer rates—typically no greater than 19.2 kbit/s.

Once again, sending data at a rate of 19.2 kbit/s may seem fast. After all, this translates to a transfer rate of 2400 characters per second (19,200/8 bits per character), and no one can type in an E-mail message that fast. However, for other applications, this speed is not sufficient. File transfers, database updates, and color graphics (to mention a few) need much greater transfer rates.

Typical voice networks. Table 1–1 provides some examples of typical voice carrier systems. One entry has not been explained. The E1 system (also called CEPT1) is Europe's principal technology for carrier transport systems. Japan's basic technology is also based on T1, but Japan's higher capacity systems are not in alignment with either European or North American systems.

Table 1–1   Typical Voice Carrier Systems

Type	Digital Bit Rate	Voice Circuits	Age	Standard or Proprietary
DS1	1.544 Mbit/s	24	32 years	Standard*
E1	2.048 Mbit/s	30	32 years	Standard*
DS3	44.736 Mbit/s	672	31 years	Standard*

*Within national boundaries

Nonetheless, because telephone networks have historically been highly regulated within a country and controlled by one enterprise (in the United States, AT&T before divestiture, and in other countries, the Postal Telephone and Telegraph Ministries [PTTs]), a national telephone network architecture uses common standards, conventions, and protocols. Thus, interworking different vendors' equipment is relatively simple (telephones, fax devices, and answering machines are common examples). This situation is not true with the architecture for data networks, as we shall see in the next section.

Typical data networks.   In contrast to the voice world, data networks and protocols have evolved into an almost bewildering array of disparate and incompatible systems. Table 1–2 provides a summary of some of the more widely known and used standards and vendor products.

Interconnecting some of these systems is almost impossible. When it is possible, the resulting systems are very complex and very expensive; yet, these systems form the foundation for our current data networks.

As Table 1–2 shows, some systems are standardized while others are proprietary. Also, they may operate as local area networks (LANs), wide area networks (WANs), or both. Most of them were conceived over ten years ago, although all have been enhanced since their inception.

Why are so many incompatible systems in existence to do one thing: transport data between computers? The answer is simple. The data communications and computer industry, unlike the telephone industry, has had very little regulation imposed upon it. Additionally, this industry is quite young, and many systems and products were developed before standards were written by organizations such as the ITU-T, the ISO, and the Internet task forces.

Table 1–2 Typical Data Networks and Protocols

Vendor or Standard	Sponsor	Age[1]	Standard or Proprietary	WAN or LAN[2]
X.25	ITU-T & ISO	20 years	Standard*	WAN
OSI	ITU-T & ISO	10 years	Standard*	Both
TCP/IP	Internet	10 years	Standard**	Both
SNA	IBM	20 years	Proprietary	Both
DECnet	Digital	20 years	Proprietary	Both
AppleTalk	Apple	10 years	Propriety	LAN
Ethernet	Xerox, Digital, Intel	12 years	Standard***	LAN
NetWare	Novell	10 years	Proprietary	LAN

[1]Approximate ages; all have evolved and have been enhanced
[2]WAN is wide area network and LAN is local area network
*Recognized by international standards groups
**A de facto standard by virtue of its wide use
***Revised slightly to become the 802.3 standard

The current status of the evolution of the data communications industry is both good news and bad news. The good news is that the lack of a dominant player (such as "Ma Bell" in the telephone industry) has lead to much competition and the availability of some extraordinary systems and products at reasonable prices. The bad news is that most customers are saddled with single-vendor systems, because a vendor-specific system cannot operate easily with any other vendor's system.

The industry is realizing that competition can continue but under an umbrella of standards. Frankly, many of the systems and products listed in Table 1–2 do just about the same things, but they do them differently.

PRESENT AND FUTURE REQUIREMENTS

In the past few years, the processing power of an ordinary personal computer has increased so rapidly that the terms high-speed workstations and mainframe computers are losing their meanings. Small machines are becoming as powerful the once "large machines."

The reader need only take a brief glance at the daily newspaper to grasp the rapid increases in the power and functionality of the computer. At this writing, Apple Computer is implementing its PowerPC™. It introduces the first "off-the-shelf" voice recognition personal computer. Following these announcements will be the ability to develop video-on-demand through conventional TV sets (with an add-on module) as well as through PCs. Future requirements for PCs will necessitate the development of even higher-speed and more powerful systems.

The communications infrastructure to support the connection of these computers and new applications must also be upgraded. While individual homes and workstations can continue to use conventional, existing media (the coaxial TV cable), the service providers' facilities, media, and networks need more bandwidth.

Downsizing and Outsourcing: Reliance on Telecommunications

In the last few years, several industrialized countries have witnessed a trend known as downsizing. Downsizing entails businesses (mostly large businesses) shedding employees, capital resources, and, in many instances, buildings. With this downsizing comes a new trend—outsourcing. Many of these firms are hiring outside contractors to provide services, such as training, food operations, mailroom operations, and software programming, that were once provided by employees. While these companies must continue their ongoing operations, they are doing it increasingly with distributed computers and communications facilities linking their computers together.

It has long been a cliché that telecommunications is playing one of the most critical roles in our information society and, indeed, in our personal culture. This role will become even more important as more humans learn to interact with the computer and exploit its productivity potential. The trend, of course, will lead toward (this writer hopes) more open societies as the telecommunications infrastructure embeds itself into the fiber of most people's lives. So, without going into a monologue on the benefits of the telecommunications infrastructure, the next section describes some of the problems faced in current communications architecture.

Present Systems: Too Much or Too Little

Voice. For today's voice transport systems, the present structure provides adequate capacity for many applications, but as stated earlier and explained in the flagship book for this series, the capacity is insufficient for others. In addition, these transport systems suffer from the asynchronous nature of their design. In this context, asynchronous means that the components of the network are not synchronized with a common clock. Consequently, it is not unusual for errors to occur between transmitting and receiving machines because the machines are using different timing schemes. (An analogy would be a person talking too fast.)

Perhaps more serious, it is recognized increasingly that these systems have very limited operations, administration, and maintenance (OAM) capabilities, known by many people as network management capabilities. The supposition (30 years ago) of these simple designs made good sense, because the operations needed to support substantial OAM required more overhead than the limited-capacity network could bear. However, with the increased use of high-speed optical fiber and fast processors, building powerful OAM modules within new systems becomes feasible.

Wide area data networks. For data communications networks, ironically, it is believed by many network designers that the current systems (especially WANs) may be doing too much, in that they are performing a number of redundant functions of marginal benefit. We shall have more to say about this idea in subsequent chapters, but for the present, it can be stated that redundant functions are performed on the majority of user traffic. In X.25 for example, sequencing and flow control, as well as positive acknowledgments (ACKs) and negative acknowledgments (NAKs) are performed at least twice.

With the advent of relatively error-free, high-capacity networks, and with the concomitant implementation of very powerful end-user workstations, the new networks take the view that many of these operations are no longer needed in the network. Indeed, many of the functions are simply removed from the network and placed in the customer premises equipment (CPE), such as user workstations, and personal computers.

We return to these important points several times in this book. The reader may refer to Chapter 6 (Errors and Error Rates) and Chapter 7 (Pre-ATM Approach to Traffic Integrity Management and ATM Approach to Traffic Integrity Management) for immediate follow-up on these ideas.

Local area data networks. It is recognized that the processing power of personal computers and workstations is doubling about every two years. Ten MHz processors were considered state-of-the-art in 1990; 25 MHz processors were in use in 1992, and 33 and 50 MHz processors by 1993. As stated, some manufacturers, such as Apple, introduced a 100 MHz processor for the personal computer in 1994. The trend shall continue, and with it an associated need for more bandwidth to support the communications between these machines. A rule-of-thumb, long accepted in the industry, is that a well-tuned computer system has one bit of I/O (input/output) for every instruction cycle. In the not-too-distant future, workstations will appear with processors that operate with a cycle time of about 1 nanosecond, and a performance of 1 billion instructions per second. These workstations will create enormous bandwidth demands on communications networks.

LANs have not kept pace with the progress of the CPUs, and with the exception of the fiber distributed data interface (FDDI), the technology has remained in the 4 to 16 Gbit/s range. As a consequence, the last few years has seen a decrease in the number of computers attached to a LAN segment [HERM93]. This trend cannot continue; it is too expensive and complex. Therefore, a new family of LANs are evolving to meet the increased needs of the user stations. The metropolitan area network (MAN), FDDI, the copper distributed data interface (CDDI), and fast Ethernet are among these solutions. So is ATM, the subject of this book.

Costs of Leased Lines

In the past few years, LANs and WANs have been interconnected with bridges, routers, gateways, and packet-switched networks. These internetworking units connect to the LANs and WANs through dedicated communications channels (leased lines). As a general practice, leased lines are "nailed up" end-to-end through the network to the user's CPE. The user is provided with the leased line on a dedicated basis and the full transmission capacity is available 24 hours a day (with some exceptions). Therefore, the user pays for the circuit regardless of its utilization. Moreover, if a connection is needed to yet another location (say another city in the country), another leased line must be rented from the public telecommunications operators (PTOs), such as AT&T, Sprint, and MCI—once again on a end-to-end, continuous basis.

Even though leased lines are becoming less expensive, the use of these lines to connect internetworking units with LANs and WANs is still a very expensive process. Moreover, reliability problems occur because individual point-to-point leased lines have no backup capability.

A better approach is to develop a LAN/WAN-carrier network that provides efficient switching technologies for backup purposes as well as high-speed circuits—a network that will allow users to share the expensive leased lines. This concept is called a virtual network or a virtual private network (VPN).

VIRTUAL COMPANIES AND VIRTUAL NETWORKS

During the past decade, smaller companies increasingly have been competing successfully against their larger rivals. Indeed, some large companies are so unwieldy and so fraught with bureaucracy and overhead that they cannot compete in many arenas with their smaller counterparts. Of course, the value of economy-of-scale still pertains; for example, my small company is not going to spend the enormous funds needed to develop an ATM switch.

However, the term virtual company is a useful description of a growing industry of small groups or individuals working out of rented business centers or even at home. This type of operation gives the illusion of the traditional private enterprise, but it usually has few or no employees, and may not even have a receptionist! Well, the answering service/answering machine is a virtual receptionist.

An treatise on the reasons for this phenomenon is beyond the scope of this book. Nonetheless, it must be emphasized that the downsizing of companies, and the distribution of workloads to remote offices (and homes), cannot occur without the accompanying supporting communications infrastructure. Indeed, the very premise of deconstruction, downsizing, and outsourcing is based on the idea that the smaller companies and their consultants (who act as virtual employees) will have access to each other through high-speed, reliable communications facilities. Increasingly, the facilities are being implemented with a VPN (an old concept that has been renamed and taken off the shelf for use in today's networks).

The VPN is so named because an individual user or enterprise shares communications channels and facilities with other users. Switches are placed on these channels to allow an end user to have access to multiple end sites. Ideally, users do not perceive that they are sharing a network with each other, thus the term *virtual private network*—you think you have it, but you don't.

Figures 1–1 and 1–2 illustrate the concepts of VPNs and their advantage over dedicated systems. In Figure 1–1(a), four customer sites from company A are connected to each other through dedicated channels (leased lines). While effective, this approach is very expensive, and it is unlikely that these lines are used on a continuous basis. Company B in Figure 1–1(b) has a separate arrangement connecting its four offices with dedicated lines in the same cities as company A.

In contrast, through the use of a VPN (Figure 1–2), the two companies can share the communications facilities. The VPN provider provides

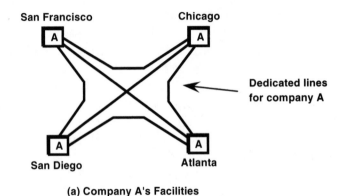

Figure 1–1
Leased lines.

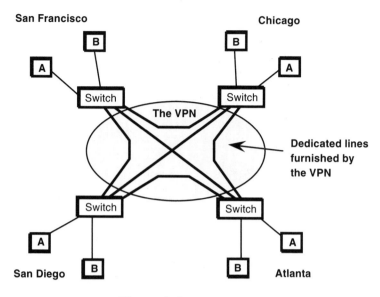

Figure 1–2
Virtual private networks.

a network for multiple users. This approach allows the traffic to be routed to various endpoints and does not require the end-user devices to "nail up" private leased lines. In some implementations, companies migrating to a VPN have reduced their costs by 30 percent vis-à-vis leased lines.

The difference between fully meshed leased lines and VPNs is even more dramatic when another location is added to a private network. If the user (say company A) wishes full connectivity to all sites, this approach requires the leasing of long-distance lines to all cities. Of course, with a fully meshed VPN, the same number of private lines are required between the switches, but the switches are relaying traffic from multiple users. So, if company A adds an office in Dallas, then it would only require the leasing of one dedicated local loop to the most convenient VPN switch. The number of dedicated lines would remain the same as long as additional switches are not added to the network.

VPN is a relatively new term in the computer/communications industry. Yet, this new term describes an old concept; the ideas behind the VPN are not new at all. Public X.25 networks have offered VPN services for years, and switched T1 services also offer VPN-like features. However, we shall see that ATM offers more powerful VPNs than these older technologies.

The first part of this chapter has described some of the problems and challenges that exist in our present climate. The remainder of the chapter describes some solutions, notably ATM and SONET.

FAST RELAY NETWORKS AND ATM

Much of the emerging technology is based on the idea of relaying traffic as quickly as possible. This idea is often called fast packet relay or fast packet switching. These names are considered generic terms in this book and are used in a variety of ways in the industry. Therefore, we will use the term fast relay systems. Currently, fast relay comes in two forms: frame relay and cell relay. Figure 1–3 shows the relationships of these two forms of fast relay systems.

Frame relay uses variable sized protocol data units (PDUs), which are called frames. The technology is based on the link access procedure for the D channel (LAPD) that has long been used in integrated services digital network (ISDN) systems. Most frame-based implementations are using LAPD as the basic frame format for the relaying of the traffic across permanent virtual circuits (PVCs). Recently, a modified version of

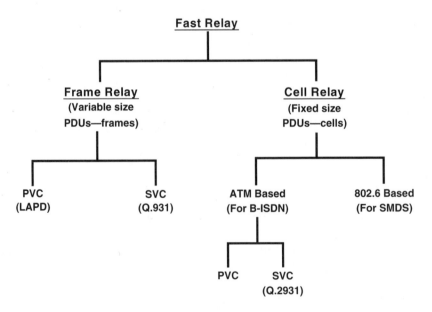

Figure 1–3
Types of relay systems.

ISDN's Q.931 has been introduced into the industry for control signaling, and to set up connections between the user and the network. Although not used much in frame relay today, Q.931 can form the basis for public switched offerings (switched virtual calls [SVCs]). The reader may refer to Chapter 4 for a tutorial on LAPD and Q.931.

In contrast to frame relay, cell relay uses a fixed length PDU, which is called a cell. The cell usually consists of a 48-octet payload with a 5-octet header, although some implementations use different cell sizes. This cell (with slight variations) is being used on both the asynchronous transfer mode (ATM) and the IEEE 802.6 standard, more commonly known as the MAN specification. In turn, the 802.6 standard is being used as a basis for the switched multimegabit data service (SMDS).

The industry is still divided on the advantages and disadvantages of the use of cell relay versus frame relay. While there are arguments for both, the trend is toward the use of the cell relay technology. The reasons are many, but before they are explained, a brief summary of cell relay technology is in order.

At the CPE, such as a computer or a PBX, a customer's traffic, which could be variable in length, is segmented into a smaller fixed length units called cells. As stated earlier, in most cell relay systems, the cells are only 53 octets in length with 5 octets devoted to a header and the remaining 48 octets consisting of user information (the payload). The term cell is used to distinguish this PDU from variable length PDUs (frames and packets).

The term "asynchronous" in asynchronous transfer mode means the cells can be used without precise timing requirements, and not necessarily on a synchronous, periodic basis. The cells may indeed be transported in a synchronous network, but they can be filled based on the needs of the application, which may be in a synchronous or asynchronous fashion. The ATM machines create a continuous stream of cells, and if no traffic is sent, the cells are empty, and are called idle cells.

Cell relay is an integrated approach to networking in that it supports the transmission and reception of voice, video, data, and other applications. This capability is of particular interest to large companies that have developed multiple networks to handle different transmission schemes. As examples, common carriers, telephone companies and Postal Telephone and Telegraph Ministries (PTTs) must support many types of applications, and historically have implemented a variety of networks to support them.

Why do many people prefer the cell technique over the frame technique? First, the use of fixed length cells provides for more predictable performance in the network than with variable length frames. Transmission delay is more predictable, as is queuing delay inside the switches. In addition, fixed-length buffers (with cell relay technology) are easier to manage than variable-length buffers. In essence, a fixed-length cell relay system is more deterministic than the use of a technology with variable length data units. Cell relay is also easier to implement in hardware than with variable length technology.

Some people have expressed concern about the high overhead of cell relay—because of the ratio of 5 octets of header to every 48 octets of user payload. But many people in the industry believe that the constant concern with efficient utilization of raw bandwidth is not a sound approach for the future. With the capacity of optical fiber and high-speed processors that are entering the marketplace, the approach of cell relay is to concentrate on superior quality-of-service features to the user. The philosophy is straightforward: Let the fast optical channels and the fast computers handle the transmission and processing of the overhead traffic.

Figure 1–3 shows several other aspects of the frame and cell relay technologies. Initial implementations of frame relay and cell relay have focused on PVCs (a logical connection to the network that is available at any time). Recent enhancements have added SVCs (a logical connection that is made available on demand, and not available at any time—similar to a dial-up telephone call).

DEVELOPMENT OF ATM

While ATM is just now appearing in the telecommunications industry, it has been the subject of research for many years. However, it was in 1993 that some nine years of work by the standards bodies came to fruition, when the ITU-T and the ATM Forum finalized their recommendations and implementors' agreements respectively. These efforts represent Phase 1 of the ATM standards, and Phase 2 is now in progress.

APPLICATIONS USE OF ATM

The ATM Forum conducted a study of 200 companies to determine their plans for the future in relation to the use of ATM and other technologies [ATM93b]. The study entailed the companies filling in a questionnaire, and then consultant John McQuillan followed up with inter-

Table 1–3   Problems That Existing Technologies Cannot Solve [ATM93b]

Problem	1st Place	2nd Place	3rd Place
1. LAN performance above 100 Mbit/s	5	4	2
2. Scalable WAN bandwidth	5	4	1
3. Integration of voice, video, and data	4	3	1
4. Network management and logistics	2	2	4
5. Uniform architecture in LANs, MANs, WANs	2	2	1
6. Bandwidth on demand (pay for use)	1	3	4
7. Network complexity	1	1	0
8. Support for multicast operations	0	1	1
9. Integration of multiple data applications	0	0	3
10. Support for isochronous applications	0	0	2

views. The numbers in the following figures represent the number of recipients responding to a particular question. The study makes no claim about its statistical validity, but purports to show accurate indications for the near future. As the reader might expect, the initial usage for ATM is focused on data applications, but voice and video will become more important in the future. Most respondents view ATM use for voice, video, and data by 1996.

The survey asked the respondents to identify current problems that existing technologies cannot solve. The responses shown in Table 1–3 are similar to those concerns that this writer hears from clients as well. Certainly, the top seven answers in this survey are what I find.

This writer also confirms the answers to the question shown in Table 1–4. Most of my findings reveal that companies are looking for ATM to solve interconnection and capacity problems in the LAN area. Even though the ITU-T originally envisioned ATM as a high-capacity wide area network technology, the local area network is seen as an area equally important for ATM use.

Table 1–4 Planned Uses of ATM [ATM93b]

Use	1st Place	2nd Place	3rd Place
1. ATM LANs for workgroups	8	1	2
2. ATM backbones for LANs	5	9	2
3. Private ATM WAN	4	1	2
4. ATM upgrades to hubs and routers	1	5	6
5. Private ATM MAN	1	2	3
6. Public national ATM service	1	1	1
7. Public metropolitan ATM service	0	2	1
8. Data ATM concentrators to public networks	0	0	2
9. ATM PBXs	0	0	1

In the past ten years, users have become increasingly wary of vendors' claims about their products. This has happened for three reasons. First, vendor products often do not deliver what the marketing people have advertised. Second, the press is more aware today, and problems are reported more than in the past. Third, users are more knowledgeable and more sophisticated.

These facts are certainly evident from the response to the question of possible barriers to the use of ATM (Table 1–5). Once again, this writer has found that the interoperability problem is "bubbling up" more and more. Users understand that systems are growing more complex, and with that come bugs, design deficiencies, and interoperability problems. Of course, the answers relating to costs are always high on the list of concerns of any manager.

The concluding chapter of this book will revisit the subject of ATM applications, and users' views of ATM. For the present, let us take a necessary diversion into SONET.

FAST RELAY NETWORKS AND SONET

At the beginning of this chapter, it was stated that for the first time in the history of the computer/communications industry, networks throughout the world are embracing a worldwide set of computer/communica-

Table 1–5   Possible Barriers to the Use of ATM [ATM93b]

Barrier	1st Place	2nd Place	3rd Place
1. Noninteroperable ATM products	7	0	2
2. High equipment costs	3	2	3
3. High communications costs	2	2	5
4. Performance problems	2	0	1
5. Incomplete ATM standards	1	3	1
6. Fear, uncertainty, doubt (FUD factor)	1	2	0
7. Lack of applications	1	2	0
8. Conservatism about untried technology	1	0	1
9. Lack of widely available public ATM networks	0	3	2
10. High operations costs	0	2	0
11. No ATM access below T3	0	1	3

tions standards. One of these standards deals with multiplexing and signaling hierarchies for carrier transport networks. Because of its importance, we shall introduce the subject here, and examine it more closely in later chapters.

During the past 30 years, three different digital multiplexing and signaling hierarchies have evolved throughout the world. These hierarchies were developed in Europe, Japan, and North America. Fortunately, all are based on the same pulse code modulation (PCM) signaling rate of 8,000 samples a second, yielding 125 microsecond sampling slots (1 second/8000 samples = .000125). Therefore, the basic architectures interwork reasonably well.

But the regions vary in how the systems are implemented, which results in extensive and expensive conversion operations, if traffic is exchanged between them (Figure 1–4). Moreover, the analog-to-digital conversion schemes also differ between North America and Europe, which further complicates interworking the disparate systems.

Japan and North America base their multiplexing hierarchies on the DS1 rate of 1.544 Mbit/s. Europe uses a 2.048 Mbit/s multiplexing scheme. Thereafter, the three approaches multiplex these payloads into larger multiplexed packages at higher bit rates, and use different values for the multiplexing integer n.

As depicted in Figure 1–4, the synchronous digital hierarchy (SDH, European term) and the synchronous optical network (SONET, North American term) support the schemes that have been in existence for many years, but specify a different multiplexing hierarchy.

The basic SDH/SONET rate is 155.52 Mbit/s. SDH/SONET then uses an x 155.52 multiplexing scheme, with x as the multiplexing factor (e.g., 155.52 * x, where x is 3, 6, etc.). Rates smaller than 155.52 Mbit/s are available at 51.840 Mbit/s. We shall have more to say about Figure 1–4 in later chapters; the other terms in this figure will be explained at that time.

At long last, worldwide agreement has been reached (with minor

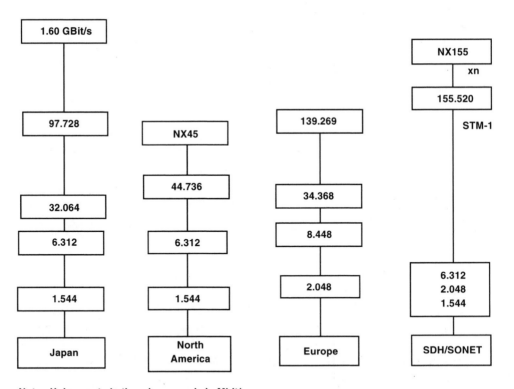

Note: Unless noted otherwise, speeds in Mbit/s

Figure 1–4
SONET and SDH hierarchies.

exceptions) on a common transport scheme. This agreement can only foster new technologies and decrease the costs of implementing them.

BROADBAND ISDN

The ITU-T describes the broadband integrated services digital network (B-ISDN) as a network built on the concepts of the ISDN model, and a network that is implemented with the ATM and SONET technologies. These two technologies are complementary to each other, as shown in Figure 1–5. In its simplest form, the SONET technology acts as the physical carrier transport system for the user payload. The user payload is carried in ATM cells. In other words, the SONET network acts as a service provider to the ATM traffic.

Figure 1–5 also shows that the ATM components can act as the user-to-network interface (UNI) with the user's CPE. This approach allows the user to negotiate a wide variety of services at the ATM node.

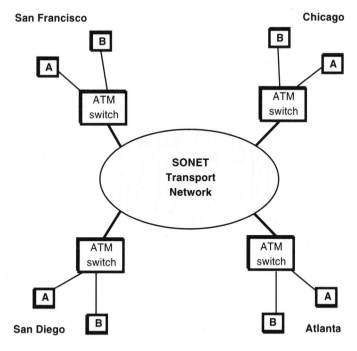

Figure 1–5
ATM and SONET.

Table 1–6   Broadband ISDN (B-ISDN)

Vendor or Standard	Sponsor	Age[1]	Standard or Proprietary	WAN or LAN
ATM	ITU-T	2–4 years	Standard	Both
SONET	ITU-T	5–6 years	Standard	Both[2]

[1]Standards are still under development

[2]Although most SONETs are deployed in WANs

In addition, a SONET system can be terminated at ATM switches. These switches relay the traffic onto outgoing SONET ports or onto local UNIs.

ATM and SONET form the "technical alliance" for B-ISDN. SONET provides extensive operations, administration, and maintenance (OAM) functions and the basic carrier transport services, and ATM provides direct services and interfaces to the user machine, as well as switching operations between SONET communications links.

As explained in subsequent chapters, one component of ATM also allows the ATM node to process and support multiapplication systems such as voice, video, data, music, and FAX.

Table 1–6 summarizes several aspects of ATM and SONET. As explained earlier, both are international standards sponsored by the ITU-T and several other national standards bodies. Although the age columns in Table 1–6 suggest they are rather mature technologies, these numbers reflect the period in which research has been conducted and implementations occurring. Indeed, SONET and ATM are still evolving as of this writing, and research on the use of these technologies continues. Both SONET and ATM can operate on WANs or LANs, although most implementations of SONET have been in large public wide area carrier transport systems.

The reader might wish to compare Table 1–6 with Tables 1–1 and 1–2, which summarize the emerged technologies. The first thing to note is that ATM and SONET are considered to be single solutions to transport and switching systems in contrast to the multiplicity of standards and proprietary implementations that the industry has fostered in the past. This writer is not suggesting that ATM and SONET are replacements for all the technologies in Tables 1–1 and 1–2. Such is not the case at all. Rather, the design goal of the B-ISDN technologies is to provide for backbone transport systems for voice, data, and video applications. Notwithstanding this goal, ATM and SONET, if implemented properly, could result in the paring down or even elimination of some of the technologies listed in Tables 1–1 and 1–2. The rationale for this statement shall be supported in other chapters of this book.

SUMMARY

It is recognized that upcoming user applications are demanding greater throughput, and lower delay from communications systems. ATM and SONET are designed to provide the capacity to support these applications.

Optical fiber systems are providing the foundation for the media support of these technologies and high-speed processors are providing the speed to process the traffic.

The movement toward world-wide standards for carrier transport technology, multiplexing techniques, and switching methodologies are at last providing the groundwork for a comprehensive and homogeneous approach to computer/communications networks.

The Nature of Analog and Digital Systems

INTRODUCTION

This chapter provides a general overview of analog and digital transmission systems. It explains how voice and data images are transported over a communications channel, and compares analog and digital networks. The concepts of analog modulation are explained, as well as analog-to-digital conversion schemes. The latter part of the chapter deals with network synchronization, timing, and clocks, and contrasts asynchronous, synchronous, plesiochronous, and mesochronous networks.

The reader who has experience with these subjects need only glance through the first part of this chapter. The latter part of the chapter deals with network synchronization, timing, and clocks. A review of this material is important for all readers (unless the reader works in this field).

ANALOG SYSTEMS

Even though telecommunications systems have evolved from single application networks (voice-only, data-only) to multiapplication networks, the legacy of voice remains in many systems. Consequently, this chapter reviews some of the pertinent characteristics of communications signals and voice transmission as they relate to the subject matter of this book.

Speech is actually a physical disturbance of the air; in effect, it is slight movements of air molecules produced by the human voice. In its essential physical nature, speech is nothing more than a pressure change in the air. Air molecules in close proximity to the mouth push against air molecules in front of them, and, in turn, these molecules push on other molecules further from the mouth. The sound propagates through the air, and gradually diminishes in intensity as the disturbance moves further away from the speaking person. The various pressure fluctuations are received by the ear, converted into nerve impulses, and interpreted by the brain as speech.

The speech pattern produces various levels of air pressure. Certain utterances create more air pressure than others. Periods of high-pressure sound signals are called condensations (the air is compressed), and periods of low sound levels are called rarefactions (the air is less dense). Human speech is a continuous train of these sound waves. The changes in air pressure are gradual (and continuous, if the speech is sustained) from high to low pressure. The shape of the signal resembles a wave and is actually called a sound wave. Talking or singing creates a complex set of waveforms that change in pressure several hundred to several thousand times per second.

The telephone handset transforms the physical speech waveform into an electrical waveform. Both waves have very similar characteristics. For example, the various heights of the sound wave are translated by the telephone into signals of continuously variable electrical voltages, or currents. The voice waveform spoken into a telephone creates an electrical alternating current: The voltage alternating reverses its polarity, which produces current that reverses its direction.

CYCLES, FREQUENCY, AND PERIOD

The wavelength measures the cycle of the wave; that is, the interval of space or time in which the waveform reaches a successive point. The cycle describes a complete oscillation of the wave. The number of oscillations of the acoustical or electrical wave in a given period (usually a second) is called the frequency (f). Frequency is expressed in cycles per second, or more commonly hertz (Hz). Frequency describes the number of cycles that pass a given point in one second (for example, our ear, a telephone mouthpiece, or a receiver in a computer). The signal travels one wavelength during the time of one cycle.

The time required for the signal to be transmitted over a distance of one wavelength is called the period (T). The period describes the duration of the cycle and is a function of the frequency:

$$T = 1/f$$

Also, frequency is the reciprocal of the period:

$$f = 1/T$$

Sound waves (as well as other waveforms such as electrical and light waves) propagate through the air or other media at a certain speed. The velocity (V) of a sound wave is about 1090 feet (332 meters) per second, measured at 0 degrees Celsius. The propagation speed of any waveform is calculated as:

$$V = f * (l)$$

Since velocity (V), frequency (f), and wavelength (l) are interrelated, if any two of the values are known, the third can be calculated:

$$V = f * l; \quad l = V/f; \quad f = V/l$$

The transmission medium also determines the propagation velocity. For example, sound travels about four times faster in water than in air and about 15 times faster in metal. Sound propagation velocity also increases with each degree increase in temperature (about 2 feet or 0.6 meters per second).

Voice signals move away from our mouths at about 1090 feet per second in a circular expanding pattern. The train of compressions and rarefactions create the waveform.

BANDWIDTH

The analog voice signal is not made up of one unique frequency. Rather, the voice signal on a communications line consists of waveforms of many different frequencies. The particular mix of these frequencies is what determines the sound of a person's voice. Many phenomena manifest themselves as a combination of different frequencies. The colors in the rainbow, for instance, are combinations of many different lightwave frequencies; musical sounds consist of different acoustic frequencies that are interpreted as higher or lower pitch. These phenomena consist of a range or band of frequencies, called the bandwidth, and stated as:

$$BW = f_1 - f_2$$

where: BW = bandwidth; f_1 = highest frequency; f_2 = lowest frequency.

As examples, a piano can produce a wide range of frequencies ranging from about 30 Hz (low notes) to over 4200 Hz (high notes). Its bandwidth is from 30 Hz to 4200 Hz. The human ear can detect sounds over a range of frequencies from around 40 to 18,000 Hz, but the telephone system does not transmit this band of frequencies. The full range is not needed to interpret the voice signal at the receiver, because most of the energy is concentrated between 300 and 3100 Hz. In fact, the vowels in speech occupy mostly the lower portion of the frequency band and the consonants, which actually contain most of the information in speech, use much less power and generally occupy the higher frequencies. Due to economics, only the frequency band of approximately 200 to 3500 Hz is transmitted across the path.

It is not necessary to reproduce the speech signals with complete accuracy on the channel, because the human ear is not sensitive to precise frequency differences, and the human brain possesses great inferential powers to reconstruct the intelligence of the speech. Even with the frequency cutoffs, 98 percent of the speech energy and 85 percent of the intelligence are still present in a transmission. Nonetheless, the bandlimited channel is one reason why voice conversations sound different on a telephone line.

The so-called voiceband (or voice-grade) channel is defined as a band of 4000 Hz. This means the channel consists of frequencies ranging from 0 to 4000 Hz. The speech signal is bandlimited to between 200 and 3500 Hz. For purposes of convenience and brevity, this book uses the value 3 kHz as the bandwidth for a voiceband channel. The other frequencies on both sides of the speech signal allow for guardbands, which lessen interference among the channels that are placed on the same physical medium, such as a wire or a cable.

We have learned that speech signals on a voiceband channel are made up of many frequencies. This also holds true for other communications circuits such as radio and television channels. The spectrum of the signal describes the range of frequencies of the signal, or its bandwidth.

Bandwidth is a very important concept in communications because the capacity (stated in bits per second) of a communications channel is partially dependent on its bandwidth. If the telephone channel were increased from a bandwidth of 3 kHz to 20 kHz, it could carry all the characteristics of the voice. The same is true for transmitting data; a higher data transmission rate can be achieved with a greater bandwidth.

The greater the bandwidth, the greater the capacity. The frequency spectrum ranges from the relatively limited ranges of the audio frequencies through the radio ranges, the infrared (red light) ranges, the visible light frequencies, and up to the X-ray and cosmic ray bands. The importance of the higher frequencies can readily be seen by an examination of the bandwidth of the audio-frequency spectrum and that of radio. The bandwidth between 10^3 and 10^4 is 9,000 Hz (10,000 − 100 = 9000), which is roughly the equivalent to three voice-grade bands. The bandwidth between 10^7 and 10^8 (the HF and VHF spectrum) is 90,000,000 Hz (100,000,000 − 10,000,000 = 90,000,000), which could support several thousand voice band circuits.

BROADBAND AND BASEBAND SIGNALS

Signals are usually categorized as either broadband or baseband. A broadband signal is identified by the following characteristics (other definitions follow):

- Uses analog waveforms
- Has a large bandwidth (typically in the megahertz to gigahertz range)
- Uses analog modulation
- Often uses frequency division multiplexing for channel sharing

A baseband signal is identified by the following characteristics:

- Uses digital signals (voltage shifts)
- Bandwidth is limited
- Does not use modulation
- May use time division multiplexing for channel sharing

Many people use the term baseband to describe an unmodulated signal. A baseband signal may be used to modulate an analog carrier signal, but the carrier need not be a broadband carrier; it may be a voiceband carrier, which is not considered a broadband signal.

Other Definitions of Broadband

The previous description of broadband is one that had been used in the industry in the past. With some of the emerging technologies, the standards groups have changed this description. Some define a broadband network as any system that operates above the T1/E1 primary rate (1.544 Mbit/s in North America/Japan, and 2.048 Mbit/s in Europe). Others define broadband as any system that utilizes ISDN architecture with transfer rates above the primary rate. Still others view broadband as any system that uses the ISDN architecture and integrates SONET/SDH and ATM into the architecture.

CHANNEL (LINK) CAPACITY

Channel capacity is determined by, dependent upon, or related to several factors:

Bandwidth

Transmission rate (bits per second)

Amount of noise on the channel

Modulation technique utilized

Encoding techniques

Let us examine the relationship of bandwidth to data rate (later we will add the other factors are discussed, but the bandwidth analysis is sufficient for the present). The greater the bandwidth of a channel, the greater the data rate (in bits per second). Conversely, the greater the data rate, the greater the bandwidth must be to support the data rate. For example, if a positive voltage represents a binary 0 and a negative voltage represents a binary 1, then a channel can support two voltage changes per cycle. The periodic waveforms can represent a 1 or 0 in each half of the cycle.

It is instructive to note that each period (t) contains a bit value of 0 or 1, so the data rate in bits per second is $2f_1$. If f_1 is 1000 Hz_1, the bit rate is 2000 bit/s, a 5th harmonic is needed to adequately shape the signal on the channel. Consequently, the bandwidth (W) requirement for 2000 bit/s is: $5f_1 - f_1 = 4$ kHz. A bandwidth of twice the data rate provides an accurate representation of the binary 1 or 0, but later discussions demonstrate that the signal can be recovered with less bandwidth.

Noiseless Channels and Harry Nyquist

Nyquist [NYQU24] showed that a channel with bandwidth W can carry 2W symbols per second. However, if a signal change takes the form of more than two states (for example, four voltage levels), then the channel capacity is 4W symbols per second. Four symbols can represent any combination of 0 and 1:

00	first symbol possibility
01	second symbol possibility
10	third symbol possibility
11	fourth symbol possibility

Eight alternative voltages per signal change (i.e., baud) can be used to provide any possible combination of 3 bits ($2^3 = 8$). Sixteen voltages per baud represent any combination of 4 bits ($2^4 = 16$) and so on.

From the above discussion, it follows that in the absence of noise, channel capacity (C) is stated as:

$$C = 2W \log_2 L$$

Generally, speaking, n bits can be transmitted by 2^n possible signaling levels. A signal with a signaling rate of 2nW bit/s can be sent through a channel with W Hz of bandwidth. The following relationship exists:

$$2^n = L \text{ therefore:}$$

$$n = \log_2 L$$

where L is the number of signaling levels (i.e., multiple amplitude levels or multiple combinations of phase changes). An 8-level transmitter (for example, a typical modem), yielding 3 bits per baud provides a C of 18,300 bit/s on a noiseless channel.

We now know how modern systems achieve such a high bit rate across a seemingly low capacity voiceband telephone line: by multilevel signaling.

The inquiring reader might wonder if this equation restricts the volume of L. Indeed, why not make L very large and achieve a very high data rate? Several factors restrict the magnitude of L value. First, the electrical properties of the line restrict L (resistance, capacitance, attenuation, etc.). Second, the larger the value of L, the smaller the increments must be between the levels within the signal. If a signal is restricted to 5 volts, a large L value means the signal voltage differences are quite small. As a result, the receiver must be very sophisticated (and expensive) to discern the small differences between the small voltages. Moreover, any slight distortion on the channel makes the voltage differences indistinguishable from each other. Third, the channel is not noiseless; the signal must manifest itself in the presence of noise, which limits C rather dramatically.

Noisy Channels

With this in mind, we must examine the characteristics of one type of noise. Then we can understand the implications of the works of Shannon [SHAN48].

The noise to which we refer is the thermal noise, and all communications conductors and electronic circuitry possess it. It cannot be eliminated. Thermal noise is called Gaussian noise, because its amplitude varies randomly around a certain level. It is also called white noise, because the noise is distributed uniformly (i.e., averaged) across the frequency spectrum, just as white light is an average of all the color frequencies.

In a conductor, such as a wire or a cable, the nonrandom movement of electrons creates an electric current that is used for the transmission signal. Along with these signals, all electrical components also experience the vibrations of the random movement of electrons. These vibrations cause the emission of electromagnetic waves of all frequencies. Other kinds of noise exist that can affect transmission quality. For example, space noise results from the sun and other stars radiating energy over a broad frequency spectrum. Atmospheric noise comes from electrical disturbances in the earth's atmosphere.

The thermal noise (N) present in an electrical conductor can be calculated as:

$$N = k\,TW$$

where k is Boltzmann's constant ($1.37 * 10^{-23}$ joules per degree), T is temperature in degrees (Kelvin), and, W is bandwidth (note that bandwidth [W] is one determinant of thermal noise).

Some twenty years after the work of Nyquist, Claude Shannon developed a set of theories that have become known as Shannon's Law. It is best known by the concept that the capacity (C) of a channel (in bit/s) is determined by its bandwidth (W) and the ratio of the power in the signal to the power in the noise:

$$C = W \log_2 (1 + S/N)$$

where S is the power in the signal and N is the power in the thermal noise.

The law is not refutable. We can certainly achieve faster data rates by increasing the bandwidth, increasing the signal power, or both. Nonetheless, Shannon's Law sets the absolute data transmission rate that can be achieved.

The Signal-to-Noise Ratio

A typical voice grade line yields a S/N ratio of 1000 to 1. Given a bandwidth of 3100 Hz, the channel could theoretically support a data transmission rate of 30.8 kbit/s (C = 3100 $\log_2$ (1 + 1000/1) = 38,894). (Many user devices do not utilize the full voiceband spectrum and are much slower.) This theoretical rate is further constrained by other factors such as signal decay (attenuation) and other types of noise. Consequently, modern powerful high speed modems operate at lesser speeds, generally from 9.6 kbit/s to 19.2 kbit/s, and add compression techniques to increase the throughput.

The signal-to-noise ratio is often used to determine an effective data rate and a permissible S/N value. This determination rests on the ratio of energy level per bit (E_b) to the energy level per Hertz (N_0), or E_b/N_0. At a given bit rate, the increase of N_0 also requires an increase in E_b. Moreover, at a given E_b/N_0, an increase in the data transmission rate increases the number of bits that will be distorted. Consequently, the ratio is important because the power level must be increased relative to noise to support an increased bit rate.

THE ANALOG-TO-DIGITAL CONVERSION PROCESS

The process of digitization was developed to overcome some of the limitations of analog systems. Several problems arise regarding the analog signal and how it is transmitted across the channel. First, the signal is relayed through amplifiers and other transducers. These devices are designed to perform the relaying function in a linear fashion; that is, the waveform representing the signal maintains its characteristics from one end of the channel to the other. A deviation from this linearity creates a distortion of the waveform. All analog signals exhibit some form of non-linearity (therefore, a distortion). Unfortunately, the intervening components to strengthen the signal, such as amplifiers, also increase the non-linearity of the signal.

Second, all signals (digital and analog) are weakened (or attenuated) during transmission through the medium. The decay can make the signal so weak that it is unintelligible at the receiver. A high-quality wire cable with a large diameter certainly mitigates decay, but it cannot be eliminated.

Digital systems overcome these problems by representing the transmitted data with digital and binary images. The analog signal is converted to a series of digital numbers and transmitted through the communications channel as binary data.

Of course, digital signals are subject to the same kinds of imperfections and problems as the analog signal—decay and noise. However, the digital signal is discrete: The binary samples of the analog waveform are represented by specific levels of voltages, in contrast to the nondiscrete levels of an analog signal. Indeed, an analog signal has almost infinite variability. As the digital signal traverses the channel, it is only necessary to sample the absence or presence of a digital binary pulse—not its degree, as in the analog signal.

The mere absence or presence of a signal pulse can be more easily recognized than the magnitude or degree of an analog signal. If the digital signals are sampled at an acceptable rate and at an acceptable voltage level, the signals can then be completely reconstituted before they deteriorate below a minimum threshold. Consequently, noise and attenuation can be completely eliminated from the reconstructed signal. Thus, the digital signal can tolerate the problems of noise and attenuation much better than the analog signal.

The periodic sampling and regeneration process is performed by regenerative repeaters. The repeaters are placed on a channel at defined intervals. The spacing depends on the quality and size of the conductor, the amount of noise on the conductor, its bandwidth, and the bit rate of the transmission. These thoughts are summarized in Figure 2–1.

Sampling, Quantizing, and Encoding

Several methods are used to change an analog signal into a representative string of digital binary images. Even though these methods entail many processes, they are generally described in three steps: sampling, quantizing, and encoding (Figure 2–2).

The devices performing the digitizing process are called channel banks or primary multiplexers. They have two basic functions: (1) con-

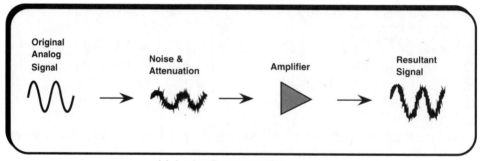

(a) Analog Reconstruction

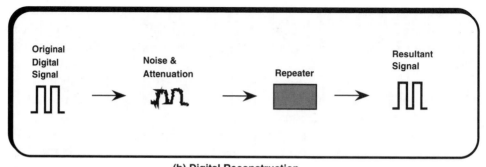

(b) Digital Reconstruction

Figure 2–1
Digital versus analog systems.

verting analog signals to digital signals (and vice versa at the other end); and (2) combining (multiplexing) the digital signals into a single time division multiplexed (TDM) data stream (and demultiplexing them at the other end).

Analog-to-digital conversion is based on Nyquist sampling theory, which states that if a signal is sampled instantaneously at regular intervals and at a rate at least twice the highest frequency in the channel, the samples will contain sufficient information to allow an accurate reconstruction of the signal.

The accepted sampling rate in the industry is 8000 samples per second. Based on Nyquist sampling theory, this rate allows the accurate reproduction of a 4 kHz channel, which is used as the bandwidth for a voice-grade channel. The 8000 samples are more than sufficient to capture the signals in a telephone line if certain techniques (discussed shortly) are used.

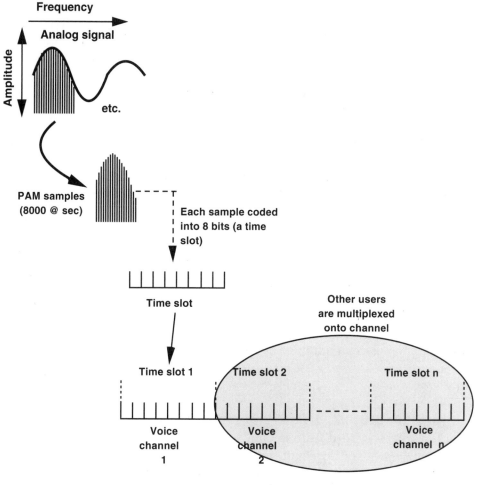

Figure 2–2
Analog-to-digital conversion.

With pulse amplitude modulation (PAM), the pulse carrier ampli-tude is varied with the value of the analog waveform. The pulses are fixed with respect to duration and position. PAM is classified as a modu-lation technique because each instantaneous sample of the wave is used to modulate the amplitude of the sampling pulse.

The 8 kHz sampling rate results in a sample pulse train of signals with a 125 microseconds (µs) time period between the pulses (1 sec-ond/8000 = .000125). Each pulse occupies 5.2 µs of this time period. Consequently, it is possible to interleave sampled pulses from other sig-nals within the 125 µs period. The most common approach in North

America utilizes 24 interleaved channels, which effectively fills the 125 µs time period (.0000052 * 24 = .000125). The samples are then multiplexed using TDM and put into a digital TDM frame. TDM provides an efficient and economical means of combining multiple signals for transmission on a common facility, and is examined in a later section of this book.

Other Coding Schemes

Differential pulse code modulation (DPCM).   Today's systems have more sophisticated approaches than the conventional PCM technique. One widely used system is differential pulse code modulation (DPCM). This technique encodes the differences between samples of the signal instead of the actual samples. Since an analog waveform's samples are closely correlated with each other (almost sample-to-sample redundant), the range of sample differences requires fewer bits to represent the signal. Studies reveal that the predictability between adjacent 8 kHz samples is 85 percent or higher. This redundancy in the PCM codes can be exploited to reduce the bit rate.

However, DPCM is subject to errors when an input signal changes significantly between samples. The DPCM equipment is not able to code the change accurately, which results in large quantizing errors and signal distortion.

Adaptive DPCM.   DPCM can be improved by assigning the 4-bit signals to represent different ranges of the signal. For example, the 4 bits can be coded to represent a change between samples. This technique is called adaptive DPCM, because the systems increase or decrease the volume range covered by each 4-bit sample value.

ADPCM uses a differential quantizer to store the previous sample in a sample-and-hold circuit. The circuit measures the change between the two samples and encodes the change. Differential PCM achieves a smaller voice digitization rate (VDR) than do the conventional PCM techniques (32 kbit/s, for example). These systems have seen extensive use in digital telephony.

Adaptive predictive DPCM.   Some DPCM systems use a feedback signal (based on previous samples) to estimate the input signal. These systems are called adaptive predictive DPCM. The technique is quite useful if the feedback signal varies from the input (due to quantization problems) and the next encoding sample automatically adjusts for the drift. Thus, the quantization errors do not accumulate over a prolonged period.

Many systems store more than one past sample value, with the last three sample values commonly used. The previous samples are then used to produce a more accurate estimate of the next input sample.

Since DPCM and ADPCM do not send the signal but the representation of the change from the previous sample, the receiver must have some method for knowing where the current level is. Due to noise, the level may vary drastically or during periods of speech silence (no talking), several samples may be zero. Periodically, the sender and receiver may be returned (referenced) to the same levels by adjusting them to zero.

TIMING AND SYNCHRONIZATION IN DIGITAL NETWORKS

With the advent of digital networks and the transmission and reception of binary pulses (1s and 0s) it became important to devise some method for sampling these signals accurately at the receiver. In older systems that operate at a relatively low bit rate, the sampling did not have to be very accurate, because the pulse did not change on the line very often. There is an inverse relationship between the number of bits on a channel (in a measured period of time), and the length of time the bit manifests itself at a receiver.

As the networks became faster and more bits per second were transmitted, the time the bits were on the channel decreased significantly. This meant that if there was a slight inaccuracy in the timing of the sampling clock, it might not detect a bit, or, more often, it might not detect several hundred bits in succession. This situation leads to a problem called "slips." Slipping is the loss of timing and the loss of the detection of bits.

PLESIOCHRONOUS NETWORKS

The early systems deployed in the early 1960s were not synchronized to any common frequency source, because they consisted of analog circuits, and did not need a precise timing setup. However, as digital networks were employed with the use of T1 technology, timing became an increasing problem. These digital networks were not synchronized to a common frequency, and thus they were called asynchronous networks. (Actually, T1 systems are plesiochronous because the timing is very tightly controlled.)

Each T1 portion of the network is synchronized to a highly accurate primary reference source (PRS) clock. These clocks operate at a stratum 1 clock level which are required to provide a minimum long-term accuracy of $\pm 1.0 * 10^{-11}$. Consequently, at the worst case, the stratum clock will experience one timing error (called a slip) every 20 weeks. Because of this performance and the fact that this technique is fairly inexpensive, PRS clocks are a cost-effective way to improve network performance.

A so-called synchronous network is distinguished by the use of one PRS called the master clock. All components derive their clocking from this master clock. Timing is derived first for the master clock, and then from a slave (for example), a toll office, and then to digital switches, digital cross connects, end offices, and so on. Timing is cascaded down to other equipment such as channel banks and multiplexers.

THE SYNCHRONOUS CLOCK HIERARCHY

Table 2–1 summarizes the synchronous network clock hierarchy and shows long-term accuracy for each stratum level, as well as typical locations of the clocking operations. A more stringent requirement rests with stratum 1 clocks, which are typically positioned as a PRS. Long-term accuracy for stratum 1 clocks is $\pm 1.0 * 10^{-11}$. The next level of accuracy is the stratum 2 clock, which is usually located in class 4 toll offices. The long-term accuracy for these clocks is $\pm 1.6 * 10^{-8}$. Next in the order of accuracy are the stratum 3 clocks, typically located in the class 5 end office or a digital cross connect (DCS). The long term accuracy of these clocks is $\pm 4.6 * 10^{-6}$. The last level of the synchronous network clock

Table 2–1   Clock Hierarchy for Synchronous Networks

Clock Stratum	Typical Location(s)	Long-Term Accuracy (Minimum)
1	Primary Reference Source (PRS)	$\pm 1.0 \times 10^{-11}**$
2	Class 4 office	$\pm 1.6 \times 10^{-8}$
3	Class 5 office, DCS	$\pm 4.6 \times 10^{-6}$
4	Channel bank, end-user Mux	$\pm 32 \times 10^{-6}$

**Also annotated as .00001 ppm (parts per million)

hierarchy is stratum 4 clock. These clocks are usually located in channel banks or multiplexers at the end-user site. Their accuracy is $\pm 32 * 10^{-6}$.

CLARIFICATION OF TERMS

The terms asynchronous networks, plesiochronous networks, synchronous networks, and mesochronous networks are used in a variety of ways. To be precise, an asynchronous network is one in which timing between the network elements is not maintained. If the timing is maintained between the components, then is it not very accurate. As an extreme example, asynchronous data communications protocols (such as XModem) have no common clocks, but derive their timing from start and stop bits in the data stream. In contrast, a synchronous network is one in which the network elements are aligned together with precise timing arrangements. The payloads can be traced back to a common reference clock. Some people use yet another term—a mesochronous network. Strictly speaking, a mesochronous network's elements are timed to the same source, and all elements are exactly the same. Mesochronous networks are expensive, and hard to achieve. Therefore, another term is used to describe a precisely timed network, or networks—plesiochronous. The term is derived from plesio, which is a Greek term meaning "nearly." Today's networks are actually plesiochronous networks in that they do not use synchronous timing, but very precise timing whose variances must fall within a very narrow range. So, in summary, a plesiochronous network is one in which network elements are timed by separate clocks with almost the same timing.

TIMING VARIATIONS

While synchronous networks exhibit very accurate timing, some variation will inevitably exist among the network elements within a network and network elements among networks. This variation, which is generally known phase variation, is usually divided into jitter and wander. Jitter is defined as a short-term variation in the phase of a digital signal, which includes all variations above 10 Hz. Causes of jitter include common noise, the bit stuffing processes in multiplexers, or faulty repeaters. In contrast, wander is the long-term variation in the phase of a signal, and includes all phase variations below 10 Hz. Wander may also include the effects of frequency departure, which is a constant frequency difference between network elements. Wander is almost inevitable in any network, due to the slight variations in clock frequency differences, transmission delay on the path, as well as bit stuffing operations.

Jitter and wander are dealt with in a digital network through the use of buffers. These buffers exist at each interface in any machine where the signal is processed (multiplexed, switched, etc.). Buffers act as windows to receive and transmit traffic. Additionally, for digital systems, they can be used to accommodate to frequency departure and phase variations. The buffers are carefully designed to handle the most common variations.

Slips—Controlled and Uncontrolled

Buffers accommodate to problems in frequency departure and phase variation by either "underflowing" or "overflowing." A underflowing buffer will repeat a block of data to compensate for slow timing. In contrast, an overflow buffer will throw away a block of data to accommodate to faster timing. In either condition, underflow or overflow operations are known collectively as slip. Obviously, slips result in errors within the network, because the overflowing or underflowing results in either a frame being deleted in the transmission scheme or being repeated.

Slips are either controlled or uncontrolled, the former being desirable and the latter being highly undesirable. As stated, underflow and overflow buffers result in a controlled slip. This term is used because this slip results in the deleting or repeating of a full frame (of 192 bits). This operation is possible because a buffer is actually larger than a frame. The extra buffer allows the most leeway to prevent frequency departure from creating slips on back-to-back frames.

The effect of a controlled slip results in one T1 frame being deleted, which means that 24 DS0 slots are deleted. Fortunately, these control slips do not affect the framing bit and therefore do not propagate to any subsequent back-to-back frames.

The reader may have noticed controlled slip occurring occasionally in a voice circuit, which can usually be detected by a very quick popping or clicking sound. This rare aberration is usually only mildly irritating on a voice signal. For data signals however, it does result in the loss of data. Additionally, if (for example) a network element such as a digital cross connect loses its master clock, it must fall back to its internal clock, which is typically a stratum 3 clock. This type of problem results in a dramatic drop in the quality of the line and an increase in the bit error rate. Evidence has shown that, in the worst case, every 13 seconds a DS0 channel will experience problems.

The next type of slip is the uncontrolled slip, also known as a change of frame alignment (COFA). This problem is also known as an unframed buffer slip. This event occurs if only a portion of a frame is either repeated or deleted, and is the result of using unframed buffers. Unframed buffers, while having the potential to present more problems, are used because they are less expensive than framed buffers. They are smaller, which decreases latency in the machine, and they are prevalent in asynchronous multiplexers as a matter of course.

COFAs are the result of excessive jitter and wander of the inputs to the asynchronous multiplexers, or any machine that uses unframed buffers. COFA affects multiple frames. The number of affected frames depends on how long it takes the receiving device to perform reframing operations. In many systems, the uncontrolled slip can result in an error of several thousand bits—some 40 to 50 times more serious than a control slip.

Bit or Clock Slips

Another form of slip that exists in digital networks is called a bit slip or clock slip. This problem describes a phase variation of only one clock signal. For example, a T1 that operates at 1/1.544 MHz could experience a bit slip of 0.648 µs.

A one part per million (ppm) frequency departure is equivalent to a one microsecond (µs) phase variation. In a T1 system, frequency departure can result in a control slip every 125 seconds. This value is derived from: 125 µs/1 µs = 125. Consequently, in a day (in which 86,400 seconds exist) a 1 ppm network can experience 691 slips (96400/125 = 691).

SUMMARY

Modern networks use digital techniques for the transport of voice, video, and data traffic. Most voice networks used plesiochronous timing in which the components are timed by separate clocks, but the clocks are almost the same.

Data networks are asynchronous networks, and the network is not synchronized to any clock. Each component runs with its own clock.

The emerging broadband networks are synchronous networks, where network components (and payload) are traced back to a common reference clock, through more than one clock.

3

Layered Protocols, the Architecture for ATM and SONET Networks

INTRODUCTION

This chapter introduces the concepts of layered protocols. The focus is on the open systems interconnection (OSI) model, because the architecture of ATM is based on OSI architecture. For this book, this model is examined in a general manner, with descriptions on the rationale for its use, and how it is used in networks. Other books treat the OSI model in more detail. Of course, in the spirit of the subject matter of this book, the OSI model is examined in relation to ATM.

The latter part of the chapter also provides an overview of several of the OSI and Internet protocols that operate at the network and transport layers in these two architectures. A knowledge of these systems is important if the reader is to understand how ATM supports data communications systems.

PROTOCOLS AND THE OSI MODEL

Machines, such as computers and switches, communicate with each other through established conventions called protocols. Since computer systems provide many functions to users, more than one protocol is required to support these functions.

A convention is needed to define how the different protocols of the systems interact with each other to support the end user. This convention is referred to by several names: network architecture, communications architecture, or computer-communications architecture. Whatever the term used, most systems are implemented with a set of protocols that are compatible, one hopes, among the communicating machines.

The open systems interconnection (OSI) model was developed in the early 1980s by several standards organizations, principally led by the ITU-T and the ISO. It is now widely used for defining how communications protocols are standardized among different vendors' equipment. This model has provided a blueprint for the design and implementation of computer-based networks.

The ITU-T publishes its OSI model specifications in the X.200–X.299 Recommendations. The X.200 documents contain slightly over 1100 pages. The ISO publishes its specifications for the OSI model in several documents, but does not use a numbering scheme that fits the mold of a simple "X.2xx" notation.

The model is organized into seven layers. Each layer contains several to many protocols that are invoked based on the specific needs of the user. However, the protocol entity in a layer need not be invoked, and the model provides a means for two users to negotiate the specific protocols needed for a session that takes place between them.

As suggested in Figure 3–1, each layer is responsible for performing specific functions to support the end-user application. One should not think of a layer as monolithic code; rather each layer is divided into smaller operational entities. These entities are then invoked by the end user to obtain the services defined in the model.

An end user is permitted to negotiate services within layers in its own machine or layers at the remote machine. This capability allows, for example, a relatively low-function machine to indicate to a relatively high-capability machine that it may not support all the operational entities supported by the high-level machine. Consequently, the machines will still be able to communicate with each other, albeit at a lesser mode of service. Conversely, if two large-scale computers, each with the full OSI stack, wish to exchange traffic within a rich functional environment, they may do so by negotiating the desired services.

This concept holds true for networks as well. For example, OSI provides rules on how services can be negotiated between the user and the network. This concept is integral to ATM, because it uses this OSI idea of allowing the user to inform the network about its needs (such as maximum delay, minimum throughput, etc.). In turn, it allows the network to inform the user if it can meet these needs, or suggest a lesser quality of service (QOS).

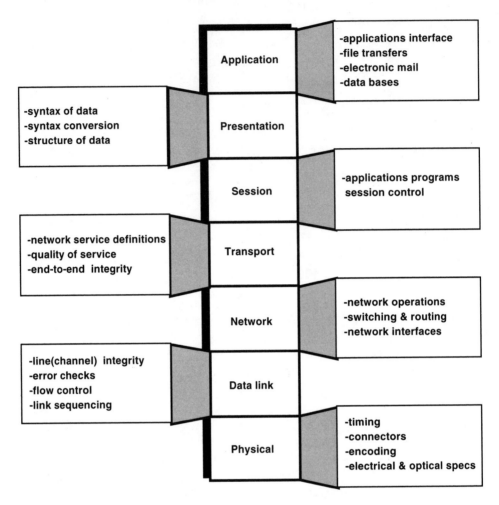

Figure 3–1
Functions of the OSI layers.

OSI Layer Operations

The layers of the OSI model and the layers of vendors' models (such as Apple's AppleTalk, IBM's SNA, etc.) contain communications functions at the lower three or four layers. From the OSI perspective, as demonstrated in Figure 3–2, it is intended that the upper four layers reside in the host computers.

This statement does not mean to imply that the lower three layers reside only in the network. The hardware and software implemented in the lower three layers also exist at the host machine. End-to-end communications, however, occurs between the hosts by invoking the upper four layers, and between the hosts and the network by invoking the lower

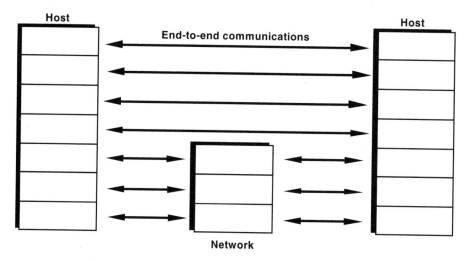

Figure 3–2
Conventional position of host and network layers.

three layers. This concept is shown in Figure 3–2 with arrows drawn between the layers in the hosts and the network. Additionally, the upper four layers may also reside in the network, for the network components to communicate with each other and obtain the services of these layers.

The end user rests on top (figuratively speaking) of the application layer. Therefore, the user obtains all the services of the seven layers of the OSI model.

CONCEPT OF A SERVICE PROVIDER

In the OSI model, a layer is considered to be a service provider to the layer above it (Figure 3–3). This upper layer is considered to be a service user to its lower layer. The service user avails itself of the functions of the service provider by sending a transaction to the provider. This transaction (called a primitive) informs the provider as to the nature of the service to be provided (at least, requested). In so far as possible, the service provider does provide the service. It may also send a transaction to its user to inform it about what is going on.

At the other machine (B in this figure), the operation at A may manifest itself by the service provider B's accepting the traffic from service provider A, providing some type of service and informing user B about the operation. User B may be allowed to send a transaction back to service provider B, which may then forward traffic back to service provider

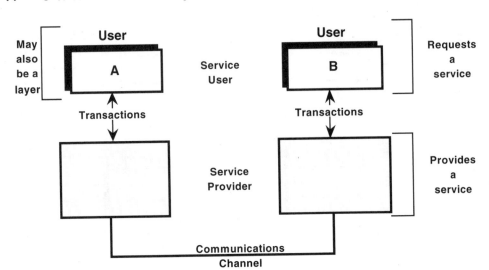

Figure 3–3
The layer as a service provider.

A. In turn, service provider A may send a transaction to user A about the nature of the operations at site B.

The OSI model provides several variations of this general scenario.

In accordance with the rules of the model, a layer cannot be bypassed. Even if an end-user does not wish to use the services of a particular layer, the user must still "pass through" the layer on the way to the next adjacent layer. This pass-through may only entail the invocation of a small set of code, but it still translates to overhead. However, every function in each layer need not be invoked. A minimum subset of functions may be all that is necessary to "conform" to the standard.

Layered network protocols allow interaction between functionally paired layers in different locations without affecting other layers. This concept aids in distributing the functions to the layers. In the majority of layered protocols, the data unit, such as a message or packet, passed from one layer to another is usually not altered, although the data unit contents may be examined and used to append additional data (trailers/headers) to the existing unit.

Each layer contains entities that exchange data and provide functions (horizontal communications) with peer entities at other computers. For example, in Figure 3–4, layer N in machine A communicates logically with layer N in machine B, and the N+1 layers in the two machines follow the same procedure. Entities in adjacent layers in the same computer interact through the common upper and lower boundaries (vertical communications) by passing parameters to define the interactions.

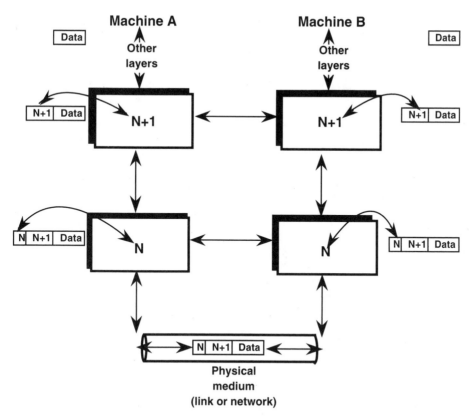

Figure 3–4
Adding header information for horizontal communications.

Typically, each layer at a transmitting station (except the lowest in most systems) adds "header" information to data. The headers are used to establish peer-to-peer sessions across nodes, and some layer implementations use headers to invoke functions and services at the N+1 or N adjacent layers.

The important point to understand is that, at the receiving site, the layer entities use the headers created by the peer entity at the transmitting site to implement predefined actions. For example, the ATM cell header created at the ATM layer at the sending machine is used by the receiving ATM layer to determine what actions it is to undertake.

Figure 3–5 shows an example of how machine A sends data to machine B. Data are passed from the upper layers or the user application to layer N+1. This layer adds a header to the data (labeled N+1 in the figure). Layer N+1 also performs actions based on the information in the transaction that accompanied the data from the upper layer.

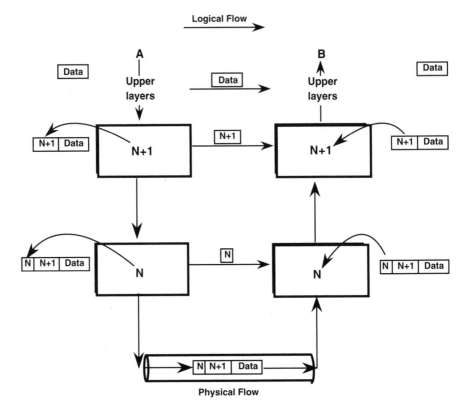

Figure 3–5
Machine A sends data to machine B.

Layer N+1 then passes the data unit with its N+1 header to layer N. Layer N performs the requested actions, based on the information in the transaction, and adds its header N to the N+1 traffic. This appended traffic is then passed across the communications line (or through a network) to the receiving machine B.

At B, the process is reversed. The headers that were created at A are used by the peer layers at B to determine that actions are to be taken. As the traffic is sent up the layers, the respective layer "removes" its header, performs defined actions, and passes the traffic on up to the next layer.

The user application at site B is presented only with user data—which was created by the sending user application at site A. These user applications are unaware (one hopes) of the many operations in each OSI layer that were invoked to support the end-user data transfer.

The headers created and used at peer layers are not to be altered by any non-peer layer. As a general rule, the headers from one layer are treated as transparent "data" by any other layer.

There are some necessary exceptions to this rule. As examples, data may be altered by a nonpeer layer for the purposes of compression, encryption, or other forms of syntax changing. This type of operation is permissible, as long as the data are restored to the original syntax when presented to the receiving peer layer.

As an exception to the exception, the presentation layer may alter the syntax of the data permanently when the receiving application layer

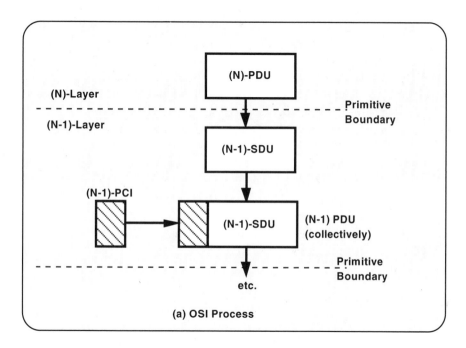

(a) OSI Process

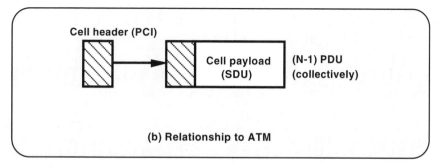

(b) Relationship to ATM

Figure 3–6
Relationship of ATM to the layered operations.

has requested the data in a different syntax (such as ASCII instead of BIT STRING).

Notwithstanding these exceptions, upper layer traffic and headers are usually sent transparently through a network. Another illustration should clarify the matter: Figure 3–6 depicts the relationship of the layers from the standpoint of how data are exchanged between them. Three terms shown in Figure 3–6(a) are important to this discussion.

- **SDU (service data unit).** User data and control information created at the upper layers that is transferred transparently through a primitive by layer (N+1) to layer (N) and subsequently to (N−1). The SDU identity (and as we just learned, its syntax) is preserved from one end of an (N)-connection to the other.
- **PCI (protocol control information).** Information exchanged by peer (the same) entities at different sites on the network to instruct the peer entity to perform a service function. PCI is also called by the names headers and trailers (which are used in this book).
- **PDU (protocol data unit).** A combination of the SDU and PCI.

At the transmitting site, the PDU becomes larger as it passes (down) through each layer by adding that layer's header and/or trailer. At the receiving site, the PDU becomes smaller as it passes (up) through each layer by stripping away that layer's header and/or trailer.

ATM AND THE MODEL

Figure 3–6(b) shows the relationship of ATM to OSI for their PCI, SDU, and PDU. ATM adds PCI to the cell payload. In OSI terms, the ATM cell header is PCI, and the cell payload is an SDU. Taken together, they form the PDU, which is called an ATM cell.

PROTOCOL ENTITIES

One should not think that an OSI layer is represented by one large monolithic block of software code. While the model does not dictate how the layers are coded, it does establish the architecture whereby a layer's functions can be structured and partitioned into smaller and more manageable modules. These modules are called entities.

The idea of the model is for peer entities in peer layers to communicate with each other. Entities may be active or inactive. An entity can be software or hardware. Typically, entities are functions or subroutines in a program. A user is able to tailor the universal OSI services by invoking selected entities through the parameters in the transactions passed to the service provider, although vendors vary on how the entities are actually designed and invoked.

SERVICE ACCESS POINTS (SAPs)

SAPs are OSI addresses and identifiers. The OSI model states: *An (N+1)-entity requests (N)-services via an (N)-service access point (SAP), which permits the (N+1)-entity to interact with an (N)-entity.*

Perhaps the best way to think of a SAP is that it is a software port (an identifier) that allows the two adjacent layers in the same machine to communicate with each other (Figure 3–7). SAPs may also be exchanged across machines in order to identify a process in the machine. In the OSI model, the SAP can identify a protocol entity that resides in a layer. For example, a SAP value could be reserved for E-mail, while a different SAP value could identify file server software. The reader may know about a UNIX socket—a concept similar to the OSI SAP.

ATM AND OSI LAYERS

Figure 3–8 introduces the ATM layers, and compares them to the OSI layered concept. The ATM operations reside in the ATM layer and the ATM adaptation layer (AAL). This chapter explains these layers in a general way. Subsequent chapters provide more detail.

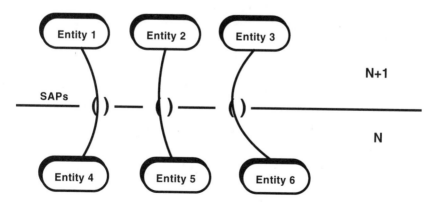

Figure 3–7
OSI service access points (SAPs).

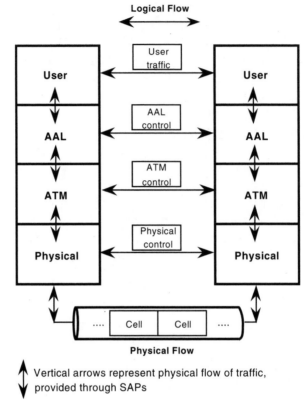

Figure 3–8
The relationship of ATM layers to the OSI model.

As the figure shows, traffic is passed physically down and up the layers through SAPs. The protocol control information (PCI) is exchanged horizontally between the peer layers of each machine. Starting at the top, the user layer contains the user application and other upper layer protocols. This layer also contains protocols for control signaling, such as network management, and protocols to set up an ATM connection between the user and the ATM network.

The AAL header is responsible for supporting the different applications in the upper layers. As such, it is quite diverse. Its operations depend upon the nature of the application that it is supporting. For example, it behaves differently when processing voice or data traffic. Among other activities, at the sending machine, it segments the user traffic into 48-byte SDUs and passes them to the ATM layer. At the receiving machine, it accepts 48-byte SDUs from the ATM layer and reassembles them into the original user traffic syntax. The AAL layer is difficult to match to the OSI model; it has some features of layers 4, 5, and 7.

The ATM layer is responsible for processing the 5-byte cell header. At the sending machine, it adds this header to the 48-byte SDU passed from the AAL. At the receiving machine, it processes this header, then passes the 48-byte SDU to the AAL. The ATM layer is also responsible for some flow control operations between machines, and for processing the various fields in the cell header. The ATM layer is roughly akin to the OSI layers 2 and 3, with a considerble number of operations removed for the purposes of speed and simplicity.

The physical layer can be implemented with a number of interfaces and protocols. Strictly speaking, ATM does not require any one type of physical layer, although the ITU-T and the ATM Forum have published specifications for ATM running of fiber, twisted pair, and so on.

THE INTERNET PROTOCOLS (TCP/IP)

In the early 1970s, several groups around the world began to address the problem of network and application compatibility. At that time, the term "internetworking," which means the interconnecting of computers and/or networks, was coined. The concepts of internetworking were pioneered by the ITU-T, the ISO, and especially the original designers of the ARPANET. (The term "ARPA" refers to the Advanced Research Projects Agency, which is a U.S. Department of Defense organization.)

Perhaps one of the most significant developments in these standardization efforts was ARPA's decision to implement the transmission control protocol (TCP) and the internet protocol (IP) around the UNIX operating system. Of equal importance, the University of California at Berkeley was selected to distribute the TCP/IP code. Because the TCP/IP code was nonproprietary, it spread rapidly among universities, private companies, and research centers. Indeed, it has become the standard suite of data communications protocols for UNIX-based computers.

In order to grasp the operations of TCP/IP, several terms and concepts must first be understood. The Internet uses the term gateway or router to describe a machine that performs relaying functions between networks, which are often called subnetworks. The term does not mean that they provide fewer functions than a conventional network. Rather, it means that the two networks consist of a full logical network with the subnetworks contributing to the overall operations for internetworking. Stated another way, the subnetworks comprise an internetwork or an internet.

An internetworking gateway is designed to remain transparent to the end-user application. Indeed, the end-user application resides in the host machines connected to the networks; rarely are user applications placed in the gateway. This approach is attractive from several standpoints. First, the gateway need not burden itself with application layer protocols. Since they are not invoked at the gateway, the gateway can dedicate itself to fewer tasks, such as managing the traffic between networks. It is not concerned with application-level functions such as database access, electronic mail, and file management. Second, this approach allows the gateway to support any type of application, because the gateway considers the application message as nothing more than a transparent PDU.

In addition to application layer transparency, most designers attempt to keep the gateway transparent to the subnetworks and vice versa. That is to say, the gateway does not care what type of network is attached to it. The principal purpose of the gateway is to receive a message that contains adequate addressing information that then enables the gateway to route the message to its final destination or to the next gateway. This feature is also attractive because it makes the gateway somewhat modular; it can be used on different types of networks.

The Internet Layers

Figure 3–9 shows the relationship of subnetworks and gateways to layered protocols. In this figure it is assumed that the user application in host A sends an application PDU, such as a file transfer system, to an application layer protocol in host B. The file transfer software performs a variety of functions and appends a file transfer header to the user data. In many systems, the operations at host B are known as server operations, and the operations at host A are known as client operations.

As indicated with the arrows going down in the protocol stack at host A, this PDU is passed to the transport layer protocol, TCP. This layer performs a variety of operations and adds a header to the PDU passed to it. The PDU is now called a segment. The traffic from the upper layers is considered to be data to the transport layer.

Next, TCP passes the segment to the network layer, also called the IP layer, which again performs specific services and appends a header. This unit (now called a datagram in Internet terms) is passed down to the lower layers. Here, a data link layer (or its rough equivalent) adds its header as well as a trailer, and the data unit (now called a frame) is launched into the network by the physical layer. Of course, if host B

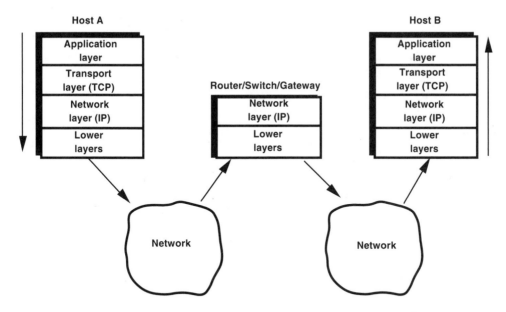

Note: The lower layers may be the traditional data link and physical layers, or the AAL, ATM, and physical layers (see Figure 3–8.)

Figure 3–9
Internet layer operations.

sends data to host A, the process is reversed and the direction of the arrows is changed.

The Internet protocols are unaware of what goes on inside the network. The network manager is free to manipulate and manage the datagram portion of the frame in any manner necessary. However, in most instances the datagram remains unchanged as it is transmitted through the subnet. The frame passes through the subnetwork until its arrival at the gateway, where it is processed through the lower layers and passed to the IP (network) layer (where it is again called a datagram). Here, routing decisions are made based on the addresses provided by the host computer.

After these routing decisions have been made, the datagram is passed to the communications link that is connected to the appropriate subnetwork (consisting of the lower layers). The datagram is re-encapsulated into the data link layer PDU (usually called a frame) and passed to the next subnetwork. As before, this unit is passed through the subnetwork transparently (usually), where it finally arrives at the host B.

Host B receives the traffic through its lower layers and reverses the process that transpired at host A. That is to say, it decapsulates the headers by stripping them off in the appropriate layer. The header is used by the layer to determine the actions it is to take; the header governs the layer's operations.

IP Functions

IP is an example of a connectionless service. It permits the exchange of traffic between two host computers without any prior call setup. (However, these two computers usually share a common connection-oriented transport protocol.) Since IP is connectionless, it is possible that the datagrams could be lost between the two end-users' stations. For example, the IP gateway enforces a maximum queue length size, and if this queue length is violated, the buffers will overflow. In this situation, the additional datagrams are discarded in the network. For this reason, a higher level transport layer protocol (such as TCP) is essential to recover from these problems.

IP hides the underlying subnetwork from the end user. In this context, it creates a virtual network to that end user. This aspect of IP is quite attractive because it allows different types of networks to attach to an IP gateway. As a result, IP is reasonably simple to install and, because of its connectionless design, it is quite robust.

Since IP is a best effort datagram-type protocol, it has no reliability mechanisms. It provides no error recovery for the underlying subnetworks. It has no flow-control mechanisms. The user data (datagrams) may be lost, duplicated, or even arrive out of order. It is not the job of IP to deal with these problems. As we shall see later, most of the problems are passed to the next higher layer, TCP.

IP supports fragmentation operations. The term fragmentation refers to an operation where a PDU is divided or segmented into smaller units. This feature can be quite useful, because all networks do not use the same size PDU.

For example, X.25-based WANs typically employ a PDU (called a packet in X.25) with a data field of 128 octets. Some networks allow negotiations to a smaller or larger PDU size. The Ethernet standard limits the size of a PDU to 1500 octets. Conversely, proNET-10 stipulates a PDU of 2000 octets.

Without the use of fragmentation, a gateway would be tasked with trying to resolve incompatible PDU sizes between networks. IP solves the problem by establishing the rules for fragmentation at the gateway and reassembly at the receiving host.

IP is designed to rest on top of the underlying subnetwork—insofar as possible in a transparent manner. This means that IP assumes little about the characteristics of the underlying network or networks. As stated earlier, from the design standpoint this is quite attractive to engineers because it keeps the subnetworks relatively independent of IP.

As the reader might expect, the transparency is achieved by encapsulation. The data sent by the host computer are encapsulated into an IP datagram. The IP header identifies the address of the receiving host computer. The IP datagram and header are further encapsulated into the specific protocol of the transit network. For example, a transit network could be an X.25 network or an Ethernet LAN.

After the transit network has delivered the traffic to an IP gateway, its control information is stripped away. The gateway then uses the destination address in the datagram header to determine where to route the traffic. Typically, it then passes the datagram to a subnetwork by invoking a subnetwork access protocol (for example, Ethernet on a LAN, or X.25 on a WAN). This protocol is used to encapsulate the datagram header and user data into the headers and trailers used by the subnetwork. This process is repeated at each gateway, and eventually the datagram arrives at the final destination, where it is delivered to the receiving station.

IP addresses. TCP/IP networks use a 32-bit address to identify a host computer and the network to which the host is attached. The structure of the IP address is:

IP Address = Network Address + Host Address.

IP addresses are classified by their formats (Figure 3–10). Four formats are permitted: class A, class B, class C, or class D. The first bits of the address specify the format of the remainder of the address field in relation to the network and host subfields. The host address is also called the local address (also called the REST field).

Class A addresses provide for networks that have a large number of hosts. The host ID field (local address) is 24 bits. Therefore, 2^{24} hosts can be identified. Seven bits are devoted to the network ID, which supports an identification scheme for as many as 127 networks (bit values of 1 to 127).

Class B addresses are used for networks of intermediate size. Fourteen bits are assigned for the network ID, and 16 bits are assigned for the host ID. Class C networks contain fewer than 256 hosts (2^8). Twenty-one bits are assigned to the network ID. Finally, class D addresses are reserved for multicasting, which is a form of broadcasting but within a limited area.

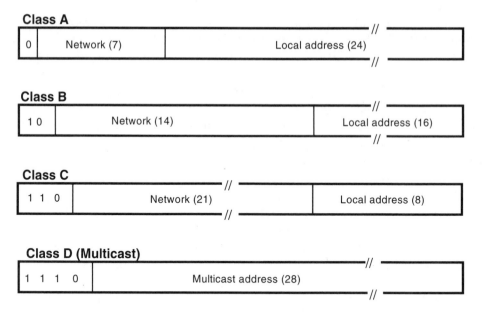

Figure 3–10
IP address formats.

TCP Operations

The internet protocol (IP) is not designed to recover from certain problems, nor does it guarantee the delivery of traffic. IP is designed to discard datagrams that are outdated, or have exceeded the number of permissible transit hops in an Internet, for example. The user datagram protocol (UDP) also is a connectionless protocol and, as such, discards traffic under similar conditions.

However, certain user applications require assurance that all datagrams have been delivered safely to the destination. Furthermore, the transmitting user may need to know that the traffic has been delivered at the receiving host. The mechanisms to achieve these important services reside in TCP. The job of TCP may be quite complex. It must be able to satisfy a wide range of applications requirements, and equally important, it must be able to accommodate to a dynamic environment within an Internet.

TCP establishes and manages sessions (logical associations) between its local users and these users' remote communicating partners. This means that TCP must maintain an awareness of the users' activities in order to support the users' data transfer through the Internet.

TCP resides in the transport layer of the conventional seven-layer model. It is situated above IP and below the upper layers. Figure 3–9 also illustrates that TCP is not loaded into the gateway. It is designed to reside in the host computer or in a machine that is tasked with end-to-end integrity of the transfer of user data. In practice, TCP is usually placed in the user host machine.

TCP is designed to run over the IP. Since IP is a connectionless network, the tasks of reliability, flow control, sequencing, opens, and closes are given to TCP. Although TCP and IP are tied together so closely that they are used in the same context (TCP/IP), TCP can also support other connectionless protocols, such as UDP.

Many of the TCP functions (such as flow control, reliability, and sequencing) could be handled within an application program. But it makes little sense to code these functions into each application. Moreover, applications programmers are usually not versed in error-detection and flow control operations. The preferred approach is to develop generalized software that provides community functions suitable for a wide range of applications, and then invoke these programs from the application software. This allows the application programmer to concentrate on solving the application problem and it isolates the programmer from the nuances and problems of networks.

TCP is a connection-oriented protocol. TCP maintains status information about each user data stream flowing into and out of the TCP module. TCP is responsible for the reliable transfer of each of the octets passed to it from an upper layer. A sequence number is assigned to each octet transmitted. The receiving TCP module uses a checksum routine to check the data for damage that may have occurred during the transmission process. If the data are acceptable, TCP returns a positive acknowledgment (ACK) to the sending TCP module. TCP also checks for duplicate data. In the event the sending TCP transmits duplicate data, the receiving TCP discards the redundant data.

TCP uses an inclusive acknowledgment scheme. The acknowledgment number acknowledges all octets up to and including the acknowledgment number less one.

The receiver's TCP module is also able to flow control the sender's data, which is a very useful tool to prevent buffer overrun and a possible saturation of the receiving machine.

TCP provides a graceful close to a virtual circuit (the logical connection between the two users). A graceful close ensures that all traffic has been acknowledged before the virtual circuit is removed.

TCP ports. A TCP upper layer user in a host machine is identified by a port address. The port address is concatenated with the IP Internet address to form a socket. This address must be unique throughout the

Internet and a pair of sockets uniquely identifies each endpoint connection. As examples:

Sending socket = Source IP address + source port number

Receiving socket = Destination IP address + destination port number

Although the mapping of ports to higher layer processes can be handled as an internal matter in a host, the Internet publishes numbers for frequently used higher level processes.

Even though TCP establishes numbers for frequently used ports, the numbers and values above 255 are available for private use. The remainder of the values for the assigned port numbers have the low-order 8-bits set to zero. The remainder of these bits are available to any organization to use as they choose. Be aware that the numbers 0 through 255 are reserved and they should be avoided.

THE OSI NETWORK AND TRANSPORT LAYER

OSI includes protocols at the network and transport layer that perform functions similar to TCP and IP. They have not yet seen extensive use in the industry, but their use is growing.

The OSI connectionless network protocol (CLNP) is quite similar to IP. Indeed, it was derived from IP. The OSI Transport Layer Protocol, class 4 (TP4) performs functions similar to TCP, but is considerably more powerful and complex. Since the basic functions of the OSI and Internet layers 3 and 4 are about the same, I shall not expend any more time on these systems.

SUMMARY

The OSI model uses the concepts of layered protocols. Key aspects of the model are service definitions for vertical communications and protocol specifications for horizontal communications. OSI is organized around the concepts of encapsulation and decapsulation, while service access points (SAPs) form the basis for OSI addressing. B-ISDN, ATM, and SONET make extensive use of the OSI model.

Emerged Technologies

INTRODUCTION

This chapter provides an overview of the communications technologies that have been in use in the industry for the past two to three decades, thus the term, emerged technologies. These technologies are covered:

- T1 and E1 carrier systems
- X.25
- Integrated Services Digital Network (ISDN)
- Signaling system number 7 (SS7)

COMPARISON OF SWITCHING SYSTEMS

Figure 4–1 summarizes the progress made in switching technologies since the 1960s. The methods of switching are compared in terms of relay technology, typical media employed with the switch, the size of the PDU (packet, message, etc.), and the delay encountered with the switching operation.

The relay techniques for earlier switching systems used a direct connection between the input and output lines, such as a crossbar switch. Later systems used buffering techniques to store the traffic on disk (a store-and-forward technology), while newer systems hold

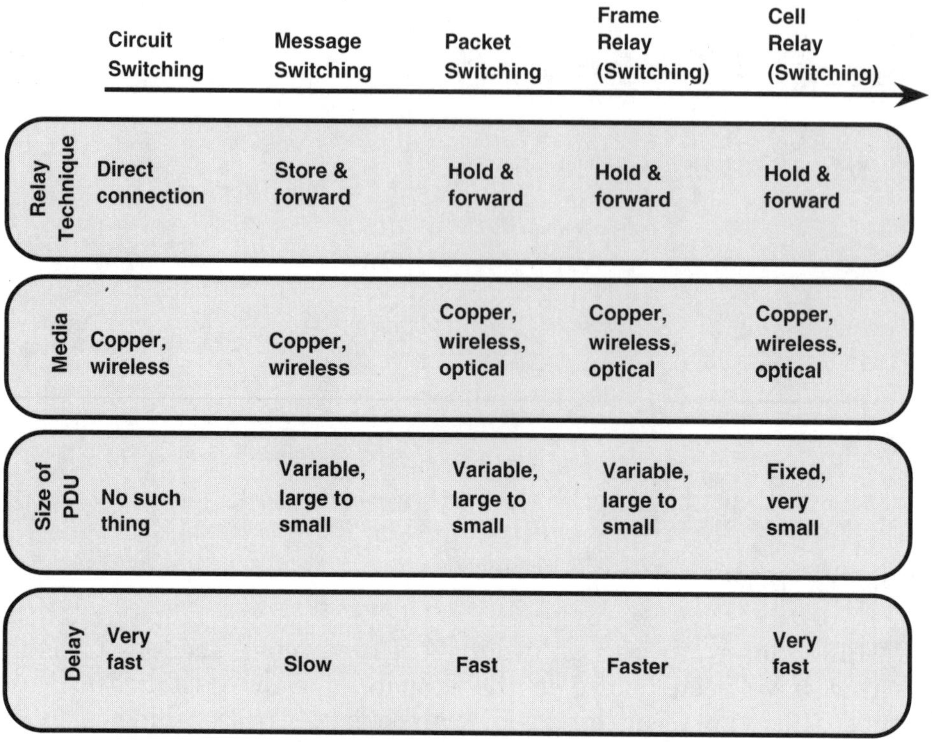

	Circuit Switching	Message Switching	Packet Switching	Frame Relay (Switching)	Cell Relay (Switching)
Relay Technique	Direct connection	Store & forward	Hold & forward	Hold & forward	Hold & forward
Media	Copper, wireless	Copper, wireless	Copper, wireless, optical	Copper, wireless, optical	Copper, wireless, optical
Size of PDU	No such thing	Variable, large to small	Variable, large to small	Variable, large to small	Fixed, very small
Delay	Very fast	Slow	Fast	Faster	Very fast

Figure 4–1
Switching technologies.

the traffic directly in memory, which is called a hold-and-forward technology.

Earlier switching systems used copper as the media for the input and output ports of the switch. With the advent of the optical fiber technology, high-capacity systems make use of optical fiber for the transmission media.

The size of the PDU has varied from nonexistent, in technologies such as circuit switching, to systems that employ a variable length PDU—ranging from a few octets to several thousand octets. Cell relay takes a different approach by using fixed, small PDUs to increase the efficiency of the operations at the switch.

Finally, older systems, with the exception of circuit switching, were somewhat slow in the delay encountered at the switch due to the processing of very large data units and to the cumbersome nature of how the CPU operated and how the software was written. These emerged technologies are being replaced by very fast switches with efficient software (and with many of the switching elements residing in silicon).

THE T1/E1 SYSTEMS

Purpose of T1 and E1

The T1/E1 systems are high-capacity networks designed for the digital transmission of voice, video, and data. The original implementations of T1/E1 digitized voice signals to take advantage of the superior aspects of digital technology. Shortly after the inception of T1 in North America, the ITU-T published the E1 standards, which were implemented in Europe. E1 is similar to (but not compatible with) T1.

These systems use asynchronous techniques; devices in the network do not operate with common clocks, and therefore, are not synchronized closely together (more on this subject later). Actually, the components operate within a specified error tolerance range, and are more accurately called plesiochronous networks. So, in most parts of the world, the present system is called the plesiochronous digital hierarchy, or PDH.

T1 is based on multiplexing 24 users onto one physical TDM circuit. T1 operates at 1,544,000 bit/s, which was (in the 1960s) about the highest rate that could be supported across twisted wire pair for a distance of approximately one mile. Interestingly, the distance of one mile (actually about 6000 feet) represented the spacing between manholes in large cities. They were so spaced to permit maintenance work such as splicing cables and the placing of amplifiers. This physical layout provided a convenient means to replace the analog amplifiers with digital repeaters.

The term T1 was devised by the U.S. telephone industry to describe a specific type of carrier equipment. Today, it is used to describe a general carrier system, a data rate, and various multiplexing and framing conventions. A more concise term is DS1, which describes a multiplexed digital signal carried by the T carrier. To keep matters simple, this book uses the term T1 synonymously with the term DS1, and the term T3 synonymously with DS3. Just be aware that the T designator stipulates the carrier system, but the digital transmission hierarchy schemes are designated as DS-n, where n represents a multiplexing level of DS1. Table 4–1 lists the more common digital multiplexing schemes used in Europe, North America, and Japan.

Today, the majority of T1/E1 offerings digitize the voice signal through pulse code modulation (PCM) or adaptive differential pulse code

Table 4–1 Carrier Systems Multiplexing Hierarchy

North America	Japan	Europe
64 kbit/s	64 kbit/s	64 kbit/s
1.544 Mbit/s 24 voice channels	1.544 Mbit/s 24 voice channels	2.048 Mbit/s 30 voice channels
6.312 Mbit/s 96 voice channels	6.312 Mbit/s 96 voice channels	8.448 Mbit/s 120 voice channels
44.736 Mbit/s 672 voice channels	32.064 Mbit/s 480 voice channels	34.368 Mbit/s 480 voice channel
274.176 Mbit/s 4032 voice channels	97.728 Mbit/s 1440 voice channels	139.264 Mbit/s 1920 voice channels

modulation (ADPCM). Whatever the encoding technique, once the analog images are translated to digital bit streams, then many T1 systems are able to time division multiplex voice and data together in 24 user slots within each frame.

Typical Topology

Figure 4–2 shows a T1 topology (the same type of topology is permitted with the E1 technology). Actually, there is no typical topology for these systems. They can range from a simple point-to-point topology shown here, where two T1 multiplexers operate on one 1.544 Mbit/s link, or they can employ with digital cross connect systems (DCS) that add, drop, and/or switch payload as necessary across multiple links.

Voice, data, and video images can use one digital "pipe." Data transmissions are terminated through a statistical time division multiplexer (STDM), which then uses the TDM to groom the traffic across the transmission line through a T1 channel service unit (CSU), or other equipment, such as a data service unit (DSU). A DSU and a CSU may be combined as well. The purpose of the CSU is to convert signals at the user device to signals acceptable to the digital line and, vice versa, at the receiver. The CSU performs clocking and signal regeneration on the channels. It also performs functions such as line conditioning (equalization), which keeps the signal's performance consistent across the channel bandwidth; signal reshaping, which reconstitutes the binary pulse stream; and loop-back testing, which entails the transmission of test signals between the DSU and the network carrier's equipment.

The bandwidth of a line can be divided into various T1 subrates. For

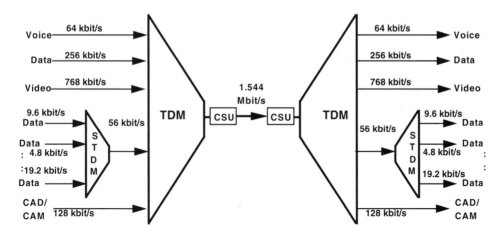

Figure 4–2
A typical T1 topology.

example, a video system could utilize a 768 kbit/s band, the STDM in turn could multiplex various data rates up to a 56 kbit/s rate, and perhaps a CAD/CAM operation could utilize 128 kbit/s of the bandwidth.

T1 and E1 Layers

In relation to the OSI model, the T1 and E1 layers reside in only one layer—the physical layer (Figure 4–3). This layer defines the connectors, signaling conventions, framing formats, and the like that are found in most physical layers.

T1/E1 PDUs

The T1 frame (or the OSI term, PDU) consists of 24 8-bit slots and a framing bit (Figure 4–4). To decode the incoming data stream, a receiver must be able to associate each sample with the proper TDM channel. At a minimum, the beginning and ending of the frame must be recognized. The function of the framing bit is to provide this delineation. The framing bit is in the 193rd bit of each frame. It is not part of the user's infor-

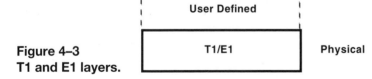

Figure 4–3
T1 and E1 layers.

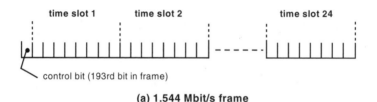

(a) 1.544 Mbit/s frame

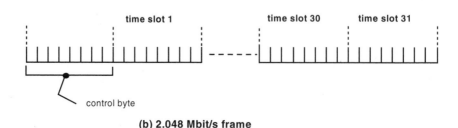

(b) 2.048 Mbit/s frame

Figure 4–4
T1 and E1 frames.

mation, but added by the system for framing. The use of this bit varies, depending on the type of the T1 system and the age of the technology.

Some T1 channel banks use the eighth bit in every 8-bit slot for control signaling. Examples of control signaling are off-hook, on-hook, ringing, busy signals, and battery reversal. During the development of the later T1 equipment, the designers recognized that every eighth bit was not needed for signaling. Consequently, later equipment, known as D2 channel banks, uses the eighth bit of every sixth and twelfth frame to provide signaling information. The least significant bit in these frames is overwritten with a signaling bit. This concept is called bit robbing, and the respective sixth and twelfth robbed frame bits are called the A and B bits.

For the transmission of data, the eighth bit is unreliable, so most vendors have chosen to ignore this bit for data signaling. As a result, the majority of T1 and related systems use a 56 kbit/s transmission rate (8000 slots/second * 7 bits per slot = 56000) instead of the 64 kbit/s rate (8000 slots/second * 8 bits per slot = 64000)

The rate for the 2.048 Mbit rate is similar to its counterpart T1 in that they both use a 125 µs time frame (Figure 4–4). However, the E1 frame is divided into 31 TDM slots and preceded by a 8-bit time slot that is used for control purposes. E1 reserves this slot in the frame for its "out-of-band" signaling, and thereby obviates the cumbersome bit robbing scheme found in T1. Robbing is not a good idea—nor is bit robbing—and therefore, the emerging technologies discussed in this book (with some minor exceptions like T1) use out-of-band signaling instead. That is to say, bandwidth is reserved for control signaling rather than robbing bits to perform the function.

Conclusions on T1/E1

The T1/E1 systems have served the industry well. However, they are quite limited in their management operations and they provide very little support for end-user control for the provisioning of services. In the old days, the use of bandwidth (control headers) for network management was not encouraged due to the limited transmission capacity of the facilities to accommodate this overhead traffic. Today, the prevailing idea is to exploit the high capacity of optical fibers and the processors, and allocate a greater amount of bandwidth (larger control headers) to support more network management services.

These older technologies also use awkward multiplexing schemes. Due to their asynchronous timing structure (each machine runs its own clock, instead of using a central clock in the network for all machines), timing differences between machines are accommodated by stuffing extra bits (bit stuffing) periodically in the traffic streams. These bits cannot be unstuffed when the traffic is demultiplexed from the higher rates (see Table 4–1) to the lower rates. Indeed, the traffic must be completely demultiplexed at the multiplexers and/or switches to make the payload accessible for further processing.

One should be careful about criticizing a technology that was conceived and implemented over thirty years ago. In retrospect, T1 and E1 were significant steps forward in the progress of the telecommunications industry. But like most everything else in this industry (thankfully, not life), things do not improve with age, and must be replaced. As we shall see, SONET/SDH are those replacements. But, like EIA-232, T1/E1 will be with us for a very long time.

X.25

Purpose of X.25

X.25 was designed to perform a function similar to that of the ISDN (discussed later): to provide for an interface between an end-user device and a network. However, for X.25, the end-user device is a data terminal and the network is a packet-switched data network; for ISDN, the end-user device was (originally) a voice terminal (telephone) and the network was (originally) a circuit-switched voice network. The comparison is apt, because both protocols have similar architectures, as will be explained in this section.

The idea of the X.25 interface, as conceived by the ITU-T study groups in the early 1970s, was to define unambiguous rules about how a public packet data network would handle a user's payload and accommodate to various QOS features (called X.25 facilities) that were requested by the user. X.25 was also designed to provide strict flow control on user payloads and to provide substantial management services for the user payload, such as the sequencing and acknowledgment of traffic.

The ITU-T issued the X.25 Recommendation in 1974. It was revised in 1976, 1978, 1980, 1984, and the last revision was made in 1988. Since 1974, the standard has been expanded to include many options, services, and facilities, and several of the newer OSI protocols and service definitions operate with X.25. X.25 is now the predominant interface standard for wide area packet networks. Unlike, T1/E1, X.25 uses STDM techniques and is designed as a transport system for data—not voice.

Typical Topology

The placement of X.25 in packet networks is widely misunderstood. X.25 is *not* a packet switching specification. It is a packet network interface specification (Figure 4–5). X.25 says nothing about operations within the network. Hence, from the perspective of X.25, the internal network operations are not known. For example, X.25 is not aware if the network uses adaptive or fixed directory routing, or if the internal operations of the network are connection-oriented or connectionless. The reader may have heard of the term "network cloud." Its origin is derived from these concepts.

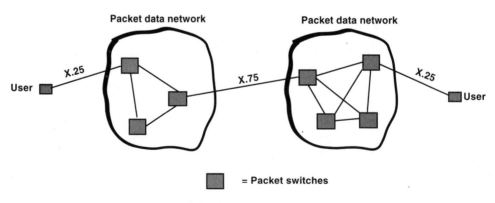

Figure 4–x5
Typical X.25 topology.

It is obvious from an examination of Figure 4–5 that X.25 is classified as a user network interface (UNI). It defines the procedures for the exchange of data between a user device (DTE) and the network (DCE). Its formal title is "Interface between Data Terminal Equipment and Data Circuit Terminating Equipment for Terminals Operating in the Packet Node on Public Data Networks." In X.25, the DCE is the "agent" for the packet network to the DTE.

X.25 establishes the procedures for two packet-mode DTEs to communicate with each other through a network. It defines the two DTE sessions with their respective DCEs. The idea of X.25 is to provide common procedures between a user station and a packet network (DCE) for establishing a session and exchanging data. The procedures include functions such as identifying the packets of specific user terminals or computers, acknowledging packets, rejecting packets, initiating error recovery, flow control, and other services. X.25 also provides for a number of QOS functions, such as reverse charge, call redirect, and transit delay selection, which are called X.25 facilities.

X.75 is a complementary protocol to X.25. X.75 is a internetworking interface, although it is used often today for other configurations such as amplifying and enhancing an interface on ISDN systems to support X.25-based applications.

X.25 Layers

The X.25 Recommendation encompasses the lower three layers of the OSI model. Like ISDN, the lower two layers exist to support the third layer. Figure 4–6 shows the relationships of the X.25 layers. The

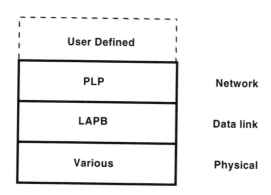

Various: V Series, X.21, X.21*bis*, etc.

Figure 4–6   LAPB: Link access procedure, balanced
The X.25 layers.   PLP: Packet layer procedures

physical layer (first layer) is the physical interface between the DTE and DCE, and is either a V-Series, X.21, or X.21*bis* interface. Of course, X.25 networks can operate with other physical layer interfaces (as examples, V.35, the EIA 232-D standard from the Electronic Industries Association, and even high-speed 2.048 Mbit/s interfaces). X.25 assumes the data link layer (second layer) to be link access procedure, balanced (LAPB). The LAPB protocol is a subset of HDLC.

X.25 PDUs

The X.25 packet is carried within the LAPB frame as the I (information) field (Figure 4–7). LAPB ensures that the X.25 packets are transmitted across the link, after which the frame fields are discarded (stripped), and the packet is presented to the network layer. The principal function of the link layer is to deliver the packet error-free despite the error-prone nature of the communications link. In this regard, it is quite similar to LAPD in ISDN. In X.25, a packet is created at the network layer and inserted into a frame that is created at the data link layer.

The network layer, also called packet layer procedures or PLP, is responsible for establishing, managing, and tearing down the connections between the communicating users and the network.

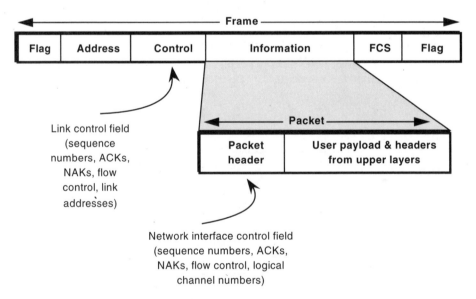

Figure 4–7
X.25 PDUs (packet and frame).

Figure 4–7 illustrates that sequence numbers, ACKs, NAKs, and flow control techniques are implemented in two different fields residing in the X.25 PDU. First, the control field in the link header is used at layer 2 (LAPB) to control operations on the link between the user device and network node. Second, the packet header is used at layer 3 (PLP) and contains sequence numbers, ACKs, and so on to control each user session running on the link between the user device and network node. As we shall see in this book, some of the emerging technologies take the stand that these operations are either redundant or unnecessary, and so they are either eliminated or decreased substantially.

Other Noteworthy Aspects of X.25

X.25 uses logical channel numbers (LCNs) to identify the DTE connections to the network. An LCN is really nothing more than a virtual circuit identifier (VCI). As many as 4095 logical channels (i.e., user sessions) can be assigned to a physical channel. In practice, however, not all numbers are assigned at one time because of performance considerations. The LCN serves as an identifier (a label) for each user's packets that are transmitted through the physical circuit to and from the network. Typically, the virtual circuit is identified with two different LCNs—one for the user at the local side of the network and one for the user at the remote side of the network.

X.25 defines quite specifically how logical channels are established, but it allows the network administration considerable leeway in how the virtual circuit is created. Notwithstanding, the network administration must "map" the two LCNs together from each end of the virtual circuit through the network so they can communicate with each other. How this is accomplished is left to the network administration, but it must be done if X.25 is to be used as specified.

The concept of labels, fostered by X.25, is also used by ATM. The reader might make a mental note to return to this section of the book when the subject of ATM labels is discussed.

X.25 interface options. X.25 provides two mechanisms to establish and maintain communications between the user devices and the network:

- Permanent virtual circuit (PVC)
- Switched virtual call (SVC)

A sending PVC user is assured of obtaining a connection to the receiving user and of obtaining the required services of the network to support the user-to-user session. X.25 requires that a PVC be established before a session can begin. Consequently, an agreement must be reached by the two users and the network administration before the PVC is allocated. Among other things, agreement must be made about the reservation of LCNs for the PVC session and the establishment of facilities.

A SVC requires that the originating user device must transmit a Call Request packet to the network to start the connection operation. In turn, the network node relays this packet to the remote network node, which sends an Incoming Call packet to the called user device. If this receiving DTE chooses to acknowledge and accept the call, it transmits to the network a Call Accepted packet. The network then transports this packet to the requesting DTE in the form of a Call Connected packet. To terminate the session, a Clear Request packet is sent by either DTE. It is received as a Clear Indication packet, and confirmed by the Clear Confirm packet.

Conclusions on X.25

One could surmise that any data communications technology developed during the 1970s cannot be appropriate to fulfill the requirements of modern applications. Additionally, a substantial segment of the telecommunications industry believe that X.25 is ineffective as an UNI, because of its "overly connection-oriented nature."

It should be remembered that X.25 is old. It was designed to support user traffic on error-prone networks, with the supposition that most user devices were relatively unintelligent. Moreover, X.25 was designed to operate on physical interfaces that are also old (and therefore inherently slow), such as EIA-232-D and V.28.

Nonetheless, X.25 usage continues to grow throughout the world because (1) it is well understood, (2) it is available in off-the-shelf products, (3) extensive conformance tests are available for the product, and (4) it is a cost-effective service for bursty, slow-speed applications, of which there are many.

If one cares for one's data and wishes to maintain some type of control over it, then there must be a connection-oriented data management protocol residing somewhere in the protocol suite—but it need not exist at the network layer. This idea is central to the behavior of several of the emerging technologies explained in this book: Yes, one needs to take care of the user's data (payload), but the network is not the place to do it. It is more appropriate for the user computer to perform this function. Later chapters will examine the rationale for this premise.

The last part of this chapter describes why (with specific examples)

ATM behaves differently than other connection-oriented systems, such as X.25.

INTEGRATED SERVICES DIGITAL NETWORK (ISDN)

Purpose of ISDN

The initial purpose of the integrated services digital network (ISDN) was to provide a digital interface between a user and a network node for the transport of digitized voice and (later) data images. It is now designed to support a wide range of services. In essence, all images (voice, data, television, facsimile, etc.), can be transmitted with ISDN technology.

ISDN has been implemented as an evolutionary technology, and the committees, common carriers, and trade associations who developed the standards wisely recognized that ISDN had to be developed from the long-existing telephone-based integrated digital network (IDN). Consequently, many of the digital techniques developed for T1 and E1 are used in ISDN. This includes signaling rates (32 or 64 kbit/s), transmission codes (bipolar), and even physical plugs (the jacks to the telephone). Thus, the foundations for ISDN have been in development since the mid-1970s.

Typical Topology

The user interface to ISDN is a very similar topology to that of X.25. An end-user device connects to an ISDN node through a UNI protocol. Of course, the ISDN and X.25 interfaces are used for two different functions. The X.25 UNI provides a connection to a packet-switched data network, while ISDN provides a connection to an ISDN node, which can then connect to a voice, video, or data network.

Before we begin an analysis of ISDN, two terms must be defined: functional groupings and reference points. Functional groupings are sets of capabilities needed in an ISDN user-access interface. Specific functions within a functional grouping may be performed by multiple pieces of equipment or software. Reference points are the interfaces dividing the functional groupings. Usually, a reference point corresponds to a physical interface between pieces of equipment. With these thoughts in mind, please examine Figure 4–8, which shows several possibilities for setting up the ISDN components at the SNI (others are permitted).

The reference points labeled R, S, T, and U are logical interfaces between the functional groupings, which can be either a terminal type 1 (TE1), a terminal type 2 (TE2), or a network termination (NT1, NT2) grouping. The purpose of the reference points is to delineate where the

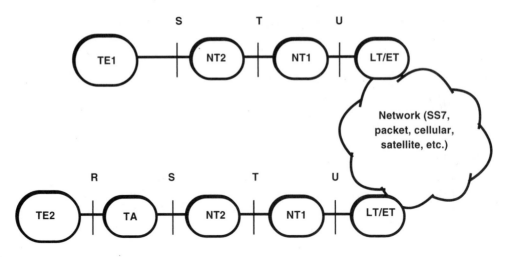

Figure 4–8
Typical ISDN topology.

responsibility of the network operator ends. If the network operator responsibility ends at reference point S, the operator is responsible for NT1, NT2, and LT/ET.

The U reference point is the reference point for the 2-wire side of the NT1 equipment. It separates a NT1 from the line termination (LT) equipment. The U interface is a national standard, while interfaces implemented at reference points S and T are international standards. The R reference point represents non-ISDN interfaces, such as EIA-232-D and V.35.

The end-user ISDN terminal is identified by the ISDN term TE1. The TE1 connects to the ISDN through a twisted pair 4-wire digital link. Figure 4–8 illustrates other ISDN options—one is a user station called a TE2 device, which represents the current equipment in use, such as IBM 3270 terminals, Hewlett-Packard and Sun workstations, and telex devices.

The TE2 connects to a terminal adapter (TA), which is a device that allows non-ISDN terminals to operate over ISDN lines. The user side of the TA typically uses a conventional physical layer interface, such as EIA-232-D or the V-series specifications, and it is not aware that it is connected into an ISDN-based interface. The TA is responsible for the communications between the non-ISDN operations and the ISDN operations.

The TA and TE2 devices are connected to either an ISDN NT1 or NT2 device. The NT1 is a device which connects the 4-wire subscriber wiring to the conventional 2-wire local loop. ISDN allows up to eight terminal devices to be addressed by NT1. The NT1 is responsible for the physical layer functions, such as signaling synchronization and timing. NT1 provides a user with a standardized interface.

The NT2 is a more intelligent piece of equipment. It is typically found in a digital PBX and contains the layer 2 and 3 protocol functions. The NT2 device is capable of performing concentration services in that it multiplexes 23 B+D channels onto the line at a combined rate of 1.544 Mbit/s or 31 B+D channels at a combined rate of 2.048 Mbit/s. The NT1 and NT2 devices may be combined into a single device called NT12. This device handles the physical, data link, and network layer functions.

In summary, the TE equipment is responsible for user communications and the NT equipment is responsible for network communications.

As illustrated in Figure 4–9, the TE1 connects to the ISDN through a twisted pair 4-wire digital link. This link uses TDM to provide three channels, designated as the B, B, and D channels (or 2 B+D). The B channels operate at a speed of 64 kbit/s; the D channel operates at 16 kbit/s. The 2 B+D is designated as the basic rate interface (BRI). ISDN also allows up to eight TE1s to share one 2 B+D link. The purpose of the B channels is to carry the user payload in the form of voice, compressed video, and data. The purpose of the D channel is to act as an out-of-band control channel for setting up, managing, and clearing the B channel sessions.

In other scenarios, the user DTE is called a TE2 device. As explained earlier, the TE2 device is the current equipment in use, such as IBM 3270 termi-

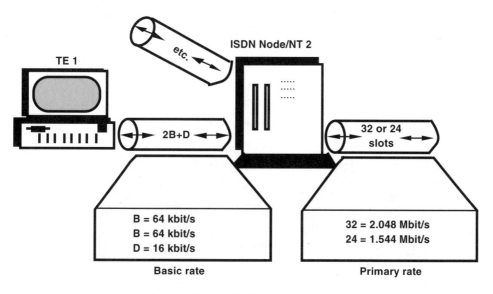

Figure 4–9
ISDN configuration.

nals and telex devices. The TE2 connects to a TA, which is a device that allows non-ISDN terminals to operate over ISDN lines. The user side of the TA typically uses a conventional physical layer interface, such as EIA-232-D or the V-series specifications. It is packaged like an external modem or as a board that plugs into an expansion slot on the TE2 devices.

As explained earlier, ISDN supports yet another type of interface called the called the primary rate interface (PRI). It consists of the multiplexing of multiple B and D channels onto a higher speed interface of either 1.544 Mbit/s (used in North America and Japan) or 2.048 Mbit/s (used in Europe). The 1.544 Mbit/s interface is designated as 23 B+D, and the 2.048 Mbit/s interface is designated as 31 B+D to describe how many B and D channels are carried in the PRI frame.

ISDN Layers

The ISDN approach is to provide an end-user with full support through the seven layers of the OSI model, although ISDN confines itself to defining the operations at layers 1, 2, and 3 of this model. In so doing, ISDN is divided into two kinds of services: the bearer services, responsible for providing support for the lower three layers of the seven-layer standard; and teleservices (for example, telephone, Teletex, Videotex message handling), responsible for providing support through all seven layers of the model and generally making use of the underlying lower-layer capabilities of the bearer services. The services are referred to as low-layer and high-layer functions, respectively. The ISDN functions are allocated according to the layering principles of the OSI model.

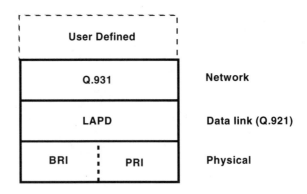

Figure 4-10
The ISDN layers.

BRI: Basic rate interface (I.430)
PRI: Primary rate interface (I.431)
LAPD: Link access procedure for D channel

Table 4–2   ISDN Layer 3 Messages

Call Establishment Messages	Call Disestablishment Messages
ALERTING	DETACH
CALL PROCEEDING	DETACH ACKNOWLEDGE
CONNECT	DISCONNECT
CONNECT ACKNOWLEDGE	RELEASE
SETUP	RELEASE COMPLETE
SETUP ACKNOWLEDGE	

Call Information Phase Messages	Miscellaneous Messages
RESUME	CANCEL
RESUME ACKNOWLEDGE	CANCEL ACKNOWLEDGE
RESUME REJECT	CANCEL REJECT
SUSPEND	CONGESTION CONTROL
SUSPEND ACKNOWLEDGE	FACILITY
SUSPEND REJECT	FACILITY ACKNOWLEDGE
USER INFORMATION	FACILITY REJECT
	INFORMATION
	REGISTER
	REGISTER ACKNOWLEDGE
	REGISTER REJECT
	STATUS
	STATUS ENQUIRY

a NNI. Table 4–2 lists these messages, and a short explanation is provided later in this section about the functions of the more significant messages.

The Q.931 messages all use a similar format. Figure 4–12 illustrates this format. The message contains several parameters to define the circuit connection. It must contain these three parameters:

- *Protocol discriminator:* Distinguishes between user-network call control messages and others, such as other layer 3 protocols (X.25, for example)

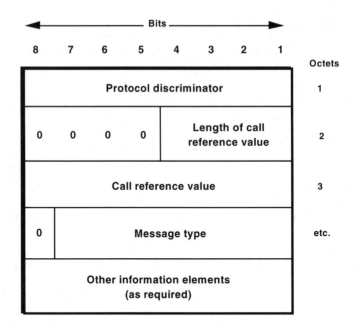

Figure 4–12
The Q.931 message

- *Call reference:* Identifies the specific ISDN call at the local UNI. It does not have end-to-end significance
- *Message type:* Identifies the message function, such as a SETUP, DIS-CONNECT, or the like

The other information elements field may consist of many entries, and its contents depend on the message type.

The SETUP message is sent by the user or the network to indicate a call establishment. In addition to the fields in the message just described, as options, other parameters include the specific ISDN channel identification, originating and destination address, an address for a redirected call, and the designation for a transit network.

The SETUP ACKNOWLEDGE message is sent by the user or the network to indicate the call establishment has been initiated. The parameters for this message are similar to the SETUP message.

The CALL PROCEEDING message is sent by the network or the user to indicate the call is being processed. The message also indicates the network has all the information it needs to process the call.

The CONNECT message and the CONNECT ACKNOWLEDGE messages are exchanged between the network and the network user to indicate the call is accepted between either the network or the user. These messages contain parameters to identify the session as well as the facilities and services associated with the connection.

To clear a call, the user or the network can send a RELEASE or DISCONNECT message. Typically, the RELEASE COMPLETE is returned, but the network may maintain the call reference for later use, in which case, the network sends a DETACH message to the user.

A call may be temporarily suspended. The SUSPEND message is used to create this action. The network can respond to this message with either a SUSPEND ACKNOWLEDGE or a SUSPEND REJECT.

During an ongoing ISDN connection, the user or network may issue CONGESTION CONTROL messages to flow-control USER INFORMATION messages. The message simply indicates if the receiver is ready to accept messages.

The USER INFORMATION message is sent by the user or the network to transmit information to a (another) user.

If a call is suspended, the RESUME message is sent by the user to request the resumption of the call. This message can invoke a RESUME ACKNOWLEDGE or a RESUME REJECT.

The STATUS message is sent by the user or the network to report on the conditions of the call, or other administrative matters. The STATUS ENQUIRY is sent by the user or the network (but usually the user) to inquire about a state or operation.

ISDN also allows other message formats to accommodate equipment needs and different information elements. This feature provides considerable flexibility in choosing other options and ISDN services.

Conclusions on ISDN

ISDN cannot be considered successful, based on its performance since inception in the early 1980s. In North America, the progress of ISDN has been much slower than in Europe because of the lack of a cohesive nationwide implementation policy. This situation has changed in the past few years with the regional Bell Operating Companies (RBOCs) and Bellcore aggressively implementing "National ISDN" throughout the United States. This is leading to extensive central office implementations in both primary and basic rate offerings. Nonetheless, the progress has still been slow.

Notwithstanding, ISDN can be judged successful in another way. It has served the industry well with its specifications of LAPD and the Q.931 messaging protocol. Indeed, these two protocols are found throughout the communications industry. For example, LAPD has been one of the foundation technologies for frame relay as well as the link access procedure for modems (LAPM), and Q.931 is used extensively in other signaling systems such as mobile radio, frame relay, and ATM.

SIGNALING SYSTEM NUMBER 7 (SS7)

Purpose of SS7

We now turn our attention to Signaling System Number 7 (SS7), a clear channel signaling specification published by the ITU-T. SS7 is the prevalent signaling system for telephone networks for setting up and clearing calls and furnishing services such as 800 operations. It is designed also to operate with the ISDN UNI.

SS7 defines the procedures for the set-up, ongoing management, and clearing of a call between telephone users. It performs these functions by exchanging telephone control messages between the SS7 components that support the end-users' connection. Table 4–3 provides a summary of the major functions of SS7.

The SS7 signaling data link is a full duplex, digital transmission channel operating at 64 kbit/s. Optionally, an analog link can be used with either 4 or 3 kHz spacing. The SS7 link operates on both terrestrial and satellite links. The actual digital signals on the link are derived from pulse code modulation multiplexing equipment, or from equipment that employs a frame structure. The link must be dedicated to SS7. In accordance with the idea of clear channel signaling, no other transmission can be transferred with these signaling messages and extraneous equipment must be disabled or removed from an SS7 link.

Typical Topology

Figure 4–13 depicts a typical SS7 topology. The subscriber lines are connected to the SS7 network through the service switching points (SSPs). The purpose of the SSPs is to receive the signals from the CPE and perform call processing on behalf of the user. SSPs are implemented at end offices or access tandem devices. They serve as the source and destination for SS7 messages. In so doing, SSP initiates SS7 messages either to another SSP or to a signaling transfer point (STP).

The STP is tasked with the translation of the SS7 messages and the routing of those messages between network nodes and databases. The STPs are switches that relay messages between SSPs, STPs, and service control points (SCPs). Their principal functions are similar to the layer 3 operations of the OSI model.

The SCPs contain software and databases for the management of

Table 4–3   Examples of SS7 Functions

- Set up and clear down a telephone call
- Provide the called party's number (caller id)
- Indicate that a called party's line is out of service
- Indicate national, international, or other subscriber
- Indicate that called party has cleared
- Identify nature of circuit (satellite/terrestrial)
- Indicate that called party cleared, then went off-hook again
- Use echo-suppression
- Notify to reset a faulty circuit
- Provide status identifiers (calling line identity incomplete; all addresses complete; use of coin station; network congestion; no digital path available; number not in use; blocking signals for certain conditions
- Check circuit continuity
- Provide call forwarding (and previous routes of the call)
- Provide for an all digital path
- Provide security access calls (called closed user group [CUG])
- Identify malicious calls
- Request to hold the connection
- Provide charging information
- Indicate that a called party's line is free
- Monitor call setup failure
- Provide subscriber busy signal
- Identify: circuits signaling points, called and calling parties, incoming trunks, and transit exchanges

the call. For example, 800 services and routing are provided by the SCP. They receive traffic (typically requests for information) from SSPs via STPs and return responses (via STPs) based on the query.

Although Figure 4–13 shows the SS7 components as discrete entities, they are often implemented in an integrated fashion by a vendor's equipment. For example, a central office can be configured with a SSP, a STP, and a SCP or any combination of these elements. These SS7 components are explained in more detail later in this section.

SS7 Layers

Figure 4–14 shows the layers of SS7. The right part of the figure shows the approximate mapping of these layers to the OSI model. Beginning from the lowest layers, the message transfer part (MTP) layer

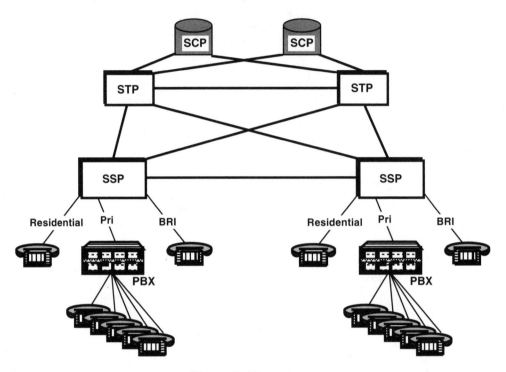

Figure 4–13
Typical SS7 topology.

1 defines the procedures for the signaling data link. It specifies the functional characteristics of the signaling links, the electrical attributes, and the connectors. Layer 1 provides for both digital and analog links, although the vast majority of SS7 physical layers are digital. The second layer is labeled MPT layer 2. It is responsible for the transfer of traffic between SS7 components. It is quite similar to an HDLC-type frame and indeed was derived from the HDLC specification. The MPT layer 3 is somewhat related to layers 3 of ISDN and X.25 in the sense that this layer provides the functions for network management, and the establishment of message routing, as well as the provisions for passing the traffic to the SS7 components within the SS7 network. Many of the operations at this layer pertain to routing, such as route discovery and routing around problem areas in an SS7 network.

Layer 3 of SS7 is organized into functional modules. Their functions are:

- *Message routing:* Selects the link to be used for each message
- *Message distribution:* Selects the user part at the destination point
- *Message discrimination:* Determines at each signaling point if the

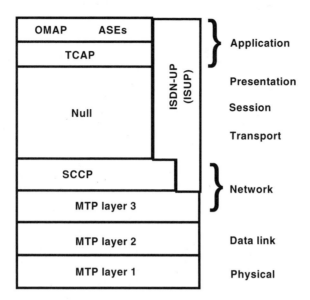

OMAP: Operations, maintenance, administration and provisioning

ASEs: Application service elements

TCAP: Transaction capabilities part

ISDN-UP: ISDN user part

SSCP: Signaling connection part

MTP: Message transfer part

Figure 4–14
The SS7 layers.

message is to be forwarded to message routing or to message distribution

- *Signaling traffic management:* Controls the message routing functions of flow control, rerouting, changeover to a less faulty link, and recovery from link failure
- *Signaling link management:* Manages the activity of the layer 2 function and provides a logical interface between layer 2 and layer 3
- *Signaling route management:* Transfers status information about signaling routes to remote signaling points

The signaling connection control point (SCCP) is also part of the network layer, and provides for both connectionless and connection-oriented services. The main function of SCCP is to provide for translation of addresses, such as ISDN and telephone numbers, to identifiers used in the SS7 network.

The ISDN user part (ISUP) is responsible for transmitting call control information between SS7 network nodes. In essence, this is the call control protocol, in that ISUP sets up, coordinates, and takes down trunks within the SS7 network. It also provides features such call status checking, trunk management, trunk release, calling party number information, privacy indicators, and detection of application of tones for busy conditions. ISUP works in conjunction with ISDN Q.931. Thus, ISUP translates Q.931 messages and maps them into appropriate ISUP messages for use in the SS7 network.

The transaction capabilities application part (TCAP) is an application layer running in layer 7 of the OSI model. It can be used for a variety of purposes. One use of TCAP is the support of 800 numbers transferred between SCP databases. It is also used to define the syntax between the various communicating components. It uses a standard closely aligned with OSI transfer syntax, called the basic encoding rules (BER), which code each field of traffic with (a) syntax type, (b) length of contents field, and (c) contents field (the information).

Finally, the OMAP and ASEs are used respectively for network management and user-specific services. Both are beyond this general text.

SS7 PDUs

ITU-T Recommendation Q.703 of SS7 describes the procedures for transferring SS7 signaling messages across one link. It performs the operations that are typical of layer two protocols. As shown in Figure 4–15, Q.703 has many similarities to the HDLC protocol. For example, both protocols use flags, error checks, and sending/receiving sequence numbers.

The messages are transferred in variable length signal units (SUs), and the primary task of this layer is to ensure their error-free delivery. The SUs are one of three types:

- Message signal unit (MSU)
- Link status signal unit (LSSU)
- Fill-in signal unit (FISU)

The MSU carries the actual signaling message forward to the user part (UP). Q.703 transfers the MSU across the link, and determines if the message is uncorrupted. If the message is damaged during the transfer, it is retransmitted. The LSSU and FISU do not transport UP signals;

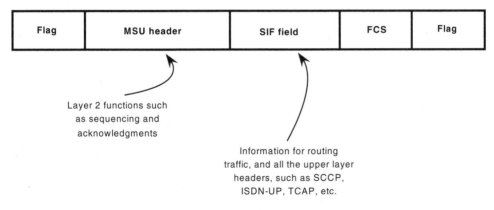

Figure 4–15
SS7 PDUs.

they are used to provide layer 2 control and status signal units between the layer 2 Q.703 protocols at each end of the link.

The SS7 layer 3 functions are called signaling network functions and fall into two categories:

- *Signaling message handling functions:* Directs the message transfer to the proper link or user part
- *Signaling network management functions:* Control the message routing and the configuration of the SS7 network

A message is generated at the originating point and then sent to the destination point. The intermediate nodes are signaling transfer points (STPs).

The STPs use information in the message to determine its routing. A routing label contains the identification of the originating and destination points. A code is also used to manage load sharing within the network. The routing label is used by the STP in combination with predetermined routing data to make the routing decisions. The route is fixed unless failures occur in the network. In this situation, the routing is modified by layer 3 functions. The load-sharing logic (and code in the label) permit the distribution of the traffic to a particular destination to be distributed to two or more output signaling links.

Conclusions on SS7

SS7 has been a huge success in the industry. It is implemented in public telephone networks by practically all carriers throughout the world. Of course, its success was almost assured because its predecessors were woefully inadequate for supporting control signaling in telephone networks. Additionally, features of SS7 have found their way into other systems such as GSM and even satellite signaling. Later in this book, examples are cited of SS7 operating with some of the emerging technologies.

ATM AND SONET: REDUCTION OR ENHANCEMENT OF FUNCTIONS IN NETWORKS

From the perspective of the ITU-T, ATM and SONET form the foundation for the broadband ISDN (B-ISDN). The implementation of these technologies provides for greatly enhanced OAM capabilities from the SONET perspective, and greatly reduced capabilities of the networks' responsibility for traffic integrity from the ATM perspective. While the ideas behind these two statements may seem contradictory, they in fact are complementary. By employing SONET/ATM components of high reliability and integrity, the loss of payload is rare and those rare instances or errors can be corrected in a more efficacious manner at the user endpoint. Therefore, from the X.25 perspective, B-ISDN scales down a network, but from the T1 network perspective, B-ISDN enhances a network.

SUMMARY

T1 and E1 were first implemented over thirty years ago, yet remain as the prevalent option for digital carrier systems. Their use will continue, with SONET/SDH eventually replacing them in carriers' backbone networks.

The implementation of the ISDN has been slow, but its components, especially LAPD and Q.931, have been quite successful, and are used in a variety of other systems, such as frame relay and ATM. However, the long-term viability of a 144 kbit/s 2 B+D offering is not assured, due to the increasing bandwidth needs of user workstations.

X.25, while being an old technology, remains a viable option for many user applications, especially low-speed, asynchronous systems. It is embedded in many systems and products and will remain an option for many years. Nonetheless, some X.25 users will migrate to ATM in the future.

SS7, while an emerged technology, has no competition by any of the emerging communications technologies and will remain as the prevalent out-of-band signaling protocol in the telecommunications industry. Its use will continue to increase, and it is being adapted for use in other technologies.

The Broadband Integrated Services Digital Network (B-ISDN) Model

INTRODUCTION

The chapter provides a description of the Broadband Integrated Services Digital Network (B-ISDN), as published by the ITU-T. The B-ISDN user, control, and management planes are described, as well as how an ATM network uses these planes. A summary is provided of possible B-ISDN services, and a classification scheme for these services. The reader new to the subject of ISDN should read the tutorial in Chapter 4. Also (and once again), be aware that the ITU-T and the B-ISDN Recommendations use the term SDH, and not SONET.

ISDN AND B-ISDN

In the early 1980s when ISDN standards were being established, the former CCITT concentrated on the H1 channel for the primary rate interface (PRI) and the 2 B+D interface for the basic rate interface (BRI). Interest shifted in the mid-1980s to higher-speed channels due to the recognition of the need and the inadequacies of the BRI and PRI technologies. The various standards groups recognized the value of the architecture of ISDN and believed that higher capacity specifications could use the basic concepts of the work performed in the 1980s.

Thus, B-ISDN started out as an extension of ISDN and has many concepts similar to ISDN. For example, functional groupings still consist of TE1, TE2, NT1, NT2, and TA. Reference points are still R, S, and T. As shown in Figure 5–1, these are conveniently tagged with the letter B in front of them to connote the broadband architecture.

It should be emphasized that the similarities between ISDN and B-ISDN are only in concept and work well enough for a general model. In practice, the ISDN and B-ISDN interfaces are not compatible. It is impossible to "upgrade" an ISDN interface by simply supplementing it with B-ISDN functional groups and reference points. Therefore, the reader should consider these terms as abstract conceptions still useful for understanding the overall B-ISDN architecture.

Another point that should be noted is that most of the specifications (Recommendations) developed by the ITU-T are written from the view of the network provider, and not the network user. This approach merely reflects the slant of the ITU-T, which historically has been to publish standards for use by public telecommunications operators (PTOs, such as AT&T, British Telecom, MCI, Sprint, etc.).

B-ISDN Configurations

According to the ITU-T I.413 Recommendation, two options exist for configurations at the T_B reference point: a cell-based physical layer, and an SDH-based physical layer. As described in I.413, these configuration options are confusing. The idea of the options is to give the network designer the option of using both ATM and SDH at T_B. Only one interface per B-NT1 is permitted at the T_B reference point. One or more S_B interfaces per B-NT2 are permitted. The ITU-T I.413 Recommendation

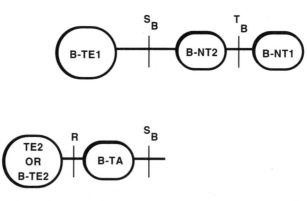

Figure 5–1
B-ISDN functional groups and reference points.

describes other interface options at the reference points, but as of this writing, several are for further study.

ATM AND THE B-ISDN MODEL

The B-ISDN reference model is based on the OSI reference model and the ISDN standards. Figure 5–2 shows the layers of B-ISDN. The physical layer could consist of different media, even though the ITU-T has encouraged the use of ATM with the SDH/SONET technology.

The B-ISDN model contains three planes. The user plane (U-plane) is responsible for providing user information transfer, flow control, and recovery operations. The control plane (C-plane) is responsible for setting up a network connection and managing the connections. It is also responsible for connection release. The control plane is not needed for permanent virtual circuits (PVCs).

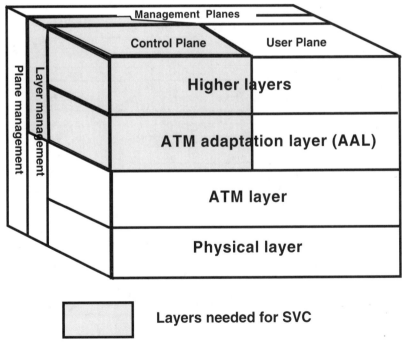

Figure 5–2
ATM and the B-ISDN reference model.

The management plane (M-plane) has two functions: plane management and layer management. Plane management has no layered structure. It is responsible for coordination of all the planes. Layer management is responsible for managing the entities in the layers and performing operation, administration, and maintenance services (OAM). The shadowed parts of Figure 5–2 include the functions needed for the implementation of SVC services.

The rather abstract view of B-ISDN and ATM in Figure 5–2 can be viewed in a more pragmatic way. The three planes depicted in Figure 5–2 (control, user, and management) are shown in Figure 5–3 with the placements of likely protocols residing in the layers. Strictly speaking, the B-ISDN model defines SDH for the physical layer, although Figure 5–3 shows other choices.

The ATM adaptation layer (AAL) is designed to support different types of applications, and different types of traffic, such as voice, video, and data. The AAL plays a key role in the ability of an ATM network to support multiapplication operations. It isolates the ATM layer from the myriad operations necessary to support diverse types of traffic. AAL is divided into a convergence sublayer (CS) and a segmentation and reassembly sublayer (SAR). CS operations are tailored, depending on the type of application being supported. SAR operations entail the segmenta-

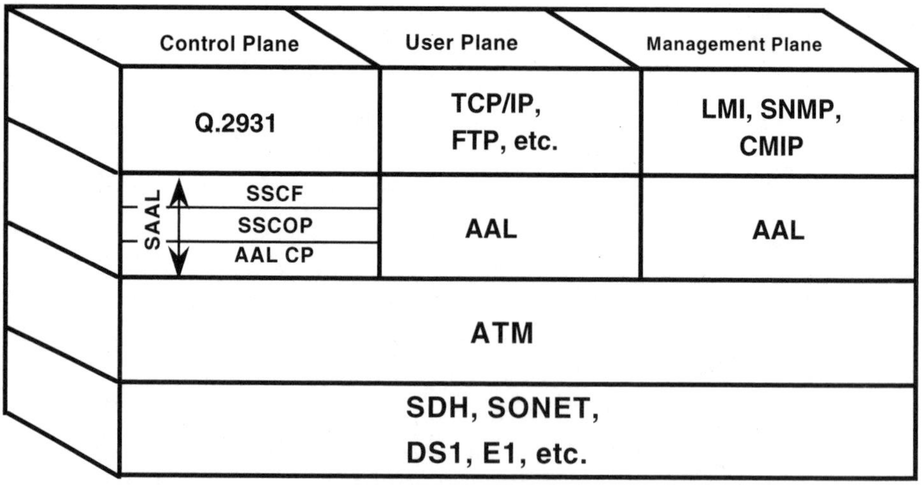

Control Plane	User Plane	Management Plane
Q.2931	TCP/IP, FTP, etc.	LMI, SNMP, CMIP
SAAL { SSCF / SSCOP / AAL CP }	AAL	AAL
ATM		
SDH, SONET, DS1, E1, etc.		

Figure 5–3
Examples of protocol placement in B-ISDN layers.

tion of payload into 48-octet SDUs at the originating SAR and reassembling the SDUs into the original payload at the receiver.

The ATM layer's primary responsibility is the management of the sending and receiving of cells between the user node and the network node. It adds and processes the 5-octet cell header.

On the left side of Figure 5–3 is the C-plane. It contains the Q.2931 signaling protocol, which is used to set up connections in the ATM network (Q.2931 is a variation of Q.931). The layer below Q.2931 is the signaling ATM adaptation layer (SAAL). SAAL supports the transport of the Q.2931 messages between any two machines running ATM SVCs. SAAL contains three sublayers (the full definitions of these sublayers have not been completed by the ITU-IS). Briefly, they provide the following functions. The AAL common part (AAL CP) detects corrupted traffic transported across any interface using the C-plane procedures. The service specific connection-oriented part (SSCOP) supports the transfer of variable length traffic across the interface, and recovers from errored or lost service data units. The service specific coordination function (SSCF) provides the interface to the next upper layer, in this case, Q.2931.

In the middle of the figure is the U-plane, which contains user and applications-specific protocols, such as TCP/IP or FTP. These protocols are chosen arbitrarily, as examples of typical user protocols. The invocation of the user plane protocols take place only if (1) the C-plane has set up a connection successfully, or (2) the connection was preprovisioned.

The M-plane provides the required management services, and is implemented with the ATM local management interface (LMI, discussed later in this book). The internet simple network management protocol (SNMP), and/or the OSI common management information protocol (CMIP) can also reside in the C-plane.

Examples of the Operations between Layers in the B-ISDN Planes

Figure 5–4 shows how the layers in the planes in the user machine communicate with the network machine, or another user machine. The user device is represented by the stacks of layers on the left side of Figure 5–4, and the network node is represented by the stacks of the right side.

In accordance with conventional OSI concepts described in Chapter 3, each layer in the user machine communicates with its peer layer in the network node, and vice versa. The one exception to this statement is

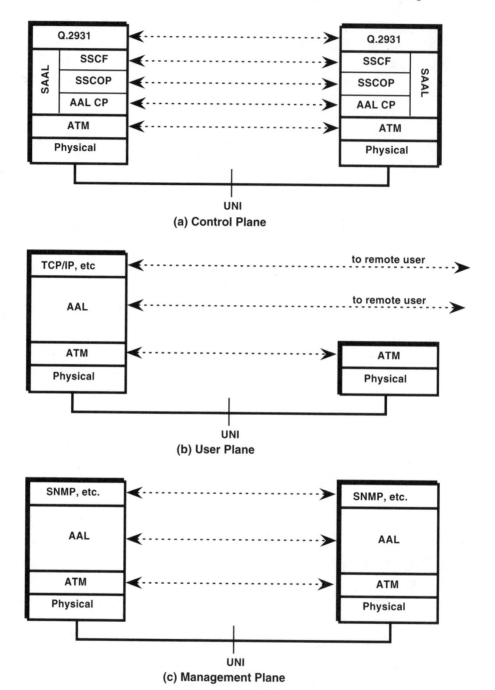

Figure 5–4
Relationships of the B-ISDN peer layers.

at the U-plane. The ATM node (and ATM network) does not process the PDUs of the AAL, and the user-specific protocols. This traffic is passed through the network to the corresponding peer layers on the remote side of the network. Once again, this concept is in the spirit of the OSI model, with its encapsulation/decapsulation techniques and the notion of the transparent aspect of a service data unit (SDU). To the ATM network, AAL and upper layer operations are SDUs. Subsequent chapters explain these three protocol stacks in greater detail.

B-ISDN FUNCTIONS

Figure 5–5 summarizes the ITU-T I.321 view of the major functions of the layers and sublayers of B-ISDN, which are also examined in more detail in subsequent chapters. The functions are listed on the left side of the figure, and the layers or sublayers in which the functions operate are shown in the right side of the figure.

The physical layer (PL) contains two sublayers: the physical medium sublayer (PM) and the transmission convergence sublayer (TC). PM functions depend upon the exact nature of the medium (single mode fiber, microwave, etc.). The physical layer is responsible for typical physical layer functions, such as bit transfer/reception and bit synchronization.

TC is responsible for conventional physical layer operations that are not medium dependent. It is organized into five major functions:

- *Transmission frame generation/recovery* is responsible for the generation and recovery of PDUs (called frames in B-ISDN).
- *Transmission frame adaptation* is responsible for placing and extracting the cell into and out of the physical layer frame. The exact operation depends on the type of frame that is used at the physical layer, such as an SDH envelope or a cell without an SDH envelope.
- *Cell delineation* is responsible for originating an endpoint to define the cell boundaries in order for the receiving endpoint to recover all cells.
- *Cell header processing* is responsible for generating a header error control (HEC) field at the originating endpoint and processing it

Layer functions   Names of layers

	Convergence	CS	AAL
	Segmentation & reassembly	SAR	
	Generic flow control		
	Cell header processing		
	VPI/VCI processing	ATM	
	Cell muxing & demuxing		
	Cell rate decoupling		
	HEC header processing		
	Cell delineation	TC	PL
	Transmission frame adaptation		
	Transmission frame generation/recovery		
	Bit timing	PM	
	Physical medium		

(Left vertical label: **Layer management**)

CS	Convergence sublayer
SAR	Segmentation and reassembly sublayer
AAL	ATM adaptation layer
ATM	Asynchronous transfer mode
TC	Transmission convergence sublayer
PM	Physical medium sublayer
PL	Physical layer

Figure 5–5
B-ISDN layer functions.

at the terminating endpoint in order to determine if the cell header has been damaged in transit.

- *Cell rate decoupling* inserts idle cells at the sending end and extracts them at the receiving end in order to adapt to the physical level bandwidth capacity.

The ATM layer is independent of the physical layer operations, and conceptually does not care if an ATM cell is running on fiber, twisted pair, or other mode. However, we shall see that this layer operates best if fiber is the physical medium. At any rate, the ATM layer is organized into four major functions.

- *Cell muxing and demuxing* is responsible for multiplexing (combining) cells from various virtual connections at the originating endpoint and demultiplexing them at the terminating endpoint.
- *VPI/VCI processing* is responsible for processing the labels/identifiers in a cell header at each ATM node. ATM virtual connections are identified by a virtual path identifier (VPI) and a virtual channel identifier (VCI).
- *Cell header processing* creates the cell header (with the exception of the HEC field) at the originating endpoint and interprets/translates it at the terminating endpoint. The VPI/VCI may be translated into a SAP at this receiver.
- *Generic flow control* is responsible for creating the generic flow control field in the ATM header at the originator and acting upon it at the receiver.

The functions of the AAL, CS, and SAR are described earlier in this chapter.

The AAL acts as the interface to the higher layers. It accommodates to the requirements of different applications (voice, data, etc.) and segments all user traffic PDUs in to 48-octet units for sending to the ATM layer. At the receiving node, it reassembles these units back into the original user PDUs.

B-ISDN SERVICE ASPECTS

The ITU-T Recommendation I.211 describes the services offered by B-ISDN. The services are classified as either interactive services or distribution services. Interactive services, as the name implies, entail an ongoing dialogue between the service user and service provider. The distribution services also entail a dialogue between the service provider and service user, but the dialogue is oriented toward a batch or remote job entry (RJE) basis.

As depicted in Figure 5–6, interactive services are further classified as (1) conversational services, (2) messaging services, and (3) retrieval services. Distribution services are further classified as distribution ser-

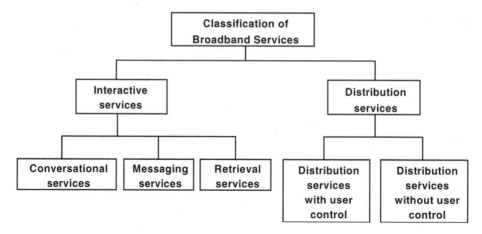

Figure 5–6
Classification of broadband services.

vices without user individual presentation control, and distribution services with user individual presentation control.

Conversational services are interactive dialogues with real-time operations. In this context, real time means that there is no store-and-forward operations occurring between the service user and service provider. For example, interactive teleshopping, ongoing message exchanges between two people, LAN-to-LAN communications, and building surveillance fall into the conversational services category.

Messaging services include user-to-user communications, such as video mail service or document mail service, which can be done on a conversational basis, or on demand.

Retrieval services fall into the store-and-forward category where a user can obtain information stored for public use. This information can be retrieved on an individual basis from the service provider to the service user. Archival information is a good example of retrieval services.

Distribution services without user individual presentation control include conventional broadcast services such as television and radio. As the reader might expect, this service provides continuous flows of information where service users can obtain unlimited access to the information.

In contrast, distribution services with user individual presentation control allows the central source to distribute the information to a large or small number of users based on some type of cyclical repetition. Obviously, the B-ISDN category of interest here is the emerging video-on-demand market.

SUMMARY

The B-ISDN reference model is organized on the original ISDN recommendations published by the ITU-T. The functional groupings and reference points of ISDN are still pertinent to B-ISDN, except on a broadband basis.

The B-ISDN protocol stacks consist of the C-plane, M-plane, and U-plane. The invocation of these protocol stacks depends on the needs of the user and the network. The ITU-T also defines the major functions of each protocol stack and, in so doing, divides some of the protocol layers into sublayers. The upper layers of the U-plane and M-plane may be user-defined.

The B-ISDN services are classified as interactive services and distribution services, and these services are divided further into specific categories.

Asynchronous Transfer Mode (ATM) Basics

INTRODUCTION

This chapter introduces the major functions of the asynchronous transfer mode (ATM) protocol. ATM cells and the user-network interface (UNI) are explained, as well as the ATM multiplexing and routing operations. The rationale for the 53-octet size cell is analyzed, and the issues of delay, error correction/detection, and synchronization are examined. Emphasis is placed on the ATM Forum activities, since this body has assumed the lead role in defining ATM architecture.

THE PURPOSE OF ATM

To review briefly the earlier parts of this book, the purpose of ATM is to provide a high-speed, low-delay multiplexing and switching network to support any type of user traffic, such as voice, data, or video applications.

ATM segments and multiplexes user traffic into small, fixed-length units called cells. The cell is 53 octets, with 5 octets reserved for the cell header. Each cell is identified with virtual circuit identifiers contained in the cell header. An ATM network uses these identifiers to relay the traffic through high-speed switches from the sending customer premises equipment (CPE) to the receiving CPE.

ATM provides no error detection operations on the user payload inside the cell. It provides no retransmisson services, and few operations are performed on the small header. The intention of this approach—small cells with minimal services performed—is to implement a network fast enough to support multimegabit transfer rates.

The ITU-T, ANSI, and the ATM Forum have selected ATM to be part of the broadband ISDN (B-ISDN) specification to provide for the convergence, multiplexing, and switching operations introduced in Chapter 1. ATM resides on top of the physical layer of a conventional layered model, but it does not require the use of a specific physical layer protocol. The physical layer could be implemented with SONET/SDH, DS3, FDDI's physical layer, CEPT4, and others. However, for large public networks, SONET/SDH is the preferred physical layer.

PERTINENT STANDARDS

A number of documents are pertinent to ATM. Most of these documents are published by the ITU-T, ANSI, and the ATM Forum, and are listed in Table 6–1. The ATM standards have been under development since 1984, and the ITU-T as well as the ATM Forum completed many of their documents in 1993. The ATM Forum has also published a B-ISDN intercarrier interface (B-ICI) for inter-LATA operations in the United States.

AN ATM TOPOLOGY

Before an ATM topology is examined, several definitions are in order. As just stated, ATM is part of an B-ISDN that is designed to support public or private networks. Consequently, ATM comes in two forms for the user-to-network interface (UNI):

- A *public UNI* defines the interface between a public service ATM network and a private ATM switch.
- A *private UNI* defines an ATM interface with an end-user and a private ATM switch.

This distinction may seem somewhat superficial, but it is important because each interface will likely use different physical media and span different geographical distances.

Table 6–1   ATM Standards and ATM Forum Specifications

T1S.1/92-185 "Broadband ISDN User-Network Interfaces: Rates and Formats Specification," ANSI Draft Standard, March 1992.

T1S1.5/92-002R3 "Broadband ISDN ATM Aspects—ATM Layer Functionality and Specification," ANSI Draft Standard, May 1992.

ITU-T Recommendation I.413 B-ISDN User-Network Interface," Matsuyama, December 1990.

ITU-T COM SVIII-R91-E "Annex 3 of Report of Study Group XVIII/8," Melbourne, February 1992, pp 103–105.

ITU-T Recommendation I.610 "OAM Principles of B-ISDN Access," Matsuyama, December 1990.

ITU-T COM SV111-R91-E "Annex 3 of Report of Study Group XVIII/8," Melbourne, February 1992, pp 85–102.

ITU-T COM XV111-R56-E "Report of Working Party XVIII/8—General B-ISDN Aspects," January 1991.

ITU-T COM SV111-R70-E "Report of Working Party SVIII/8—General B-ISDN Aspects," January 1991.

ITU-T COM SV111-R91-E "Annex 3 of Report of Study Group XVIII/8," Melbourne, February 1992, pp 85–102.

ITU-T Q.2931 "B-ISDN Call Control"

ITU-T Q.SAAL "Signaling AAL"

ITU-T Q.SSCOP "Service Specific Connection-Oriented Protocol"

The ATM Forum, ATM User-Network Interface Specification, 3.1 July 21, 1994.

The ATM Forum, B-ISDN Intercarrier Interface (B-ICI), Version 1.0, June 1, 1993.

The ATM topology depicted in Figure 6–1 is a conceptual model, as viewed by the standards groups and the ATM Forum. At this embryonic stage in the evolution of ATM, there is no such thing as a typical typology (but Figure 6–2, explained shortly, shows a likely topology).

It is obvious from a brief glance at Figure 6–1 that the ATM interfaces and topology are organized around the ISDN model, introduced in Chapter 5. The UNI can span across public or private S_B, T_B, and U_B interfaces (where $_B$ means broadband). Internal adapters may or may not be involved. If they are involved, a user device (the B-TE1 or B-TE2) is connected through the R reference point to the B-TA. B-NT2s and B-NT1s are also permitted at the interface with B-NT2 considered to be

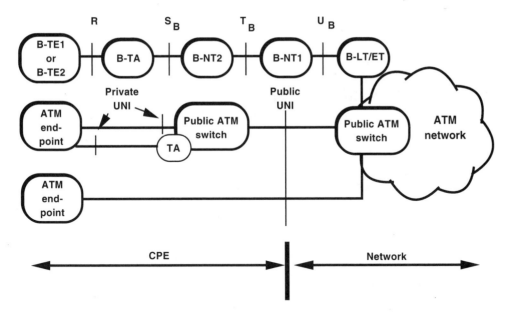

Figure 6–1
An ATM ISDN-based topology. [ATM92a]

part of the CPE. For purposes of simplicity, the picture shows only one side of an ATM network. The other side could be a mirror image of the side shown in Figure 6–1, or could have variations of the interfaces and components shown in the figure.

Figure 6–2 shows a possible ATM-based topology. The topology is a star, point-to-point topology, but nothing precludes the use of other topologies, such as multipoint configurations. As stated briefly in the introduction to this chapter, ATM is designed to support multiapplication service. Its convergence functions permit the relaying of voice, video, and data traffic through the same switching fabric. The interconnection of LANs can also be supported by the ATM technology, because it has convergence and segmentation reassembly (C/SAR or C/S) operations for connectionless data. Convergence services are also provided for fixed bit rate video and variable bit rate video and voice operations.

The WAN in Figure 6–2 could be a public network offered by a public telecommunications operator (PTO, such as AT&T, MCI, or Sprint). The ATM nodes at this interface use a public UNI to the CPE ATM nodes. In turn, the CPE ATM nodes connect with private UNIs to LANs, PBXs, and the like.

ATM allows multiple users to share a line at the UNI by a subscrip-

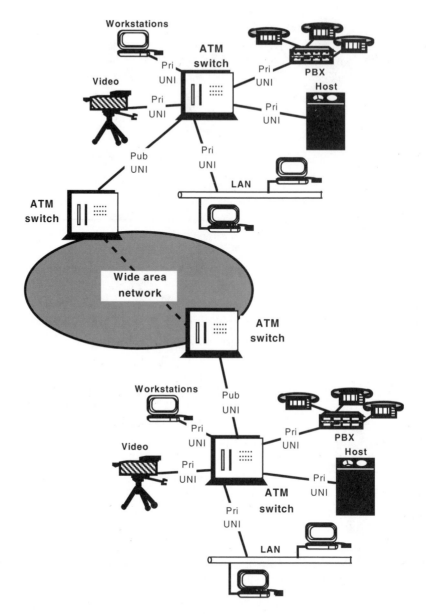

Figure 6–2
A possible ATM topology.

tion agreement with each ATM customer (subscriber). This agreement defines the amount of traffic that the network must support, as well as several QOS features, such as delay and throughput. The agreement also restricts how much traffic the subscriber can submit to the network during some measured period.

The VPI and VCI Labels

The ITU-T Recommendation requires that an ATM connection be identified with connection identifiers that are assigned for each user connection in the ATM network. The connection (at the UNI) is identified by two values in the cell header: the virtual path identifier (VPI) and the virtual channel identifier (VCI). The VPI and VCI fields constitute a virtual circuit identifier. Users are assigned these values when the user enters into a session with a network as a connection-on-demand, or when a user is provisioned to the network as a PVC.

Figure 6–3 shows examples of how the VPI/VCI values can be used. Three applications are connected to each other through the network: a video conference, a data session between a workstation and a host computer, and a telephone call. Each connection is associated with a VPI/VCI value on each side of the network. For example, the video session's connection is associated with VPI 4/VCI 10 at one UNI and VPI 20 and VCI 33 at the other UNI. The manner in which VPI/VCI values are established and managed is left to the network administrator. In this example, VPI/VCI numbers have local significance at each UNI. Of course, the network must assure that these local VPI/VCI values at each UNI are "mapped together" through the network.

ATM services can be obtained as a PVC or as an SVC. The term SVC is not used in some of the ATM specifications, and is gradually being replaced with the term connection-on-demand, which does convey the idea well. One colleague stated that two terms are needed. The first, "connection-on-demand" is from the user perspective. The other, "connection-on-request" is from the network provider perspective.

In addition, perhaps a better term to describe the ITU-T view of a PVC is that it is a semi-permanent virtual circuit technology. That is, users of two connecting endpoints are preprovisioned in the network, and then given a session (connection) when requested by the user—*if* the session can be supported by the network. That is, if the network has sufficient bandwidth available to meet the needs of the user session.

The ATM Forum and the ITU-T have published specifications for

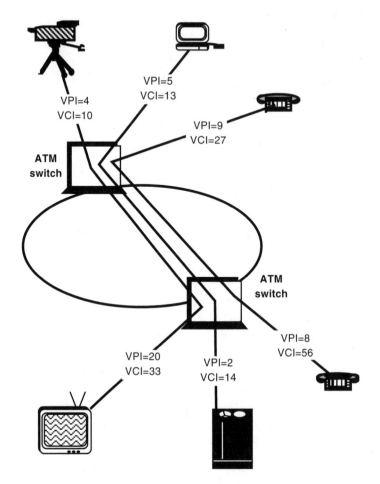

Figure 6–3
Examples of VPI and VCI operations.

ATM connections on demand, or SVCs [ATM93a], which are explained in Chapter 10.

The VPIs and VCIs are also used in the ATM network. They are examined by switches in order to determine how to route the cell through the network. The manner in which the VPI/VCIs are processed in the network is not yet defined in the ATM standards. As depicted in Figure 6–3, from the perspective of these standards, the VCI/VPI has local significance at the UNI only.

Thus, the VPI/VCI labels are similar to data link connection identifiers (DLCIs) used in frame relay networks, and logical channel numbers (LCNs) used in X.25-based networks.

ATM LAYERS

As illustrated in Figure 6–4, the ATM layers are similar to the layers of some other emerging communications technologies (the metropolitan area network [MAN] and the switched multimegabit data service [SMDS]). ATM provides convergence functions at the ATM adaptation layer (AAL) for connection-oriented and connectionless variable bit rate (VBR) applications. It supports isochronous applications (voice, video) with constant bit rate (CBR) services.

A convenient way to think of the AAL is that it is actually divided into two sublayers, as shown in Figure 6–4. The segmentation and reassembly (SAR) sublayer, as the name implies, is responsible for processing user PDUs that are different in size and format into ATM cells at the sending site and reassembling the cells into the user-formatted PDUs at

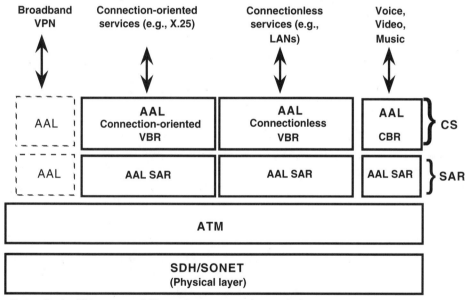

Note: Dashed box means AAL services may not be needed

AAL	ATM adaptation layer
CBR	Constant/continuous bit rate
VBR	Variable bit rate
SAR	Segmentation and reassembly
SDH	Synchronous Digital Hierarchy
SONET	Synchronous Optical Network

Figure 6–4
The ATM layers.

the receiving site. The other sublayer is called the convergence sublayer (CS), and its functions depend upon the type of traffic being processed by the AAL, such as voice, video, or data.

The SAR and CS entities provide standardized interfaces to the ATM layer. The ATM layer is then responsible for relaying and routing the traffic through the ATM switch. The ATM layer is connection-oriented and cells are associated with established virtual connections. Traffic must be segmented into cells by the AAL before the ATM layer can process the traffic. The switch uses the VPI/VCI label to identify the connection to which the cell is associated.

Broadband virtual private networks (VPNs) may or may not use the services of the ATM adaptation layer. The decision to use this service depends on the nature of the VPN traffic as it enters the ATM device.

ATM Layers and OSI Layers

The ATM layers do not map directly with the OSI layers. The ATM layer performs operations typically found in layers 2 and 3 of the OSI model. The AAL combines features of layers 4, 5, and 7 of the OSI model. It is not a clean fit, but then, the OSI model is over ten years old. It should be changed to reflect the emerging technologies.

The physical layer can be a SONET or SDH carrier. It may also be other carrier technologies, such as DS3, E3, or FDDI.

A user CPE may use the AAL to provide convergence support for different kinds of traffic across virtual connections. If virtual private networks provide services that are compatible with ATM, then the AAL services are not needed. For the foreseeable future, the AAL will be quite prevalent in ATM UNI services.

The relationship of the user connections to the AAL and ATM layers is shown in Figure 6–5. The figure also shows that VPI/VCIs can be assigned bidirectionally; that is, bandwidth and QOS need not be the same in both directions of the traffic flow for a connection. For example, consider a client-server application in which the client is obtaining a file transfer from the server. While the initial dialogue between the two endpoints requires about the same amount of bandwidth in both directions, after the file transfer begins, the server needs more bandwidth than does the client, since most of the traffic (the file) is flowing from the server to the client. ATM provides procedures to set up asymmetrical bandwidth for the virtual connection.

Whatever the implementation of AAL at the user device, the ATM network is not concerned with AAL operations. Indeed, the ATM bearer

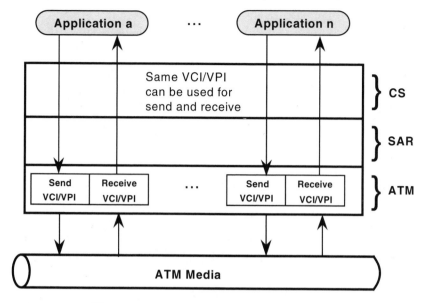

Figure 6–5
Applications and VPI/VCI assignments.

service is "masked" from these CS and SAR functions. The ATM bearer service includes the ATM and physical layers. The bearer services are application independent, and AAL is tasked with accommodating to the requirements of different applications.

These ideas are amplified in Figure 6–6. For the transfer of user

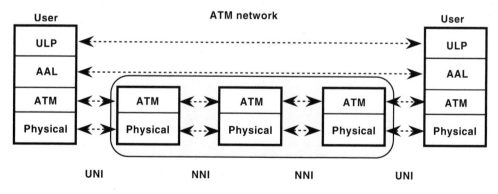

ULP   Upper layer protocols

Figure 6–6
Relationship of user and network layers (for transfer of user payload).

payload, upper layer protocols (ULP) and AAL operations are not in-voked in the ATM network functions. The dotted arrows indicate that logical operations occur between peer layers at the user nodes and the ATM nodes. Therefore, the ULP headers, user payload, and the AAL headers are passed transparently through the ATM network. Of course, as we learned in Chapter 5, AAL must be invoked for the C-plane and M-plane, because AAL must be available to assemble the payload in the cells back to an intelligible ULP PDU.

RELATIONSHIP OF AAL, ATM, AND THE NETWORK

It is evident that the AAL is responsible for acting as the interface between user applications and the ATM layer. As such, it is expected to enhance the services provided by the ATM layer, based on the specific re-quirements of the application. It has the task of supporting different user operations such as voice, video, and data.

Figure 6–7 illustrates several of the major functions of AAL, the ATM layer, and the ATM network. User traffic, digitized images of vari-ous payload types (again, voice, video, or data), is segmented by AAL into PDUs of 48 octets. However, these octets do not contain solely user pay-load. Headers (H), and perhaps trailers (T), use part of these 48 octets. The contents and structure of these headers and trailers vary, depending on the type of payload.

The ATM layer expects to receive and transmit fixed length data units to and from the AAL. Among other tasks, the transmitting ATM layer adds a 5-octet cell header (CH) to the 48-octet AAL PDU and the receiving ATM layer processes this header, then strips it away before passing the 48-octet PDU to the receiving AAL.

The AAL is responsible for operations beyond the SAR functions just described. For example, fixed rate video applications require the AAL to maintain a concise and fixed time relationship for the transferral of data units between the source and destination applications. As an-other example, connectionless data applications require that the AAL provide flexible buffering arrangements for these bursty-type transac-tions.

The ITU-T and other standards groups do not define all the activi-ties and functions that may be invoked at the AAL or between the AAL and the upper layer protocol, because they may already be defined by standards that exist in the upper layer protocols, or they may be left to vendor-specific solutions. As examples not defined in AAL: (1) the exact

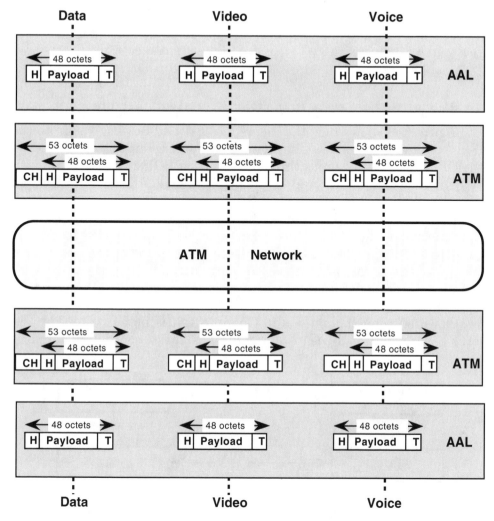

Figure 6–7
Relationships of AAL, ATM layer, and ATM network.

manner in which a receiving AAL entity must adjust to delay variations of arriving voice PDUs; (2) how video compression is accomplished; and (3) how different queues are managed. These types of operations are left to either a vendor-specific solution or they are defined in other standards.

The ATM network processes the ATM PDU header (the 5-octet header). It receives the cells from the ATM and physical layers (physical layer is not shown in this figure) at the local UNI, and transports these cells to the remote UNI through the use of the ATM cell header. Here, the cells are presented to the user node, where the cell and PDU are processed by the physical, ATM, and AAL layers respectively.

Relationship of Layers to the OSI Layered Architecture

Figure 6–8 shows how the layers of ATM and SONET relate to the OSI model. As discussed in Chapter 3, the layers communicate with each other between two machines through the use of PDUs. At the ATM layer, the PDUs are called cells, and at the physical layer, the PDUs are called frames.

The service definitions define the interactions between adjacent layers in the same machine, and use service access points (SAPs) to identify the source and destination communicating parties. The service definitions are known as primitives and are actually implemented with computer-specific operations, such as C function calls, UNIX system library calls, etc.

Based on the explanations in Chapter 3, it is noted that ATM networks use conventional encapsulation/decapsulation concepts. Therefore,

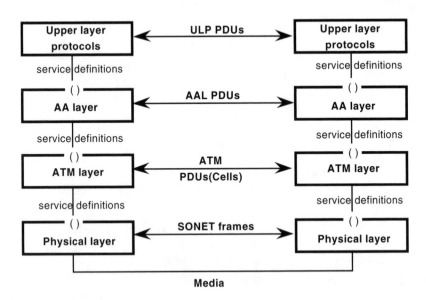

Note: ( ) represents a service access point (SAP)

Figure 6–8
B-ISDN PDUs and service definitions.

we shall not dwell on the subject further. The interested reader can refer to Chapter 3.

Where to Find Service Definitions and Primitives

In order to simplify the description of the aforementioned topics, the service definitions and primitive calls between (1) the ULP and the AAL, and (2) the AAL and the ATM layer are explained in Chapter 7 (see "The AAL/ATM Primitives"). The service definitions and primitive calls between the AAL and the physical layer are described in Chapter 14 (see "The ATM/Physical Layer Primitives"). The service definitions and primitive calls at the M-plane and ATM (not shown in Figure 6–8) are described in Chapter 13 (see "The Layer Management/ATM Primitives").

TYPICAL PROTOCOL STACKS

Figure 6–9 is an example of a typical configuration at the user host machines, routers, and the ATM network nodes. A router is included in this example, because many of the current implementations are using a router (or something similar to a router) to provide the ATM UNI. The configuration keeps the end-user equipment isolated from the ATM operations, and allows the use of a high-speed, cell-based ATM network to transfer traffic between user applications, but does not require the integration of the ATM technology into the architecture of the workstation.

This figure may require some study on the part of the reader, and may require revisiting some material in earlier chapters. As a starter, the tutorial on layered protocols in Chapter 3 is key to understanding this figure. Additionally, as the legend in the figure explains, the AAL and upper layers are not invoked at the ATM node for the transfer of user payload (the U-plane), and these ideas are summarized in this chapter and explained also in Chapter 5.

The protocols and their headers, emanating from the host on the left side of the figure, are received by the router. The data link and physical layer headers (D and P in the figure) used at the local host-router interface are removed by the router. The header of the network layer (N in the figure) is used by the router to determine the destination address of the destination host (for example, this header could be an IP datagram header, and the destination address could be an IP address).

In this example, a routing table stored at the router reveals that the next node to process the datagram is an ATM node. Therefore, the router

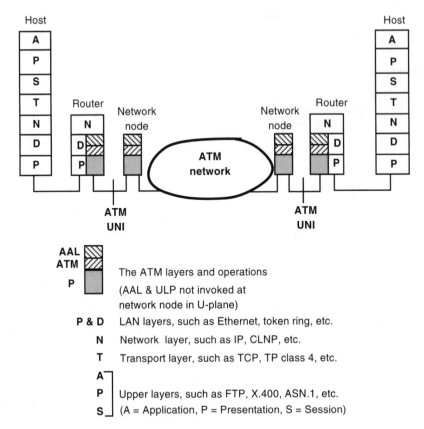

Figure 6–9
Typical protocol stacks (M-plane and C-plane).

must invoke the ATM protocol stack, and create the cells for transport to the ATM network node. The manner in which the cells are created, and how the router (or any user machine) interacts with the ATM network are explained further in Chapters 9, 10, and 11.

The cells containing the IP datagram, the headers of the upper layers, and the user payload are transported through the ATM network across the remote UNI to the terminating router. Here, the process is reversed: the cells are reassembled into the original datagram, placed inside the headers and trailers of the physical and data link layers of the remote router-host interface, and sent to the terminating host—up through the layers of the user host machine to the end-user application (A).

Figure 6–10 shows the relationships of the layer interactions for M-plane and C-plane operations. The horizontal arrows depict that the layers at each end of the arrowed line are communicating with each

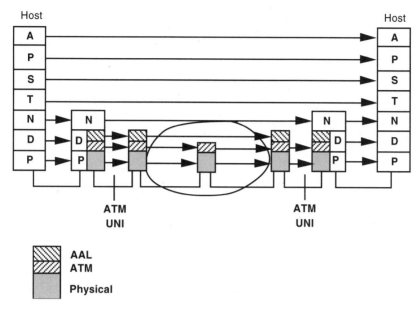

Figure 6–10
Interactions of the protocol stacks (M-plane and C-plane).

other. The direction of the arrow indicates that the endpoint protocol (at the end of the arrow) receives a header and processes it according to the rules of the particular protocol of that specific layer.

For this example, the AAL is invoked (for a M-plane, or C-plane operations). Notice that the AAL is not invoked inside the network. Additionally, if the example were a U-plane operation, AAL would not be invoked at the ATM nodes at the local and remote UNIs.

ATM PDUS (CELLS)

The ATM PDU is called a cell. It is 53 octets in length, with 5 octets devoted to the ATM cell header, and 48 octets used by AAL and the user payload. As shown in Figure 6–11, the ATM cell is configured slightly differently for the UNI than for the NNI. Since various OAM functions operate only at the UNI interface, a flow control field is defined for the traffic traversing this interface, but not at the NNI. The flow control field is called the generic flow control (GFC) field. If GFC is not used, this 4-bit field is set to zeros.

Most of the values in the 5-octet cell header consist of the virtual circuit labels of VPI and VCI. A total of 24 bits are available with 8 bits

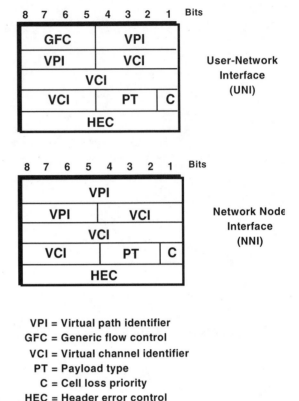

Figure 6–11
The ATM PDU (cell) headers.

assigned to VPI and 16 bits assigned to VCI. For the NNI, the VPI field contains 12 bits. A combination of the VPI and VCI field is called the VPCI field.

Use of Two Identifiers

Most of the VPI and VCI overhead values are available for use as the network administrator chooses. Here are some examples of how they can be used. Multiple VCs can be associated with one VP. This approach can be used to assign a certain amount of bandwidth to a VP, and then allocate it among the associated VCs. "Bundling" VCs in VPs allows one OAM message to be transmitted that provides information about multiple VCs, by using the VPI value in the header. Some implementations do not use all the bits of VPI/VCI to avoid processing all the bits in the VP and VC fields. Some implementations examine only the VPI bits at intermediate nodes in the network.

A payload type (PT) identifier field identifies the type of traffic residing in the cell. The cell may contain user traffic or management/control traffic. The ATM Forum has expanded the use of this field to identify other payload types (OAM, control, etc.). One of particular interest is a payload type that indicates that either the cell contains user data and the cell receiver is notified of congestion problems, or the cell contains user data and the cell receiver is notified that congestion has not been experienced. In other words, this field is now used for congestion notification operations, which is similar to the congestion notification bits (FECN and BECN bits) in frame relay. Interestingly, the GFC field does not contain the congestion notification codes, because the name of the field was created before all of its functions were identified. The flow control fields (actually, congestion notification) are contained in the PT identifier field. Chapter 13 describes how the GFC, PT, and the remainder of the first four octets are defined by the ATM Forum to identify OAM and other control signaling at the UNI.

The cell loss priority (C) field is a 1-bit value. If C is set to 1, the cell is subject to being discarded by the network. Whether the cell is discarded depends on network conditions and the policy of the network administrator. Whatever the policy of the administrator may be, the C bit set to 0 indicates a higher priority of the cell to the network. It must be treated with more care than a cell in which the C bit is set to 1. The C bit is quite similar to the frame relay discard eligibility (DE) bit in frame relay.

The header error control (HEC) field is an error check field, which can also correct a 1-bit error. It is calculated on the 5-octet ATM header, and not on the 48-octet user payload. ATM employs an adaptive error detection/correction mechanism with the HEC. The transmitter calculates the HEC value on the first four octets of the header. The 1-octet result becomes the HEC field. The value is the remainder of the division (Modulo 2) by the generator polynomial x^8+x^2+x+1 for the x^8, multiplied by the content of the header. The pattern 01010101 is XORed with the 8-bit remainder, and this result is placed in the last octet of the header. The complementary calculation is performed at the receiver on all five octets.

Metasignaling Cells and Other Cells

The VCI, VPI, and other parts of the first four octets of the cell can be coded in a variety of formats to identify nonuser payload cells. One such convention is called metasignaling. It is used to establish a session with the network and negotiate session services. Another convention is called broadcasting. With this feature, the VPI and VCI are coded to indicate that the cell is to be broadcast to all stations on the UNI. Other conventions provide for management services, the identification of idle cells (cells that are empty), and unassigned cells. Unassigned cells are sent when the ATM module has no user payload to send, a process called cell decoupling. Thus, the continuous sending of cells at the sender and the continuous reception of cells at the receiver allow the network to operate synchronously, yet support bursty, asynchronous services. Metasignaling is described in Chapter 13.

The ATM Forum has defined an additional coding for octets 1-4 to identify a network management cell. This coding convention is part of the Forum's interim local management interface (ILMI) specification (available in the ATM UNI Specification (v. 2.0) [ATM92a]. The ILMI also is covered in Chapter 13.

RATIONALE FOR THE CELL SIZE

The reader might wonder why a user payload of 48 octets was chosen. Why not 32? Why not 64? The 48-octet size was a result of a compromise between various groups in the standards committees. The compromise resulted in a cell length that is (1) acceptable for voice networks, (2) adaptable to forward error correction operations, (3) able to minimize the number of bits that must be retransmitted from the user device in the event of errors, and (4) able to work with ongoing carrier transport equipment. The small cell also avoids the delay inherent in the processing of long PDUs.

We shall see in Chapter 12 that the SONET/SDH STS-3 payload accommodates the bit rate requirement for high-quality video, even when the video images are carried inside the payload of the ATM cell. In this section of this chapter, the cell size is examined in relation to transmission errors, equipment processing errors, transmission delay, and equipment processing delay.

Ideally, one would like to have a choice of the size of a PDU, based on the quality of the circuits. For error-prone links, it is desirable to have small PDUs because the number of bits retransmitted are small. For high-quality links, it is desirable to have larger PDUs in order to increase the ratio of user payload to the cell header. Moreover, it is well known that variable-length PDUs provide greater transmission efficiency than fixed-length PDUs (a demonstration of this fact will follow shortly). However, transmission efficiency is not the only criterion that should be used in making the decision on fixed or variable length PDUs. Equally important is the effect a fixed/variable length PDU has on switching speed and network delay. An analysis of these factors vis-à-vis transmission efficiency led the ITU-T to the decision to use fixed cells.

The transmission efficiency of a protocol can be calculated as: $TE = L_i / (L_i + L_o)$, where TE = transmission efficiency; L_i = length of information field (user traffic); L_o = length of control header. Various studies reveal that the TE is better for variable length PDUs than for fixed length PDUs. It is common sense that the more bits in the information field, the better the TE for a given L_o. However, a large I field entails overhead at a switch, because it takes longer for the cell to be processed and to leave the switch. Indeed, one of the reasons for the migration from message switching systems in the 1970s to packet switching systems was the attractive feature of being able to process a small packet more quickly than a large message. Figure 6–12 shows that for an ATM cell with 10 percent of overhead (the 5 byte header), delay is less than 2 ms for a 64 kbit/s voice transmission. Figure 6–13 amplifies these ideas by contrasting overhead and delay.

Therefore, the ITU-T had to balance conflicting factors in choosing a fixed or variable length PDU, and the size of the SDU. After a lengthy

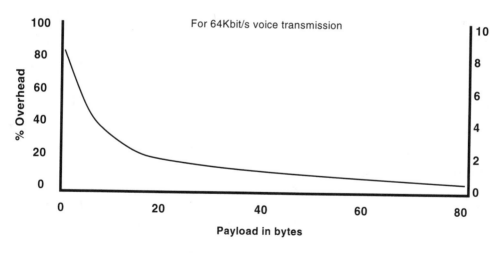

Figure 6–12
Overhead and delay.

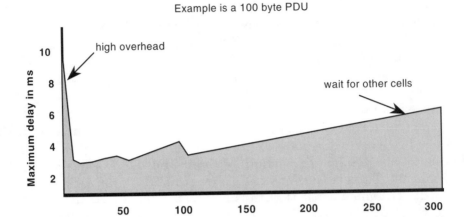

Figure 6–13
Overhead and delay. [ATM94a]

analysis, with Europe opting for a cell size of 32 octets (and 4-octet header), and the United States and Japan opting for a cell size of 64 octets (with 5-octet header), the difference was split, and the size of 48 octets was selected at the 1989 Group XVIII Geneva meeting.

After extensive deliberations in the standards working groups, it was agreed that a user payload size between 32 and 64 octets would perform satisfactorily because it (1) worked with ongoing equipment (did not require echo cancellers), (2) provided acceptable transmission efficiency, and (3) was not overly complex to implement. As stated, the United States favored a cell size with 64 octets of user payload; Europe favored a size of 32 octets.

The size of the cell is quite important for speech and video because of the concept of cell length (the duration of the cell on the channel). Cell length is a function of the number of bits in the cell, the compression ratio (if any) reflected in these bits, and the coding rate of the signal (for example, 64 kbit/s). Studies reveal [JAYA81] that losing traffic that is 1 or 2 ms long is disturbing to the listener, because it has the effect of impulse noise. Traffic loss of around 32 to 64 ms is quite disruptive, because it means the loss of speech phonemes. On the other hand, cell loss of a duration of some 4 to 16 ms is not very noticeable or disturbing to the listener or viewer. Therefore, a payload size of anywhere around 32 to 64 octets would be acceptable to an audio listener or video viewer. As examples, consider a digitized voice image with a coding rate of 64 kbit/s:

- 32 octets * 8 bits per octet = 256 bits
  256/64,000 = .004
- 48 octets * 8 bits per octet = 384 bits
  384/64,000 = .006
- 64 octets * 8 bits per octet = .512 bits
  512/64,000 = .008

Therefore, a cell loss for a 64,000 bit/s signal with 32, 48, or 64 octets in the payload of the cell results in traffic loss of 4 ms, 6 ms, or 8 ms respectively. Eventually, a compromise was reached and the 48-octet size was adapted (less the 5-octet header). Subsequent material describes other factors that contributed to these decisions.

Network Transparency Operations

This section delves into more detail about the ATM cell and its relationship to errors, delay, and the size of the cell. The service data unit (SDU) is a useful OSI term for this discussion. The reader can refer to Chapter 3 if the concept of the SDU is not familiar. Three concepts are examined in this discussion:

Semantic transparency:	Transporting the user's SDUs without error from source to destination
SDU size transparency:	Accommodating the user's variable size SDUs
Time transparency:	Transporting the user's SDUs with a fixed delay between source and destination

Errors and Error Rates

Errors are impossible to eliminate completely in a communications network. As reliable as optical fiber is, noise, signal dispersion, and other impairments will persist. Errors also will occur in equipment due to the malfunctioning of hardware and imperfections in component design, as two examples.

Communications network error rates are measured with a simple formula called the bit error rate (BER). It is calculated as follows:

$$BER = errored\ bits\ received\ /\ total\ bits\ sent$$

BER is measured over a period of time, which smoothes out the randomness of errors on communications channels. Generally, measurement periods are several orders of magnitude more than the actual BER value.

Another useful statistic is called the block error rate (BLER), which defines the number of blocks sent in relation to the number of blocks received in error. The term block is generic; for this discussion, a block refers to a cell. BLER is calculated as:

$$BLER = errored\ blocks\ received\ /\ total\ blocks\ sent$$

Other error statistics are important. One that is pertinent to ATM is called the loss rate, which is the ratio of lost or inserted cells in relation to the total number of cells sent. Lost cells are any cells that are damaged and cannot be corrected, cells that arrive too late to be useful (as in a video application), or cells that are discarded by the network. Inserted cells are cells that are received by a user when they were supposed to go to another user.

These error rate statistics play a key role in the design of the network. As errors increase, user payload (data) must be retransmitted from the user CPE. The end effect is the creation of more traffic in the network. Ideally, one wishes to design a network that is cost effective from the standpoint of its incidence of errors as well as efficient in its treatment of errors. This brings us to the subject of error rates on optical fiber and the size of an ATM cell.

AT&T [ATT89a] conducted a study on the error rates of optical fiber. This study is summarized in Figure 6–14. Under normal operating conditions, most errors occuring on optical fiber are single-bit errors. As this figure illustrates, 99.64 percent of the errors are a single bit. Although not shown in this figure, AT&T also conducted a study on the error rate during maintenance conditions. For example, during switchover operations on a device, the single bit error probability dropped to 65 percent. Figure 6–14 also reveals that the ATM error handling operations is based on the fact that 6 bits are needed to correct a single bit error for 40 bits of a header, and 8 bits will correct a single bit error and detect 84% of multiple bit errors. Therefore, a cell header of five bytes, which are the protected bits, is a resonable compromise in relation to the HEC field of one byte, which are the protection bits.

These studies and others paved the way for a more detailed analysis of the effect of using forward error correction (FEC) to correct a one-bit

Bit Error Rates on Optical Fiber

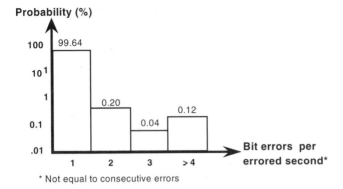

* Not equal to consecutive errors

Header size:

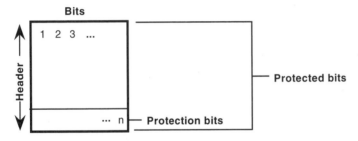

- 6 bits needed to correct a single bit error for 40 bits
- 8 bits will correct a single bit error and detect 84% of multiple bit errors

Figure 6–14
Bit error rates (BER) on optical fiber. [ATT89a]

error. Subsequent research has confirmed that small cell headers experiencing a one-bit error can be corrected, which obviates (1) retransmitting data cells and (2) discarding voice/video cells. Since errors are rare on optical fiber, ATM does not execute cumbersome retransmission schemes, it will *correct* headers with one-bit errors and *discard* headers with multiple-bit errors.

However, it is also recognized that errors on optical fiber are actually a mix of single-bit errors and errors that have long bursts. Consequently, some implementations may not invoke the error correction feature, which is ineffective on media exhibiting errors that damage a long string of bits.

Error Correction and Detection

The ATM HEC operations protect the cell header and not the 48-octet payload. The HEC field of 8 bits was selected because it allows the correction of a single bit error and the detection of multiple bit errors. Figure 6–15 depicts the general logic of the correction and detection functions. Initially, the HEC operation is in the correction mode. If it detects either single-bit or multiple-bit errors in the header, it moves to the detection mode. A single bit error is corrected, and a multiple-bit error results in the discarding of the cell. Once in the correction mode, all cells that have errors are discarded. When a cell with no error is detected, the operation returns to the correction mode. Figure 6–16 shows how a cell is treated if it is either corrupted or uncorrupted, and if the operation is in a correction or detection mode. Refer to the legend in this figure for the explanation.

ATM uses an adaptation of the Hamming code technique known as the Bose-Chadhuri-Hocquenghem (BHC) codes. These codes provide error correction/detection schemes based on the ratio of protection bits in the HEC field (for example) to the protected bits in the cell header (for example). Without delving into error coding theory, which is best left to theoretical texts, it is instructive to note that a 40-bit field (the cell header of 5 octets * 8 bit per octet = 40 bits) needs at least 6 protection bits to correct a single bit. The 6 bits will also detect 36 percent of multiple-bit errors. Improvements to an 84 percent detection rate of multiple-bit errors can be attained if 8 protection bits are used [dePr91]. Of course, this is a good arrangement if optical fiber media are employed,

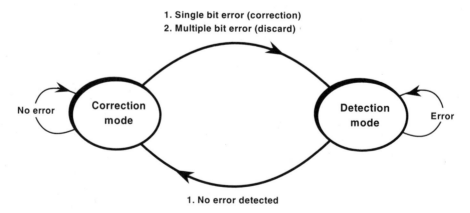

Figure 6–15
Header protection in the HEC field.

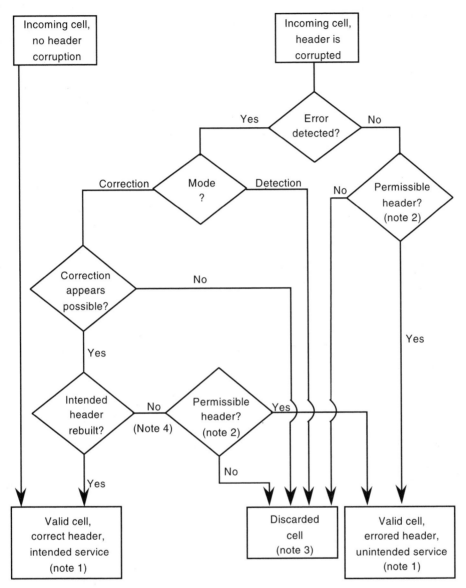

Note 1: Valid cell means cell is free of errors
Note 2: A cell that is not permissible depends on implementation (e.g., invalid VPI/VCI, etc.)
Note 3: Header invalid or not permitted
Note 4: Error correction is not invoked (depends on implementation)

Figure 6–16
ITU-T I.432 view of error handling.

due to optical fiber error characteristics. The HEC field of 8 bits was selected because of these characteristics.

Probability of Discarding Cells

Figure 6–17 illustrates the probability of the ATM network discarding cells in relation to the random bit error rate of a communications channel, as published by the ITU-T in I.432. By examining one point on the graph in this figure, even a modest random bit error probability of $10E^{-7}$, the probability of a discarded cell occurring is $10E^{-11}$.

Conclusions. It can be concluded that the ATM approach of using small cells and small cell headers lends itself to efficient error correction/detection schemes. The next questions are: What size should the full cell be? And, if it is to be small, can it be variable in length or must it be fixed? These two questions are answered in the next two sections.

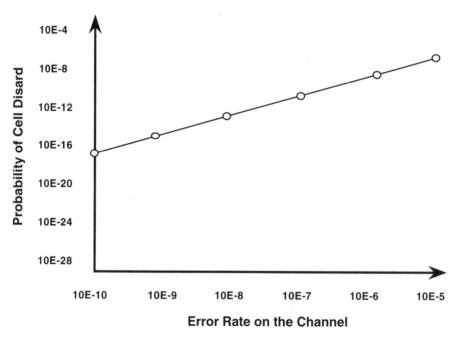

Figure 6–17
Probability of discarding cells.

Overhead of the Cell Approach

The issue of cell overhead is visited in later in Chapter 7. For this discussion, it is noted that the use of small cells (which exhibit a high ratio of overhead to payload) requires an ATM node (switch) to operate at very high speeds, if multiple applications are to be supported simultaneously. Given the same amount of traffic in networks that carry small PDUs (cell networks) versus networks that carry large PDUs (frame networks), the cell networks simply must process more headers and more cells, because, given a steady flow of traffic, there is an inverse ratio between the PDU arrival rate at a node, and the size of the PDU.

For example, consider a frame relay network that transports frames. A typical payload is 512 octets, and frame relay adds a 2-octet header to this payload. Thus, the ratio of overhead to payload in this frame relay example is only .39 percent (16 bits of header / [512 octets × 8 bits per octet] = .0039). In contrast, a typical ATM network carried an overhead ratio of 10.4 percent (40 bits of header / [48 octets × 8 bits per octet] = .1041). Since frames are larger than cells, a node must process more cells than frames, even though the basic link speed into the node is the same for both cell and frame relay interfaces.

Actually, the ratio is worse if data transmissions are used as a comparison (which is reasonable, since frame relay, at this time, supports only data). The ATM 48-octet payload uses four of these octets for managing and identifying the user traffic at the ATM adaptation layer (AAL). Thus, the ratio of overhead to payload in a typical ATM data network transmission is 70 bits of overhead to 352 bits of data, resulting in an overhead ratio of almost 20 percent.

Of course, one must also take into consideration the overhead at the physical layer, and if SONET is used, approximately 4 percent of the channel bandwidth is taken for SONET overhead. Then, one must add in the headers of the upper layer protocols, which are for data transmissions and which can range from 12 to 30 octets for *each* user PDU.

The overhead cited in the previous paragraph is not an issue in the comparisons of cell and frame relay. Notwithstanding, three observations are appropriate:

- ATM must utilize fast processors and high bandwidth channels to compensate for its overhead.
- Even with high bandwidth channels and fast processors, compression operations will still be quite important in ATM networks.

- Comparing the ratio of the overhead bits of all layers to the user bits will reveal that, on occasion, actual user traffic is passed though a communications channel.

Transmission Delay

Previous discussions in this book have explained how certain applications require a predictable and fixed delay of traffic between the source and destination, such as video and voice applications. The task is to design a network that provides time transparency for user payload. This concept means that (for certain applications) the user's payload has a fixed and nonvariable delay between the sender and receiver. In effect, an ATM network must emulate circuit networks, which are designed to provide a fixed delay of voice and video traffic from source to destination.

The ATM layer is not tasked with providing time transparency services to the end-user application. This service is delegated to the AAL and the application running on top of AAL. It entails conditioning the received user payload (typically holding the user payload in a buffer) to achieve a fixed delay from the source to the endpoint(s). For isochronous traffic, the ITU-T requires that transmissions from source to destination shall not incur an overall delay greater than 199 ms. (This number is not cast in stone. Many studies reveal a round-trip tolerance, in the absence of echoes, for audio of 600 ms [EMLI63] and [KITA91].

As illustrated in Figure 6–18, a number of factors contribute to the delay of a cell. At the sender, delay is incurred when voice and video traffic are translated and segmented into cells by convergence services and segmentation and reassembly (C/SAR) services. At the receiver, delay is incurred for the opposite operations.

Each transmission channel in the end-to-end path incurs a delay in the transport of the cell between the user device or the switch(es). This is shown in Figure 6–18 as propagation delay (PD). While ranges vary on the exact delay in the transmission, it is predictable, because it depends on the distance between the transmitting station and the receiving station. ITU-T provides guidance with ranges running between 4 to 5 µs per km. The IEEE uses a 4.2 µs delay on CSMA/CD coaxial-based networks.

At the switch, two forms of delay are incurred: queuing delay (QD) and switching delay (SD). Because the switches are performing STDM operations, and since traffic arrives asynchronously at the switches, it is necessary to build queues to accommodate peaks in traffic. Obviously,

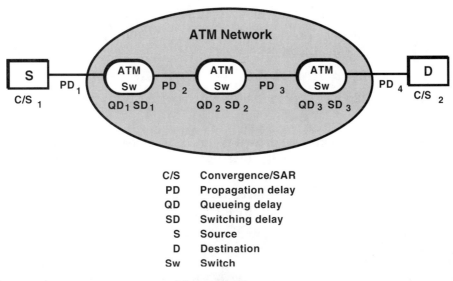

C/S	Convergence/SAR
PD	Propagation delay
QD	Queueing delay
SD	Switching delay
S	Source
D	Destination
Sw	Switch

Figure 6–18
Factors in delay.

delay varies in relation to the amount of traffic in the network and the time required to process the traffic at the switch.

The second factor at the switch is the speed at which traffic is relayed through the switch. SD varies depending on the type of switching operation employed, but it is a fixed delay vis-à-vis the size of the cell. Generally, switches today can process a cell within a broad range of 2 and 100 μs, and the ITU-T's Q.507 Recommendation stipulates an average SD of smaller than 450 μs.

Additional delay may be incurred to remove jitter by queuing the traffic slightly longer at each receiver. Notwithstanding, jitter can usually be accommodated during the queuing process. Thus, delay through an ATM network entails the summation of the delays incurred at the user devices, the switches, and on the communications links.

It is noted that switching can be performed faster than the line speed. Consequently, switching speed is usually limited by the communications lines (155 Mbit/s, etc.) that are input into the switch (unless excessive queuing occurs).

Given the assumptions and estimates cited above, end-to-end delay of a cell traveling from the sending machine to the receiving machine (in Figure 6–18) is 14.297 ms, well within the ITU-T requirements of 199 ms for digitized voice. This value was derived by the following assumptions:

C/S   12000 µs (6000 µs each at source and destination)

PD   2000 µs (assuming a distance of 500 km between source and destination)

SD   72 µs (24 µs at each switch, with 3 switches)

QD   225 µs (75 µs at each switch, with 3 switches)

Several conclusions are drawn from this discussion. First, it is obvious that propagation delay (PD) is a significant factor when compared to some of the other ingredients of delay. In older systems with slow processors, this factor was not considered significant because of the relatively large QD, C/S, and SD values. In newer systems, the PD remains the same, of course, but the ratios change.

The second conclusion is the C/S functions may consume considerable overhead if voice and video must be converted to digital signals and then segmented at the transmitter (and have the complementary yet opposite functions performed at the receiver).

The third conclusion is that in a pure ATM network, the C/S functions are performed only twice: at the source and destination points. If other networks reside between these two machines, like an intervening synchronous network (such as SONET/SDH), additional mapping and convergence functions must be performed to enter and exit the synchronous network. Consequently, the C/S functions play an important role at this additional interface. Finally, be aware that C/S, SD, and QD will vary between machines, and QD is a function of the amount of traffic entering the switch and the size of the queues.

The surface has only been touched regarding the design considerations in providing the ATM user semantic, SDU size, and time transparency services. Notwithstanding, we can now move forward to a more detailed examination of the ATM virtual circuits, and the ATM multiplexing and switching operations. Later, the transparency services are revisited in their relation to traffic management in an ATM network.

ATM LABELS

Earlier discussions explained that an ATM connection is identified through two labels called the virtual path identifier (VPI) and virtual channel identifier (VCI). In each direction, at a given interface, different virtual paths are multiplexed by ATM onto a physical circuit. The VPIs and VCIs identify these multiplexed connections.

As shown in Figure 6–19 virtual channel connections can have end-to-end significance between two end users, usually between two AAL entities. The values of these connection identifiers can change as the traffic is relayed through the ATM network. For example, in a switched virtual connection, a specific VCI value has no end-to-end significance. It is the responsibility of the ATM network to "keep track" of the different VCI values as they relate to each other on an end-to-end basis. Perhaps a good way to view the relationship of VCIs and VPIs is to think that VCIs are part of VPIs; they exist within the VPIs.

Routing in the ATM network is performed by the ATM switch examining both the VCI and VPI fields in the cell, or only the VPI field. This choice depends on how the switch is designed and if VCIs are terminated within the network—a topic covered in Chapter 8.

The VCI/VPI fields can be used with switched or nonswitched ATM operations. They can be used with point-to-point or point-to-multipoint operations. They can be pre-established (PVCs) or set up on demand, based on signaling procedures, such as Q.2931, derived from the ISDN network layer protocol.

Additionally, the value assigned to the VCI at the user-network interface (UNI) can be assigned by (1) the network, (2) the user, or (3) through a negotiation process between the network and the user.

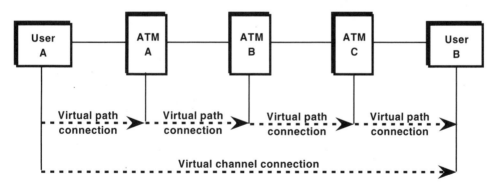

VPC   Virtual path connection
VCC   Virtual channel connection

Figure 6–19
Types of ATM connections.

Multiplexing VCIs and VPIs

So, to review briefly, the ATM layer has two multiplexing hierarchies: the virtual channel and the virtual path. The virtual path identifier (VPI) is a bundle of virtual channels. Each bundle must have the same endpoints. The purpose of the VPI is to identify a group of virtual channel (VC) connections. This approach allows VCIs to be "nailed-up" end-to-end to provide semipermanent connections for the support of a large number of user sessions. VPIs and VCIs can also be established on demand.

The VC is used to identify a unidirectional facility for the transfer of the ATM traffic. The VCI is assigned at the time a VC session is activated in the ATM network. Routing might occur in an ATM network at the VC level, but VCs are usually mapped through the network without further translation. If VCIs are used in the network, the ATM switch must translate the incoming VCI values into outgoing VCI values on the outgoing VC links. The VC links must be concatenated to form a full virtual channel connection (VCC). The VCCs are used for user-to-user, user-to-network, or network transfer of traffic.

The VPI identifies a group of VC links that share the same virtual path connection (VPC). The VPI value is assigned each time the VP is switched in the ATM network. Like the VC, the VP is unidirectional for the transfer of traffic between two contiguous ATM entities.

As shown in Figures 6–20 and 6–21, two different VCs that belong to different VPs at a particular interface are allowed to have the same VCI value (VCI 1, VCI 2). Consequently, the concatenation of VCI and VPI is necessary to uniquely identify a virtual connection.

CELL RELAY BEARER SERVICE (CRBS)

The type of ATM services offered to two communicating users is known as the Cell Relay Bearer Service (CRBS) [MINO93].[1] In accordance with the OSI term "bearer" service, CRBS offers only basic lower layer services—in this instance, specific services at the ATM layer.

---

[1]This material was prepared as part of ANSI working papers and a proposal prepared under the authorship of Dan Minoli, of Bellcore. CRBS is not yet part of the international standards, although some of these ideas are part of the ATM Forum specifications.

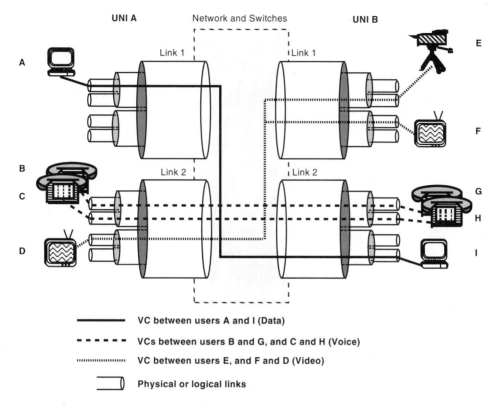

Figure 6–20
ATM connections.

The most valuable aspect to CRBS is the descriptions of how the transfer of cells occur between the ATM users. In this section, we describe these operations:

- Bidirectional symmetric point-to-point (BSPP) service
- Unidirectional point-to-point (UPP) service
- Bidirectional point-to-multipoint (BSPM) service
- Bidirectional asymmetric point-to-multipoint (BAPM) service
- Unidirectional point-to-multipoint (UPM) service
- Bidirectional symmetric multipoint-to-multipoint (BSMM) service
- Bidirectional asymmetric multipoint-to-multipoint (BAMM) service
- Unidirectional multipoint-to-multipoint (UMM) service

The term bidirectional means cells are transferred in both directions between the communicating users; unidirectional means cells are

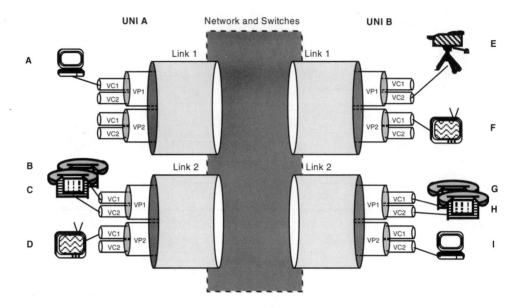

Virtual Circuits:

    A to I: UNI A, Link 1, VCI 1, VPI 1 ↔ UNI B, Link 2, VCI 2, VPI 2

    B to G: UNI A, Link 2, VCI 1, VPI 1 ↔ UNI B, Link 2, VCI 1, VPI 1

    C to H: UNI A, Link 2, VCI 2, VPI 1 ↔ UNI B, Link 2, VCI 2, VPI 1

    E to F and D: UNI B, Link 1, VCI 2, VPI1 → UNI A, Link 2, VCI 1, VPI 2,

        and → UNI B, Link 1, VCI 1, VPI 2

Figure 6–21
ATM connection identifiers.

transferred in one direction only. The term symmetric means the amount of bandwidth, and the QOS (delay, throughput, etc.) are the same in both directions between the users. Asymmetric means these operations may be different in each direction of the virtual connection. The term point-to-point means cells are transferred from one user to one other user. Point-to-multipoint means the cells are transferred from one user to more than one user. Most of these terms and their underlying concepts are self-evident. However, a few comments about point-to-multipoint and multipoint-to-multipoint services should prove useful.

Point-to-Multipoint and Multipoint-to-Multipoint Services

In order to support applications such as telephone conference calls, downline loading of video programs, and video conferencing operations, ATM provides a service called point-to-multipoint connections. From a technical standpoint, a point-to-multipoint connection is nothing more than a collection of associated VC or VP links with their associated endpoints.

In a point-to-multipoint service, the endpoints have a link that serves as the root in a logical tree topology. This approach means that when a root node sends traffic, all of the remaining nodes (which are leaf nodes) receive copies of this traffic. In the present evolution of ATM and the ATM standards, the root node communicates directly with the leaf nodes. The leaf nodes (as of this writing) may not communicate with each other. A multipoint-to-multipoint service assumes a group of users need to be connected to one another, such as in a telephone conference call. Many of the issues surrounding these two services need further study.

ATM INTERFACES

Multiple protocols are required to support full ATM operations. The number of protocols required depends upon where the user traffic is being transported. Figure 6-22 shows that four different protocols and procedures may be invoked.

The user network interface (UNI) is the most important protocol, because it defines the procedures for the interworking between the user equipment and the ATM node. As the figure shows, two forms of UNI are supported, and private UNI and a public UNI. The major difference between these interfaces pertains to the physical communications links between the machines. A private UNI would likely have a link such a private fiber, or twisted pair. A public UNI would likely consist of SDH/SONET, DS3, or E4, for example. Also, a private UNI might not have the elaborate monitoring and policing procedures that exist at the public UNI.

The network node interface (NNI) can exist as both a public or private interface as well. "I" defines the interworking of the ATM network nodes. As of this writing, it has not been completed by the ITU-T, or the ATM Forum.

The intercarrier interface (ICI) is an internetworking protocol. As such, it defines the operations and procedures that exist between networks.

The data exchange interface (DXI) has been developed by the ATM Forum to provide a standard procedure for the interfacing of current equipment into an ATM node. The DXI is a very simple protocol, and allows an easy migration into ATM.

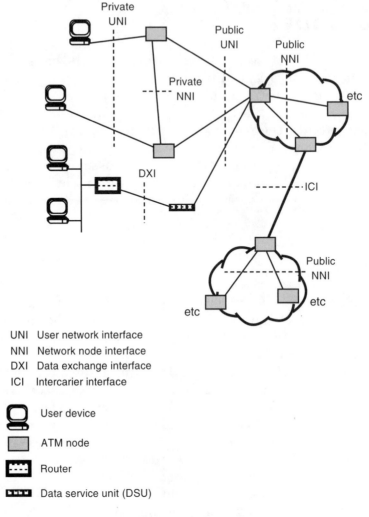

UNI   User network interface
NNI   Network node interface
DXI   Data exchange interface
ICI   Intercarier interface

◻   User device

▢   ATM node

▣   Router

▦   Data service unit (DSU)

Figure 6–22
ATM interfaces.

While four separate interfaces may be invoked, they all are similar (except for the DXI), and use many of the concepts found in the UNI.

PRINCIPAL SPECIFICATIONS FOR ATM

Figure 6–23 should prove helpful to you as you read the remainder of this book. We will examine each of the depicted operations/functions in this figure, because they provide the basis for the specifications and standards from which ATM products are developed and implemented.

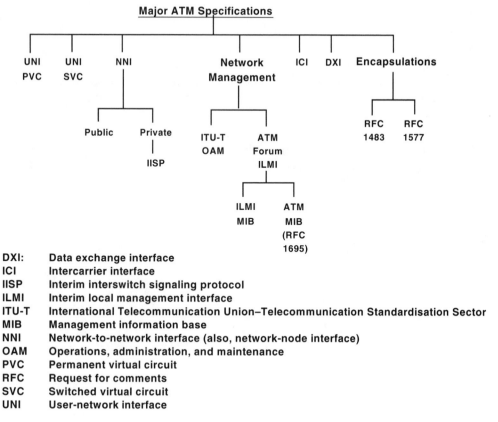

Figure 6–23
Principal standards and specifications for ATM.

DXI:	Data exchange interface
ICI	Intercarrier interface
IISP	Interim interswitch signaling protocol
ILMI	Interim local management interface
ITU-T	International Telecommunication Union–Telecommunication Standardisation Sector
MIB	Management information base
NNI	Network-to-network interface (also, network-node interface)
OAM	Operations, administration, and maintenance
PVC	Permanent virtual circuit
RFC	Request for comments
SVC	Switched virtual circuit
UNI	User-network interface

Specific parts of the book will also give you an update on the status of each of these areas.

As a general statement, the network-node interfaces (network-to-network) (NNI) are still under development by the ATM Forum and the ITU-T. The ITU-T operations, administration, and maintenance (OAM) standards are not yet complete. All others have been completed and are at various stages of implementation.

SUMMARY

ATM is a high-speed, low-delay multiplexing and switching technology. It supports any type of user traffic, such as voice, data, and video applications.

ATM uses small, fixed-length units called cells. Each cell is identified with VPIs and VCIs that are contained in the cell header. An ATM network uses these identifiers to relay the traffic through high-speed switches.

ATM provides limited error detection operations. It provides no re-transmission services, and few operations are performed on the small header. The intention of this approach is to implement a network that is fast enough to support multimegabit transfer rates.

ATM also has a layer that operates above it, called the ATM adaptation layer (AAL). This layer performs convergence as well as segmentation and reassembly operations on different types of traffic.

The ATM Adaptation Layer (AAL)

INTRODUCTION

This chapter examines the ATM adaptation layer (AAL). The AAL classes of traffic are explained and related to the types of AAL protocol data units (PDUs). The rationale for the size and format of the AAL headers and trailers is analyzed.

Before we begin, a quick review of AAL is in order. The point has been made in earlier discussions that AAL is an essential part of the ATM network because it "converges" (adapts) the user traffic to the cell-based network. It is also important to remember that for transfer of user traffic (the B-ISDN U-plane), the AAL operates at the endpoints of the virtual connection and does not operate within the ATM backbone network. For C-plane and M-plane traffic, AAL must be invoked at the network node of the UNI.

PRINCIPAL TASKS OF THE AAL

The AAL is designed to support different types of applications and different types of traffic, such as voice, video, and data. At first glance, it might appear that the integration of voice, data, and video is a simple matter. After all, once the analog signals have been converted to digital images, all transmissions can be treated as data-bit images. However, if we examine the transmission requirements of voice and data, we find that they are quite different. Be aware the AAL standards do not define completely how to manage and support these requirements. These important functions are either defined in other standards or are vendor-specific.

Voice and lower-quality video transmissions exhibit a high tolerance for errors. If an occasional cell is distorted, the quality of the voice or video reproduction is not severely affected. In contrast, data transmissions have a low tolerance (more often, no tolerance) for errors. One corrupted bit changes the meaning of the data.

Yet another difference between voice, data, and video transmissions deals with network delay. For the voice or video cell to be translated back to an analog signal in a real-time mode, the network delay for these cells must be constant and generally must be low. Some studies shows that a two-way speech communication can tolerate round-trip delays of up to 600 ms, in the absence of echoes. Other studies show that the perceived quality is better with lower delays—around 200 ms [EMLI63] and [KITA91].

For data traffic, the network delay can vary considerably. Indeed, data can be transmitted asynchronously through the network, without regard to precise timing arrangements between the sender and the receiver. To complicate matters further, specific data applications exhibit different delay requirements. For example, LAN-to-LAN traffic is more delay-sensitive than say, E-mail traffic. In contrast, video transmissions must maintain a precise timing relationship between the sender and the receiver.

Since voice and video traffic can afford (on occasion) to be lost or discarded, packets may be discarded in the event of excessive delays and/or congestion in the network. Again, the loss does not severely affect voice fidelity if the lost packets are not detected by a human—who is the ultimate judge of the voice, video, and audio quality. As discussed before, data can ill afford to be lost or discarded.

As explained in Chapter 6, the tolerance for cell loss in audio systems is a function of (1) the number of bits in the cell, (2) the compression ratio (if any) reflected in these bits, and (3) the coding rate of the signal (for example, 32 kbit/s), because the length of a cell loss is the important component in judging the quality of speech and audio. Indeed, a fine line exists in selecting an acceptable length of cell loss. Studies [JAYA81] reveal that losing several samples is disturbing to the listener because it has the effect of impulse noise. Traffic loss of around 32 to 64 ms is quite disruptive, because it means the loss of speech phonemes. On the other hand, cell loss of a duration of some 4 to 16 ms is not very noticeable or disturbing to the listener.

Finally, voice and video transmissions require a short queue length at the network nodes in order to reduce delay, or at least to make the delay more predictable. The short voice packet queue lengths can experience overflow occasionally, with resulting packet loss. However, data packets require the queue lengths to be longer to prevent packet loss in overflow conditions.

THE AAL SUBLAYERS

The ATM adaptation layer (AAL) plays a key role in the ability of an ATM network to support multiapplication operations. The type of user payload is identified at the AAL. Therefore, AAL must be able to accommodate to a wide variety of traffic—from connectionless, asynchronous data to connection-oriented, synchronous voice and video applications.

The ATM standards groups decided that the AAL should be divided into two sublayers: the convergence sublayer (CS) and the segmentation and reassembly sublayer (SAR). The rationale for this structure is explained in Chapter 6. This layered architecture is in consonance with the conventional OSI layered architecture approach described in Chapter 3. So, we continue these discussions in the next section of this chapter.

Creating and Processing the AAL PDU

As depicted in Figure 7–1, AAL is responsible for accepting the user traffic, which could range from one octet to several thousand octets, and placing a header and trailer around it. The length of the header and trailer vary depending on the technology. It could be as small as 6 octets and can range as high as approximately 40 octets. Be aware that this initial header and trailer may not be added by all AAL implementations, it will depend on the type of traffic.

Once the header and trailer have been added to the user payload, the traffic is then segmented into data units ranging in size from 44 to 47 octets. The size varies depending on the type of traffic, such as voice, video, or data. The next function entails adding another header and, possibly, a trailer to each data unit. Once again, the nature of the header and the possible use of the trailer will vary depending on the type of payload that is being supported. In any event, the final data unit from this operation is always a 48-octet PDU.

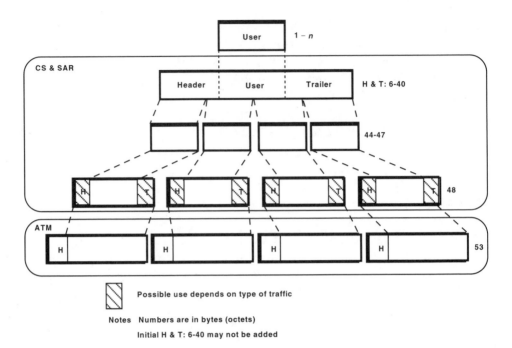

Figure 7–1
AAL convergence and SAR.

As discussed earlier, the choice of the 48-octet payload was based on several factors. One factor is cell loss for voice transmissions. Given a payload of 384 bits (48 octets $*$ = 384), samples of a digitized voice image (at 64 kbits/s) results in a 1-cell loss of 6 ms—well within the tolerances cited earlier (382 / 64000 = .006).

Moreover, later discussions in this chapter reveal that methods and standards exist to allow the selective shedding of *parts* of a sample for voice and video, and not an entire sample. This approach results in a very flexible and efficient means to (1) compensate for cell loss, (2) maintain a high-quality signal, and (3) ameliorate potential congestion by reducing the number of bits processed by the network.

The last operation shown in Figure 7–1 is performed by the ATM layer, which adds a 5-octet header to the 48-octet payload, resulting in a 53-octet ATM cell.

In accordance with the ideas of layered protocols, the reverse of these operations take place at the receiving machine.

CLASSES OF TRAFFIC

AAL is organized around a concept called service classes, which are summarized in Table 7–1. The classes are defined with regards to the following operations:

- Timing between sender and receiver (present or not present)
- Bit rate (variable or constant)
- Connectionless or connection-oriented sessions between sender and receiver
- Sequencing of user payload
- Flow control operations
- Accounting for user traffic
- Segmentation and reassembly (SAR) of user PDUs

As of this writing, the ITU-T had approved four classes, with labels of A through D. We will now summarize these classes and their major

Table 7–1   AAL Classes of Traffic

Purpose: Convert and aggregate different traffic into standard formats to support different user applications

- **Class A**
  Constant bit rate (CBR)
  Connection-oriented, e.g., CBR for video
  Timing relationship between source and destination: Required

- **Class B**
  Variable bit rate (VBR)
  Connection-oriented, e.g., VBR video for voice
  Timing relationship between source and destination: Required

- **Class C**
  Variable bit rate (VBR)
  Connection-oriented, e.g., bursty data services
  Timing relationship between source and destination: Not required

- **Class D**
  Variable bit rate (VBR)
  Connectionless, e.g., bursty datagram services
  Timing relationship between source and destination: Not required

- **Class X**
  Traffic type and timing requirements defined by the user (unrestricted)

Table 7–2   Support Operations for AAL Classes

Class	A	B	C	D
Timing	Synchronous		Asynchronous	
Bit transfer	Constant	Variable		
Connection mode		Connection-oriented		Connection-less

features. Table 7–2 is provided to assist the reader during this discussion.

Classes A and B require timing relationships between the source and destination. Therefore, clocking mechanisms are utilized for this traffic. ATM does not specify the type of synchronization—it could be a timestamp and/or a synchronous clock. This function is performed in the application running on top of AAL. Classes C and D do not require precise timing relationships. A constant bit rate (CBR) is required for class A; and a variable bit rate (VBR) is permitted for classes B, C, and D. Classes A, B, and C are connection-oriented; while class D is connectionless.

It is obvious that these classes are intended to support different types of user applications. For example, class A is designed to support a CBR requirement for high-quality video applications. On the other hand, class B, while connection-oriented, supports VBR applications and is applicable for VBR video and voice applications. Class B service could be used by information retrieval services in which large amounts of video traffic are sent to the user and then delays occur as the user examines the information.

Class C services are the connection-oriented data transfer services such as X.25-type connections. Conventional connectionless services, such as datagram networks, are supported with class D services. Both of these classes also support (final decisions by ITU-T still pending) the multiplexing of multiple end users' traffic over one connection.

As of this writing, other classes are under study and undergoing revisions through ITU-T working groups. This work has been published in ITU-T recommendation I.363 Annex 5.

Last, the ATM Forum has specified class X, which is an unrestricted service where the requirements are defined by the user.

RATIONALE FOR AAL TYPES

In order to support different types of user traffic and provide the classes of service just described, AAL employs several protocol types. Each type is implemented to support one or a number of user applications, such as voice, data, and so on. Each type consists of a specific SAR and CS. As a general statement, the type 1 protocol supports class A traffic, type 2 supports class B traffic, and so on, but other combinations are permitted, if appropriate.

The point has been made several times in this book that the very nature of emerging technologies makes it difficult to write about the subject matter as if the protocols were cast in stone. The AAL is no exception. Initially, the ITU-T published four AAL types to support four classes of traffic. However, as the standards groups became more attuned to the tasks at hand, it was recognized that this approach needed to be modified. Also, little interest was shown in defining type 2 traffic for class B applications, and it was also acknowledged that a user-specified class of traffic should be included, as well as a provision for interworking frame relay into ATM. So, modifications were made to the specifications to reflect these changes. This chapter includes the latest changes made to AAL, and at the time this book went to press, it is up to date.

One of the major changes is that VBR applications are serviced at the AAL by a common part (CP), and a service specific part (SSP). As the names of these parts imply, the CP is somewhat generic and pertains to a set of VBR applications, and the SSP pertains to a VBR application that requires additional and specific services. With these thoughts in mind, the next part of this chapter provides a review of the AAL protocol types.

DIVIDING CS INTO FURTHER SUBLAYERS

As the AAL has been further defined and refined, the CS has been divided for the support of type 3/4 and 5 traffic. Figure 7–2 shows this change. The two sublayers are the service specific CS (SSCS) and the common part of CS (CPCS). As their names imply, SSCS is designed to support a specific aspect of a data application, and CPCS supports generic functions common to more than one type of data application.

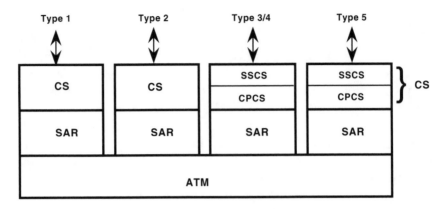

SSCS   Service specific CS

SPCS   Common part CS

Figure 7–2
Dividing the CS into sublayers.

Specific examples of these sublayers are provided later in this chapter and in Chapter 10.

AAL NAMING CONVENTIONS

Before we launch into an examination of the AAL details, a few words are in order about the AAL structure and the naming conventions. Chapter 3 provides the basics for the ensuing discussion. Figure 7–3 shows the conventions for the ATM and AAL layers, as well as the placement of service access points (SAPs), and the naming conventions. Based on the information in Chapter 3, this figure is largely self-explanatory. It can be seen that the naming conventions follow the OSI conventions, and use the concepts of service access points (SAPs), service data units (SDUs), protocol data units (PDUs), primitives, encapsulation, decapsulation, and protocol control information (headers and trailers).

AAL TYPE 1 (AAL 1)

As we just learned, for class A traffic, the bit rate does not vary over time. The term fixed bit rate means that the bit rate is (1) constant and (2) synchronized between sender and receiver (see Figure 7–4). Each sample of the analog image results contains the same number of bits.

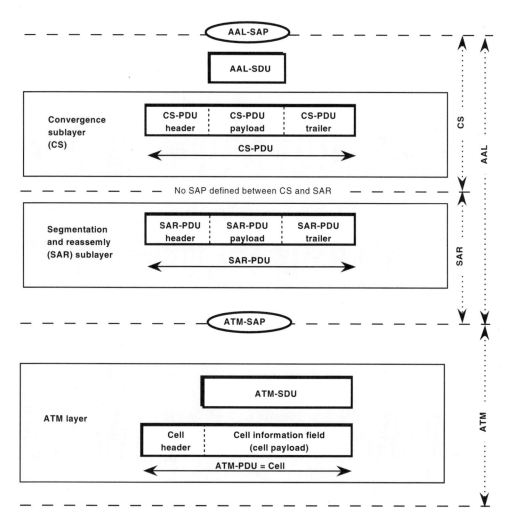

Figure 7–3
AAL general data unit conventions.

THE AAL 1 PDU

The AAL uses type 1 PDUs to support applications requiring a CBR transfer to and from the layer above AAL. It is divided into the CS and SAR sublayers. The CS needs a clock for some of its operations. According to I.363, the clock can be derived from the S_B or T_B interface, but in practice, the clock can be derived from other sources (see Chapter 2 for a discussion on clocking). CS is responsible for the following tasks:

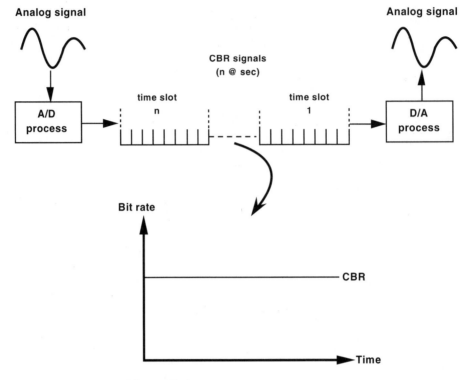

Figure 7–4
Constant bit rate (CBR) applications.

- Accomomodating to cell delay variation, and delivering AAL-SDUs to the user at a constant bit rate
- Detecting lost or missequenced cells
- Providing source clock frequency recovery at the receiver (if needed)
- Providing forward error correction (FEC) Δ172on user payload for high-quality video/audio applications
- Providing FEC on the AAL 1 header

The SAR has the job of receiving a 47-octet PDU from CS and adding a 1-byte header to it at the transmitting side and performing the reverse operation at the at the receiving side.

As depicted in Figure 7–5, the AAL 1 PDU consists of 48 octets with 47 octets available for the application payload. The AAL 1 header consists of four bits in the two fields. The first field is a sequence number (SN) and is used for detection of mistakenly inserted cells or lost cells. The SN protection (SNP) field performs error detection on the SN.

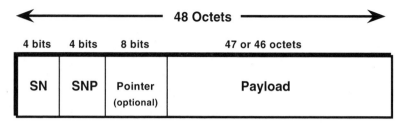

SN   Sequence number (1 bit CSI, 3 bits sequence count)
SNP   Sequence number protection
CSI   Convergence sublayer indication
      (0 = no pointer; 1 = pointer)

Note: Optional timestamp uses 1 bit of CSI in four
successive PDUs

**Figure 7–5
AAL 1 PDU.**

As mentioned earlier, AAL 1 CS is responsible for clock recovery for both audio and video services. This operation can be accomplished through the use of real-time synchronization or through the use of time-stamping.

The SN in not used to request the sender to retransmit the PDU, because of the unacceptable delay this operation would entail. Rather, the detection of traffic loss with the SN can be used as feedback information to the sender to modify its operations (with a knowledge of the nature of the loss [WADA89]).

One bit in the SN field is called the convergence sublayer indication (CSI), and is used to indicate that an 8-bit pointer exists. This pointer capability allows a cell to be partially filled if the user application so requires in order to reduce delay in assembling and processing additional bits or octets.

AAL 1 Modes of Operation

CBR traffic can operate in one of two modes: (a) the unstructured data transfer (UDT) mode, or the structured data transfer (SDT) mode. The former is a bit-stream operation that has an associated bit clock, and the latter is a byte stream (8 bit octets) operation with a fixed block length that has an associated clock. As of this writing, these modes had not been completely defined, but the intent of the structured mode is to allow the sending of 8-bit samples (or multiple samples in the 8-bit byte for ADPCM coding schemes, etc.).

Synchronization and Clock Recovery

Clock recovery can be provided by a timestamp or an adaptive clock. The first method is called the synchronous residual timestamp (SRTS). The RTS information (4 bits) is carried in a serial bit stream by the CSI bit in successive headers of the AAL PDUs. This value is used at the receiver to determine the frequency difference between a common reference clock (fn) to the local service clock (fs). A derived network clock frequency (fnx) is obtained from the fn. For example, assume an fn for SONET of 155.520 MHz. The fnx for is fn * 2^{-k}, where K is a specified integer. For 64 Kbit/s, K = 11, so the fnx is 155.520 * 2^{-11}, or 75.9375 kHz.

The number of derived clock cycles (mq) is obtained at the sender and conveyed to the receiver in the timestamp field, which allows the receiver to reconstruct the service clock of the sender.

The term "residual" stems from the fact that this method actually sends a value representing the residual part of mq. The residual part is fequency difference information, and can vary. The timestamp represents y, where $y = N * fnx/fs * e$ (N is the period of RTS in cycles of fs, and e is the service clock tolerance $\mp$ e). This approach is used because it is assumed the nominal part of mq is known at the receiver, so only the residual part mq is conveyed.

The SRTS method assumes the availability of a common synchronous network clock from which sender and receiver can reference. Plesiochronous operations that do not have a common reference clock are not standardized, and vary between vendors and countries.

Other aspects and rules for the SRTS are explained in G.823, G.824, and I.363, if you want to know more about the SRTS method. I.363 also describes the FEC mechanism for unidirectional video services.

For the adaptive clock method, the local CS simply reads the buffer of the incoming traffic with a local clock. The level of the buffer (its fill level) contols the frequency of the clock. The measure of the fill level drives a mechanism to control the local clock.

Running AAL 1 Traffic on a T1 Link

As of this writing, no standard has been published on running voice over ATM. The ITU-T plans to finalize a standard in 1995. In the meantime, vendors are using their own proprietary approaches. Figure 7–6 shows an example of how AAL 1 is used to support 64 kbit/s voice traffic. The ATM cells are run over a 1544 Mbit/s T1 link. In this situation, the T1 line is unchannelized: It is simply providing the raw bandwidth, and the notion of 24 fixed slots per T1 frame does not exist.

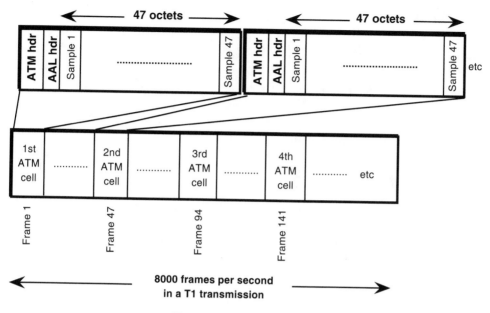

Figure 7–6
Running AAL 1 over T1.

Assuming that 47 samples are placed into one cell, an ATM voice call requires 171 cells per second, because 8000 samples per second / 47 samples per cell = 171 (170.212). A system must allocate a cell in every 47th frame on the T1 channel, since 8000 frames a second/171 cells = 47 (46.783). Therefore, a cell is sent in every 47th frame.

This example assumes that the equipment is designed to handle a constant playout at the receiver, and that timing has been provided. The residual timestamp can be used, if necessary. One last point, the 171st cell would not fill the AAL PDU. Therefore, the AAL 1 PDU pointer is employed to identify the samples from the remainder of the bytes in the PDU, which are used as padding to achieve a full 48-byte boundary.

AAL TYPE 2 (AAL 2)

AAL 2 is employed for VBR services where a timing relationship is required between the source and destination sites. Class B traffic, such as VBR audio or video, falls into this category. The standards bodies have not defined AAL 2 fully, so this explanation reflects the state of its standardization.

The type 2 category of service requires that timing information be maintained between the transmitting and receiving sites. It is responsible for handling variable cell delay, as well as the detection and handling of lost or missequenced PDUs. Since a cell may be only partially filled because of the bursty aspect of VBR operations, the SAR, in addition to its segmentation and reassembly operations, also maintains a record of how many octets in the user payload area actually contain traffic.

In earlier implementations of digitized voice, all systems used fixed bit-rate schemes. The same statement holds true for earlier video A/D operations. However, shortly after the advent of the analog-to-digital process, research indicated that it would be efficacious to compress the resulting digitized images so that a reduced number of bits would be transmitted through the communications channel.

The manner in which the compression algorithms operate on the data leads to the traffic's exhibiting VBR characteristics. This means that the bit rate varies in time, as depicted in the Figure 7–7. VBR coding is widely employed in video systems to take advantage of visual irrelevancy and variable redundancy. Visual irrelevancy describes the inability of the human eye to comprehend the full details of an image—especially moving images. For example, in television, pictures are actually displayed on the screen between 25 and 30 times a second. However, the human eye is not capable of perceiving these fixed images. Furthermore, due to the analog nature of digital signals, there is a high correlation between adjacent images and, indeed, adjacent pixels within images. So, compression schemes take advantage of variable redundancies.

To code the visual digital images, Huffman coding, which uses variable length encoding of the samples, is employed. This coding scheme uses a small number of bits to represent signals with the highest probability of occurring in the image and a larger number of bits to represent signals that occur rarely in the image.

This same scheme is also used in facsimile transmission and is used to compress long occurrences of white or black pixels (images) on a sheet of paper.

The AAL 2 PDU

The PDU for AAL 2 traffic consists of both a header and a trailer (see Figure 7–8). The header consists of a SN as well as an information type (IT) field. The length of these fields and their exact functions have not been determined as of this writing. Obviously, the SN will be used for detection of lost or mistakenly inserted cells. The IT field may contain

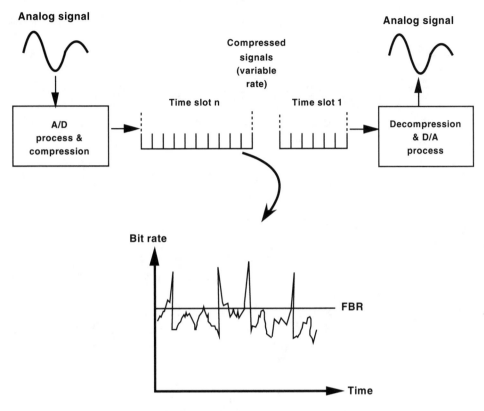

Figure 7–7
Variable bit rate (VBR) applications.

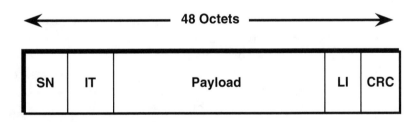

SN   Sequence number
IT   Information type
LI   Length indicator
CRC Cyclic redundancy check

Figure 7–8
AAL 2 PDU.

the indication of beginning of message (BOM), continuation of message (COM), or end of message (EOM), which could be used to chain all samples of a burst together. It may also contain timing information for audio or video signals.

The AAL 2 trailer consists of a length indicator (LI) that will be used to determine the number of octets residing in the payload field. And finally, the cyclic redundancy check (CRC) will be used for error detection (and perhaps error correction) of the user payload.

VOICE PACKETIZATION

Further discussion on AAL 2 and how it can interact with a user application to support voice traffic can provide the reader with additional relevant information. The AAL does not define the syntax of the payload inside the AAL 1 or 2 PDU, and the manner in which the voice or video image is digitized is defined in other standards, or in a vendor's proprietary package. This section explains how these voice packets can be created and placed in an AAL PDU that supports VBR traffic, based on [CCIT90a] and [SRIR93]. The latter reference is based on the research that led to AT&T's Integrated Access and Cross-Connect System (IACS).

The term "packet" is used in this discussion in deference to industry practice; it defines a group of bits that contain samples of a voice image. Whatever the term used, the voice packet is placed inside the AAL PDU.

Previous discussions in this book have explained that a certain amount of traffic loss (packet discard, misrouting, etc.) for voice is tolerable and acceptable. The amount of loss that can occur is quite variable, ranging from 0.1 percent to 10 percent, depending on (1) how the voice images are sampled, (2) how they are coded in the packet, and (3) how they may be discarded. For systems that do not selectively discard traffic, the tolerable loss is low; for systems that selectively discard traffic, the tolerable loss is high. However, for video traffic, the loss of a single cell might cause degradation of the picture if synchronization is lost. Therefore, cell loss must be rare. Studies have shown that a high-quality television signal operating at 155 Mbit/s, in which a cell is not lost for about two hours requires a bit error rate of 10^{-12} and a cell error rate of 10^{-10} [LEE93]. As discussed in Chapter 6, these levels of performance are obtainable with optical fiber.

Grouping Samples into Blocks

To explain the rationale for these three suppositions, we will use an example of a digitized voice image of 32 kbit/s. This technique carries 4 bits per sample (4 * 8000 samples per second = 32,000). As shown in Figure 7–9, the voice samples for a 32 kbit/s image are placed into a packet with the 4 bits of each sample grouped together based on the arithmetic significance of each bit in each sample. That is, the least significant bits (- - -X) are grouped together, followed by the next least significant bits (- -X-), and so on. Since ADPCM (adaptive pulse code modulation) uses 4 bits per sample, the packet contains 4 blocks, one for each bit of the 4-bit sample, and a control header, which is explained shortly.

Assume the following coding for two of the samples in the packet of 4 bits: One sample is 15_{10}, or 1111_2, and the other sample is 7_{10}, or 0111_2. Of course, if a full sample is discarded, all 4 bits of the sample are not available for the digital-to-analog conversion process at the receiver. However, since the bits are not encoded in the packet on a sample-by-sample basis, but rather on the arithmetically significant positions of the bits in the samples, the selective discarding of bits is not so severe.

To see why, consider that an ATM node is measuring congestion, and determines that it must shed traffic. The packet header contains a block-dropping indicator field to track the status of the blocks. (This indicator is explained shortly.) So, the block in the packet containing the

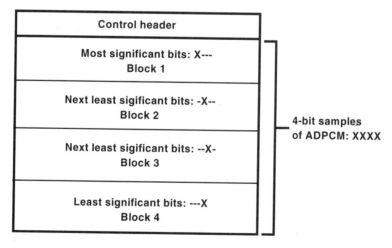

Figure 7–9
Grouping the bits of the samples.

least significant bit is dropped. The effect of the samples is (where x is the discarded bit of the samples):

$$15_{10} \text{ or } 1111_2 \text{ is now } 14_{10} \text{ or } 111x_2$$

$$7_{10} \text{ or } 0111_2 \text{ is now } 6_{10} \text{ or } 011x_2$$

This slight change in the sample translates to a different PAM pulse at the receiver, but the distortion is not severe.

The speech stream is coded into the packet (shown in Figure 7–10) in 16 ms time slots. Each packet contains 128 4-bit samples. This coding convention results in a 32 kbit/s transmission stream, based on the following calculations (and depicted graphically in Figure 7–10):

$$1 \text{ second } / 8000 \text{ samples per second} = \text{a } .000125 \text{ sample interval}$$

$$.000125 * .016 = .016 \text{ packet interval}$$

The packet in Figure 7–10 is 64 octets in length (512 bits). Therefore, the 32 kbit/s transmission stream is derived by:

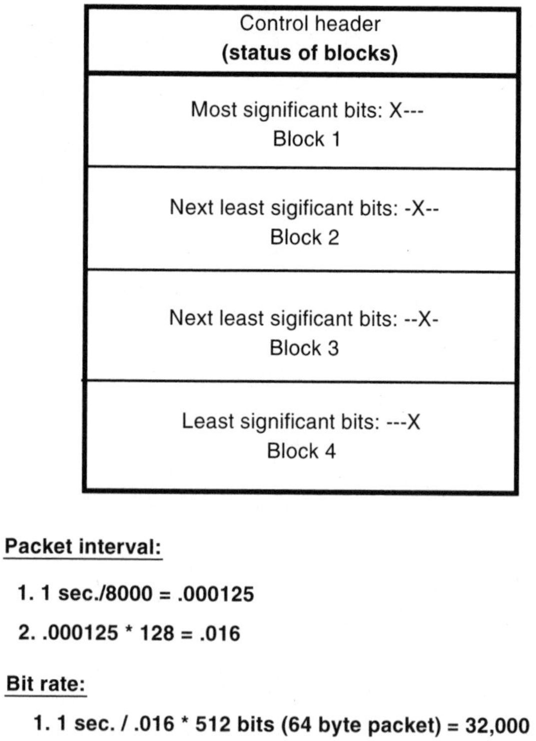

Control header **(status of blocks)**
Most significant bits: X--- Block 1
Next least sigificant bits: -X-- Block 2
Next least sigificant bits: --X- Block 3
Least significant bits: ---X Block 4

Packet interval:

1. 1 sec./8000 = .000125

2. .000125 * 128 = .016

Figure 7–10
Voice packet interval and bit rate.

Bit rate:

1. 1 sec. / .016 * 512 bits (64 byte packet) = 32,000

$$1 \text{ second} / .016 = 62.5$$

$$62.5 * 512 \text{ bits} = 32,000$$

The number of blocks in the 16 ms interval depends upon the type of coding used. For example, if 8 bits were carried per sample, then 8 blocks would be needed, and a 64,000 bit rate is required. Table 7–3 shows the number of blocks collected during the 16 ms interval, based on the coding type used.

A packet size of 64 octets means that the samples are contained in more than one ATM cell. An AAL 1 PDU could be used, and the pointer could locate the payload in the payload field. However, using an AAL 2 PDU is preferable, because it contains a length field (if it is finally approved with these fields by the ITU-T), as well as the BOM, COM, EOM, and SSM indicators, which are essential for proper identification of the related samples of the signal. Nothing precludes the use of an AAL 3/4 PDU, since it also contains these fields, as long as the traffic is treated synchronously.

Most voice packet systems also employ digital speech interpolation (DSI), which does not generate packets during periods of silence in a

Table 7–3 Blocks Collected during the Packetization Interval

Coding Type	Number of Blocks
8 bits/sample	8
1 bits/sample	1
2 bits/sample	2
3 bits/sample	3
4 bits/sample	4
5 bits/sample	5
6 bits/sample	6
7 bits/sample	7
8 bit PCM (A-law or μ-law)	8
2 bits/sample ADPCM	2
3 bits/sample ADPCM	3
4 bits/sample ADPCM	4
5 bits/sample ADPCM	5
(4,2) embedded ADPCM	4
(5,2) embedded ADPCM	5
(8,6) embedded ADPCM	8

voice conversation. This allows more voice channels to be multiplexed on any given media. Thus, a system such as AT&T's IACS uses a combination of ADPCM and DSI to multiplex 96 voice channels onto a DS1 1.544 Mbits/s channel, and 120 voice channels onto a CEPT1 2.048 Mbits/s channel.

Furthermore, block dropping decreases the bursty aspect of digitized voice by smoothing the queues. It has also been demonstrated that this process increases the system capacity by some 20 to 25 percent [SRIR90b].

Combining voice and data. This procedure can transport data as well. For data applications, the block dropping indicator field is coded to show that the data blocks are nondroppable. When data are supported, the node's physical interface must be able to detect modem signals, determine the modem line speed (in bit/s), and assign a coding rate to support the line speed. For example, the node can assign 32 kbit/s ADPCM code to low-speed modems running 1.2 to 2.4 kbit/s rates, and a conventional PCM code to higher speed modems, say from 7.2 kbit/s rates and higher. Furthermore, the node is able to receive and transmit G3 facsimile signals.

The Voice Packet

The format for the ITU-T G.764 voice packet is shown in Figure 7–11. To simplify this discussion, Figure 7–8 does not show octet and bit positions. The packet is encapsulated into an HDLC-type header, which contains an address field, a command/response bit (not used), and a frame type field. The address field is a conventional data link connection identifier (DLCI). The frame type is an HDLC unnumbered information type (UI), and can also be coded to indicate if a cyclic redundancy check (CRC) with the frame check sequence is performed on the frame header and packet header or on the entire frame. The former is called the unnumbered information with header check (UIH).

This option does not protect the voice bits, because the dropping of blocks does not require the recalculation of the CRC, and retransmissions in the event of an error are not performed due to the sensitivity of voice traffic to delay.

The protocol discriminator is preset to 01000100. The block dropping indicator contains several fields. One field contains two bits, labeled as C1 and C2. These bits are set to indicate how many blocks are droppable as follows: 00 = no droppable blocks; 01 = one droppable block; 10 = two droppable blocks; 11 = three droppable blocks. C1 and C2 are

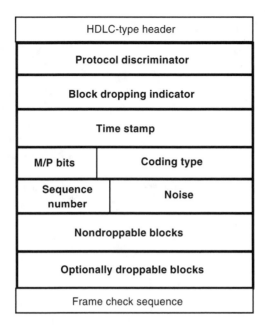

HDLC-type header
Protocol discriminator
Block dropping indicator
Time stamp

M/P bits	**Coding type**
Sequence number	**Noise**

Nondroppable blocks
Optionally droppable blocks
Frame check sequence

Figure 7–11
Format of G.764 voice packet.

changed when a block is dropped to indicate how many blocks are still available for dropping.

The timestamp field records the cumulative delay encountered as the packet makes its journey through the network. Its value is not to exceed 200 ms.

The coding type field indicates the specific analog-to-digital technique used. The coding of this field must adhere to the ITU-T conventions shown in Table 7–4.

The M bit (more data bit) is set to 1 for all packets of a voice burst, except the last packet in the burst. The receiver uses this bit to learn that all samples have arrived. The P bit (poll bit) is not used and is set to zero.

The sequence number (SN) is used at the receiver during the building of the voice burst. It is used to note the first packet in the burst, and also to note if a packet has been lost. The value is incremented by 1 for each subsequent packet in the signal. The SN is used with the time-stamp to assure that variable delay is removed for the process.

Since this technique uses DSI, a noise field indicates the level of background noise that is to be played in the absence of packets. These bits must be coded in accordance with the ITU-T specifications, shown in Table 7–5.

Table 7–4   Coding Type (CT) Format

Bit Number					Coding Type
5	4	3	2	1	
0	0	0	0	0	8 bit/sample
0	0	0	0	1	1 bit/sample
0	0	0	1	0	2 bit/sample
0	0	0	1	1	3 bit/sample
0	0	1	0	0	4 bit/sample
0	0	1	0	1	5 bit/sample
0	0	1	1	0	6 bit/sample
0	0	1	1	1	7 bit/sample
0	1	0	0	0	8 bit A-law PCM
0	1	0	0	1	8 bit μ-law PCM
0	1	0	1	0	2 bit/sample ADPCM
0	1	0	1	1	3 bit/sample ADPCM
0	1	1	0	0	4 bit/sample ADPCM
0	1	1	0	1	5 bit/sample ADPCM
0	1	1	1	0	Reserved for future use
0	1	1	1	1	Reserved for future use
1	0	0	0	0	Reserved for future use
1	0	0	0	1	Reserved for future use
1	0	0	1	0	Reserved for future use
1	0	0	1	1	Reserved for future use
1	0	1	0	0	(4,2) embedded ADPCM
1	0	1	0	1	(5,2) embedded ADPCM
1	0	1	1	0	Reserved for future use
1	0	1	1	1	Reserved for future use
1	1	0	0	0	(8,6) embedded ADPCM
1	1	0	0	1	Reserved for future use
		...			
		...			
1	1	1	1	1	Reserved for future use

Finally, the blocks fields contain the samples that were described earlier.

Packet Buildout at the Receiver

To properly decode voice packets, they must arrive at the receiver (terminating endpoint) experiencing nonvariable delay. However, since variable delay is inevitable due to queuing and switching operations in

Table 7–5   Noise Field Format

Bit Number	Noise Level
4321	(dBmc0)
0000	Idle code
0001	16.6
0010	19.7
0011	22.6
0100	24.9
0101	26.9
0110	29.0
0111	31.0
1000	32.8
1001	34.6
1010	36.2
1011	37.9
1100	39.7
1101	41.6
1110	43.8
1111	46.6

the network, the receiver masks the variability of the delay through the use of the timestamp (TS) value in the packet header.

For this operation to work correctly, the system must define a maximum allowable delay. This can be defined when a PVC is provisioned, when an SVC is created, or in any manner deemed appropriate by the network administrator. Whatever the value chosen, it must be ≤ 199 ms, as established by ITU-T G.764. Additionally, the terminating endpoint must check the TS value in the packet as part of this operation and compare it to a predefined constant delay value, and determine if the packet is to be buffered, released to the decoding application, or discarded (buildout operations).

Figure 7–12 shows four possible scenarios that may occur when cells (with voice packets) reach the receiver. After the cell and AAL headers are processed, the terminating endpoint compares the timestamp to the CDV (100 ms in this example). In scenario 1, the packet has arrived

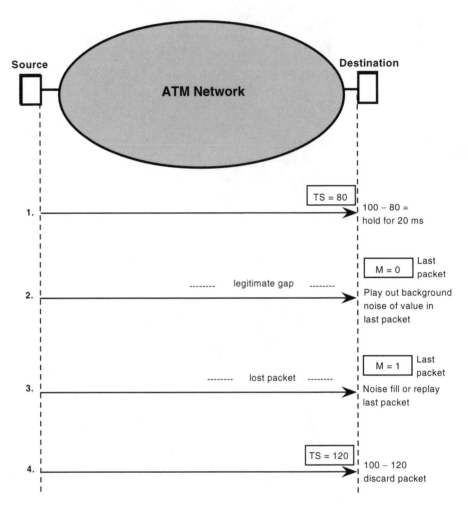

Figure 7–12
Buildout operations at the receiver.

with TS = 80 ms, which means it took 80 ms to traverse the network from the originating endpoint to the terminating endpoint. Since 100 − 80 = 20, the packet is held for 20 ms before being given to the decoding application.

In scenario 2, the endpoint has no packets to play out. So, it examines the M bit of the previous packet for this speech signal (which it must buffer). If M = 0, the gap is legitimate, and the noise field in the previous packet is used to play out appropriate background noise.

Scenario 3 is the same as scenario 2 in that the endpoint has no packets to play out. In this case, the M bit of the previous packet is 1. Therefore, a packet is lost, and the terminating endpoint creates a noise fill, replays the previous packet, and so on. This interpolation procedure has not yet been defined in any of the standards, and the ITU-T cites it as for "further study."

In scenario 4, the packet arrives later than the constant delay value (120 ms in the timestamp), and the packet is discarded.

In effect, a buffer at the receiver must eliminate jitter (varying arrival times of the cells, due to variable delay). The application reads out of the receiving buffer based on a local clock. The handling of delay, such as the examples in this section, is usually implemented differently by each network designer. Nonetheless, a scenario such as the one described here is common to some implementations.

AAL TYPES 3, 4, 3/4, AND 5 (AAL 3, AAL 4, AAL 3/4, AND AAL 5) FOR DATA

Pre-ATM Approach to Traffic Integrity Management

Before an analysis is made of ATM support for data payloads, it will be helpful to pause and reflect on the way (and the reasons why) an ATM network transports data. This section continues the discussions in Chapter 6 on bit error rates and the rationale for the size of the ATM header and payload.

Many of the data communications networks in operation today provide extensive services to the user (which will be called traffic integrity management in this discussion), such as:

- Sequencing the traffic to make certain it arrives in the proper order at the end destination. In the event it arrives out of order, the traffic is stored in a buffer, resequenced, and presented to the end user in the proper order. This operation is quite useful. For example, it ensures that the records of, say, a file transfer, arrive in order.
- Performing error checks on the traffic to make certain the bits in the traffic stream were not distorted due to transmission impairments, such as noise or crosstalk, for example.
- Sending acknowledgments to the sender of the traffic. Based on an error check operation, the acknowledgment is either positive (ACK), or negative (NAK).

- Retransmitting the traffic in case the originator receives a NAK from the receiver.
- Performing flow control on the user application to prevent the user from saturating the network with too much workload.

As seen in Figure 7–13, in some networks the operations of sequencing, error checking, acknowledgments (positive and negative), retransmissions, and flow control are performed more than once. These operations are performed at the data link layer (L2), the network layer (L3), the transport layer (L4), and perhaps the application layer (L7) (not shown in this figure), and even again at the network layer *inside* the network (also not shown in this figure).

Most likely, the reader is wondering why these operations are duplicated. A useful question is, Why should these functions, however useful, be replicated in several layers? Generally, they should not be replicated. Figure 7–14 shows the fields present in the PDU for these three layers. Although the names vary, all layers are performing sequencing with N(S), N(R), P(S), P(R), T(S), and T(R) values, where (S) represents a send SN and (R) represents a receiving SN. All layers are performing ACKs, NAKs, and flow control with receive not ready (RNR) and receive ready (RR).

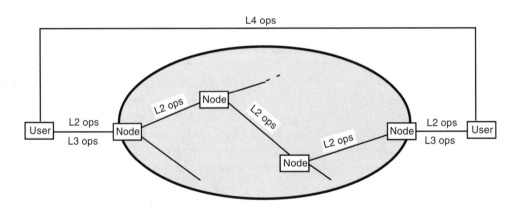

Ln ops   The operations at the n layer

    L2   Link layer

    L3   Network layer

    L4   Transport layer

Figure 7–13
Data integrity operations.

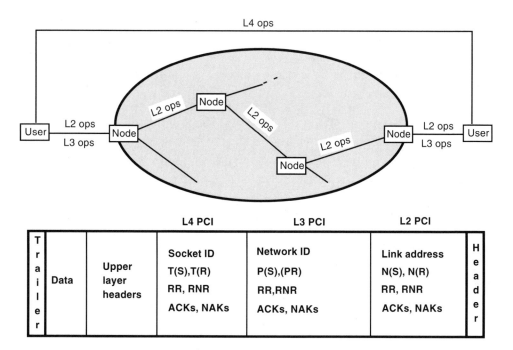

Figure 7–14
Contents of headers.

Notwithstanding, and in deference to past technologies, it has made good sense to perform these operations in several layers, because communications links were (and still are in *many* systems) quite error-prone, and performing error checks (with ACKs and NAKs) was an effective means to ensure that the traffic on the links was error-free. Thus, layer two (L2) performs a error check on the received data on each link and returns an ACK or NAK to the sender.

Moreover, many data communications protocols are implemented with the well-founded notion that the services provided by other protocols in a network cannot be assumed. For example, the data link layer (L2 in this figure) is usually tasked with performing an error check on the incoming traffic to determine if a transmission impairment (noise, crosstalk, etc.) has distorted the data. However, some data link layer implementations perform these services, and others do not. So, a prudent network layer (L3 in this figure) protocol designer must build error detection and resolution capabilities into the network layer, which operates above the data link layer.

Moreover, the L2 operations affect all users on the link. The layer makes no distinction about what is carried in the L2 frame. Its job is to deliver the frame safely to the destination station on that one link.

On the other hand, the network layer (L3) header identifies *each* user on the link *at the UNI* with a network ID, such as a virtual circuit number. Therefore, a finer granularity of control is achieved with this layer. For example, an RNR issued at the link layer affects all users on that link, but an RNR issued at the network layer only affects a selected user—one that is identified by a virtual circuit number.

A transport layer (L4 in this figure) designer can also implement these operations. After all, the L4 operations are not aware of the lower layer operations, and it cannot be assumed that sequencing, flow control, ACKs, and NAKs are performed in an internet in which traffic may be transported across unknown networks. However, the transport operations occur between the end-user stations; they do not operate on the link or in the network. In other words, the transport layer provides end-to-end traffic integrity management. The transport header is sent through the network and links transparently—these lower layers do not examine the syntax of this header. The transport layer uses socket IDs or OSI service access points (SAPs) to identify each user's traffic between the end-user workstations.

Some network vendors perform an end-to-end acknowledgment yet once more between the boundaries of the network cloud. The reason? The network cannot afford to assume that traffic integrity management operations are taking place *outside* the network. This practice is especially important for connection setup and disconnect messages.

So, the manner in which many data communications systems have evolved during the past twenty years is for each layer to assume that the other layers are not doing any integrity management operations. The end result is that these operations may occur at least once (for certain) and maybe five times: (1) L2; (2) L3 at the UNI; (3) L3 inside the network; (4) L4; (5) L7.[1]

ATM Approach to Traffic Integrity Management

ATM eliminates almost all of these functions at L2 and L3 (see Figure 7–15). In addition, the headers in these layers are combined into the ATM cell header. The reasons for these changes are:

---

[1]In an OSI network, some of these operations are even defined at the session layer (L6).

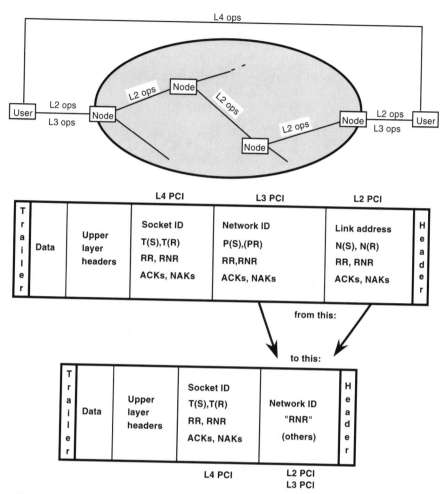

Figure 7–15
ATM approach to the use of headers.

- ATM assumes the transmission media to be relatively error-free. Therefore, the conventional link layer operations of ACKs and NAKs become less necessary.
- Even if L2 ACKs and NAKs are believed to be important, they are not feasible for certain types of traffic that cannot afford the delay in waiting for a retransmission (voice and video traffic). It is inefficient for the ATM network to distinguish between data and voice/video traffic in deciding if NAKs and ACKs should or should not be performed.

- ATM still performs an error check for each cell upon its arrival at each receiving node, but it does not ACK or NAK. In the event of an uncorrectable error, it discards the cell.
- ATM does not eliminate all of the L3 operations. It still uses an ID to identify each user's traffic, which we learned is called the VPI/VCI in ATM networks. Nonetheless, conventional L3 operations, such as closed user groups, call collects, and call redirects, are eliminated at the UNI.
- Sequencing, flow control, ACKs, and NAKs are also eliminated or reduced at L3. One of the main reasons for this scaled-down UNI is that L4 is performing these operations on an end-to-end basis, and the L3 functions become somewhat redundant.

In a nutshell, most of the traffic integrity functions for data applications are removed from the data link and network layers and passed to the transport layer, which resides in the customer's workstation. This approach allows the user to implement any type or level of integrity function deemed necessary for that application. It also makes for a much faster network, because the network is not spending as much time and overhead in processing the user payload.

THE ORIGINAL AAL TYPES 3 AND TYPE 4 (AAL 3, AAL 4)

The original ATM standards established AAL 3 for VBR connection-oriented data operations, and AAL 4 for VBR connectionless data operations. These two types have been combined and are treated as one type. This section of the book describes the initial AAL 3 and AAL 4, and then explains the revised approach.

AAL 3 is used to support connection-oriented VBR services. These bursty-type data services do not require any precise timing relationships to be maintained between the source and destination. Obviously, AAL 3 can support class C traffic.

The AAL 4 cell is used to support either message-mode service or stream-mode service for data systems (not voice or video). It is designed also to support connectionless services, although the ITU-T also provides for this type to give assured operations in which lost traffic can be retransmitted. With assured operations, flow control is a mandatory feature. In addition, AAL 4 operations may also provide non-assured operations in which lost or discarded traffic is not recovered, nor is flow control provided.

AAL 3/4

As the AAL standard has matured, it became evident that the original types were inappropriate. Therefore, AAL 3 and AAL 4 were combined because of their similarities. AAL 3/4 is the preferred type for internetworking ATM with SMDS or MAN.

Naming Conventions for AAL 3/4

Figure 7–16 shows the naming conventions for AAL 3/4. The convergence sublayer is divided into the common part convergence sublayer (CPCS) and the service specific convergence sublayer (SSCS). The SSCS is used to support different user applications, and thus, multiple SSCSs may exist. The SSCS may be null if it is not needed. In this case, it is used only to map primitives of the user upper layer to/from CPCS. The various SDUs, PDUs, headers and trailers in Figure 7–16 are self-explanatory.

The AAL 3/4 PDU

As shown in Figure 7–17, the AAL 3/4 PDU carries 44 octets in the payload and 5 fields in the header and trailer. The 2-bit segment type (ST) is used to indicate the beginning of message (BOM = 10), continuation of message (COM = 00), end of message (EOM = 01), or single segment message (SSM = 11). The SN is used for sequencing the traffic. It is incremented by one for each PDU sent, and a state variable at the receiver indicates the next expected PDU. If the received SN is different from the state variable, the PDU is discarded. The message identification (MID) subfield is used to reassemble traffic on a given connection. The length indicator (LI) defines the size of the payload. And, finally, the cyclic redundancy check (CRC) field is a 10-bit field used to determine if an error has occurred in any part of the PDU.

AAL 3/4 Headers and Trailers

The AAL 3/4 layers and their functions closely resemble their counterparts in MAN and SMDS. As depicted in Figure 7–18, AAL 3/4 consists of a CS/SAR. CS is responsible primarily for error checking, and

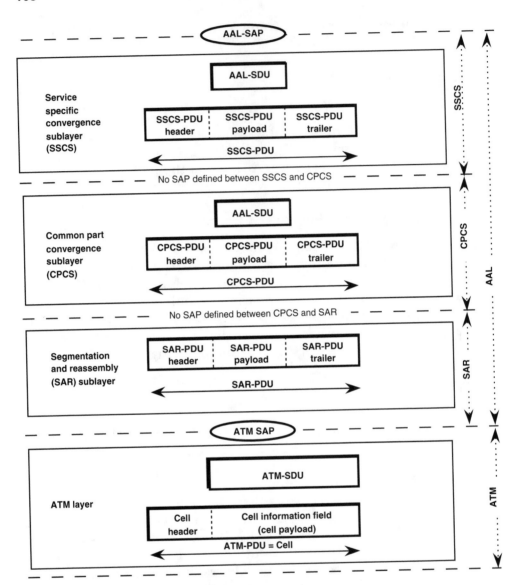

Figure 7–16
AAL 3/4 general data unit.

SAR is responsible for segmentation and reassembly operations. AAL 3/4 can accept and process a user PDU of up to 65,535 octets. Like MAN and SMDS, the traffic is segmented into 53 octet cells for transmission on the media.

As mentioned earlier, AAL 3/4 operations support two types of data transfer requirements: a message-mode service and a stream-mode ser-

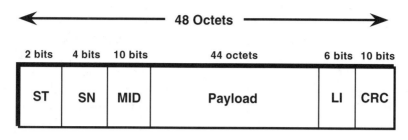

ST   Segment type
SN   Sequence number
MID   Message identifier
LI   Length indicator
CRC   Cyclic redundancy check

Figure 7–17
AAL 3/4 PDU.

vice. The message-mode service allows a single SDU to be segmented into smaller pieces for transmission. In the stream-mode service, one or more fixed size SDUs are transported as one AAL convergence function PDU. The stream-mode will allow a SDU to be as small as one octet.

The CS_PDU headers and trailers are shown in Figure 7–18. The header contains three fields. The common part identifier (CPI) field (one octet) identifies the type of traffic and certain values that are to be im-

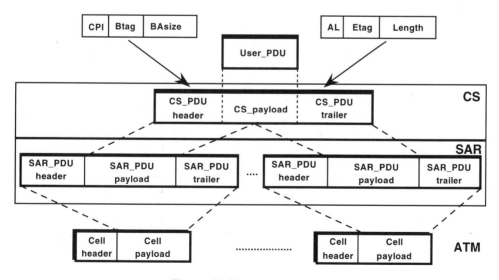

Figure 7–18
AAL 3/4 layers and PDUs.

plemented in the other fields of the headers and trailers. The Btag field (one octet) is used to identify all CS_PDUs that are associated with a session. The buffer allocation size field (BAsize, two octets) defines the size of the buffer to receive the CS_PDU at the receiver. The trailer also contains three fields. The alignment field (AL) is a filler to 32-bit align the trailer. The Etag (one octet) is used with the Btag in the header to correlate all traffic associated with the CS_payload. Finally, the length field specifies the length of the CS_payload (in octets).

AAL 3/4 Sequencing and Identification Operations

Figure 7–19 provides an example of how the various fields in the headers and trailers are used to assure all traffic is received and re-assembled correctly at the terminating AAL entity. The first PDU always contains the header created by CS at the originating AAL entity: the CPI, Btag, and BAsize. This header is used by the receiving AAL to iden-tify (1) the type of traffic coming in (CPI); (2) the size of the buffer that is to receive all PDUs (BAsize); (3) the tag that will allow the detection of the last PDU (Btag). In this example, the Btag is 44 and the BAsize is 880.

The AAL PDU header contains the segment type field to indicate the BOM, COM, and EOM PDUs. The SN field is incremented by 1 for each successive PDU. In this example, 20 PDUs are sent, so numbers 1 through 15 are placed in the PDUs and a wraparound counter allows the SN values to be reused. The message identification field (MID) is set to 68 in this example to uniquely identify all associated PDUs. The last PDU has its ST set to 01 for EOM. The last PDU has SN = 5, which

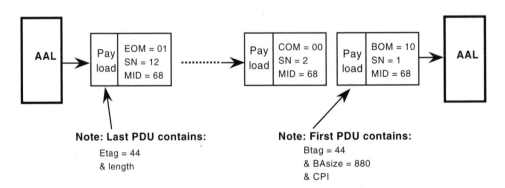

Figure 7–19
Example of AAL 3/4 sequencing and identification operations.

means the SN wraparound counter started at 1, and wrapped around to 5 for the last PDUs.

During the reassembly process, if any PDU is not received correctly, then all associated PDUs must be dropped. If one PDU is lost, none are retained at the receiver.

If 16 successive PDUs are lost, the 4-bit SN alone will not allow the detection of this type of problem. The BAsize can be used to recover. When the last PDU arrives (EOM set in the segment type field), the receiver detects that the buffer is not filled. It knows something is amiss and discards the buffer.

Figure 7–20 shows other aspects of AAL 3/4 operations. Each SAR-PDU that belongs to one SAR-SDU is sequenced, by incrementing the sequence number by one, with each succeeding SAR-PDU. Successive SAR-SDUs belonging to one MID are not necessarily sequenced together. The receiver does not correlete the sequence numbers of successive SAR-SDU, only the SAR-PDUs within the SAR-SDU. So, send can set the sequence number field to any value (0–15) in the first SAR-PDU on the segmented SAR-SDU. Furthermore, Figure 7–20 also shows that the Btag and Etag do not have to be continuous sequence numbers for successive transfers of CPCS-PDUs. For simplicity of implementation, they may indeed be in sequence, but the receiver does not make this check.

A Complete SAR-PDU and CPCS-PDU Example

Figure 7–21 shows the structure and format for the combined SAR and CPCS PDU for AAL 3/4 operations. This figure represents a single-segment PDU (SSM), which is used for this example because it contains

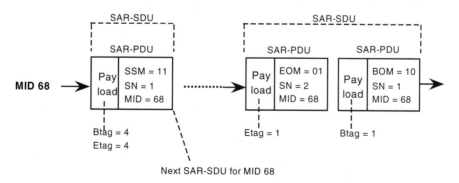

Figure 7–20
Relationship of sequence numbers and Btag/Etag values.

SSM SAR-PDU

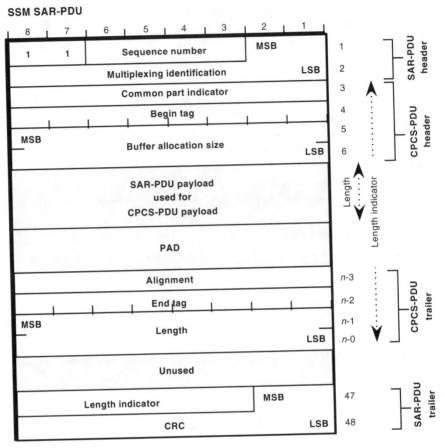

Figure 7–21
Combined SAR and CPCS-PDU: SSM.

all the headers and trailers, whereas BOM, COM, and EOM only contains parts of them. In this example, an original SDU is not long enough to warrant more than one segmented PDU. Therefore, the SAR header contains the SSM bits of 11 in bits 8, 7 of the first octet of the header. It must contain the SAR-PDU header and trailer, as well as both the CPCS-PDU header and CPCS-PDU trailer. The header also contains the sequence number (SN), which is followed by the message identification field (MID).

The CPCS-PDU header follows with the common part indicator (CPI), the Btag, and the BAsize fields. Next is the user payload, which is followed by CPCS-PDU trailer of the alignment field (AL), the Etag, and the length field. Then follows the SAR-PDU trailer, consisting of the length indicator (LI), and the cyclic redundancy check field (CRC).

Functional Model for AAL 3/4

ITU-T I.363, Annex C describes a functional model for AAL 3/4. It is included here because it provides a good example of the relationships of the SAPs, layers, and data units. Figure 7–22 depicts this model on the send side. The blocks in this figure support a user connection. Each SAR

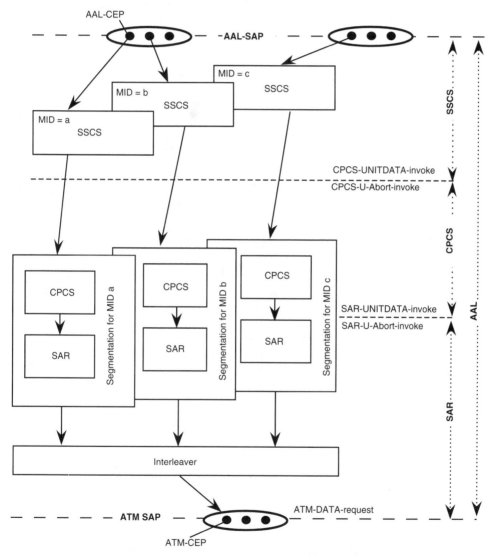

Figure 7–22
AAL 3/4 functional model on the send side. [ITUT-TI3.63]

and CPCS pairs represent a segmentation state machine. The interleaver is responsible for allocating the AAL SAR-PDUs from the state machines across the ATM SAP. How this is done is an internal matter.

The receiver side model is a mirror image of the send side, as shown in Figure 7–23. Of course, the operations are reversed. The ATM layer

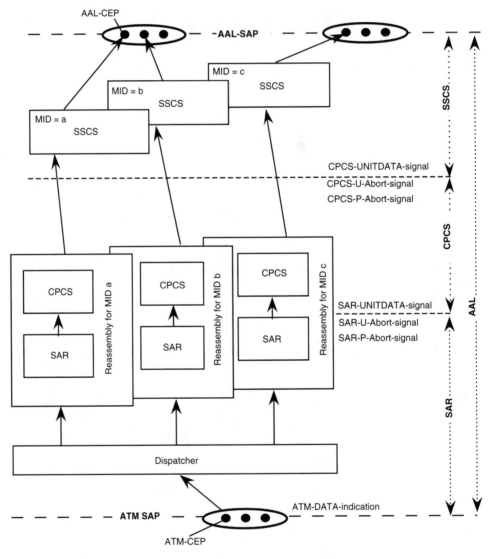

Figure 7–23
AAL 3/4 functional model on the receive side type.
[ITU-TI.363]

presents the SDUs to the AAL dispatcher, which uses the MID field to route the traffic to the proper reassembly state machine.

AAL TYPE 5 (AAL 5)

The purpose of AAL 5 is to provide guidance for transporting upper layer protocols over ATM. It was conceived because AAL 3/4 was considered to contain unnecessary overhead; it was judged that multiplexing

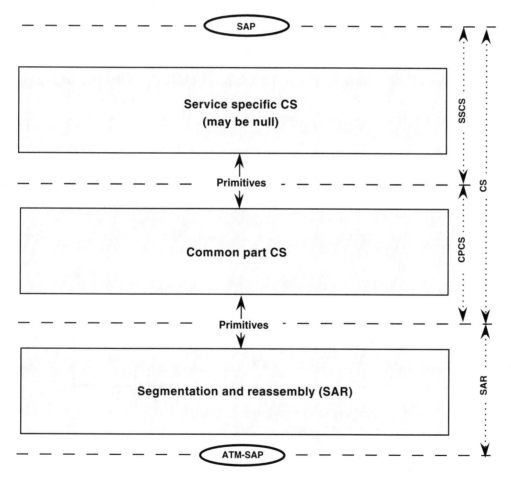

Figure 7–24
The AAL 5 structure.

could be pushed up to any upper layer, and that the BAsize operations to preallocate buffers at the receiver were not needed.

Structure of AAL 5

As shown in Figure 7–24, the AAL 5 structure is similar to the structure for AAL 3/4, but is simpler. It contains the convergence sublayer, which is divided into the common part convergence sublayer (CPCS) and the service specific convergence sublayer (SSCS)—obviously, this part is identical to AAL 3/4. The SSCS is used to support different user applications, and thus, multiple SSCSs may exist. The SSCS may be null if it is not needed. In this case, it is used only to map primitives of the user upper layer to/from CPCS.

The AAL 5 PDU

Figure 7–25 shows the format of the AAL 5 PDU. It consists of an 8-octet trailer. The PAD field acts as a filler to fill out the PDU to 48 octets. The CPCS-UU field is used to identify the user payload. The common part indicator (CPI) has not been fully defined in ITU-T I.363. The Length field (L) defines the payload length, and the CRC field is used to detect errors in the SSCS PDU (user data).

AAL 5 is a convenient service for frame relay because it supports connection-oriented services. In essence, the frame relay user traffic is given to an ATM backbone network for transport to another frame relay user. Discussion of AAL 5 and its relationship to the ATM Forum activi-

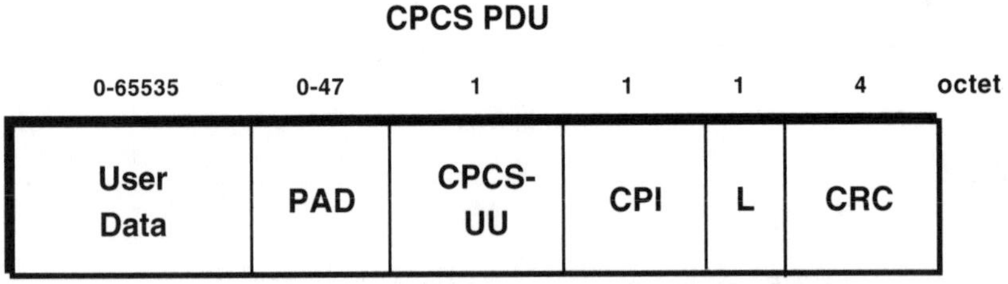

CPCS PDU

0-65535	0-47	1	1	1	4	octet
User Data	PAD	CPCS-UU	CPI	L	CRC	

CPCS-UU   Common part convergence sublayer
CPI   Common part indicator
L   Length
CRC   Cyclic redundancy check

Figure 7–25
The AAL 5 PDU.

ties is covered in Chapter 11 (see "Internetworking with ATM Networks").

A NEW TYPE—AVAILABLE BIT RATE (ABR)

As of this writing, the ATM Forum is in the process of defining a new type of service, called the available bit rate (ABR). Its purpose is to provide a mechanism for controlling traffic flow from LAN-based workstations, and the routers that service these workstations. Since LAN devices have no "contract" with a network, no easy method is available to relate the AAL CBR and VBR idea to a LAN environment. Since this new type is concerned principally with traffic management, I shall defer further discussion on the subject to Chapter 9.

THE AAL/ATM PRIMITIVES

Chapter 3 explains service definitions and primitives. This section continues that discussion, focusing on the operations between the AAL and ATM layers, the user application and the AAL, as well as the CS and SAR within the AAL. Remember that primitives specify the type of function call or system library call that is invoked between two layer entities, as well as the arguments (the primitive parameters) that are conveyed with the call. This section should be of particular interest to software designers and programmers, but it is presented in a general fashion for all.

Figure 7–26 shows the ATM Forum view of how the primitives are exchanged between the AAL and ATM layers, as well as their associated parameters. Two primitives are exchanged, the ATM-DATA.request and the ATM-DATA.indication. The response and confirm primitives are not used at this layer boundary.

The ATM-DATA.request transfers an ATM_SDU from AAL to ATM over an existing connection at the sending machine. The ATM-SDU parameter contains this SDU. Two other parameters are associated with the request primitive. The SDU-type is used to distinguish between two types of ATM-SDUs that are associated with the connection. The meaning of this parameter is implementation specific. The submitted loss-priority parameter indicates the importance of this SDU. It can take on

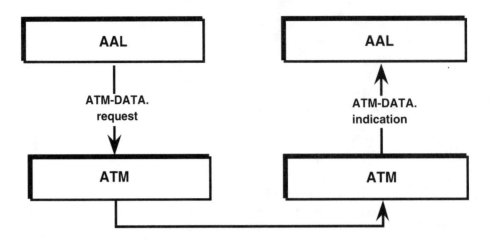

Parameter	Associated Primitives	Meaning	Valid Values
ATM-SDU	ATM-DATA.request ATM-DATA.indication	48-byte pattern for transport	Any 48 byte pattern
SDU-type	ATM-DATA.request ATM-DATA.indication	End-to-end cell type indicator	0 or 1
Submitted Loss-priority	ATM-DATA.request	Requested cell loss-priority	High or low priority
Received Loss-priority	ATM-DATA.indication	Received cell loss priority	High or low priority
Congestion-experienced	ATM-DATA.indication	EFCN indication	True or False

Figure 7–26
The AAL-ATM primitives.

two values: high priority or low priority. This parameter can be used by the ATM layer to set the cell loss priority (CLP) bit in the cell header.

The ATM-DATA.indication transfers the ATM_SDU at the receiving machine's ATM layer to the AAL. It, of course, contains the ATM-SDU parameter, the SDU-type parameter, and two others. The received loss-priority parameter reflects value of the CLP bit (it is implementation-specific) in the cell header. The congestion indication parameter indicates that the ATM-SDU has passed through at least one network node that experienced congestion.

The primitives for class A CBR traffic are shown in Figure 7–27.

Two primitives are used, the AAL-DATA.request and the AAL-DATA.indication. The time intervals between the invocations of these primitives must be constant in order to preserve the synchronous nature of the connection and information transfer exchange.

The parameters in the primitives are also shown in Figure 7–27. The AAL_SDU contains one bit of user payload. The structure parameter is used to support structured information transfer for 8-bit octets. It is set to start to indicate the beginning of a block of traffic; otherwise it is set to continuation. The status parameter is used in the indication primitive to inform the AAL user if AAL judges the AAL_SDU to be errored or not in error. It may also be used to indicate that the AAL_SDU is not relevant (a dummy AAL_SDU, for example).

The CS/SAR primitives for Class A traffic are shown in Figure 7–28. Two primitives are invoked between these two sublayers: the SAR-DATA.invoke and the AAL-DATA.signal. The figure also shows the parameters used in the primitives. The CSDATA parameter contains the 47-octet CS_SDU transferred between the two layers. The SCVAL parameter contains the SN for the CS_SDU. The CSIVAL parameter contains the value for the CSI bit. The SNCK parameter is present in the indica-

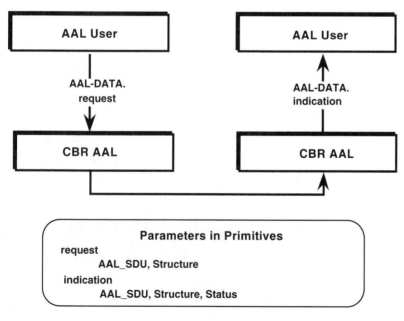

Figure 7–27
The user-AAL CBR primitives.

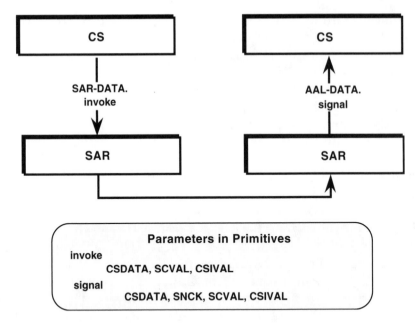

Figure 7–28
The AAL CS/SAR primitives for class A traffic.

tion primitive. It is used by SAR to inform CS of the results of the error check performed on the SN.

SUMMARY

The ATM adaptation layer (AAL) is designed to support different types of applications, and different types of traffic, such as voice, video, or data. The AAL is divided into two sublayers: the convergence sublayer (CS) and the segmentation and reassembly (SAR) sublayer. For some implementations, CS is divided further into the service specific CS (SSCS) and the common part of CS (CPCS). SSCS is designed to support a specific aspect of a data application, and CPCS supports generic functions common to more than one type of data application.

8

ATM Switching Operations

INTRODUCTION

This chapter examines ATM switching operations. It also explains how the VPI and VCI are used by a switch to make routing decisions. Since switching is not part of the ATM standards and vendors use a wide variety of techniques to build their switches, this chapter focuses on the prevalent methods in use today. In most implementations, this part of the ATM node is quite proprietary; vendors put a large amount of research and development into the switching fabric. In most instances, the author was able to obtain the general architectural descriptions from several vendors. Therefore, this chapter reflects examples of ATM switches as well as a description of current research on cell switching.

Several approaches to cell switching are examined in this chapter. The topic of ATM switching is worthy of an entire book, so the goal of the chapter is more modest, and is designed to give the reader a general overview of cell switching architecture and the major components of an ATM switch. Be aware that there is no "best way" to build an ATM switch, and the ATM standards wisely do not address this aspect of the technology.

ATM SWITCHING

One of the most important components of ATM is the switch and how fast it relays cells (without cell loss). ATM must accept asynchronous and synchronous traffic, as well as connection-oriented and connectionless traffic. Queuing delay and switching delay must be minimized if the ATM network is to perform satisfactorily in its support of the input and output lines operating (perhaps) at 155 Mbit/s. Consequently, the ATM switch requires not only a processor capable of supporting high-speed ports, but also switches with a capacity of up to 2 Gbit/s (which are readily available today). This speed will be modest in a few short years.

One purpose of the ATM switch is to adapt gracefully to changing network traffic profiles with the ability to adjust to increased or decreased input traffic (within limits, however). Since the switch of an ATM network must receive traffic that is somewhat unpredictable, the ATM switch must be able to adjust to changing network conditions. All these problems and their solutions are not defined in the ATM standards. Vendors are free to implement the techniques they deem appropriate for their product.

Routing with the Cell Header

As described in earlier chapters, the virtual channels are aggregated through multiplexers and switched (routed) through the network. Two types of switches are used in an ATM network for the multiplexing/demultiplexing and routing of traffic (see Figure 8–1). Conceptually, a virtual path switch is only required to examine the VPI part of the header for multiplexing/demultiplexing and routing. Virtual channel switches, on the other hand, must examine the whole routing field; that is to say, the VCI and the VPI.

The intent of this approach is to speed up switching and routing at intermediate points. Instead of requiring the switch (in some instances) to examine the entire routing field (which could entail overhead and processing delays), the VCI value can be transported transparently through a virtual path connection. Please note that while the VPI/VCI can be used as the routing label, nothing precludes a switch designer from placing a special routing label onto the cell for its processing through the switch.

In Figure 8–1(b), two virtual path connections exist from user A to ATM B and from ATM B to user B. Virtual path connections can be thought of as using leased lines for connecting nodes. A node can use the VCI identifier on any virtual path connection (with the use of the VCI). Also, as suggested in Figure 8–1(b), virtual path connections exist between the user and the network and within the network itself. This approach could be applied to the North American carrier system in which the VCI 14 could exist in one operator and VCI 23 could exist in another

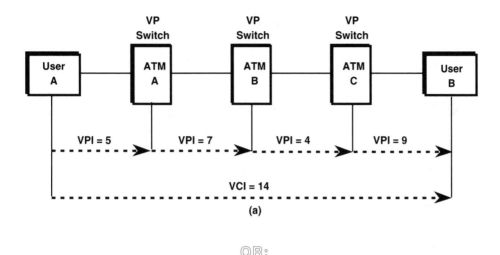

(a)

OR:

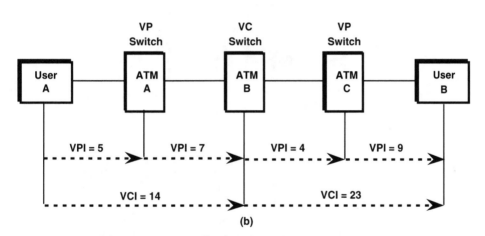

(b)

Figure 8–1
ATM switches: virtual path and virtual channel switches.

operator. This approach is a "clean" interface and also lends itself to relatively small lookup tables.

The VP and VC switches actually treat virtual path and virtual
channel connections the same in the sense that they can be set up on a
demand basis or they can be set up on a permanent basis. The network
also can use QOS features, such as traffic usage, to associate with either
a virtual channel or a virtual path.

Figure 8–2 provides an example of how VPIs and VCIs are translated and mapped at the switch. Figure 8–2(a) is an example of VPI

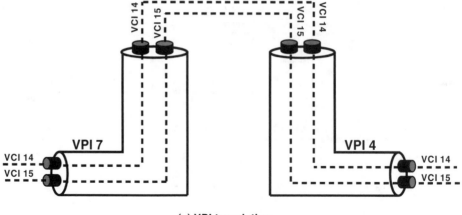

(a) VPI translation

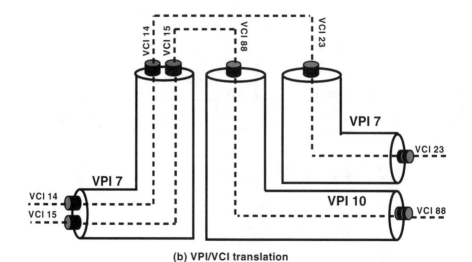

(b) VPI/VCI translation

Figure 8–2
VPI/VCI switching.

switching. The VCIs are passed unaltered through the switch, and VCIs 14 and 15 remain bundled in a VPI. The incoming VPI 7 is translated to outgoing VPI 4, but the VCI values are not altered.

In contrast, Figure 8–2(b) shows both VPIs and VCIs being translated and mapped to different values. VCI 14 (in the incoming VPI 7 bundle) is translated and mapped to outgoing VPI 7 with the VCI value changed to 23. The incoming VCI 15 (also bundled into VPI 7) is translated and mapped into VCI 88 and bundled into outgoing VPI 10.

SPACE AND TIME SWITCHING

Switching has been defined for many years to encompass two realms: space switching and time switching (see Figure 8–3). In either case, the objective of the operation is to transport traffic from an input port (an inlet) to an output port (an outlet). Stated another way, a switch transports traffic from n inlets to m outlets. The ATM switch functions like classical switching systems in that traffic is physically moved from input ports to output ports. This concept is called space switching in the sense that different input and output lines are utilized.

The other realm is called time switching (shown in Figure 8–3(b)), and it has long been used in time slot interchange (TSI) switches. With time switching, the information and time slots are switched to different slots from the inlets to the outlets. The difference with ATM is that the time slots do not exist for identification purposes such as in a straight TDM switch. The slot is identified by an ATM label (VCI/VPI). Because

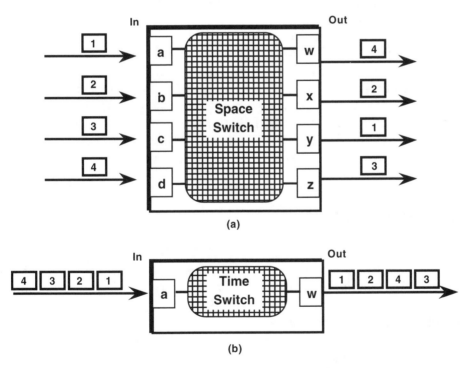

Figure 8–3
Space and time switching.

ATM switches do not use TSI operations, it is possible that the staging switches could contend with each other for the same time slot. Therefore, ATM uses queuing to ameliorate this problem.

In managing the cells, a switch must consider two kinds of priorities. The first deals with time priority, and must accommodate to cells with varying delay requirements. The second deals with space priority, and must accommodate to cells with varying loss requirements.

DIGITAL CROSS CONNECTS

ATM uses several of the concepts found today in digital cross connect equipment. The switch uses line and trunk identifers to map incoming connections to outgoing connections. Figure 8–4 shows a line side and a trunk side of a cross connect switch. Each 64 kbit/s DS0 channel is associated with a DS1 number and a physical port (line) number. A mapping table correlates this channel with an outgoing channel. An end-to-end digital circuit is made up of a set of DS1 and DS0 at each physical interface between two end users.

Figure 8–4 shows the mapping table at the bottom of the figure. The top part of the figure shows two examples of how the cross connect table is used. The two sets of arrows should aid you in these two examples. In the first example, DS0 #1 of DS1 #1 on line 1 is mapped to trunk 2, DS1 #1 and DS0 #5. In the second example, DS0 #2 of DS1 #1 on line 1 is mapped to trunk 1, DS1 #2 and DS0 #2. As we shall see in the next section, ATM uses the line and trunk switching concept for its VCI and VPI mapping and switching operations.

THE SWITCHING FABRIC

Before delving into the details of ATM switching, several definitions are needed. First, a switching fabric describes the components of the switch, which include its hardware and software architecture. Second, a network element is a part of the overall switching fabric, such as a software or hardware component.

Figure 8–5 shows a general depiction of ATM switch operation. Later discussions examine specific implementations. The ATM machine receives a cell on an incoming port (inlet) and reads the VCI/VPI value. This value has been reserved to identify a specific end user for a virtual

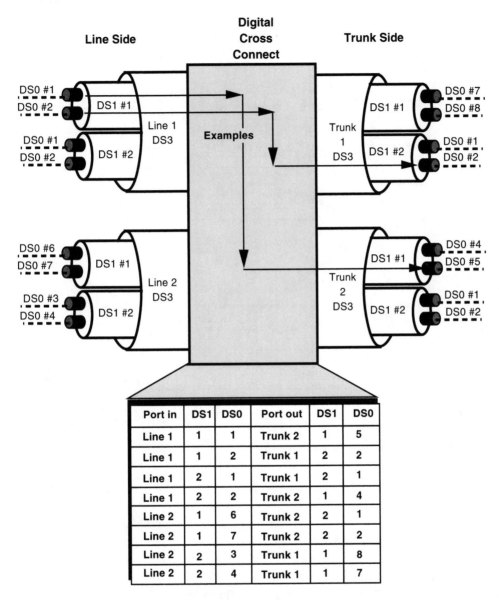

Figure 8–4
A digital cross connect.

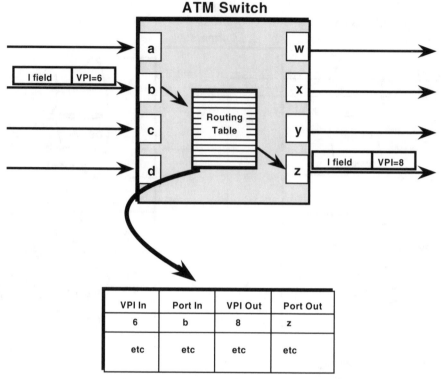

VPI   Virtual path Identifier
Note: VPI *and* VCI may be examined at the VCI/VPI switch

Figure 8–5
ATM routing operations.

circuit. It also identifies the outgoing port (outlet) for the next node that is to receive the traffic. The ATM switch then examines a routing table for the match of the incoming VPI number and corresponding incoming port to that of an outgoing VPI number and corresponding outgoing port. Some implementations do not make use of a routing table, but rely on the switching fabric to be self-routing; these switches are explained later.

The header in the outgoing cell is changed with the new VPI value placed in a field of the cell header. The new VPI value is used by the next ATM switch to perform subsequent routing operations.

This approach requires the routing tables to be established in advance; that is, this approach uses connection-oriented operations. Nothing precludes a connectionless implementation to support dynamic switching and adaptive routing in the event of problems, but ATM is designed around the concepts of connection-oriented virtual circuits.

MULTIPLEXING AND LABEL MAPPING

An ATM switch also performs multiplexing functions. The information from the inlets are multiplexed onto the outlets. The operations also include switching—the traffic from the inlets is switched to different outlets. While the cells are switched through the switching fabric from input to output ports, their header values are also translated from one incoming value to another outgoing value. It can be seen in Figure 8–5 that the headers uniquely identify the users' traffic, although the virtual circuit identifiers can be reused even if they are on different physical ports.

Figure 8–6 shows that an ATM switch is performing space switching by moving traffic from inlets a, b, c, d to outlets w, x, y, z. The switch

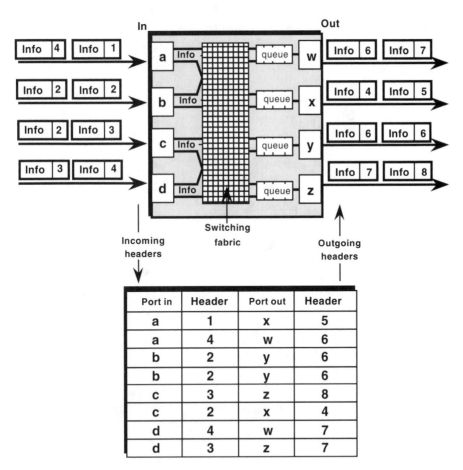

Port in	Header	Port out	Header
a	1	x	5
a	4	w	6
b	2	y	6
b	2	y	6
c	3	z	8
c	2	x	4
d	4	w	7
d	3	z	7

Figure 8–6
Routing and header translation.

is also performing header translation, which is sometimes called header switching. This figure also shows the use of buffers (in this example, these are called output buffers because they exist at the outlet). These buffers are used to assure (most of the time) that cells do not arrive at the same outlet at the same time.

The figure also depicts how the VPIs in the cell headers are used to determine the output port for the incoming cell. For example, a cell with VPI 1 arrives at port a. Routing operations reveal that the cell is be relayed to outport x, and its VPI changed to 5. As another example, a cell with VPI 3 arrives at port c. It is relayed to output port z and its label is mapped to VPI 8.

This figure summarizes the major functions of the ATM switch. It performs space switching, routing, multiplexing, and queuing. It also provides header mapping (header translation) by mapping the VPI values (and possibly the VCI values as well).

Figure 8–7 shows how the VPI/VCIs are used at the ATM switches (nodes) to set up a connection and to create the routing table entries. In

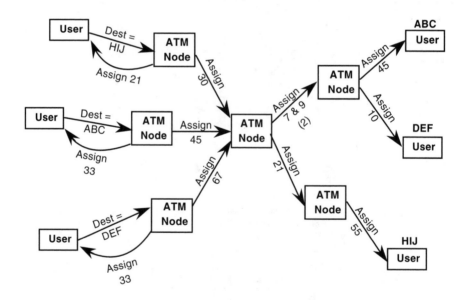

Note: Destination address (Dest = n) is sent to each ATM node to determine the route & is also sent to end-user node at terminating UNI

(2): Two connections are mapped at this node for end
     points ABC & DEF

Figure 8–7
Setting up the path through the ATM swtiches.

this example, three connections are created by three originating end users, by sending Q.2931 messages to the network. These messages contain a wide variety of information which are examined in Chapter 10, Call and Connection Control.

Among the fields in the Q.2931 connection request message is a destination address. This address is used by the ATM node to determine the route that is to be established for the connection. Each node accepts the Q.2931 message, examines the destination address and then consults a routing table to determine the next node that should receive the message.

A routing table is stored at each node and reflects the state of the network, the available bandwidth at each node, and other such information. It is updated periodically as conditions in the network change. Consequently, when the Q.2931 message is received by an ATM node, it knows the "best route" for this connection—at least to the next neighbor node.

These operations are dependent on how a vendor chooses to perform route discovery and maintain routing tables. The network may search for available bandwidth, and then set up the VPI/VCIs, or it may set them up on a link-by-link basis.

As each node sets up the calls, it reserves a VPI/VCI for each connection. Given an input VPI/VCI value, it selects an unused VPI/VCI value for the output port. The next node receives this value, selects the route, and chooses the VPI/VCI values for its output port, and so on, to the final terminating UNIs. It is the job of the network to select values that are not being used on the same physical interface. This approach allows the VPI/VCI values to be reused.

After the connection is established, only the VPI/VCI values are needed, not the destination address. This figure also shows that the originating users do not give the network a VPI/VCI at the originating UNI. The network assigns these values to the user, usually after the connection is completed and verified through the network to the terminating endpoint. This practice varies, but the ATM Forum specification requires that the network take responsibility for assigning VPI/VCIs. The originating end user can be informed of the values it is to use when the network returns a connection confirm message to the user.

SWITCHING TECHNOLOGIES

This section provides an overview of several prominent switching technologies. Vendors often design their switches with a combination of the variety of technologies described here.

Shared Memory Switch

The shared memory switch, as its name implies, provides a common memory for the storage of the cells and the switching fabric (see Figure 8–8). As we learned earlier in this chapter, these cells are organized into separate queues and are routed based on the VPI/VCI values in the header. This illustration shows the use of a multiplexer and demultiplexer at the input ports and output ports, respectively. The cells arriving at the receiving multiplexer are placed onto a single line to the switch, and the switching functions move the traffic from the input queues to the output queues and to the output port(s).

Shared Bus Switch

Figure 8–9 shows a functional view of a shared bus switch architecture. It also shows the switch supporting both frame relay PDUs and ATM PDUs. In most implementations such as shown here, the switch is implemented with two busses for fully redundant operations. The busses actually operate in the cell mode, and traffic is diced into 48-octet pieces with a 5-byte header attached (some implementations are using different size cells). The destination card reassembles the traffic.

Cell traffic is carried through the bus as cells, therefore, both cells or frames can be sent across the bus. As just stated, frames are converted to ATM cells and vice versa, which allows frame and cell relay services to interwork.

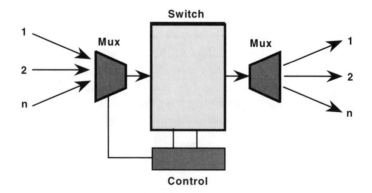

Figure 8–8
Shared memory switch.

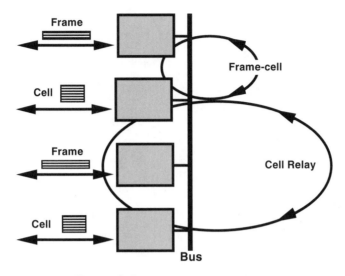

Figure 8–9
Example of a shared bus switch.

Crossbar Switch

Crossbar switching is arranged in one or a combination of three architectures: (1) concentration (more input lines than output lines), (2) expansion (more output lines than input lines), and (3) connection (an equal number of input and output lines). In its simplest form, a circuit switch is a N × M array of lines that connect to each other at crosspoints (see Figure 8–10). In a large switching office, the N lines are input from

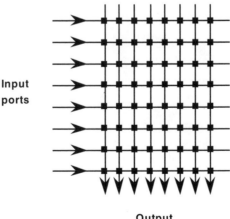

Figure 8–10
Crossbar switching.

the subscriber (terminals, computers, etc.) and the M lines are output to other switching offices. The switching fabric of a crossbar switch consists of N^2 crosspoints. Therefore, the size of the switch is limited.

Crossbar switch with arbiter (knockout switch).   A variation of the crossbar switch is shown in Figure 8–11 [DUBO94]. It is known by several names in the industry—perhaps the best known name is the knockout switch. The switch operates as a conventional crossbar switch in that the horizontal input is connected to a vertical output. Notice that each input line is connected to each output line. In addition, each output port has an arbiter. This component receives cells from the vertical output lines, and places them into a first-in, first-out (FIFO) queue. The queue allows the arbiter to decide which cells gain access to the output port.

Multistage Switching

Crossbar switching is usually performed in more than one array or stage in order to reduce the number of crosspoints. If N lines are to be connected, then N^2 crosspoints are required. Multistage switches are

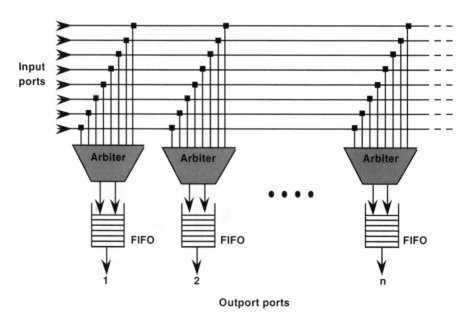

Figure 8–11
Crossbar switching with output arbiter (knockout switch).

economical for networks when $N > 16^3$ [AMOS79]. Multistage networks are designed with fewer crosspoints, yielding a more economical arrangement.

The input and output lines are divided into subgroups of N inputs and N outputs. The input first stage consists of n $\times$ k matrices. The k output is connected to one of the k center matrices. The third stage consists of k $\times$ n matrices connected from the center stage to the n outlets. The center stage matrices are all N/n by N/n arrays that permit connections from any first stage to any third stage.

The total number of crosspoints for this three-stage switch is [BELL82]:

$$N_x = 2Nk + k\ (N/n)^2$$

where: N_x = total number of crosspoints; N = number of input and output lines; n = size of each input/output group; k = number of center stage arrays.

Banyan and Delta Switching Networks

A technique that is often employed in high-speed switches is the Banyan network [GOKE73]. As illustrated in Figure 8–12, this switch is characterized by only one path existing between an input to the final output port. With this approach, routing operations are quite simple and straightforward, but cells may be blocked (collide) if more than one arrives at a switching element at the same time.

Banyan networks are classified further into subgroups. An (L)-level Banyan network is one in which only the adjacent elements are connected, so each path passes through the same number of L states. A special Banyan implementation is a delta network. It is characterized by having an equal number of inputs lines to outputs lines, with each output identified with a unique value (for example, a destination address). Each digit in an address identifies a next stage of a switching element in the switching fabric.

A number of switching technologies have been proposed for ATM. Some of these proposals and implementations are based on the concept of single-state networks where a single stage of switching element is connected to the inputs and outputs of the switch. Multistage networks (in which several stages of switching elements are connected by various links to form the switching fabric) have also seen use. As of this writing, it is certain that ATM switching will be a melding of several switching

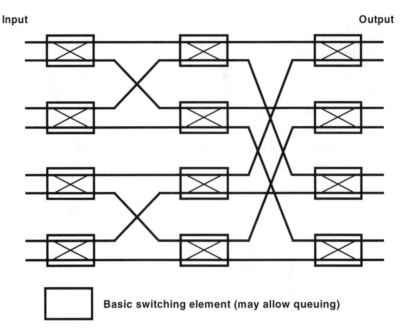

Figure 8–12
The Banyan-Delta switching fabric.

techniques, and these techniques will form a switching element that is reproduced and interconnected to form the switching fabric

Figure 8–13 shows a multistage delta network, called a 3-stage folded network. With this approach, traffic that arrives through the input lines (inlets) are examined by (in this example) three decision stages (switching elements). The traffic is passed to subsequent stages on output lines (outlets) based on an analysis of the address (which could be a tag used at the switch). Each stage is responsible for examining one bit in the address, typically from the most significant bit (MSB) to the least significant bit (LSB). In this example, a 3-bit address is used for simplicity.

The resulting address resolution is made one stage at a time in each bit of the address. As Figure 8–13 shows, the resultant output is based on the 3-bit address analysis of the three stages.

Figure 8–14 provides an example of an address resolution performed by the Banyan multistage switch. The bold line indicates the decision processes performed at the various stages. The destination address (010) is examined by each of the three stages on a bit-by-bit basis from the MSB to the LSB. The traffic, with its associated header, and address of 010 is routed to the output line identified as 010.

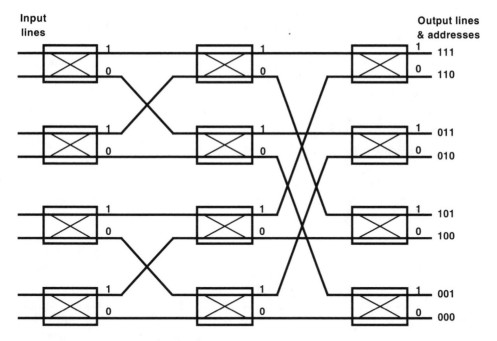

Figure 8–13
A 3-stage folded delta network.

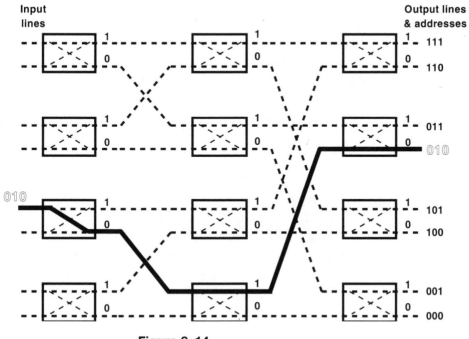

Figure 8–14
Example of address resolution.

Collisions may occur in a delta network if cells arrive at a switching element at the same time. These cells may collide at an intermediate element, even though they are destined for the same output line, or they may collide at the final element. The probability of collisions occurring can be reduced by placing buffers in each switching element and allowing the buffers to queue arriving cells, which is an approach that is implemented in a number of high-speed switches. Alternately, the switch can operate at a higher speed than the inlets, thus giving an arrival time at the switching elements with no collision probability. Other mechanisms may be employed, and systems today can operate at a cell loss rate of 10^{-10}.

Figure 8–15 shows three alternatives for the use of buffers and queues within the switching fabric. The first approach places the buffers on the inlet side. Each inlet has a dedicated buffer, which is serviced on a first-in, first-out (FIFO) operation. Logic in the buffer determines when the buffer is to be served and when the cell is to be out-queued to the bus. This approach encounters collisions if two cells at the head of the queue in different buffers are destined for the same switching element. Also, if a queued cell is awaiting the availability of a line to a switching element, subsequent cells in the queue are also blocked even though an inlet may be available.

Output buffers are yet another alternative. This approach requires that a single cell can be served only by an outlet, which also could create output collisions and contention. Collisions can occur only if the switching fabric operates at the same speed as the incoming lines to the switching elements. In other words, several cells are contending for the same outlet. As discussed earlier, using different speeds within the switching fabric vis-à-vis the communications lines can reduce this problem. So, if collision is not to occur, cell transfer must be performed at n times the speed of the inlets, where n = the number of possible lines.

The last illustration shows central queuing, which entails nondedicated buffers between the inlets and the outlets; that is to say, a central memory element is used by all inlets to the outlets. This process does not work on the FIFO discipline, because the inlet traffic is placed into a single queue. To service the queues efficiently and fairly, there must be some mechanism to access the entries in the queues and to index the traffic in either sequential or random access operation.

Network switches can be developed that use parallel switching techniques. Figure 8–16 shows a parallel Banyan switch, also called vertical stacking. While switching techniques vary with parallel switching, as a general rule, the ATM cells that belong to the same connection are

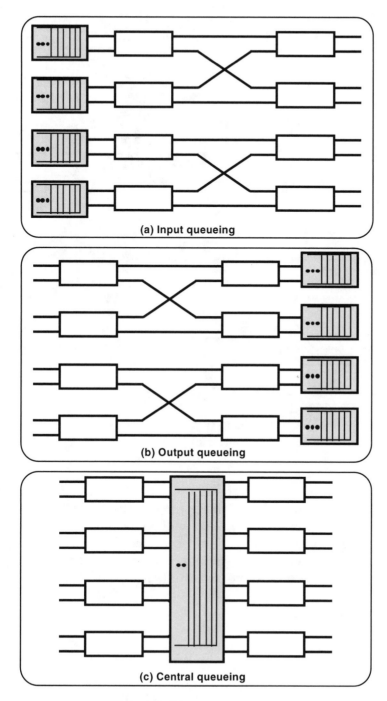

(a) Input queueing

(b) Output queueing

(c) Central queueing

Figure 8–15
Switch buffers and queues.

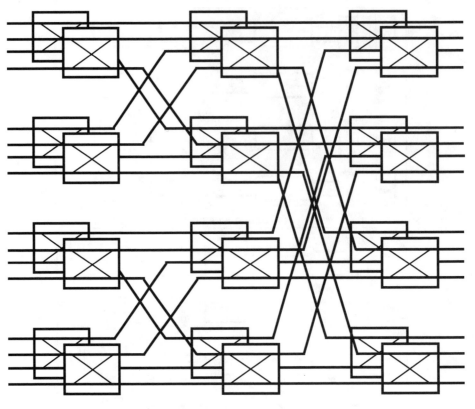

Figure 8–16
A parallel Banyan switch.

passed on the same plane of the multi-dimensioned switch. How this is determined varies among switch designers. During call establishment, decisions are made as to which plane will be used for the connection. The switch contains logic that examines each incoming call, places it on the appropriate plane, and then switches it to the appropriate output line. This approach has proved to be highly efficient, and it provides very high throughput.

EXAMPLE OF AN ATM SWITCH

Figure 8–17 shows an example of a commercial ATM switch [NORT94]. The switch fabric module (SFM) switches cells from the inlets to the outlets. The 8×8 switching fabric supports eight ports operating

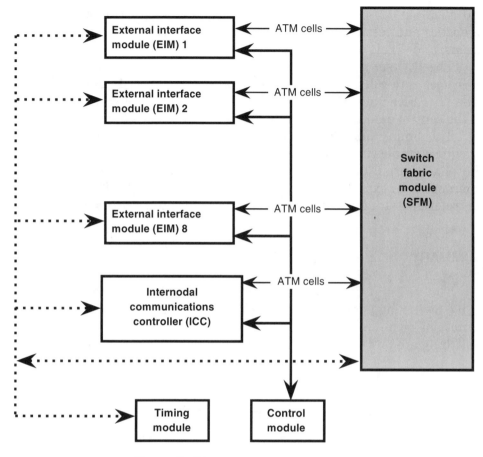

Figure 8–17
ATM switch components. [NORT94]

at 155.52 Mbit/s. The basic fabric operates at 1.2 Gbit/s, with a nonblocking architecture. Input and output buffers are connected with bytewide busses.

The external interface modules (EIMs) provide UNIs or NNIs for: (1) DS3, (2) OC-3c, (3) unframed T-1, SF1 (superframe), or ESF T-1 (extended superframe). The EIM adds a node tag to each cell as it enters the switch. The tag is used to control the routing through the SFM. The tag is discarded as it leaves the switch.

The control module is a UNIX-based Sun SPARCstation that operates the node control software. It is also tasked with sending and receiving messages to and from other switches via the internodal communications controller (ICC). It provides the following functions: (1) node initialization, (2) port configuration, (3) connection or call setups, (4) diagnostics and testing, (5) selection of timing source, (6) switch over operations, and (7) alarms and statistics.

The ICC supports interswitch communication. It segments the ICC messages into cells, and sends these cells onto the link along with user cells. The receiving ICC reassembles the cells and delivers the message to the control module. ICC uses AAL 3 or AAL 5 operations.

The timing module receives commands from the control module to provide a stable timing reference for all operations in the switch. It locks the phases of all output clock generators, based on one of three source references: an external clock recovered from any of the EIMs, an external reference standard, or an external reference to Stratum 3 accuracy.

SUMMARY

The VPI and VCI are used by an ATM switch to make routing decisions. Switching is not part of the ATM standards, so vendors use a wide variety of techniques to build their switches. Several approaches to cell switching are now implemented, but research continues in this area.

CHAPTER 9

Traffic Management

INTRODUCTION

This chapter examines several methods for managing user traffic in an ATM network. The emphasis is placed on the operations at the user-network interface (UNI). Ideas on queue management and queue servicing for different applications are explored, as well as how an ATM node must adjust its behavior to varying traffic loads. The chapter includes a description of the work done by the ATM Forum and ITU-T on traffic control and congestion control.

TRAFFIC MANAGEMENT IN AN ATM NETWORK

Digitizing analog images is an easy task with today's technology. These techniques have been around for over thirty years, and are now found in common devices such as personal computers and even children's toys. A more formidable task is the management of the digital images of voice, video, and data applications in a coherent and integrated fashion.

A properly constructed ATM network must manage traffic fairly and provide effective allocation of the network capacity for different sorts of applications, such as voice, video, and data. The ATM network must also provide cost effective operations relative to the service level (quality of service, QOS) stipulated by the network user, and it must be able to support the different delay requirements of the applications, an important support function known as cell delay variation (CDV) management.

The ATM network must be able to adapt to unforeseen traffic patterns; for example, unusual bursts of traffic from the various end-user devices or applications. Also, the network must be able to shed traffic in certain conditions to prevent or react to congestion. In so doing, it must be able to enforce an allowable peak cell rate for each VPI/VCI connection. This means that when a user's traffic load is presented to the network beyond a maximum peak rate, then it may be discarded.

In addition to these responsibilities, the network must be able to monitor (police) traffic. It must be able to monitor all VPI/VCI connections, and verify their correctness (that they are properly mapped into the network and operate effectively). The network must be able to detect problems, and emit alarms when certain troubling events are encountered.

An effective ATM network must be designed with an understanding that both the user and the network assume responsibility for certain QOS operations between them. The user is responsible for agreeing to a service contract with the ATM network that stipulates rules on the use of the network, such as the amount of traffic that can be submitted in a measured time period. In turn, the network assumes the responsibility of supporting the user QOS requirements.

The Natural Bit Rate

All applications exhibit a natural bit rate [dePr91]—the rate at which the application generates and/or receives a certain number of bits per second (bit/s) based on its "natural requirements." For example, digitized voice using conventional ITU-T standards exhibits a natural bit rate of 32 kbit/s. Large data transfer systems have a fluctuating natural bit rate, depending on the nature of the traffic, but ranging from a few kbit/s to several hundred kbits/s. High definition television (HDTV) has a natural bit rate of approximately 100 to 150 kbit/s, depending on the coding schemes employed on the signals.

The challenge of the ATM network is to support the natural bit rates of all applications being serviced. Because of variable traffic profiles, it may be imperative to discard traffic from certain users if the network experiences congestion problems. This situation is illustrated in Figure 9–1(a). For a brief period of time the user exceeds the transfer rate permitted in the network with a burst of traffic. The shadowed portion of the graph is the "burstyness" of the traffic, which exceeds, mo-

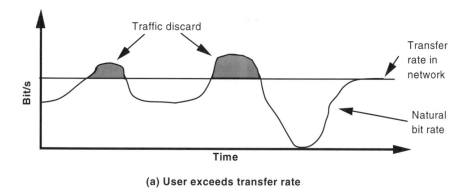

(a) User exceeds transfer rate

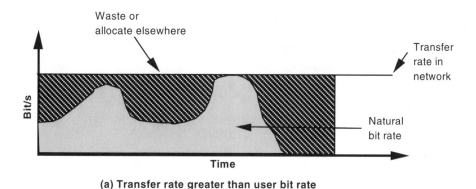

(a) Transfer rate greater than user bit rate

Figure 9–1
Bandwidth allocations. [dePr91]

mentarily, the permitted rate of the network. With ATM networks, this traffic will be tagged for possible discard.

An application's natural bit rate (because of its burstyness) may not use the full rate allocated by the network to this application. The possibility of wasted bandwidth occurring is shown in the striped area of Figure 9–1(b). Therefore, some systems (such as an ISDN terminal adapter) can stuff bits into the application's data stream such that it appears to be the same as the transfer rate in the network (or more likely, the transfer rate of the communications link on which the traffic is to be sent). Or, the network can attempt to allocate this bandwidth to other applications.

With these discussions in mind, the remainder of this chapter examines some approaches to the management of multiapplication traffic.

TRAFFIC CONTROL AND CONGESTION CONTROL

In a B-ISDN, the terms traffic control and congestion control describe different aspects of ATM operations. We concern ourselves with the latter term first. Congestion is defined as a condition that exists at the ATM layer in the network elements (NEs) such as switches, transmission links, or cross connects where the network is not able to meet a stated and negotiated performance objective. In contrast, traffic control defines a set of actions taken by the network to avoid congestion; traffic control takes measures to adapt to unpredictable fluctuations in traffic flows and other problems within the network.

The objectives of both traffic control and congestion control are to protect the network and at the same time provide the user with its stated service contract objectives. For B-ISDN, this includes formally stated QOS objectives. ATM is not designed to rely on AAL to provide any type of traffic control or congestion control measures. While AAL may indeed perform these functions, the design of the ATM network does not assume this service.

Functions to Achieve Traffic Control and Congestion Control

To meet the objectives of traffic control and congestion control, the ATM network must:

- Perform a set of actions called connection admission control (CAC) during a call setup to determine if a user connection will be accepted or rejected. These actions may include acquiring routes for the connection.
- Establish controls to monitor and regulate traffic at the UNI; these actions are called usage parameter control (UPC).
- Accept user input to establish priorities for different types of traffic, through the use of the cell loss priority (CLP) bit.
- Establish traffic shaping mechanisms to obtain a stated goal for managing all traffic (with differing characteristics) at the UNI.

These concepts are described in the following sections.

ALLOCATION OF BANDWIDTH

Since an ATM network is expected to support a wide variety of applications, the network designer must answer the questions of how the natural bit rate of user applications can be accommodated vis-a-vis the transfer rate of the network. Or stated another way, How should the CAC and UPC be established and managed effectively for each user connection? The term "effectively" has two aspects:

1. What is effective for an individual user may not be effective from the network perspective.
2. And, of course the opposite is true—what is effective for the network may not be perceived as effective for the user.

The ATM standards do not stipulate all the specific rules for the CAC and UPC operations. Notwithstanding, this section of the chapter summarizes several approaches that can lead to a fair and effective allocation of the network's bandwidth.

The network exhibits a finite transfer rate, as does each link in the network. Not only must ATM traffic management manage the limited bandwidth within the network, but it also must allocate traffic to *each* communications link within the network.

To examine the second issue, Figure 9–2 depicts a typical traffic stream that a ATM node might receive (assuming the machine is truly a multiapplication node). Regardless of the capacity of the network, the aggregate transfer rates of all the input lines n (inlets) must not exceed the transfer rate of the output line m (outlet)—at least not for a prolonged period (in fractions of milliseconds). Notwithstanding, some buffering of traffic at the multiplexer (ATM node) allows n to exceed m for a few milliseconds.

Each queue must be serviced by the multiplexer in a fair and equitable manner. Queue servicing operations should result in appropriate delays, and acceptable traffic losses vis-à-vis the application. As examples, (1) CBR video queues should be serviced between 1 and 2 ms; (2) VBR voice queues should not allow the loss of traffic to exceed 1 to 10 percent of the samples (the range depends on how traffic is dropped; see Chapter 7); (3) data queues should allow for no loss of traffic; and (4) the signaling queue contains OAM information and should receive the highest consideration of any of the other queues.

As Figure 9–2 shows, the queues are serviced on a cyclical basis (the queue service cycle). Each queue is examined, payload is extracted and transported through the 155 Mbit/s output link. The next queue is examined, payload is extracted, and so on, until the last queue is examined and the process starts over again on the first queue.

The manner in which the queues are set up is not defined in the

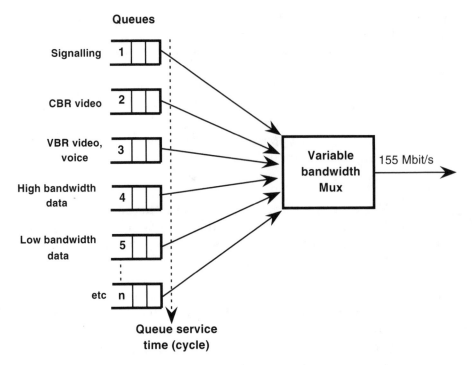

Figure 9–2
Allocating bandwidth using multiple queues.

ATM specifications. Typically, a separate queue is established for each voice and video connection. This approach simplifies queue management.

The queue service cycle must assure that delay-sensitive traffic is serviced within 1 to 2 ms. Given this requirement, let us assume a cycle time of 1.5 ms, which translates to 666.6 service cycles per second (1 second/.0015 = 666.6). Further, assume that the 155.52 output link can accept 353,207 cells per second (155,520,000 [less overhead of the 155.52 Mbit/s frame yields a rate of 149.760 Mbit/s]/424 bits in a 53-octet cell = 353,207). Therefore, this configuration can service 529 cells per service cycle (353,207/666.6 = 529).

Figure 9–3 shows that all queues are serviced during the service cycle. The multiplexer must adjust to the changes in the number of calls and the resultant queues, and vary the service times on the queues accordingly. Therefore, it must be able to add/delete queues and adjust its queue extractions accordingly.

The example in Figure 9–2 is based on the use of a SONET STS-3c 155.52 Mbit/s link. Other links with different bit rates obviously affect

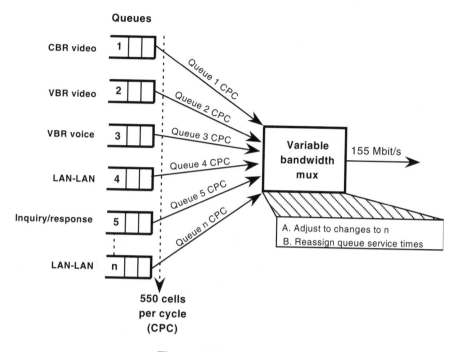

Figure 9–3
Servicing the queues.

the value of the cells per service cycle. For example, if the output link were a 44.736 DS3 link, the cells could use 40.704 Mbit/s of this capacity—the other bits are overhead. Therefore, 40,704,000/424 = 86,914 for the number of cells that can be transported per second across the DS3 link. This configuration supports 130 cells per service cycle (86,914/666.6 = 130).

The task now is to determine which queues are to have their cells withdrawn during the service cycle, and at what rate the cells will be withdrawn from the queues. The general strategy is simple [SRIR90a] and [SRIR90b]:

- The signaling queue is given the highest priority, and should experience little or no delay and experience no loss.
- Delay-sensitive queues are serviced next, if cells are in the queues, for T_1 ms, or until these queues are empty.
- Next, delay-insensitive queues are serviced for T_2 ms.
- In some installations, the absence of talkspurts allows data queues to be serviced more frequently.

- When the signaling queue is serviced, either T1 or T2 is suspended, and resumed (not restarted) when this queue service is finished.

Thus, all queues are guaranteed an established and minimum bandwidth of (T1/{T1+T2})B for delay sensitive traffic and (T2/{T1+T2})B, delay insensitive traffic, where B is the transfer rate of the output link.

The manner in which the queues are serviced depends on how many cells must be withdrawn per service cycle. Be aware that the number of cells serviced per cycle varies, not only between voice, video, and data, but within those applications as well. For example, a conventional 64 kbit/s voice call operates at about 166 cells per second. In marked contrast, a 32 kbit/s voice call using selective cell discard and compression of silent periods needs only about 38 cells per second. Therefore, the variable bandwidth mux must know how to service each queue in regard to the cell withdrawal rate. Once again, these decisions are vendor-specific.

Computing the Parameters for Queue Servicing

[SRIR93] defines three equations for computing the parameters to be used for servicing the queues.

The first equation assures queue $_i$ that a fraction f_i of the output link bandwidth is available:

$$f_i = \frac{T_i}{\sum\limits_{i=0}^{n} T_i}, \ 0 \le i \le n,$$

The second equation assures that all the bandwidth assigned to all queues cannot exceed a fraction of $(1 - f_0)$ for the output link capacity:

$$\sum_{i=0}^{n} f_i \le 1 - f_0$$

The third equation shows that the cycle time for all queues should be from 1 to 2 ms, in order to guarantee consistent service to delay-sensitive traffic.

$$\sum_{i=0}^{n} T_i \le D_c \, ms (D_c \approx 1 \text{ to } 2 \text{ ms}),$$

where: n is number of queues; f_n is a fraction of the bandwidth of the output link; T_n is the time parameter for servicing the queue n; $D_c = M_c t$ is the service cycle time; Mc is the number of cells withdrawn from the queue during the service cycle time; and t is the cell transmission time on the link.

The reader is encouraged to follow up on this general discussion by pursuing the references and sources cited in this section. Sriram's ongoing work [SRIR93] is especially recommended.

DEALING WITH VARIABLE DELAY

Traffic management operations occur not only at the source UNI but also at the destination node itself. The manner in which traffic management is implemented depends on the type of traffic. Assuming that the traffic has been granted admission at the source UNI into the network, upon its arrival at the end-user device, further traffic management decisions on how to "outplay" the traffic to the user application must be made.

As Figure 9–4 shows, different types of traffic must be handled in different ways. The classes of traffic, 1A, 1B, 2, and 3, represent one method of categorization. The traffic with high bandwidth requirements using isochronous timing is buffered at the receiver if the traffic arrives sooner than a predetermined time. If it arrives after this time, it is discarded. Type 1B traffic, which is delay-sensitive nonisochronous, high-bandwidth traffic, is handled depending on the specific kind of traffic. For example, LAN-to-LAN traffic would be buffered, whereas variable bit-rate video would be buffered if the traffic arrives early and discarded if the traffic arrives late. Type 2 traffic, which is delay-insensitive, nonisochronous, high-bandwidth type traffic, again is handled differently depending of the specific subtype. Data traffic is buffered and delayed VBR video traffic (video that must be delivered at a later time) is handled like any type of VBR video traffic that, if it is early, is buffered, but if it arrives late is discarded.

Finally, class 3 traffic, which is delay insensitive not isochronous, is handled differently for voice than for data. As the reader might now expect, early arriving voice packets are buffered until a payout time is reached, and then late arriving packets are discarded.

In essence, any type of traffic involving data is buffered and held in the buffer for quite some time to prevent discarding it. In contrast, video

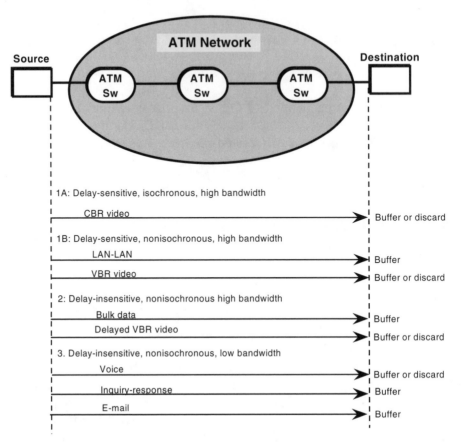

Figure 9–4
Processing the payload at the receiver. [SRIR93]

and voice will be discarded if it arrives too late and it will be buffered (to meet a standard arrival time) if it arrives too early.

The reader may wish to review "Voice Packetization" in Chapter 7 for examples of queue management and outplay operations.

CONNECTION ADMISSION CONTROL (CAC) PROCEDURES

CAC is a set of procedures that operate at the UNI, encompassing actions taken by the network to grant or deny a connection to a user. A connection is granted when the user's traffic contract is examined, revealing that the connection can be supported through the whole network at its required QOS levels (see Figure 9–5).

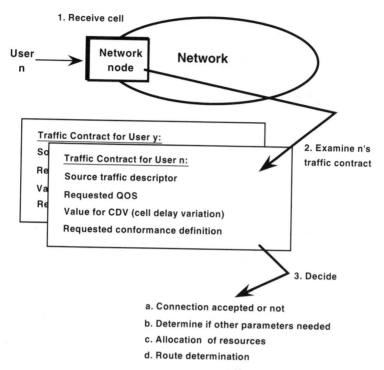

Figure 9–5
Connection admission control (CAC).

The Traffic Contract should contain sufficient information to allow the network to make an intelligent decision about the granting or denial of the connection. This information includes:

- *Source traffic descriptor:* Values such as the peak cell rate, the sustainable cell rate, burst tolerance, etc. They may vary with each connection.
- *Quality of service for both directions:* While several QOS parameters are still under study, parameters such as cell error ratio, cell loss ratio, cell misinsertion rate, etc. have been established.
- *Cell delay variation:* Amount of end-to-end variation that can occur with the cells of the connection.
- *Requested conformance definition:* Values describing the conformance of cells for the connection. Values include peak cell rate and sustainable cell rate (SCR) with the cell loss priority (CLP) bit set to either 0 or 1.

USAGE PARAMETER CONTROL (UPC)

After a connection is granted, and the network has reserved resources for the connection, each user's session is monitored by the network. This is the UPC operation, which is designed to monitor and control traffic, and to check on the validity of the traffic entering the
network. UPC maintains the integrity of the network and makes sure
that only valid VPIs and VCIs are entering the network (see Figure 9–6).

According to the ATM Forum, several other features are desirable
for UPC:

- The ability to detect noncompliant traffic
- The ability to vary the parameters that are checked
- A rapid response to users violating their contracts
- To keep the operations of noncompliant users transparent to com-
  pliant users

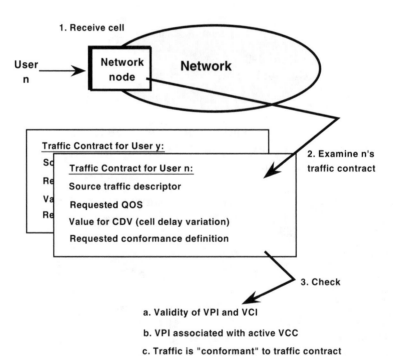

Figure 9–6
Traffic policing with usage parameter control (UPC).

PERFORMANCE PARAMETERS AT THE UNI

ITU-T Recommendation I.35B

ITU-T Recommendation I.35B defines a number of performance parameters for ATM-based networks. Figure 9–7 summarizes these categories, which are: (1) successfully delivered cells, (2) lost cells, (3) inserted cells, and (4) severely damaged cells.

As shown in Figure 9–7(a), any error-free cell that arrives (Δ t) before its maximum allowed time (T) is considered to be a successfully delivered cell (Δ < T). This cell must be "conformant," in that it is intelligible to the receiver. In Figure 9–7(b), cell loss occurs when a cell arrives later than time T (Δ t > T). Even though the cell arrived safely, it is still considered lost, because in some applications, such as voice and video, a late-arriving cell cannot be used in the digital-to-analog conversion process. In Figure 9–7(c), the cell is defined as lost when it is either lost or discarded in the network. Cell loss can occur if an error in the VPI/VCI is not detected, which results in a new or duplicate VPI/VCI being injected into the network, which of course results in the original cell disappearing from the network and the correct virtual circuit. It is also possible to experience a cell loss when a single-bit error results in the incorrect rebuilding of the header, which also results in a new VPI/VCI being injected in to the network, and a cell disappearing from the network and the virtual circuit. In Figure 9–7(d), the cell is defined as lost when the cell has an error of more than one bit in the header. The header error correction function cannot correct errors of more than one bit. In Figure 9–7(e), an inserted cell error occurs when a cell arrives at the destination from a source other than the virtual connection source. In Figure 9–7(f), a severely damaged cell is one in which the user I field contains bit errors.

TRAFFIC MANAGEMENT AT THE UNI—BASIC CONCEPTS

A wide number of alternatives exist for the management of traffic in an ATM network. This section provides a review of several proposals.

Eckberg Scheme

Figure 9–8 shows one proposal that has met with general approval from the ITU-T. This analysis was provided by Bell Laboratories and its Teletraffic Theory Group, which is supervised by A. E. Eckberg [ECKB92].

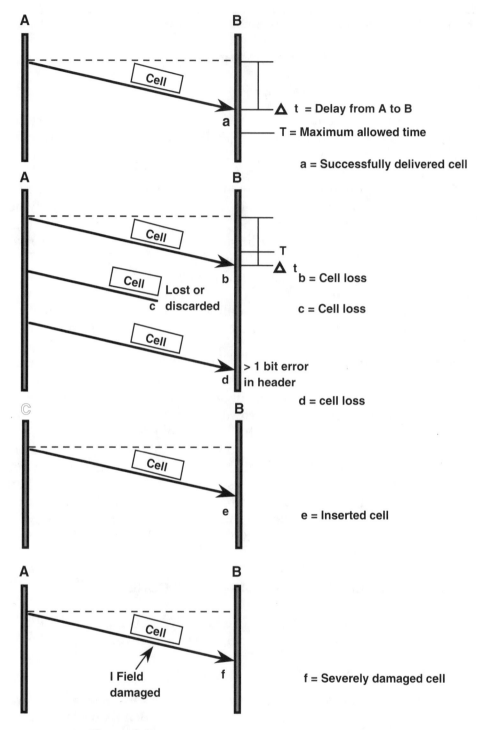

Figure 9–7
Cell transfer performance parameters. [HAND91]

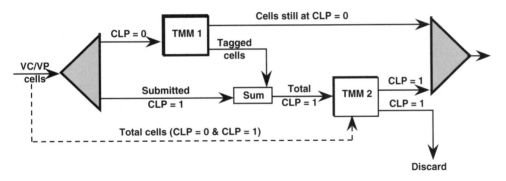

Figure 9–8
Proposed scheme for traffic management (from ITU paper CCITT 371). [ECKB92]

The scheme shown in this figure assumes that the user has a service contract with the ATM network wherein certain QOS parameters have been specified. Upon submitting traffic to the network, the user has the option of identifying individual cells with a certain precedence. This decision by the user allows the ATM network service provider to determine how to treat the traffic in the event of congestion problems.

For traffic that is considered to be essential, the network then assumes the responsibility to assure that this traffic is treated fairly vis-à-vis the type of traffic. As an illustration, if the type of traffic is more tolerant to loss, the network then assumes the responsibility of tagging this traffic as "possible loss traffic," and perhaps discarding this traffic if network congestion becomes a problem.

The major task of the ATM network is to make certain that the total cells presented to the network are consistent with the total cells processed by the network. This entails balancing the traffic submitted with CLP 0 and CLP 1 to that of the user's service contract.

On the left side of Figure 9–8, the user submits its traffic to the network node with the virtual channel and virtual path identifiers residing in the submitted cell. These identifiers are matched against the user's contract and decisions are made whether to grant the user access to the network.

A transmission monitoring machine (TMM1) is responsible for keeping track of all cells submitted by the user with CLP = 0 (those that should not be lost, such as data). In the event of unusual problems, or (more likely) if the user violates the contract with the network, the TMM1 can change the CLP of 0 to a 1. The cell that is tagged by the TMM1 is called an excessive traffic tag. TMM1 does not tag all cells. It must pass cells that are within the service contract. These cells come from the user with the CLP bit = 0. This value remains at 0 if traffic conditions are acceptable and the user is within its service contract.

The user may submit traffic to the network with CLP bit = 1 (known as externally tagged cells). The ATM network node will sum these tagged cells with the excessive traffic tagged cells and provide a total of frames with a CLP = 1 to TMM2. TMM2 then makes a decision to (1) discard some of the tagged cells or (2) permit these cells to enter the network. Also, ITU-T I.371 permits TMM2 to discard a CLP = 0 cell when necessary. This possibility is not depicted Figure 9–8.

MULTIPLEXING TRAFFIC INTO THE CELLS

The manner in which cells are multiplexed onto the communications channel is a proprietary operation, and varies from vendor-to-vendor. The examples in Figure 9–9 show how several applications' bandwidth requirements can be supported by ATM multiplexing cells into an OC-3 frame of 155.52 Mbit/s. I have included tutorial information in the examples of this figure to aid the reader in understanding each example.

The first example is for high-quality video, which requires 135 Mbit/s of bandwidth. This application would use all the cells in an OC-3 frame (allowing for the OC-3 overhead).

The second example is for T1-based video. In this application, every second frame would carry one cell of the application. However, be aware that some vendors will burst multiple cells of an application into the frame, and rely on the receiving machine to smooth the cells back to a synchronous flow vis-a-vis the application.

The third example is for heavily compressed video, which can utilize 511.7 kbit/s (depending upon the compression algorithm). This application would use one cell in every sixth OC-3 frame.

The last example shows that the cells from these applications can be multiplexed into one frame for transport across the communications link.

Token Pools and Leaky Buckets

A number of ATM implementations have adopted the "leaky bucket" approach (see Figure 9–10). The bucket is actually a number of counters that are maintained at the UNI network side for each connection. Periodically, a token generator issues values called tokens, which are placed into a token pool. The token generator can be thought of as a

High-quality video can utilize 135.168 Mbit/s
Connection 7 uses almost all cells in an OC-3 frame, because:
155.52 Mbit/s − 5.76 Mbit/s (overhead) = 149.760 Mbit/s available for payload

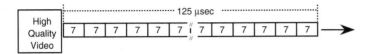

T1-based video can utilize 1.536 Mbit/s
Connection 8 uses one cell in every second OC-3 frame, because:
(1 cell/2 frames) * (8000 frames per sec) * (48 bytes * 8 bits per byte) = 1.536 Mbit/s

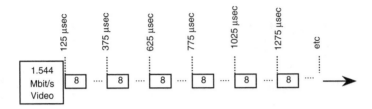

Heavily compressed video can utilize 511.7 kbit/s
Connection 9 uses one cell in every sixth OC-3 frame, because:
(1 cell/6 frames) * (8000 frames per sec) * (48 bytes * 8 bits per byte) = 511.7 Mbit/s

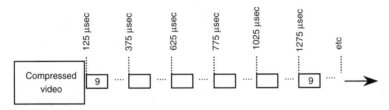

Cells from different connections may be multiplexed into one frame

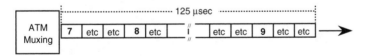

Figure 9–9
Examples of Cell Loading (calculations assume a 48 byte cell payload). [McCO94]

credit accrual timer in that its invocation gives the user credits (rights) to send cells to the network.

When cells are sent to the network, the token pool is reduced for the respective connection by the number of cells that were sent. If the user sends excessive traffic (beyond the service contract), the token pool is exhausted; that is, the user has "used up" its tokens. In such a situa-

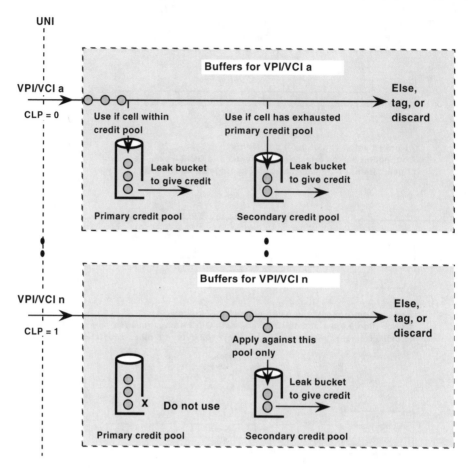

Figure 9–10
The leaky bucket approach.

tion, the cell may have its CLP bit set to 1 by the network and passed into the network, or the cell may be dropped at the UNI without further processing. These decisions depend upon the actual implementation of the specific network.

Some proposals specify two token pools for each connection. One pool is debited for cells in which the CLP bit is set to 0 by the user (a primary pool). Another pool is debited for cells in which the CLP bit is set to 1 by the user (a secondary pool). This approach gives the user some control on which cells may be dropped by the network, because the cells with CLP = 1 are not debited from the primary pool.

In later sections of this chapter, I shall return to the subject of token

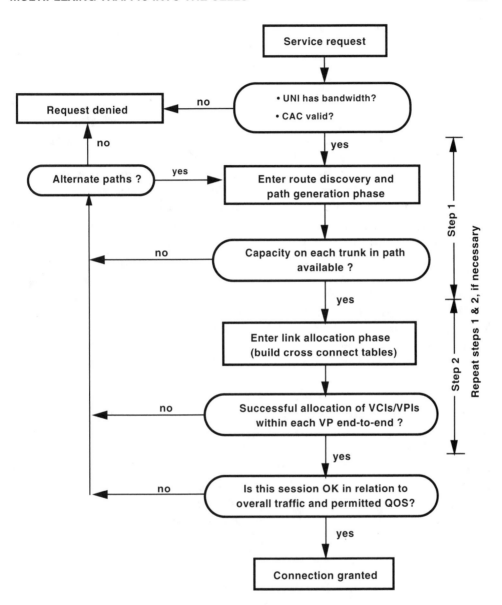

Figure 9–11
Allocation and management scheme.

pools and leaky buckets, and provide some examples of of implementations.

Allocating Resources

Figure 9–11 shows yet another proposed scheme for allocating resources in the network. It is based on the idea of a connection-on-demand, where a user's service request is matched against the current available bandwidth. Thereafter, resources are "gathered" within the network to support the user payload. The initial service request is submitted to the ingress node of the network, which makes a determination if sufficient bandwidth is available at the UNI to support the request. If bandwidth is available, the path generation phase is entered, and capacity is reserved for each trunk on the virtual path. During the path generation phase, if capacity is not available on any one trunk, the request is denied. If all goes well, the link allocation phase is entered, and VCIs/VPIs are allocated end-to-end. During the link generation phase, if VCI/VPI allocation is not successful on any one trunk, the request is denied. Finally, an analysis is made of the user request in relation to the overall network traffic and the permitted QOS. If this test is passed, a connection is granted.

Will this model work? It might seem preferable to perform the latter overall traffic pattern and QOS test *before* trunk and VCI/VPI allocation operations, because the overhead involved of the allocation procedures would be obviated if this test failed. However, to do so places the allocation process in a Catch-22 situation. If a check is made of the session in relation to overall traffic before the allocation operations, another session might seize the remaining trunk capacity while the check is being performed, which means the service request would have to start over.

ATM BEARER SERVICE ATTRIBUTES AT THE UNI

As of this writing, the ATM Forum is studying QOS attributes that will be made available at the UNI. The specific bearer service attributes have been identified but some of the specific features are not yet complete. Table 9–1 lists the attributes for private and public UNIs, some of which pertain to performance and traffic management. Most of the attributes are self-explanatory. A few warrant further explanation in the following sections.

Table 9–1 ATM Bearer Service Attributes at the UNI

Support for point-to-point PVCs

Support for point-to-point PCCs

Support for point-to-multipoint PVCs

Support for point-to-multipoint VCCs, SVC

Support for point-to-multipoint VCCs, PVC

Support for PVC

Support for SVC

Support of specified QOS classes

Support of unspecified QOS classes

Multiple bandwidth granularities for ATM connections

Peak cell rate (PCR) enforcement via the usage parameter control (UPC)

Sustainable cell rate (SCR) traffic enforcement via UPC

Traffic shaping

ATM layer fault management

Interim local management interface (ILMI)

The subjects of point-to-point and multipoint connections as well as PVC and SVCs have been covered in earlier parts of this book.

TRAFFIC CONTROL AND CONGESTION CONTROL

Earlier discussions in this chapter defined traffic control and congestion control. Traffic control specifies the actions taken by the network to avoid congestion. However, if congestion occurs, then congestion control relates to the operations taken by the network to minimize the effects of the congestion. While this distinction may seem somewhat arbitrary, it has important implications for how traffic is monitored and policed at the UNI. Whatever the case may be on the monitoring to achieve traffic control and congestion control, the B-ISDN objectives for these operations are:

- Both traffic control and congestion control must support an ATM QOS consistent with all aspects of the QOS objectives.
- ATM traffic control and congestion control reside at the ATM

layer; consequently, the ATM layer should not rely on the ATM adaptation layer (AAL) to obtain traffic control and congestion control services, nor should the ATM layer rely on any other higher layer protocols residing in the CPE.

• The ATM layer traffic control and congestion control operations should be designed to minimize network complexity.

CELL ARRIVAL RATE AND CELL INTERVAL

In any network that is demand driven, a (somewhat) unpredictable load can be imposed on the network at the UNIs. An ATM network is certainly no exception. We have learned earlier in this chapter that traffic policing and remedial action is required to ensure that traffic load does not jeopardize the performance of the network. Ideally, one would not like to impose restrictions on a user and the user's ability to present payload to the network (after all, payload is so named because it produces revenue). Moreover, in an ideal world, a network is able to accept all user traffic.

Unfortunately, such is not the case in the real world. Because of simple economics, busy signals must be returned to telephone users when the network is busy. It would be somewhat impractical for a network to be designed to accommodate all calls, for example, one that could handle all Mother's Day traffic. Therefore, any network which has an unpredictable (within limits of course) load offered to it, the network must be able to monitor this traffic and take remedial action, if required.

An ATM network provides these important operations by monitoring the cell arrival rate for each connection across the UNI. Of course, if the network were monitoring only one user and its cell arrival profile at each physical interface, the matter would be relatively simple. With the ability to multiplex (potentially) hundreds of sessions on one physical interface, it becomes quite important to monitor each user's traffic pattern and to make adjustments accordingly, which might mean shedding or flow-controlling a specific user's traffic.

Figure 9–12 shows the problem faced by an ATM network. In Figure 9–12(a) the cell arrival rate to the network node is relatively low. Due to the nature of the user's application and the behavior of the application at this instance, relatively long intervals are occurring between the arrival of successive cells at the network. Of course, this simplifies greatly the network's ability to handle the traffic.

On the other hand, in Figure 9–12(b), the cells are arriving at a

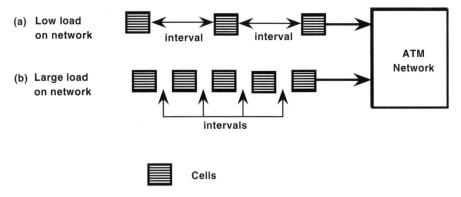

- Cell duration is 2.831 msecs: 53 octets * 8 bits per octet/155.52 Mbit/s - 5.76 Mbit/s
- A 155.52 Mbit/s link transmits 353.207 cells per second: 149.760 Mbit/s/424 bits in a 53-octet cell = 353,207

Figure 9–12
Arrival rate and interval of a user's traffic.

much faster rate, which results in the concomitant decrease in the interval between the cells. In a commercially oriented network, Figure 9–12(b) is more preferable to Figure 9–12(a), because more cells produce more income. However, for the network manager, Figure 9–12(b) presents a more challenging problem in that the network must adjust and accommodate to the higher traffic loads.

Also, the cells depicted in Figure 9–12 may be carrying traffic from different user applications (such as voice, video, and data) and traffic within these applications may require a different level of QOS support from the network. Consequently, a multi-application network must deal with issues other than simple cell arrival rates in accommodating to varying traffic loads. An ATM network must also accommodate to the different QOS emanating from each application. Granted, some applications will have the same QOS profile, which simplifies some of the policing and congestion control operations for that traffic at the UNI. Notwithstanding, the applications presented to this interface will vary significantly in their need for bandwidth-on-demand. Therefore, the network must be able to sustain those traffic bursts, guarantee the cell rate intervals, and provide such services.

With these thoughts in mind, the following sections examine some ideas of how ATM networks accommodate to a widely diverse environment where each application may exhibit different cell intervals and different cell arrival rates.

ATM CELL TRANSFER PERFORMANCE PARAMETERS

The ATM Forum [ATM93a] has defined a set of ATM cell transfer performance parameters to correspond to the ITU-T Recommendation I.350 stipulation for QOS at the UNI. These parameters are summarized in Table 9–2, and the ATM Forum cell rate algorithm is explained in the next section of this chapter. Most of these parameters are self-descriptive. Amplifying information on some of the parameters follows. For more detailed information, the reader should refer to Section 3 and the Appendix of [ATM93a].

For the severely errored cell block ratio, a cell block is a sequence of n cells sent consecutively on a given connection. A reasonable way to measure this operation is to assume that a cell block is a sequence of cells transmitted between OAM cells, although the size of a cell block is not specified in the standards.

The cell misinsertion rate value is calculated as a rate and not as a ratio, since misinsertion operations are independent of the amount of traffic transmitted.

The cell delay variation (CDV) has two performance parameters associated with it: the 1-point CDV, and the 2-point CDV. The 1-point CDV describes the variability in the arrival pattern observed at a measurement point in reference to $1/T$. The 2-point CDV describes variability in the arrival pattern observed at an output in relation to the pattern at an input.

In Table 9–3, the peak cell rate (PCR) is coded as cells per second. A

Table 9–2   Cell Transfer Performance Parameters

- *Cell error ratio:* Errored cells/ successfully transferred cells + Errored cells

- *Severely errored cell block ratio:* Severely errored cell blocks/Total transmitted cell blocks

- *Cell loss ratio:* Lost cells/Total transmitted cells

- *Cell misinsertion rate:* Misinserted cells/Time interval

- *Cell transfer delay:* Elapsed time between a cell exit a measurement point its entry at another measurement point

- *Mean cell transfer delay:* Average of a specified number of cell transfer delays for one or more connections

- *Cell delay variation (CDV):* Describes the variability of the pattern of cell arrival for a given connection

Table 9–3   Other Useful Definitions

- *Multiple bandwidth granularities:* The provision for bandwidth on demand for each UNI connection

- *Peak cell rate (PCR):* The permitted burst profile of traffic associated with each UNI connection (an upper bound)

- *Sustainable cell rate is (SCR):* A permitted upper bound on the average rate for each UNI connection, i.e., an average throughput

- *Traffic shaping:* Altering the stream of cells emitted into a virtual channel or virtual path connection (cell rate reduction, traffic discarding, etc.)

further discussion of this parameter is deferred until further related definitions are clarified.

A network operator may or may not provide bearer services to its subscribers. However, some of these services must be implemented if the cell relay network is to operate efficiently. As examples, peak rate traffic enforcement and traffic shaping must be part of the network's ongoing functions in order to keep congestion under control.

Table 9–3 defines several other terms and parameters that are used later in this chapter.

ATM LAYER PROVISIONS FOR QUALITY OF SERVICE (QOS)

The performance parameters discussed in the previous section serve as the basis for measuring the QOS provided by the ATM network. The parameters in Table 9–3 are used to assess the QOS in regards to:

Cell error ratio	accuracy
Severely-errored cell block ratio	accuracy
Cell loss ratio	dependability
Cell mis-insertion rate	accuracy
Cell transfer delay	speed
Mean cell transfer delay	speed
Cell delay variation	speed

As reliable as an ATM network may be, errors will occur. Software bugs, excessive traffic, uncorrectable errors in the header, and user payload corruption are examples of common problems that will lead to dis-

Table 9–4   QOS Degradation Factors

Attribute	A	B	C	D	E
Propagation delay				Y	
Media errors	Y	Y	Y		
Switch architecture		Y		Y	Y
Buffer capacity		Y		Y	Y
Number of tandem nodes	Y	Y	Y	Y	Y
Traffic load		Y	Y	Y	Y
Failures		Y			
Resource allocation		Y		Y	Y

A Cell error ratio

B Cell loss ratio

C Cell misinsertion rate

D Mean cell transfer delay

E Cell delay variation

carded traffic. As a guideline, [ATM93a] summarizes how impairments will affect five critical performance parameters (see Table 9–4).

While the information in Table 9–4 is largely self-evident, a few observations should be made. First, if possible, it is desirable to have as few as possible intermediate nodes (tandem nodes) involved in relaying the cells from the source to the destination, because each node is a potential source for the degradation of all five of the performance parameters shown in the table. The rationale behind this observation is based on well-founded design principles (and common sense). Second, traffic load (that is, excessive traffic load) is to be avoided, because it leads to the degradation of four of the performance parameters shown in the table. It does not affect the cell error ratio. Third, while propagation delay affects only the mean cell transfer delay, its effect on calculating overall delay is quite significant.

ATM FORUM AND ITU-T TRAFFIC CONTROL AND CONGESTION CONTROL

The ATM Forum and ITU-T have defined algorithms for policing the traffic at the UNI for both CBR and VBR traffic. The traffic parameters employed are: (1) PCR for CBR connections, and (2) PCR, SCR and maximum burst size (MBS) for VBR traffic. These parameters are provided by the user during the connection establishment with the SETUP message.

An additional parameter is the burst tolerance (BT), which places a restriction on how much traffic can be sent beyond the SCR before it is tagged as excessive traffic. It is calculated as:

$$BT = (MBS -1) / (1/SCR - 1/PCR)$$

Generic Cell Rate Algorithm (GCRA)

The generic cell rate algorithm (GCRA) is employed in traffic policing and is part of the user/network service contract. In the ATM Forum specification, the GCRA consists of two parameters: the increment I and the limit L. (As a note, the CCITT I.371 uses the parameters T and t respectively for I and L.) The notation GCRA (I, L) means the generic cell rate algorithm with the increment parameter set to I and the limit parameter set to L. The increment parameter affects the cell rate. The limit parameter affects cell bursts. The GCRA allows, for each cell arrival, a 1-unit leak out of the bucket per unit of time. In its simplest terms, the bucket has finite capacity, and it leaks out at a continuous rate. Its contents can be filled (incremented) by I if L is not exceeded. Otherwise, the incoming cell is defined as nonconforming. This idea is shown in Figure 9–13.

The GCRA is implemented as a continuous-state leaky bucket algorithm or a virtual scheduling algorithm. The two algorithms serve the same purpose: to make certain that cells are conforming (arriving within the bound of an expected arrival time), or nonconforming (arriving sooner than an expected arrival time).

The virtual scheduling algorithm updates a theoretical arrival time (TAT), which is an expected arrival time of a cell. If the arrival is not too early (later than TAT + L, where L is a network-specified limit parameter), then the cell is conforming. Otherwise, it is nonconforming. If cells arrive after a current value of TAT, then TAT is updated to the current time of the arrival of the cell (expressed as $t_a(k)$, where K cell arrives at time t_a + the increment I). If the cell is nonconforming, then TAT is not changed. Other aspects of the virtual scheduling algorithm are shown in Figure 9–14.

The continuous-state leaky bucket algorithm places a bound on the traffic of L + I. The conceptual bucket has a finite capacity; its contents drain out by one unit for each cell. Its contents are increased by one for each conforming cell. Simply stated, upon the arrival of a cell, if the con-

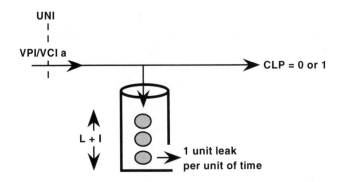

Generic Cell Rate Algorithm, GCRA(I,L):

I   Increment parameter, affects cell rate

L   Limit parameter, affects cell bursts

Leaky bucket:
- Finite-capacity bucket
- Contents leak out at a continuous rate of 1 per unit time
- Contents are incremented by I, if L is not exceeded

**Figure 9–13
The I and L parameters.**

tent of the bucket is less than or equal to the limit L, the cell is conforming. Other aspects of the continuous-state leaky bucket algorithm are also shown in Figure 9–14.

Bandwidth allocation and policing schemes are far from settled, although the ATM Forum and ITU-T approach is supported widely in the industry. Notwithstanding, new papers appear each month in trade journals, and conferences are held in an attempt to work out this difficult issue. The reader is encouraged to study the IEEE and ACM publications, and other trade journals, for more detail. Indeed, a full book could be written on this subject.

The Peak Cell Rate Reference Model

The ATM Forum specification provides a reference model to describe the peak cell rate (PCR). This model is shown in Figure 9–15. It consists of an equivalent terminal, containing the traffic sources, a multiplexer (MUX), and a virtual shaper. The term equivalent terminal means a model of a user device that performs the functions described in this discussion.

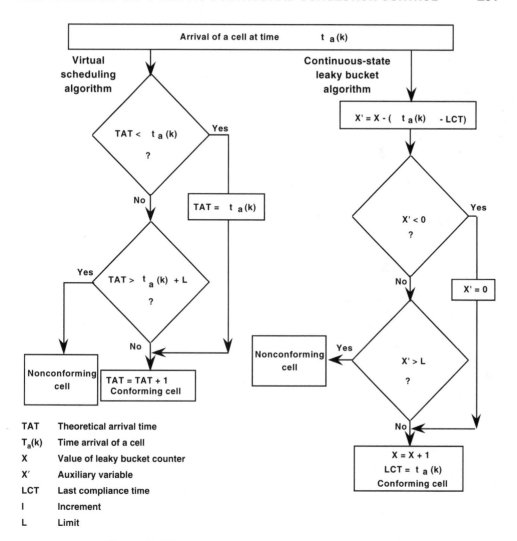

Figure 9–14
The generic cell rate algorithm (GCRA). [ATM93a]

The traffic sources offer cells to a multiplexer (MUX), with each source offering cells at its own rate. Typically, the cells are offered from the AAL through the service access point (SAP). The MUX then offers all these cells to the virtual shaper. The job of the virtual shaper is to smooth the cell flow offered to the physical layer and the ATM UNI (private UNI). Moreover, the GCRA comes into play in this model at three interfaces: (1) the boundary between the ATM layer and the physical layer (the PhSAP), (2) the private UNI, and (3) the public UNI.

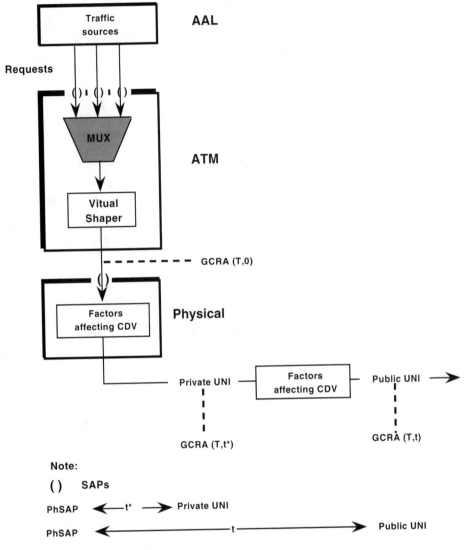

Figure 9–15
Reference model for peak cell rate (PCR). [ATM93a]

For this discussion, we define T as the peak emission interval of the connection, and the minimal interarrival time between two consecutive cells is greater than or equal to T. The PCR of the ATM connection is the inverse of the minimum arrival time between two cells.

The output of the virtual shaper at the PhSAP conforms to GCRA (T,0). The outputs at the private UNI and public UNI are different, because CDV will exist in the physical layer of the equivalent terminal (user device) and the node between this device and the network. Therefore, the private UNI conforms to GRCA (T,t*) and the public UNI conforms to GRCA (T,t), where t is the cell delay tolerance. The latter value takes into consideration the additional CDV between the PhSAP and the public UNI.

The ATM network does not set the peak emission interval T at the user device. T can be set to account for different profiles of traffic, as long as the MUX buffers remain stable. Thus, T's reciprocal can be any value that is greater than the sustainable rate, but (of course) not greater than the link rate.

Cell Delay Variation (CDV) Tolerance

A certain amount of delay is encountered when cells are vying for the same output port of the multiplexer, or when signaling cells inserted in to the stream. As a result, with the reference to the peak emission interval T, randomness is instilled in the interarrival time between consecutive cells ([ATM93a]; Appendix A).

1-point CDV.   The 1-point CDV for cell $k(y_k)$ at the measurement point is the difference between the cell's reference arrival time (c_k) and the actual arrival time (a_k) at the measurement point: $y_k = c_k - a_k$. The reference arrival time (c_k) is:

$$c_0 = a_0 = 0$$

$$c_k + 1 = \begin{cases} c_k + T & \text{if } c_k \geq a_k \text{ otherwise} \\ a_k + T \end{cases}$$

2-point CDV.   The 2-point CDV, or cell $k(v_k)$, between two measurement points MP_1 and MP_2 is the difference between the absolute cell transfer delay of cell $k(x_k)$ between the two MPs and a defined reference cell transfer delay $(d_{1,2})$ between MP_1 and MP_2: $v_k = v_k - d_{1,2}$.

The absolute cell transfer delay (xk) of cell k between MP_1 and MP_2 is the same as the cell transfer delay defined earlier. The reference cell transfer delay $(d1,2)$ between MP_1 and MP_2 is the absolute cell transfer delay experienced by a reference cell between the two MPs.

Figure 9–16 shows two examples of how the GCRA is applied [ATM94a]. Figure 9–16(a) shows smooth traffic with GCRA (1.5, .5). The vertical arrows connote the arrival of a cell across the UNI; the

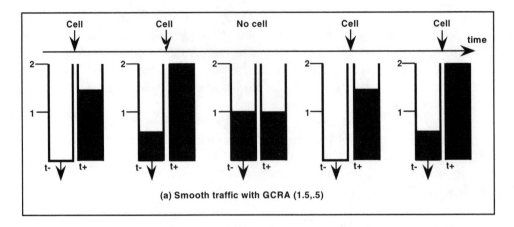

(a) Smooth traffic with GCRA (1.5,.5)

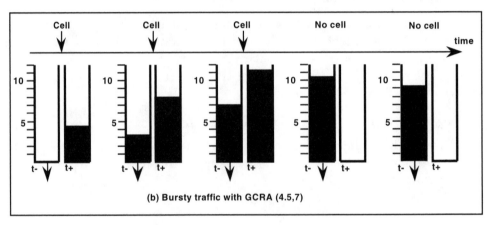

(b) Bursty traffic with GCRA (4.5,7)

Figure 9–16
Examples of the GCRA. [ATM94a]

horizontal arrows connote time. The variables t– and t+ mean the follow-ing:

    t–: State of bucket just before the arrival of a cell

    t+: State of bucket just after the arrival of a cell

For Figure 9–16(a), with the bucket at 1, at t–, L prevents the send-ing of I cells. If they are sent, they are nonconforming.

The same definitions apply to Figure 9–16(b), which shows bursty traffic for GCRA(4.5, 7). Once again, no cells are allowed (or if sent, they are nonconforming) if the bucket would overflow.

MANAGING LAN TRAFFIC WITH THE AVAILABLE BIT RATE (ABR)

Brief mention was made in Chapter 7 that the ATM Forum is in the process of defining a new type of service, called the available bit rate (ABR), which provides a mechanism for controlling traffic flow from LAN-based workstations and the routers that service these workstations. Since LAN devices have no "contract" with a network, no easy method is available to relate the AAL CBR and VBR idea to a LAN environment.

Several proposals are being considered for ABR. All entail a mechanism for informing a user about network conditions. One proposal uses a backward explicit congestion notification (BECN) signal and the forward explicit congestion notification (FECN) signal to send to downstream and upstream devices respectively. This approach is borrowed from frame relay. Another proposal uses a credit scheme to control the user device's traffic. It is anticipated that a standard will be available on ABR in 1995.

Examples of ABR Operations

The goal of the ABR service class is to provide LAN emulation service through an ATM backbone and offer the same quality of service that current LANs offer. This includes a cell loss rate of about one frame in every 10^8 cells transmitted and the ability to support to point-to-point or point-to-multipoint connections. In addition, the ABR is supposed to provide the ability to transmit up to the full line rate if the line is idle.

Currently, vendors are taking different approaches to the implementation of ABR. At the broadest level, the choices revolve around two approaches (with variations of these approaches discussed later):

1. Credit-based schemes
   a. Credits for each connection
   b. Credits aggregated for all connections (aggregate connections)
2. Rate-based schemes
   a. Rates established for each connection
   b. Rates established for all connections (aggregate connections)

Figures 9–17 and 9–18 show the credit-based and rate-based schemes operating on individual or aggregate connections. As depicted in Figures 9–17(a) and 9–18(a), the credit-based scheme operates on a hop-

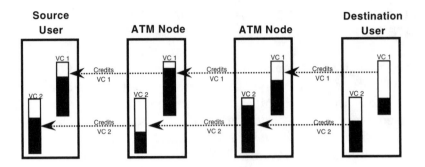

(a) Feedback loop: hop-by-hop

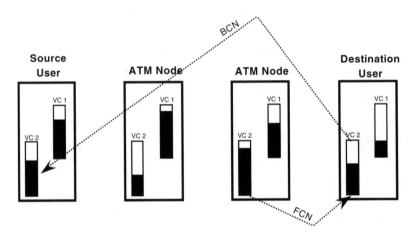

(b) Feedback loop: end-to-end

Note: Dashed lines in figure (b) show logical flow of feedback

Figure 9–17
Feedback on each connection.

by-hop (link-by-link) basis. Downstream nodes send credits to upstream nodes all the way to the source of the traffic. These credits allow a sending node to send traffic down stream. If the sending node receives no credits, then it must wait (and stop sending) until credits arrive (if they do).

The rate-based scheme (shown in Figures 9–17(b) and 9–18(b)) is quite similar to the frame relay congestion notification operations. An ATM node can send the destination a forward congestion notification signal. The destination user, in turn, sends to its source a backward notifi-

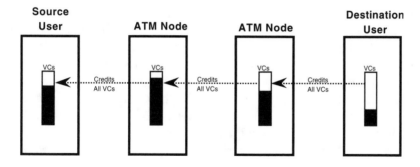

(a) Feedback loop: hop-by-hop

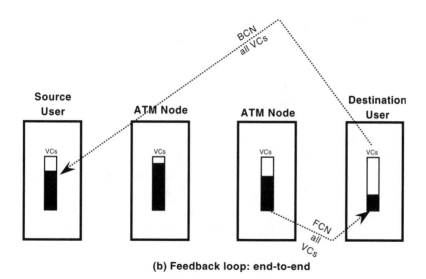

(b) Feedback loop: end-to-end

Figure 9–18
Aggregate feedback on all connections.

cation congestion signal and through some algorithm, the source will back off from sending cells.

Both approaches have their advantages and disadvantages. Credit-based schemes are much more effective in regulating bandwidth immediately but they have more overhead. Rate-based schemes are cheaper to implement but the latency of acting upon forward and backward congestion notification could result in some oscillating behavior in the network.

The granularity of feedback is also a very important consideration in ABR. As shown in Figures 9–17 and 9–18, this feedback may be aggregated over multiple connections or on each connection. Obviously, the advantages and disadvantages for these operations are that aggregate feedback does not permit the monitoring of individual connections. Consequently, cells might be marked as congestion even though they may not be part of the problem. The per-connection feedback selects only those connections that are contributing to the problem.

In addition to the granularity and feedback, granularity of buffering is also an important consideration. Granularity of buffering simply means that connections are aggregated in one buffer or an individual buffer is reserved for each connection.

Types of Feedback

Three types of feedback information can be implemented with ABR, and are depicted in Figure 9–19:

1. Binary rate feedback
2. Explicit rate feedback
3. Explicit burst feedback

With the binary rate feedback mechanism, a network node determines that congestion is occurring on a node and sets bits in a cell heading downstream to the destination. The destination uses these cells to send notifications back to the source. This means the source can stop, speed up, or slow down traffic based on receiving or not receiving this feedback. The term binary is used in this procedure because the amount of flow control that is performed in not determined. It is simply a binary yes or no to express if congestion is or is not occurring. Therefore, no further information is contained within the notification cell itself.

Explicit rate feedback allows a network node to examine each connection to determine that each connection receives its fair share of the available bandwidth. Periodically, a source node will sent a OAM cell containing an initial bandwidth rate value for a particular connection. As the cell passes through a node, if the node's current storage of the fair share value of the connection is less than the value in the cell, the value in the cell is updated. The destination device returns this control cell back to the source. The source must adjust its flow relative to the point where the OAM cell was updated; i.e., to the most severe bottleneck in the virtual circuit. Thereafter, the source transmits at the new rate.

Explicit burst feedback is credit based scheme. A burst size is placed in an OAM cell and this burst size informs the transmitter (upstream node) its specified burst size. Therefore, when a network node has avail-

- **Binary Rate Feedback**
    Amount of flow not specified.
    A bit is on or off.

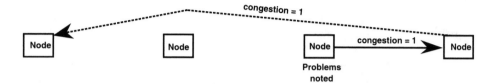

- **Explicit Rate Feedback**
    Each node determines each connection's fair share of resources.
    Periodically source device sends an OAM cell containing its current rate.
    Any node can reduce or expand this value, which is returned to the source.
    The source must adjust accordingly.

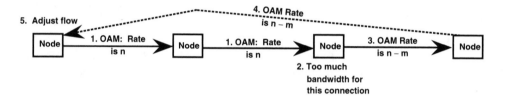

- **Explicit Burst Feedback**
    Number of cells a transmitter can send is limited by a burst size.
    Downstream node sends upstream node a credit.
    If upstream node uses up the credit, it must wait for a new credit.

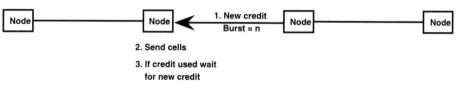

Figure 9–19
Types of feedback information.

able buffer for forwarding cells, it forwards an OAM cell to the next up-stream node. The upstream node uses this information to update its credit balance by forwarding cells. The upstream node reduces its credit balance by one with each cell sent. Therefore, once the node (or for that matter, the end user) has exhausted its balance, it must wait for the next credit update from the receiver.

Presently, vendors vary on how feedback is provided. The ATM Forum is working through the issues and will eventually publish a standard on feedback mechanisms. By the time this book is published, it is likely that the Forum will have decided on these issues.

BUILDOUT DELAY PROCEDURES
AT THE RECEIVING ENDPOINT

Most of this chapter has discussed how the ATM network manages user traffic at the UNI to the entrance of the network. At the receiving UNI, the ATM network passes the cells to the user. The user processes the traffic based on the schemes explained earlier.

For voice packets, ITU-T Recommendation G.764 defines a method to define a maximum allowed time in an end-to-end transmission time. This method masks any delay that may have occurred in the network. The maximum delay must be less than 200 ms. Any packet that arrives at 200 ms or later is discarded. The reader may recall that this operation is described in some detail in Chapter 7, and can be reviewed again, if necessary (see the section titled, "Packet Buildout at the Receiver" in Chapter 7).

SUMMARY

A wide variety of methods have been proposed for the management of traffic in an ATM network. The manner in which traffic is managed will eventually become a standardized operation. Traffic policing functions have been published by the ATM Forum, to provide guidance on how traffic can be tagged, *but* the decision on how to act upon the tag is not defined by the ATM Forum. Nor should it be. The manner in which a network manages user payload must rest with the network.

Call and Connection Control

INTRODUCTION

This chapter examines the ATM call and connection control operations. Emphasis is placed on how connections are set up on demand between users and the ATM network. This procedure is also known as a switched virtual call (SVC) in older technology. The Q.2931 connection control protocol is explained, and the Q.2931 messages and their contents are analyzed. The ATM address is also examined in this chapter, as is the ATM use of the OSI address.

ATM CONNECTIONS ON DEMAND

Early ATM efforts focused on PVC implementations, with user service available at any time. The ATM Forum has reached a consensus that connections on demand are quite important and has issued specifications for this operation [ATM93a]. This section describes the specification, known as "Phase 1."

Like all connections-on-demand (SVCs), a user-to-user session through an ATM network requires both a connection setup procedure and a disconnection procedure. With connection setup, the user must furnish the network with the calling and called party addresses and the QOS needed for the session. In the event of a network failure, connection-on-demand sessions may not be automatically reestablished, although they may remain active for an arbitrary amount of time.

The ATM connection control procedures are organized around the ISDN Q.931 layer 3 operations (explained in Chapter 4), and a subset of Q.931, called Q.2931, that is in development [ITU93a]. Phase 1 signaling must support fourteen capabilities at the UNI. They are listed in Table 10–1, and summarized herein. Several of the descriptions of the demand connections are self-explanatory, others are not; more detail is provided for the ambiguous titles.

Connections on demand simply means that the ATM UNI must support switched channel connections. They are established with signaling procedures discussed shortly in this chapter. Permanent connections are not supported at this time, although they are under study.

The ATM UNI supports both point-to-point single connection and point-to-multipoint connections. A point-to-multipoint connection is defined as a collection of associated VC and VP links that are associated with endpoint nodes. One ATM link is designated as the root link, which serves as the root in a tree topology. When the root receives information, it sends copies of this information to all leaf nodes on the tree. Communications must occur between the leaf nodes through the root node. Connections are established initially through the root node and

Table 10–1   Capabilities of ATM Demand Connections

- Connections on demand (switched)
- Point-to-point and point-to-multipoint connections
- Symmetric or asymmetric bandwidth requirements
- Single connection calls
- Specific procedures for call setup, request, answer, clear and out-of-band signaling
- Support of class A, C and X transport services
- Nonnegotiation of QOS between users
- Specification of VPI/VCI ranges
- Designation of an out-of-band signaling channel
- Mechanisms for error recovery
- Guidelines for addressing formats
- Client registration procedures
- Methods of identifying end-to-end capability parameters
- Nonsupport of multicasting operations

then one leaf node, then other nodes can be added with "add party" operations, one leaf entry at a time.

The UNI supports either symmetric or asymmetric connections for bandwidth allocation. Bandwidth is specified independently in each direction across the virtual connection. Forward direction is from the calling party to the called party; backward direction is from the called party to the calling party.

The UNI also defines specific procedures for the requesting and setting up of connections and the clearing of the connections (and the reason for clearing) as well as an out-of-band channel used for control purposes.

Phase 1 supports ATM class A and class C transport services, as well as class X procedures, which are published by the ATM Forum. Class X is a user-defined QOS operation. The reader may wish to refer to the section titled "Classes of Traffic" in Chapter 7.

For phase 1, QOS cannot be negotiated between users. A user may request a certain level of service and can send the QOS parameters in the connection setup request. The receiver merely indicates if these values can be accommodated. It is not allowed to return any traffic suggesting a negotiation procedure.

The specification also defines a range for the use of VCI and VPI. For phase 1, there is a one-to-one mapping between a VCI and a VPI; therefore, values beyond 8 bits are not permitted. As part of the designation for the VPI/VCI ranges, an out-of-band signaling channel has been designated with the values of VCI = 5 and VPI = 0.

The phase 1 specification contains several mechanisms for handling error recovery procedures. Among these are provisions for the signaling of nonfatal errors (errors that can be recovered), procedures for recovering from resets, procedures for forcing VCCs into an idle state, and other diagnostic information pertaining to error recovery and call clearing.

One important capability at the UNI is the provision for addressing format guidelines. These guidelines are organized around OSI network service access points (NSAPs), which are specified in ISO 8348 and ITU-T X.213 Annex A. The phase 1 specification requires the use of these formats in accordance with registration procedures contained in ISO 10589. This feature of the standard will facilitate the interworking of different vendors' systems.

The ATM demand connections capabilities also include a client registration procedure that allows users to exchange address information across the UNI, as well as other administrative information. This procedure allows an ATM network administrator to load network addresses dynamically into the port.

Also supported is the ability to identify end-to-end capability parameters. Capability means that provisions are available to identify what protocol is running inside the ATM PDU; that is to say, what protocols are operating above the ATM services. This capability allows the two end users to run various types of protocol families across an ATM-based network, and use this identifier to separate and demultiplex the traffic to the respective protocol families at the receiving machine.

Finally, the fourteenth capability is really not a capability, in that the phase 1 specification does not support multicast operations at this time.

THE ATM ADDRESS

With the addition of SVCs to ATM operations, it is important to have a standardized convention for coding destination and source addresses. Addressing is not an issue with PVCs, because connections and endpoints (destination and source) are defined, and a user need only provide the network with a preallocated VCI/VPI. However, for SVCs, the destination connection can change with each session; therefore, explicit addresses are required. After the call has been mapped between the UNIs, the VCI/VPI values then can be used for traffic identification.

The ATM address is modeled on the OSI network service access point (NSAP), which is defined in ISO 8348 and ITU-T X.213, Annex A. A brief explanation of the OSI NSAP and its relationship to ATM addressing (see Figure 10–1) follows.

The ISO and ITU-T describe a hierarchical structure for the NSAP address, as well as the syntax for the NSAP address. It consists of four parts:

Initial domain part (IDP): Contains the authority format identifier (AFI) and the initial domain identifier (IDI).

Authority format identifier (AFI): Contains a one octet field to identify the domain specific part (DSP). For ATM, the AFI field is coded as:

39 = DCC ATM format

47 = ICD ATM format

45 = E.164 format

Initial domain identifier (IDI): Specifies the addressing domain and the network addressing authority for the DSP values. It is interpreted according to the AFI (where AFI = 39, 47, or 45). For ATM, the IDI is coded as (1) a data country code (DCC) in accordance with ISO

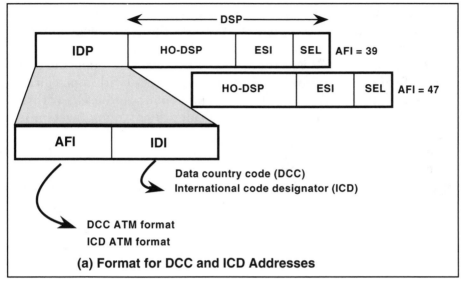

(a) Format for DCC and ICD Addresses

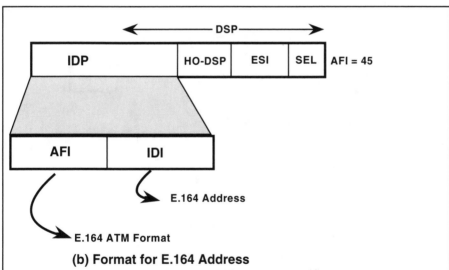

(b) Format for E.164 Address

Figure 10–1
The OSI/ATM address formats.

3166; (2) the international code designator (ICD), which identifies an international organization and is maintained by the British Standards Institute; or (3) an E.164 address, which is a telephone number.

Domain specific part (DSP): Contains the address determined by the network authority. For ATM, the contents vary, depending on value of the AFI. The domain format identifier (DFI), specifies the syntax and other aspects of the remainder of the DSP. The administrative authority (AA) is an organization assigned by the ISO that is responsible for the allocation of values in certain fields in the DSP.

The high order DSP is established by the authority identified by the IDP. This field might contain a hierarchical address (with topological significance, see RFC 1237), such as a routing domain and areas within the domain. The end system identifier (ESI) identifies an end system (such as a computer) within the area.

The selector (SEL) is not used by an ATM network. It usually identifies the protocol entities in the upper layers of the user machine that are to receive the traffic. Therefore, the SEL could contain upper layer SAPs.

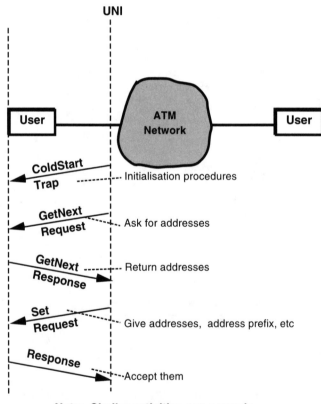

Note: Similar activities can occur in
the reverse direction

Figure 10–2
Address registration.

ATM public networks must support the E.164 address and private networks must support all formats.

Address Registration

The ATM Forum UNI signaling specification provides a procedure for the user and the network to register the ATM address or addresses. The procedure begins with the network initializing its address table as empty. Then, as shown in Figure 10–2, it sends an SNMP ColdStart Trap message to the user side. It can issue GetNext Request to obtain addressing information. Next, it sends an SNMP SetRequest message to the user side, which contains a network prefix. The user side is expected to "register" this address in its address MIB. Although not shown in this figure, the user side can also send GetNext and Set responses to the network side to register addresses.

Table 10–2   ATM Connection Control Messages

Message	Function
Call establishment	
SETUP	Initiate the call establishment
CALL PROCEEDING	Call establishment has begun
CONNECT	Call has been accepted
CONNECT ACKNOWLEDGE	Call acceptance has been acknowledged
Call clearing	
RELEASE	Initiate call clearing
RELEASE COMPLETE	Call has been cleared
Miscellaneous	
STATUS ENQUIRY (SE)	Sent to solicit a status message
STATUS (S)	Sent in response to SE or to report error
Global call reference	
RESTART	Restart all VCs
RESTART ACKNOWLEDGE	ACKS the RESTART
Point-to-multipoint operations	
ADD PARTY	Add party to an existing connection
ADD PARTY ACKNOWLEDGE	ACKS THE ADD PARTY
ADD PARTY REJECT	REJECTS the ADD PARTY
DROP PARTY	Drops party from an existing connection
DROP PARTY ACKNOWLEDGE	ACKS THE DROP PARTY

THE CONNECTION CONTROL MESSAGES

Table 10–2 lists the ATM messages and their functions employed for demand connections at the UNI. Because these messages are derived from Q.931, which was discussed in Chapter 4, this section will concentrate of the use of these messages vis-à-vis the ATM UNI operation.

These messages contain the typical Q.931 fields such as protocol discriminator, call reference, message type, and message length. The information content of the field, of course, is tailored for the specific ATM UNI interface.

CONNECTION SETUPS AND CLEARS

This section shows some examples of the use of the connection management messages. The connection establishment procedures begin by a user issuing the SETUP message (see Figure 10–3). This message is sent by the calling user to the network and is relayed by the network to the called user. This message contains several information elements (fields) to identify the message, specify various AAL parameters, calling and called party addresses, requirements for QOS, selection of the transit network (if needed), and a number of other fields. The notations in the boxes in Figure 10–3 depict the main information elements that are transferred in the messages. Other information elements may be present, depending on the specific implementation of a system.

Upon receiving the SETUP message, the network returns a CALL PROCEEDING message to the initiating user, forwards the SETUP message to the called user, and waits for the called user to return a CALL PROCEEDING message. The CALL PROCEEDING message is used to indicate that the call has been initiated and no more call establishment information is needed, nor will any be accepted.

The called user, if it accepts a call, will then send to the network a CONNECT message. This CONNECT message will then be forwarded to the calling user. The CONNECT message contains parameters that deal with some of the same parameters in the SETUP message, such as call reference and message type, as well as the accepted AAL parameters and several other identifiers created as a result of the information elements in the original SETUP message.

Upon receiving the CONNECT messages, the calling user and the

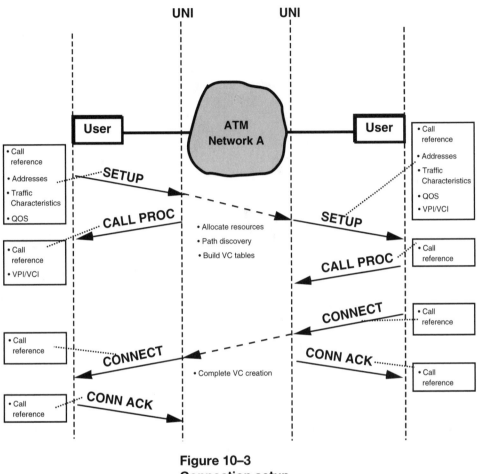

Figure 10–3
Connection setup.

network return the CONNECT ACKNOWLEDGE to their respective parties.

As Figure 10–4 illustrates, either user can initiate a disconnect operation. To do so requires the user to send to the network the RELEASE message. The effect of this message clears the end-to-end connection between the two users and the network. This message only contains the basic information to identify the message across the network. Other parameters are not included because they are not needed to clear the state tables for the connection. In consonance with the practice we established in Figure 10–3, the notations in the boxes in Figure 10–4 depict the main information elements that are transferred in the messages. Other infor-

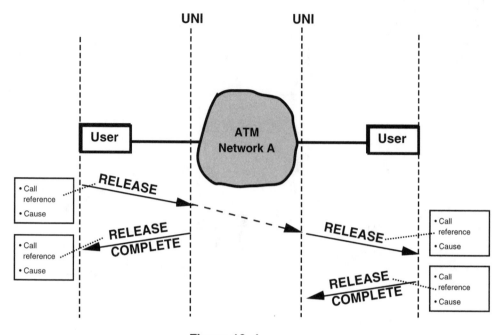

Figure 10–4
Connection release.

mation elements may be present, depending on the specific implementation of a system.

The receiving network and receiving user are required to transmit the RELEASE COMPLETE message as a result of receiving the RELEASE message.

Q.2931 TIMERS AND STATES

Most networks that provide connections on demand use timers at both the user and network nodes to define reasonable wait periods for completion of certain actions (such as completion of a setup, completion of a restart, etc.). The ATM UNI signaling interface provides ten timers at the network side and ten timers at the user side. These timers and their general operations are summarized in Tables 10–3 and 10–4.

Each connection is controlled by states. For example, a user enters into a "call present" state when a call establishment request has been received but the user has not yet responded to the request. Various states can be entered and exited as a call is processed, some of which are gov-

Table 10–3   Timers in the Network Side

Timer Number	Cause for Start	Normal Stop
T301	Not supported in this Implementation Agreement	
T303	SETUP sent	CONNECT, CALL PROCEEDING, OR RELEASE COMPLETE received
T308	RELEASE sent	RELEASE COMPLETE or RELEASE received
T309	SAAL disconnection	SAAL reconnected
T310	CALL PROCEEDING received	CONNECT or RELEASE received
T316	RESTART sent	RESTART ACKNOWLEDGE received
T317	RESTART received	Internal clearing of call references
T322	STATUS ENQUIRY sent	STATUS, RELEASE, or RELEASE COMPLETE received
T398	DROP PARTY sent	DROP PARTY ACKNOWLEDGE or RELEASE received
T399	ADD PARTY sent	ADD PARTY ACKNOLWEDGE, ADD PARTY REJECT, or RELEASE received

erned by timers. In the event an action does not take place before a designated timer expires, various remedial actions are dictated, such as issuing retries and/or moving to other states.

CONNECTION CONTROL EXAMPLES

Before discussing and providing some examples of connection control operations, it is helpful to distinguish between three terms: (1) connected virtual channels, (2) disconnected virtual channels, and (3) released virtual channels. A virtual channel is considered connected when all parties, including network and users, have agreed to the connection. A virtual channel is disconnected when it is no longer a part of the connection but is not yet available for a new connection. A channel is consid-

Table 10–4   Timers in the User Side

Timer Number	Cause for Start	Normal Stop
T303	SETUP sent	CONNECT, CALL PROCEEDING, OR RELEASE COMPLETE received
T308	RELEASE sent	RELEASE COMPLETE or RELEASE received
T309	SAAL disconnection	SAAL reconnected
T310	CALL PROCEEDING received	CONNECT or RELEASE received
T313	CONNECT sent	CONNECT ACKNOWLEDGE received
T316	RESTART sent	RESTART ACKNOWLEDGE received
T317	RESTART received	Internal clearing of call references
T322	STATUS ENQUIRY sent	STATUS, RELEASE, or RELEASE COMPLETE received
T398	DROP PARTY sent	DROP PARTY ACKNOWLEDGE or RELEASE received
T399	ADD PARTY sent	ADD PARTY ACKNOWLEDGE, ADD PARTY REJECT, or RELEASE received

ered to be released when not only is the channel not part of a connection, but is also available for another connection.

Connection Setup

Figure 10–5 shows the timers invoked for the establishment of a connection. Three timers are involved in the process and perform the following functions.

Timer T303 is invoked when ATM issues a SETUP message to the network on the local side of the network and is invoked by network node at the remote side when it passes the SETUP message to the user. The timer is stopped when the remote end user returns a CALL PROCEEDING message. This message is relayed to the local network side, which also sends it to the originating user. Although not illustrated in this figure, timer T303 can also be stopped if either a CONNECT message or a

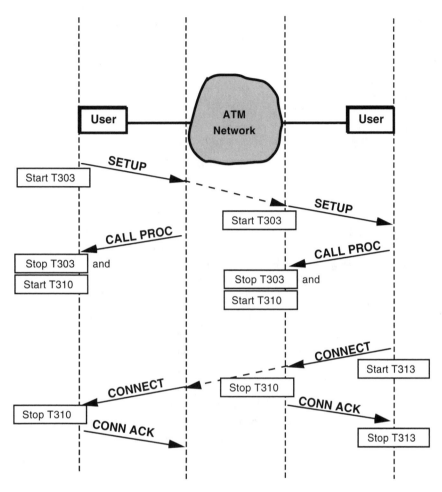

Figure 10–5
The connection setup procedure.

RELEASE COMPLETE message is received. If the timer expires before the reception of a CALL PROCEEDING message, a SETUP message may be retransmitted or, if the network does not support SETUP retransmissions, the potential connection is cleared and a null state is entered. The ATM specifications require that only one retry may be attempted after which a null state must be entered.

Upon receiving the CALL PROCEEDING message, the local user and remote network node turn off their T303 timers and turn on their T310 timers. This timer waits for the CONNECT message to be sent to either party. Upon successful reception of the CONNECT message, timer T310 is turned off and the recipients of this message respond with a CONNECTION ACKNOWLEDGMENT of this message. If the CONNECTION ACKNOWLEDGMENT message is not received before timer T310 expires, the connection must be cleared.

The remote user also invokes timer T313 when it sends the CONNECT message to the network. This timer is turned off upon receiving the CONNECT ACKNOWLEDGMENT message.

The SETUP message must contain all the information required for the network and the called party to process the call. This information must include the QOS parameters, the cell rate parameters (called the traffic descriptor in more recent documents), and any bearer capabilities that the network may need at either side. The user is not allowed to fill in the connection identifier information element in the SETUP message. If it is included, the network ignores it. This means that the network selects the VPI/VCI for the connection. This information is returned to the user in the CALL PROCEEDING message.

A similar procedure is performed on the remote side of the network in that the network node is responsible for allocating the VPI/VCI value and placing this value in the SETUP message before it sends this message to the called user. Likewise, when the called user accepts the message, it maps these VPI/VCI values into its virtual circuit identifier (VCI) table and returns a CALL PROCEEDING message.

In the event a call is not completed, either party can send a number of diagnostics citing the reason for the inability to complete the connection.

Connection Release

As illustrated in Figure 10–6, the connection release operation entails only timer T308. Either the network or the user can invoke the connection release by sending the RELEASE message to the respective party. This operation turns on timer T308, which remains on until the RELEASE message is received. If T308 expires for the first time, the RELEASE message is retransmitted. If a response is not returned on this second try, the user must release the call reference and return to the null state (no connection exists). The manner in which this operation is then handled is not defined in the standard but is network- or user-specific.

In the event that a RELEASE message is received by the network or the user at the same time that the respective node sends a RELEASE (this procedure is called a clear-clear collision), the affected party stops

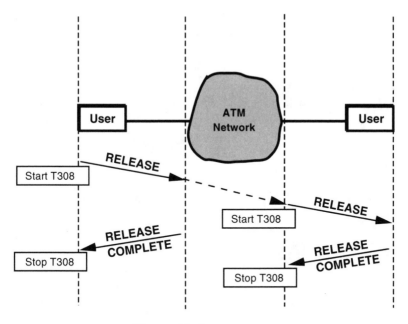

Figure 10–6
The release procedure.

timer T308, releases the call reference as well as the virtual channel, and enters into the null state.

Restart Procedure

The network or user can initiate restart operations for any number of reasons. Failure of any component can result in the restart procedure being invoked, and information elements in the header cite the reason for the restart. As illustrated in Figure 10–7, the initiation of the restart by the user invokes timer T316 by the originator's sending the RESTART message to the recipient. In turn, the recipient (network side shown) starts timer T317 upon receiving the RESTART message. After processing the RESTART message and taking any necessary actions, the recipient issues a RESTART ACKNOWLEDGE and stops T317.

Next, the network issues a RELEASE to the destination and starts timer T308. The destination acknowledges the RELEASE message by returning the RELEASE COMPLETE. A RESTART ACKNOWLEDGE is sent to the originator, which then stops T316. The field in the RESTART message labeled restart indicator determines if an indicated virtual

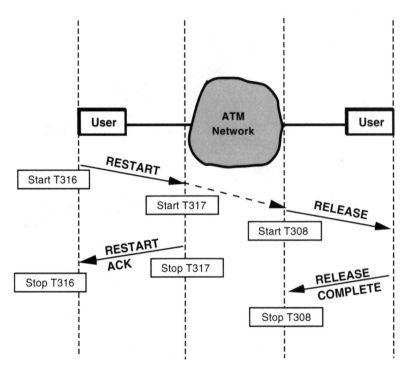

Figure 10–7
The restart procedure.

channel is to be restarted or all channels controlled by this layer 3 entity are to be restarted.

Status Inquiry

The status inquiry procedure is invoked by either the network or the user to determine the state of a connection, such as the call state, the type of connection being supported, or the end state of a point-to-multipoint connection. As indicated in Figure 10–8, timer T322 controls this procedure. Either party may invoke the STATUS INQUIRY message by turning T322 on. Upon receipt of the STATUS or STATUS COMPLETE message, this timer is turned off. Be aware that a status enquiry only operates on a link basis.

Add Party

Because of the importance and wide use of telephone conference calls and video conferencing operations, the ATM designers developed procedures to support these types of applications. This capability is im-

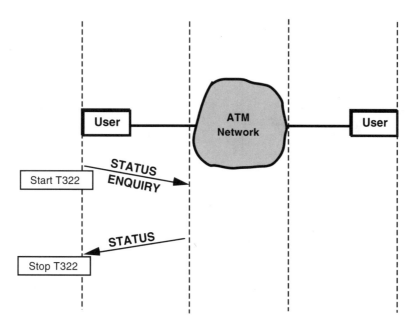

Figure 10–8
The status inquiry procedure.

plemented through the add-party procedure as shown in Figure 10–9. This illustration shows the addition of only one party, but multiple parties may be connected with this operation. The originating site issues an ADD PARTY message across the UNI to the network. The network forwards this message to the destination in which the destination network node, issues a SETUP across the UNI to the destination user. The SETUP message is used if procedures must begin from scratch. That is to say, this UNI is currently not participating in the call. Not shown in this figure is the possibility of issuing the ADD PARTY message across the remote UNI for situations where a call is already in place and another calling party needs to be added.

The operation is controlled with timer T399 at the sending site. This timer is turned off upon receiving a CONNECTION ACKNOWLEDG-MENT, an ADD PARTY, ADD PARTY ACK, REJECT, or a RELEASE. In this example, the remote side uses the initial setup operation, discussed earlier. The point-to-multipoint operation is also controlled by party-states. These states may exist on the network side or the user side of the interface. They are summarized as follows:

- *Null:* A party does not exist; therefore an endpoint reference value has not been allocated

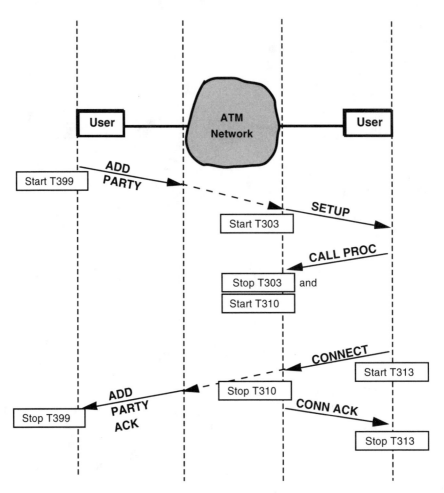

Figure 10–9
The add party procedure.

- *Add party initiated:* An ADD PARTY message or a SETUP message has been sent to the other side of the interface for this party
- *Add party received:* An ADD PARTY message or a setup message has been received by the other side of the interface for this party
- *Drop party initiated:* A DROP PARTY message has been sent for this party
- *Drop party received:* A DROP PARTY message has been received for this party
- *Active:* On the user side of the UNI, an active state is when the user has received an CONNECT ACKNOWLEDGE, ADD PARTY ACKNOWLEDGE, or a CONNECT. On the network side an ac-

tive state is entered when it has sent a CONNECT, CONNECT ACKNOWLEDGE, or an ADD PARTY ACKNOWLEDGE; or when the network has received an ADD PARTY ACKNOWL-EDGE from the user side.

Drop Party

As the reader might expect, the drop party procedure provides the opposite function of the add-party procedure discussed in the previous section. With this operation, one party or multiple parties can be dropped from the connection. These operations are illustrated in Figure 10–10. The activity is controlled by the T398 and T308 timers. In this example, the RELEASE and RELEASE COMPLETE messages are used at the remote side. Under certain conditions the drop party is also activated at the remote side.

Signaling AAL Reset and Failure

The AAL request operation occurs when the AAL entity issues a AAL-establish-indication primitive to ATM (no figure is shown). This resets a current connection but does not affect other connections on the in-

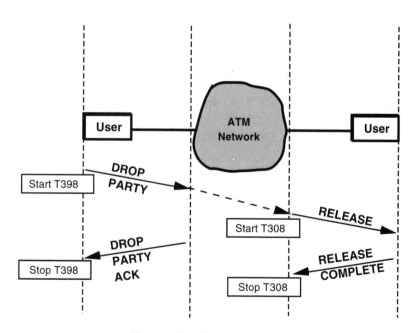

Figure 10–10
The drop party procedure.

terface. Another AAL operation is titled the AAL failure. In this situation any parties that are not in the active party state must be cleared.

FUNCTIONS OF Q.2931 MESSAGES AND INFORMATION ELEMENTS

We have learned that the messages for the ATM call and connection control are derived from the Q.931 protocol, the layer 3 specification for ISDN. The purpose of Q.931 is to establish connections for B channels at the ISDN basic rate interface (BRI). Q.2931 is used to set up and tear down a connection through the ATM network. The next three sections of this chapter provide a summary of the three major types of Q.2931 messages. Then, the fourth section describes the functions of the information elements that may reside in the messages. A fifth section shows coding examples of the messages and the information elements.

Messages for Call Control

Table 10–5 summarizes the information elements (fields) that are present in the messages. A key is provided with Table 10–5 to identify the message information elements. The reader will find this table handy as the information elements are described.

Messages for Restart Operations

The global call reference messages are used by the network or user to request the restart of a virtual channel or all virtual channels controlled by the signaling virtual channel. This channel is reserved with VCI = 5 and VPCI = 0.[1] It is used for all signaling in phase 1 of SVC. Metasignaling is not supported in phase 1.

The messages used for the global call reference are listed in Table 10–6, as well as the information elements that are used in these messages.

Messages for Adding and Dropping Parties

The ATM SVC supports both point-to-point connections and point-to-multipoint connections. The point-to-multipoint message allows one ATM link (the root link) to send information to any remaining nodes on

---

[1]The ATM Forum uses the virtual path connection identifier (VPCI) instead of a VPI for certain forms of signaling. The issue is for further study. Currently, VPI and VPCI are the same.

Table 10–5 ATM Call and Connection Control Messages

Information Element	Message							
	1.	2.	3.	4.	5.	6.	7.	8.
Protocol discriminator	✓	✓	✓	✓	✓	✓	✓	✓
Call reference	✓	✓	✓	✓	✓	✓	✓	✓
Message type	✓	✓	✓	✓	✓	✓	✓	✓
Message length	✓	✓	✓	✓	✓	✓	✓	✓
AAL parameters		✓		✓				
AMT user traffic descriptor				✓				
Broadband bearer capability				✓				
Broadband high layer information				✓				
Broadband repeat indicator				✓				
Broadband low layer information		✓		✓				
Called party number				✓				
Called party subaddress				✓				
Calling party number				✓				
Calling party subaddress				✓				
Call state							✓	
Cause					✓	✓	✓	
Connection identifier	✓	✓		✓				
QOS parameter				✓				
Broadband sending complete				✓				
Transit network selection				✓				
Endpoint reference	✓	✓		✓			✓	✓
Endpoint state							✓	

1 CALL PROCEEDING
2 CONNECT
3 CONNECT
  ACKNOWLEDGE

4 SETUP
5 RELEASE
6 RELEASE
  COMPLETE

7 STATUS
8 STATUS ENQUIRY

Table 10–6   Global Call Reference Messages

Information Element	Message		
	Restart	Restart Acknowledge	Status
Protocol discriminator	✓	✓	✓
Call reference	✓	✓	✓
Message type	✓	✓	✓
Message length	✓	✓	✓
Call state			✓
Cause			✓
Connection identifier	✓	✓	
Restart indicator	✓	✓	
Endpoint reference			✓
Endpoint state			✓

the connection. These nodes are called leaf nodes and receive copies of all information sent by the root link. The add party messages (as their names imply) are to add a party to an existing connection and to acknowledge that the add party request was successful. The add party request can also be rejected.

The drop party messages (again, as the name implies) are used to drop a party from an existing point-to-multipoint connection.

The messages used with ATM point-to-multipoint call and connection control are shown in Table 10–7, as well as the information elements present in the messages.

Descriptions of the Information Elements

This section describes the functions of the information elements, several of which are self-explanatory. To simplify matters, the functions of the information elements are summarized in Table 10–8, followed by additional comments on some of the entries in the table. Many of the entries listed in Table 10–8 are briefly explained following the table and are noted with the "see below" notation. The information in this section is amplified in the next section with examples.

Addresses and other identifiers in the messages.   ATM uses a num- ber of labels, addresses, and identifiers to keep track of the various

Table 10–7   Point-to-Multipoint Call and Connection Control Messages

Information Element	Message 1.	2.	3.	4.	5.
Protocol discriminator	✓	✓	✓	✓	✓
Call reference	✓	✓	✓	✓	✓
Message type	✓	✓	✓	✓	✓
Message length	✓	✓	✓	✓	✓
AAL parameters	✓				
Broadband high layer information	✓				
Broadband low layer information	✓				
Called party number	✓				
Called party subaddress	✓				
Calling party number	✓				
Calling party subaddress	✓				
Cause			✓	✓	✓
Broadband sending complete	✓				
Transit network selection	✓				
Endpoint reference	✓	✓	✓	✓	✓

1 ADD PARTY   4 DROP PARTY

2 ADD PARTY ACKNOWLEDGE   5 DROP PARTY ACKNOWLEDGE

3 ADD PARTY RESET

connections in the network. These values are placed in several of the ATM messages to be used for connection control. These values are listed in Table 10–5:

- Call reference
- Connection identifier
- Endpoint reference
- Called and calling party number
- Called and calling party subaddress

The call reference value identifies the call at the local UNI. It is used to associate incoming and outgoing messages with the proper connection. The call reference has local significance only and is not mapped

Table 10–8   Functions of the Information Service Elements

Protocol discriminator	Distinguishes different types of messages within ITU-T standards and standards bodies throughout the world
Call reference	Uniquely identifies each call at the UNI (see below)
Message type	Identifies type of message, such as SETUP, STATUS, etc.
Message length	Length of message excluding the three elements above and this element
AAL parameters	AAL parameters selected by user
ATM user traffic descriptor	Specifies set of traffic parameters
Broadband and bearer capability	Indicates several network bearer services (end-to-end-timing, CBR, VBR, point-to-point, multipoint services) (see below)
Broadband high layer information	End-user codes, passed transparently through ATM network; identifies upper layer protocols or a vendor-specific application (see below)
Broadband repeat indicator	Used to allow repeated information elements to be interpreted correctly
Broadband low layer information	End-user codes, passed transparently through ATM network; identifies lower layer protocols and their configurations
Called party number	Called party of the call (see below)
Called party subaddress	Called party subaddress (see below)
Calling party number	Origin party number (see below)
Calling party subaddress	Calling party subaddress (see below)
Call state	One of 12 values to describe status of a call (active, call initiated, etc.)
Cause	Diagnostic codes (see below)
Connection identifier	The VPI and VCI for the call (see below)
QOS parameter	QOS class
Broadband sending complete	Indicates the completion of the called party number
Transit network selection	Identifies a transit network (an IXC in the U.S.) (see below)

Table 10–8   Functions of the Information Service Elements (continued)

Endpoint reference	Identifies endpoints in a point-to-multiplication connection
Endpoint state	Indicates state of each endpoint (add party initiated, received, active, etc.) (see below)
Restart indicator	For a restart, identifies which virtual channels are to be restated

to other side of the network UNI. The values are assigned by the user on the originating side of the call and by the network on the other side of the call. They are unique at each local interface and exist only for the duration of the connection. Unlike other connection-oriented systems, such as X.25, identical call reference values may exist on the same virtual channel because the call reference value contains a flag identifying which end of the signaling channel originated the call. The originating side sets the call flag to 0 and the destination side sets the call flag to 1. This approach avoids call collisions (simultaneous use of the same value) that exist in older types of networks.

The connection identifier contains the VPI and VCI values. Within certain limitations (published by the ITU-T and ATM Forum), most of the VPI/VCI values can be used in any manner deemed necessary by the network.

The endpoint reference identifier is not an identifier as such, but is used to identify a state of an endpoint in a point-to-multipoint connection. As examples, this value could indicate that an add party operation has been initiated, a drop party has been initiated, or that a party is now active.

The called and calling party numbers must be coded in messages dealing with connection setups. Without these numbers, the network would not know where to route the call. The party number is actually two fields, one for called party and the other for the calling party. These numbers are either a telephone number, which typically is an ISDN E.164 value, and/or an OSI address known as the network service access point (NSAP).

The last identifier is the network party called and calling party subaddress and is employed only if a network supports only an E.164 address. The purpose of the subaddress is to provide a field for the OSI NSAP address.

To clarify the difference between the party number and the party subaddress, the party number may have embedded in it the full OSI addressing plan, including NSAPs and E.164. If it does not have this full number and contains only the E.164 telephone number, then the additional party subaddress field can contain the OSI subaddress. The reason for this addition is that it is possible for traffic to be routed to an address signified by E.164 and delivered to the proper user station (computer, PBX, etc.), when the E.164 address is insufficient to define fully which entity inside the receiver station is to receive the traffic, such as file transfer server or an E-mail server. The OSI NSAP contains information that permits these operations to occur.

ATM AAL parameters.　The parameters in the AAL information element indicate the AAL values for the connection. Listed below are some of the major parameters:

- Type of traffic (1, 3/4, 5, or user-defined)
- Subtype of traffic (circuit emulation, high-quality audio, video, etc.)
- Maximum SDU size for AAL 3/4
- CBR rate (64 kbit/s, DS1, E1, n × 64 kbit/s, etc.)
- Clock recovery type for AAL 1
- Mode for AAL 5 (message mode or streaming mode)
- Error correction method for AAL 1

ATM user traffic descriptor.　The parameters in the traffic descriptor information element indicate: (1) forward and backward peak cell rates; (2) forward and backward sustainable cell rates; and (3) forward and backward maximum burst sizes. The term forward describes the direction of traffic flow from the calling user to the called user, and the term backward indicates the direction of traffic flow from the called user to the calling user. A subfield in this information element allows the user to indicate if tagging is requested, for either forward or backward flows.

Broadband bearer capability and higher layer information.　Two information elements indicate a wide variety of services requested for the connection at a B-ISDN bearer service (the lower three layers of OSI) and the upper layers (the top four layers of OSI). These parameters have no effect on the ATM network, and are passed transparently to the end-user node.

Examples of the bearer parameters are an indication that timing is or is not required and an indication of CBR/VBR traffic. Examples of higher layer information are the identification of the user layers (protocol entities) that are to operate over ATM at the end-user station; or for X.25/X.75 traffic, the default packet size of the user payload or information on the layer 2 protocol, such as HDLC.

Chapter 11, Internetworking with ATM Networks, shows how these fields can be employed to facilitate internetworking between ATM and other networks, with ATM acting as the backbone transport network for the other networks.

Quality of services (QOS).   This information element contains values to request (and maybe receive) certain QOS operations. QOS is requested for both directions of the connection.

ATM QOS is organized around the ITU-T I.362 service classes A, B, C, and D (see Chapter 7). This information element is coded to request a QOS that meets one of the service class performance requirements. It may also be coded as unspecified, in which case the network may establish a set of objectives for the connection.

Cause parameters.   This information element contains diagnostic information and the reasons that certain messages are generated. Diagnostics such as user busy, call rejected, network out of order, QOS unavailable, user traffic descriptor not available, and the like are coded in this information element. Table 10–9 lists the cause values currently published [ATM93a].

Table 10–9   Cause Value Meaning

Unallocated (unassigned) number

No route to specified transit network

No route to destination

VPCI/VCI unacceptable

User busy

No user responding

Call rejected

Number changed

User rejects all calls with calling line identification restriction (CLIR)

Destination out of order

Invalid number format (address complete)

(continued)

Table 10–9   Cause Value Meaning (continued)

Response to STATUS ENQUIRY

Normal, unspecified

Requested VPCI/VCI not available

Network out of order

Temporary failure

Access information discarded

No VPCI/VCI available

Resource unavailable, unspecified

Quality of service unavailable

User traffic descriptor not available

Bearer capability not authorized

Bearer capability not presently available

Service or option not available, unspecified

Bearer capability not implemented

Unsupported combination of traffic parameters

Invalid call reference value

Identified channel does not exist

Incompatible destination

Invalid endpoint reference

Invalid transit network selection

Too many pending add party requests

AAL parameters cannot be supported

Mandatory information element is missing

Message type nonexistent or not implemented

Information element nonexistent or not implemented

Invalid information element contents

Message not compatible with call state

Recovery on timer expiry

Incorrect message length

Protocol error, unspecified

Transit network selection. This parameter is important in the United States for traffic that is sent across LATAs. It allows the user to choose the interexchange carrier (IXC) for the session.

EXAMPLES OF Q.2931 MESSAGES

The Q.2931 specification defines many rules for coding messages and information elements. This discussion will acquaint the reader with some of the principal features of the message coding, and will provide some examples of the information elements. Other examples can be found in Chapter 11. Be aware that this discussion does not explain all formats of all the messages.

It is recognized that some readers will not care to delve into the bit-level of these messages, and knowing the bit structure is not required to understand the functions of the messages. Other readers want the bit-level detail. Whatever the needs of the reader, an examination of these messages will help in understanding how the ATM connections are managed, and will shed light on many of the functions of the ATM layer and the ATM adaptation layer.

One final point, it will become evident that the messages follow a common convention. Therefore, the first few examples will explain this convention, down to the bit level. Subsequent examples will elevate the level of detail. I hope this satisfies all readers.

Figure 10–11 shows the basic organization of the Q.2931 message. Most of the contents of this message have been explained earlier. Some additional comments are appropriate. The protocol discriminator field can be coded to identify the Q.2931 message, or other layer 3 protocols. Obviously, it is coded in this protocol to identify Q.2931 messages. The call reference identifies each call, and is assigned by the originating side of the call (the user at the local side, and the network at the remote side). The message type identifies a SETUP, ADD PARTY, and other messages. The information elements contain the fields that are used to control the connection operation.

Coding Conventions

In order to understand the coding structure of the ATM messages, a few rules must be explained. All information elements contain a header, which identifies (1) the type of information element (IE), (2) a coding standard, (3) an IE instruction field, (4) a length field (length of the in-

Bits

8	7	6	5	4	3	2	1	Octets
Protocol discriminator								1
0	0	0	0	Length of call reference				2
Flag	Call reference value							3
Call reference value (continued)								4
Call reference value (continued)								5
Message type								6
Message type (continued)								7
Message length								8
Message length (continued)								9
Variable length information elements								n

Figure 10–11
Organization of a Q.2931 message.

formation elements), and (5) the actual information element (IE). The coding standard is usually set to 00 to identify an ITU-T standard. The IE instruction field values vary, depending on the specific information element. Generally, this field is not explained in our general description in this chapter.

An octet number may be repeated in the figure (for example, see Figure 10–13). The specific octet number identifies an octet group. Octets are extended in a group by appending .1, .2, .3, or .a, .b, .c, . . . behind the octet value. In Figure 10–13, octet 6 is extended by the notation 6.1. The groups can be identified and/or extended through the use of bit 8 in each octet as follows: 0 = another octet follows; 1 = last octet of this group.

AAL Parameters

Figure 10–12 illustrates the first six octets of the AAL information element. These octets are used for all AAL types. Octet 1 is coded as 01011000 to identify the information element. Octet 2 is preset or not significant. Octet 5 is coded to indicate the AAL type information that follows in octets 6 through n:

Bits

8	7	6	5	4	3	2	1	Octets
ATM adaptation layer parameters								
0	1	0	1	1	0	0	0	1
Information element identifier								
1 ext	Coding Standard	IE Instruction Field						2
Length of AAL parameters contents								3
Length of AAL parameters contents (continued)								4
AAL Type								5
Further content depending upon AAL type								6 etc.

Figure 10–12
AAL information element for all AAL types.

00000001	AAL 1
00000011	AAL 3/4
00000101	AAL 5
00010000	User-defined AAL

AAL 1. Figure 10–13 shows the parameters for octet groups 6-12 for AAL 1. The subtype (octet 6.1) indicates:

00000000	Null/empty
00000001	Voiceband 64 kbit/s
00000010	Circuit emulation (synchronous)
00000011	Circuit emulation (asynchronous)
00000100	High-quality audio
00000101	Video

The CBR rate (octet 7.1) requests a bit rate for the session. It is coded as follows:

00000001	64 kbit/s
00000100	1544 kbit/s (DS1)
00000101	6312 kbit/s (DS2)
00000110	32064 kbit/s
00000111	44736 kbit/s (DS3)
00001000	97728 kbit/s

Bits

8	7	6	5	4	3	2	1	Octets
Subtype identifer								6
1	0	0	0	0	1	0	1	
Subtype								6.1
CBR rate identifier								7
1	0	0	0	0	1	1	0	
CBR rate								7.1
Multiplier identifier								8 (Note 1)
1	0	0	0	0	1	1	1	
Multiplier								8.1 (Note 1)
Multiplier (continued)								8.2 (Note 1)
Source clock frequency recovery method identifier								9
1	0	0	0	1	0	0	0	
Source clock frequency recovery method								9.1
Error correction method identifier								10
1	0	0	0	1	0	0	1	
Error correction method								10.1
Structured data transfer blocksize identifier								11
1	0	0	0	1	0	1	0	
Structured data transfer blocksize								11.1
Partially filled cells identifier								12
1	0	0	0	1	0	1	1	
Partially filled cells method								12.1

These octets are only present if octet 7.1 indicates "n x 64 kbit/s."

Figure 10–13
Parameters for an AAL 1 connection.

00010000	2048 kbit/s (E1)
00010001	8448 kbit/s (E2)
00010010	34368 kbit/s (E3)
00010011	139264 kbit/s (E4)
01000000	$n \times 64$ kbit/s

The multiplier parameter is used to define a $n \times 64$ kbit/s, with n ranging from 2 to $2^{16}-1$. The clock recovery type parameter indicates the kind of clocking operation to be employed to recover and decode the signal (timestamp, etc.). The error correction parameter identifies the type of error correction method employed to detect errors at the terminating endpoint (none, FEC, etc.). The structured data transfer identifies that this connection will or will not use structured data transfer (see Chapter 7). The partially filled cells parameter states how many of the 47 octets in the cell are in use.

AAL 3/4 and AAL 5. Figure 10–14 shows the parameters for AAL 3/4, and Figure 10–15 shows the parameters for AAL 5. The functions represented in these fields are explained in Chapter 7. Briefly, then, the service specific CS (SSCS) and the common part CS (CPCS) parameters indicate (1) the maximum CPCS-SDU sizes (forward and backward), with values ranging from 1 to 65,535 (2^{16}–1); (2) the ranges for the mes-

				Bits				
8	**7**	**6**	**5**	**4**	**3**	**2**	**1**	**Octets**
Forward maximum CPCS-SDU size identifier								6
1	0	0	0	1	1	0	0	
Forward maximum CPCS-SDU size								6.1
Forward maximum CPCS-SDU size (continued)								6.2
Backward maximum CPCS-SDU size identifier								7
1	0	0	0	0	0	0	1	
Backward maximum CPCS-SDU size								7.1
Backward maximum CPCS-SDU size (continued)								7.2
MID range identifier								8
1	0	0	0	0	0	1	0	
MID range (lowest MID value)								8.1
MID range (lowest MID value) (continued)								8.2
MID range (highest MID value)								8.3
MID range (highest MID value)(continued)								8.4
SSCS type identifier								9
1	0	0	0	0	1	0	0	
SSCS type								9.1

Figure 10–14
Parameters for an AAL 3/4 connection.

Bits								Octets
8	7	6	5	4	3	2	1	
Forward maximum CPCS-SDU size identifier								6
1	0	0	0	1	1	0	0	
Forward maximum CPCS-SDU size								6.1
Forward maximum CPCS-SDU size (continued)								6.2
Backward maximum CPCS-SDU size identifier								7
1	0	0	0	0	0	0	1	
Backward maximum CPCS-SDU size								7.1
Backward maximum CPCS-SDU size (continued)								7.2
SSCS type identifier								8
1	0	0	0	0	1	0	0	
SSCS type								8.1

Figure 10–15
Parameters for an AAL 5 connection.

sage identification field (1 to 1023); (3) a message or streaming mode; and (4) SSCS type (such as assured operations, a frame relay SSCS, etc.).

User Traffic Descriptors

The user traffic descriptors indicate the characteristics the user wishes to use for the connection (no figure shown). The parameters (see Chapter 8) define the following traffic capabilities (the cell rates are expressed in cells per second, and the burst size is expressed as a cell):

Forward peak cell rate

Backward peak cell rate

Forward sustainable cell rate

Backward sustainable cell rate

Forward maximum burst size

Backward maximum burst size

These examples have given the reader an idea of the syntax and format of the Q.2931 messages. Chapter 11 examines those that are associated with internetworking operations.

SUMMARY

The ATM call and connection control operations define how connections are set up on demand between users and the ATM network. The Q.2931 connection control protocol, based on the ISDN Q.931, is used for these operations. The ATM address utilizes the OSI address syntax. Q.2931 supports point-to-point, unidirectional connections. Future releases of Q.2931 and the ATM Forum specifications will also support multipoint-to-multipoint connections.

Internetworking with ATM Networks

INTRODUCTION

This chapter examines how ATM internetworks with other networks. Its emphasis is on the B-ISDN intercarrier interface (B-ICI). It also explains how several of the Q.2931 messages can be used to define network operations between networks that are using an ATM network as the backbone network between them. The ATM data exchange interface (DXI) is also examined. The reader who is not familiar with the basic operations of DS3 should review Chapter 4.

THE ATM NETWORK AS THE BACKBONE FOR OTHER NETWORKS

From the perspective of ATM vendors, the ATM Forum specifications, and other supporters of this technology, ATM is viewed as the backbone for interconnecting other networks. To this end, the standards bodies and the ATM Forum have published a number of recommendations and specifications that define (1) how traffic from different networks is transported through an ATM network, (2) how the header in the PDUs of these different networks is (or is not) translated into the ATM cell, and (3) how the services offered by these networks are (or are not) mapped into the ATM services.

USING Q.2931 TO SUPPORT PROTOCOL CAPABILITY (TUNNELING)

The term tunneling refers to an operation in which a transport network, such as an ATM backbone, carries traffic from other protocols and networks transparently (or almost transparently) through the transport network. If possible, the transport network does not become involved with either the syntax or the interpretation of the transported traffic. Thus, the term refers to the notion of sending traffic (say a car) through a "tunnel" without anyone in the tunnel, stopping the car, rolling down the windows of the car, and checking the contents in the passenger space.

The tunneled information is passed transparently by the ATM network between the two user parties. ATM does not examine, interpret, or act on this traffic. Its intent is to allow the two end users to inform each other about the nature of some of the communications protocols operating in their machines. The goal is to stipulate or negotiate a compatible protocol stack for the exchange of traffic between the user applications. Tunneling in ATM is performed by using the Q.2931 operations and the broadband low-layer information element that is introduced in Chapter 10.

In some systems, such as the well-known point-to-point protocol (PPP), these services are accomplished with two methods. First, during the connection setup, two end users can inform each other about which protocols are to be invoked during the session. This procedure allows the two parties to negotiate an acceptable set of protocols to be used during the session. Second, during the transfer of traffic, a protocol identifier is conveyed to indicate what type of protocol payload is being sent in the service data unit (SDU).

While Q.2931 can be configured to accomplish either method, it does not stipulate any negotiation procedures. Additional software must be written to provide full negotiation operations.

Figure 11–1 shows how the Q.2931 messages can be invoked and interpreted. The boundary of the message flow is between a calling user and a called user. In this example, the flow is between (in ITU-T terminology) interworking units (IWU)—or routers. Of course, the manner in which the end-user stations communicate with the routers is not defined by ATM, since the information flow between the end-user station and the router is not part of the ATM UNI. Nonetheless, the user station-to-router operation is well-defined in other standards, and the router need only map the information received from the user stations into the Q.2931

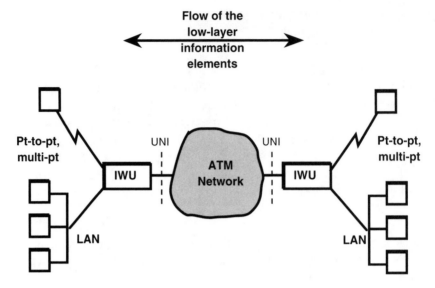

Figure 11–1
Flow of the Q.2931 low-layer information element.

message at the originating router and perform a complementary and reverse operation at the terminating router.

The identification of the layer 2 protocols must discern whether
they are running on (1) point-to-point links, (2) multipoint links, or (3)
LAN links. Some protocols, such as LAPD, can operate on a multipoint
link; others operate on only point-to-point links, such as LAPB. Still others, operate only on LAN links.

However, in this latter case for LAN links, these procedures do not
identify the type of LAN (Ethernet, token ring, etc.), because the headers
of the respective LANs are not carried across the ATM network—they
are stripped away at the originating router and reconstituted at the terminating router. This approach allows the terminating router to place
the traffic onto any type of LAN, which may be different than the LAN at
the originating site.

Figure 11–2 illustrates the various layer 2 and 3 protocols and procedures that can be identified in the Q.2931 low-layer information element. Figure 11–2(a) depicts the layer 2 protocols, and Figure 11–2(b)
depicts the layer 3 protocols. The description of all these protocols is well
beyond the subject of this book. The reader can study *X.25 and Related
Protocols, Data Link Protocols,* and *Computer Networks: Protocols,*

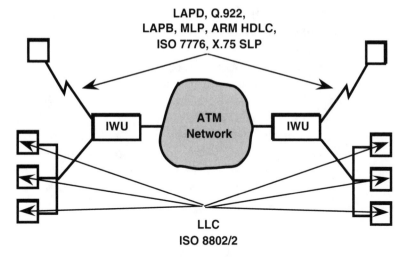

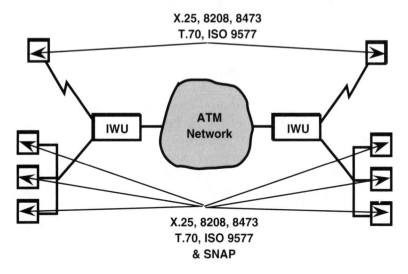

(b) Layer 3 Protocols

Figure 11–2
Layers 2 and 3 identifications.

Standards and Interfaces, all by Uyless Black [BLAC89], [BLAC91], and [BLAC93] for information on these systems. All references are highly recommended by this writer.

For the layer 3 protocols, the LAN stations ordinarily support the Internet Protocol (IP), or some vendor-specific protocol, such as Novell's IPX. The approximate equivalent in this specification is ISO 8473, the connectionless network protocol, or CLNP.

Also, the subnetwork access protocol (SNAP) is usually employed in LANs (and not WANs) to identify the layer 3 protocol residing in the data unit. Nothing precludes using other methods. The most common approach is to use SNAP on LANs, as it was so designed, and to use PPP on point-to-point links, as it was so designed.

BROADBAND LOW-LAYER INFORMATION ELEMENT

Figure 11–3 shows the format and contents of the broadband low-layer information element. Octets 1-4 are explained in Chapter 10. Octet 5 is not supported at this time in the ATM Forum specification. Octet 6, bits 1-5, are coded in accordance with the conventions shown in Figure 11–4. Octet 6a uses the mode field to define if extended (0-127) or normal sequencing (0-7) is to be employed at layer 2 (if sequencing is employed). The Q.933 field is used, based on implementation-specific rules. The window size field (k) can range from 1-127. The next occurrence of 6a defines if a user specified layer 2 protocol is employed.

Octet 7, bits 1-5 are coded in accordance with the conventions shown in Figure 11–5. The mode field in octet 7a defines if extended (0-127) or normal sequencing (0-7) is to be employed at layer 3 (if sequencing is employed). The default packet size field in octet 7b is used to define the default size of the X.25 packet (if X.25 is invoked). The packet window size is also employed for X.25 (octet 7c) for a range of 1-127.

The second occurrence of octet 7a is used to identify a user-specified layer 3 protocol, such as SNA Path Control or AppleTalk layer 3.

The remainder of the octets in this information element can be used to identify SNAP information. If so indicated by octets 7a, a 24-bit organization unique ID (OUI) and a 16-bit protocol ID (PID) are contained in the last octets of the information element. The OUI and PID are values that are registered under ISO, the IEEE, and the Internet.

Bits								Octets
8	7	6	5	4	3	2	1	
Broadband low layer information								1
0	1	0	1	1	1	1	1	
1 ext	Coding standard		IE instruction field					2
Length of B-LLI contents								3
Length of B-LLI contents (continued)								4
1 ext	0 1 Layer 1 id		User information layer 1 protocol					5
0/1 ext	1 0 Layer 2 id		User information layer 2 protocol					6
0/1 ext	Mode		0 Spare	0	0	Q.933 use		6a
1 ext	Window size (k)							6b
1 ext	User specified layer 2 protocol information							6a
0/1 ext	1 1 Layer 3 id		User information layer 3 protocol					7
0/1 ext	Mode		0	0	0 Spare	0	0	7a
0/1 ext	0 0 Spare		0	Default packet size				7b
1 ext	Packet window size							7c
1 ext	User specified layer 3 protocol information							7a
0 ext	ISO/IEC TR 9577 Initial protocol identifier (IPI) (bits 8-2)							7a
1 ext	IPI (bit1)	0	0	0	0 Spare	0	0	7b
1 ext	0 0 SNAP ID		0	0	0 Spare	0	0	8
OUI Octet 1								8.1
OUI Octet 2								8.2
OUI Octet 3								8.3
PID Octet 1								8.4
PID Octet 2								8.5

Figure 11–3
The broadband low-layer information element.

Octet 6 Bits 54321	Meaning
00001	Basic mode ISO 1745
00010	CCITT Recommendation Q.921
00110	CCITT Recommendation X.25, link layer
00111	CCITT Recommendation X.25 multilink
01000	Extended LAPB; for half duplex operation
01001	HDLC ARM (ISO 4335)
01010	HDLC NRM (ISO 4335)
01011	HDLC ABM (ISO 4335)
01100	LAN logical link control (ISO 8802/2)
01101	CCITT Recommemdation X.75, single link procedure (SLP)
01110	CCITT Recommendation Q.922
10000	User specified
10001	ISO 7776 DTE-DTE operation

Figure 11–4
Coding bits 1-5 of octet 6.

Octet 7 Bits 54321	Meaning
00110	CCITT Recommendation X.25, packet layer
00111	ISO/IEC 8208 (X.25 packet level protocol for data terminal equipment)
01000	X.223/ISO 8878 (use of ISO/ISO 8208 [41] and CCITT X.25 to provide the OSI-CONS)
01001	ISO/IEC 8473 (OSI connecionless mode protocol)
01010	CCITT Recommendation T.70 minimum network layer
01011	ISO/IEC TR 9577 (Protocol Identification in the Network Layer)
01000	User specified

Figure 11–5
Coding for bits 1-5 of octet 7.

THE NETWORK-TO-NETWORK INTERFACE

Presently, two network-to-network interfaces (NNI) are under development for ATM. (Some literature uses the term network-node interface; in this discussion, they mean the same thing). A public NNI is being developed by the ITU-T, and a private NNI is being developed by the ATM Forum (see Figure 11–6).

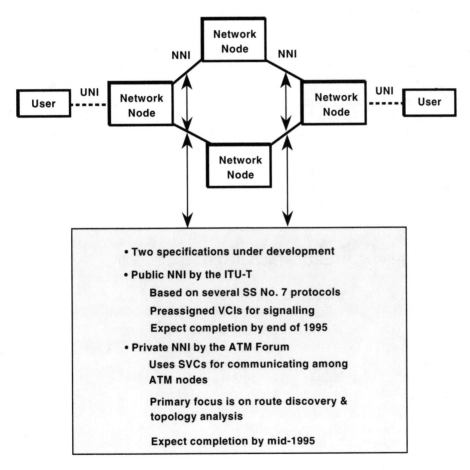

Figure 11–6
Major aspects of the network-to-network interface (NNI)
(Note: Under development).

The private NNI is due for completion by mid-year 1995. It will allow different vendors' ATM machines to communicate with each other. The communications will utilize the standard UNI switched virtual call (SVC) procedures, with additional information added in the SVC messages. The major aspects of the private UNI will focus on route discovery, building routing tables, and maintaining an awareness of "reachability" to other ATM nodes. It is based on hierarchical routing and hierarchical addresses. Advertisements are part of this specification, with information on link state metrics, and bandwidth availability.

Since the private NNI will not be available until mid-1995, the ATM Forum has published an interim specification, called the interim interswitch signaling protocol (IISP). It is a low-function protocol, with no dynamic route discovery. Tables are preconfigured, although SVC operations allow switches to request connections with each other.

The public NNI is being developed by the ITU-T. Signaling System No. 7, (SS7) has been adapted for use with this specification. As a general description, SS7's ISDN user part (ISUP), and message transfer part 3 (MTP 3) are modified for the public NNI. These protocols run on top of ATM and some type of physical layer. A special AAL called the signaling ATM adaptation layer (SAAL) rests between the ATM layer and the SS7 layers. It is anticipated that most of the public NNI standards will be in place by the end of 1995.

THE ATM B-ISDN INTERCARRIER INTERFACE (B-ICI)

The ATM Forum has published the broadband intercarrier interface (B-ICI) Version 1.0.[1] Figure 11–7 shows the relationships between the UNI and B-ICI, and the idea that the B-ICI can operate with public local exchange carrier (LEC) networks and independent LECs (ILECs). This distinction is important, because B-ICI is an interface between public ATM networks, not private networks.

---

[1]Some confusion exists regarding NNI. Some vendors/standards call it the network-node interface, and others call it the network-to-network interface. With either term, NNI is supposed to determine a switch-to-switch interface, which could be within a network or between networks. The major goal of an NNI is to allow ATM switches from different vendors to interwork with each other. Therefore, the ATM B-ICI is one aspect of an NNI specification: a carrier-to-carrier interface.

Obviously (and eventually), the NNI and the B-ICI must coexist at the ICI. But the B-ICI need not exist between two switches in the *same* network.

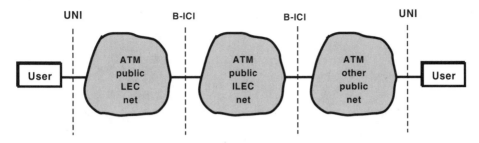

Figure 11–7
ATM and public carrier networks.

Figure 11–8 shows the relationship of the B-ICI to other interfaces and protocols, notably, frame relay service (FRS), circuit emulation service (CES) for CBR traffic, cell relay service (CRS), and SMDS. All these technologies, as well as ATM, provide for the user-to-network interface, which is called either a UNI or a subscriber-to-network (SNI).

The B-ICI is designed for multiservice operations. Traffic can be submitted to a network in ATM cells, DS1/DS3 frames, frame relay frames, or SMDSs L2_PDUs. This traffic is sent across the B-ICI in the form of (1) ATM cells over ATM connections, (2) DS1 or DS3 frames (CES), which are encapsulated into AAL 1 PDUs, (3) frame relay frames, which are encapsulated into AAL 5 PDUs and mapped into ATM cells, or (4) SMDS L2_PDUs, which are encapsulated into AAL 3/4 PDUs or mapped directly into ATM cells.

The capacity for each user is assigned based on the type of traffic. Consequently, access classes for SMDS, and the committed information rate (CIR), and excess information rate (EIR) for frame relay pertain to this interface. Presently, dynamic bandwidth allocation is not provided.

The ATM B-ICI has considerable functionality. It is (in ITU-T terms) an interworking unit (IWU), which transmits and receives traffic from different systems. The term gateway is sometimes used to describe this function. The multiservice aspect of ATM is in keeping with ATM's design to support multimedia traffic.

For cell transfer between two ATM networks, the B-ICI specification requires that the two networks retain a relationship between a B-ICI connection and a UNI connection. For the transmission of DS1/DS3 frames, the DS1/DS3 VCCs should be translated to unique VCCs at the internetworking interface in order to avoid the use of duplicate VCC values (to those at the UNI). How this is performed is not defined in the standard but is left to the implementation of the carriers.

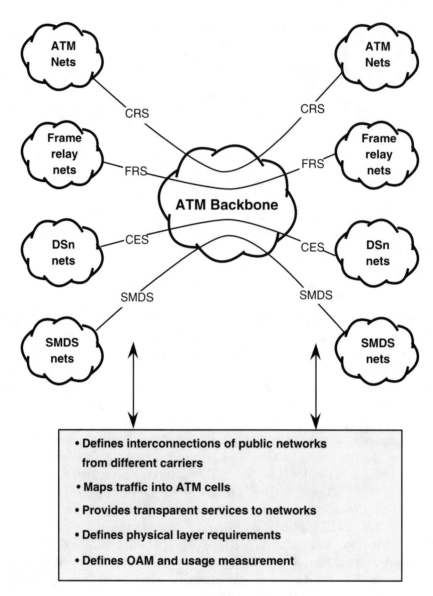

Figure 11–8
ATM B-ICI.

Frame relay frames are encapsulated into AAL 5 cells, and the DLCI is sent transparently through the networks and translated at the receiving frame relay interface. Alternately, if frames are mapped to the ATM layer, a DLCI must be translated into a VPI/VCI. Finally, SMDS L2_PDUs can be encapsulated into AAL 3 or 4 cells. Alternately, SMDS L2_PDUs can be mapped into specific VCC or VPC values.

Physical Layer Requirements at the B-ICI

The B-ICI physical layer requirements are closely aligned with the ATM UNI requirements for 155.520 Mbit/s STS3-c, 622.080 Mbit/s STS-12c, and 44.736 Mbit/s DS3. Likewise, the ATM layer at the B-ICI is almost identical to the UNI. Since these requirements are covered in other parts of this book, they will not be repeated (see Chapter 14 for this information).

Traffic Management at the B-ICI

Like the UNI, the B-ICI stipulates a traffic contract between networks—a carrier-to-carrier service contract. With few modifications, the generic cell rate algorithm (GCRA) is used at the B-ICI.

For each direction of transmission, the traffic contract consists of several parameters (some optional and some required): (1) a connection traffic descriptor, (2) a requested QOS class, and (3) a definition of a compliant ATM connection. These parameters include: peak cell rate, sustainable cell rate, burst tolerance, cell delay variability tolerance, and conformance definition based on the GCRA. The cell loss priority CLP bit may be used at the B-ICI.

Reference Traffic Loads

The B-ICI specification provides guidance on how the network operator can identify and manage traffic loads in view of complying with the performance objectives of a service contract. The approach is to characterize traffic loads by a utilization factor for a specific type of physical circuit at the B-ICI, as well as the type of traffic being carried on the circuit. Table 11–1 shows the reference traffic loads for three types of traffic: traffic load type 1 represents CBR traffic (DSn emulation), and traffic load types 2 and 3 represent VBR traffic. These traffic types are examined with three types of physical links: DS3 with PLCP cell mapping, SONET STS-3c, and SONET STS-12c. Table 11–1 also shows the number of active traffic sources that leads to the link utilization factor.

Table 11–1   Reference Traffic Loads for PVC Performance [ATM93a]

Reference Traffic Load Type	Link's Capacity	Number of Active Traffic Sources to Provide Link Utilization Factor	Link Utilization Factor
1	DS3 PLCP	20	0.86
1	STS-3c	73	0.85
1	STS-12c	292	0.85
2	DS3 PLCP	Not applicable	0.85
2	STS-3c	Not applicable	0.85
2	STS-12c	Not applicable	0.85
3	DS3 PLCP	66	0.70
3	STS-3c	242	0.70
3	STS-12c	969	0.70

To illustrate how the reference traffic load is used, consider the requirement for generating reference traffic load type 1. Apply the number of active sources listed in Table 11–1 to each link being tested. The utilization factor is derived from the total traffic from the active sources, with each source producing cells at a rate of 4,106 cells per second ([4106 = 1.544 Mbit/s] / [47 * 8 bits per cell]). For CBR traffic, the traffic from the same source must have a uniform distribution over a 244 μs interval (244 μs = 1/4106 cells a second). This source traffic type is compatible with the requirements for AAL 1, because of its support of 4,106 cells/sec. Other reference traffic loads are explained in section 5.1 of the ATM Forum B-ICI documents.

B-ICI Layer Management Operations

The B-ICI layer management operations use the B-ISDN/SONET/SDH F4 and F5 operations, administration, and maintenance (OAM) information flows. This topic is covered in Chapter 13 of this book, so it is not repeated here. On another level, the management operations are grouped into two categories of fault management and performance management. Fault management concerns itself with alarm surveillance and the verification of ongoing VP and VC connections. Performance management concerns itself with monitoring lost or misinserted cells, cell delay variations, and bit errors. The reader can refer to the section in Chapter 13 titled, "Operation and Maintenance (OAM) Operations" for more information on the F4 and F5 information flows.

SPECIFIC INTERNETWORKING SERVICES

We now turn our attention to the four specific services supported by the B-ICI. These four services are examined in this order:

PVC cell relay service (CRS)

PVC circuit emulation service (CES)

PVC frame relay service (FRS)

SMDS service

PVC Cell Relay Service (CRS)

The CRS is the most straightforward of the B-ICI multiapplication services. The physical interfaces are the same as those for a UNI, and performance and QOS is based on ITU-T I.35B and the ATM Forum UNI, which includes specifications on cell transfer delay, cell delay variation (CDV), misinsertion rate, error ratio, loss ratio, mean time between service outages, and mean time to restore. The interfaces and layers for CRS are depicted in Figure 11–9.

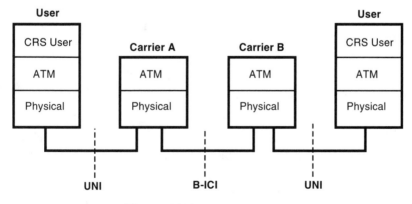

Figure 11–9
CRS layers and interfaces.

PVC Circuit Emulation Service (CES)

The CES supports operations for inter-carrier DS1 and DS3 across the B-ICI. The grooming of these rates are not supported. Figure 11–10 shows three examples of CES configurations. These cases represent examples only, and other configurations are possible and permitted. In all three cases, AAL 1 is required to support unstructured data transfer (UDT: Traffic is not organized into blocks). As described in the AAL chapter, the AAL 1 convergence sublayer (CS) performs its typical operations of organizing the traffic into 47 octet PDUs, providing clocking operations, and supporting sequencing functions. At the receiver, CS also generates dummy AAL_SDUs to the user application in the event of DS1 or DS3 alarm indication signals (AIS). The segmentation and reassembly layer (SAR) generates (at the sender) the 1-octet header and processes this header at the receiver.

Referring once again to Figure 11–10, in case a, the DSn operations, and AAL1 occur at the user's customer premises equipment (CPE). For case b, Carrier B operates with an interworking unit (IWU). The reason for the placement of interworking functions in another machine is to monitor and measure (1) buffer overflows, (2) cell loss, (3) absence of user traffic (a starvation condition), and (4) length and time of the starvation on behalf of the CPE. Finally, for case c, IWUs are placed in the equipment of both carriers.

The interworking functions also compensate for loss of traffic that may occur when the ATM layer is not supporting the transfer rate of AAL 1. The IWU must be able to detect the loss of signal (LOS), loss of frame (LOF), and alarm indication signals (AIS) signals on the DSn channel (discussed in Chapter 13). As illustrated in Figure 11–11, these detections are mapped into ATM OAM cells, transported through the ATM network(s), and mapped into DS3 alarm signals for receipt by the other DS3 interface component.

PVC Frame Relay Service (FRS)

Figure 11–12 shows the structure and layers for internetworking frame relay networks with ATM networks. The interworking unit processes frames at the frame relay UNI with the user device using the Frame Relay Q.922 core procedures.

The IWF assumes the job of mapping functions between the frame relay network and the ATM network. At a minimum the following functions must be supported:

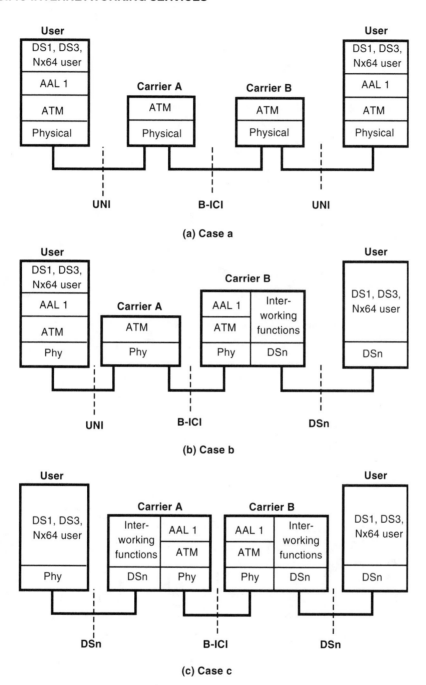

Figure 11–10
CES layers and interfaces.

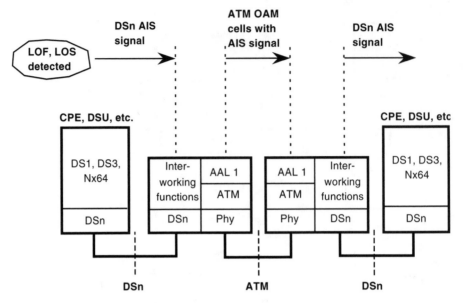

Figure 11–11
Mapping a DSn AIS into the ATM OAM cell.

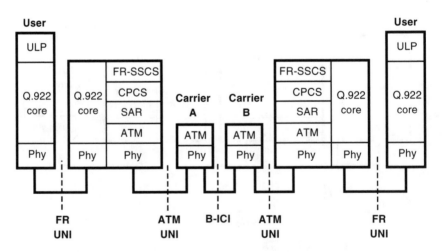

Figure 11–12
FRS layers and interfaces.

- *Variable length PDU formatting and delimiting:* Using AAL 5, support the frame relay 2 octet control field (required), and the 3 and 4 octet control field (optional)
- *Error detection:* Using CRC-32, provide error detection over the FR PDU
- *Connection multiplexing:* Associating one or multiple frame relay connections with one ATM VCC
- *Loss priority indication:* Mapping the frame relay discard eligibility bit and the ATM cell loss priority bit
- *Congestion indication:* Support of the frame relay forward and backward congestion notification features (within certain rules)

The FR-SSCS (frame relay-service specific convergence sublayer) FR-SSCS supports variable length frames at the FR UNI over preestablished connections (i.e., PVCs). Each FR-SSCS connection is identified with a Frame Relay data link connection identifier (DLCI: equivalent to the ATM VPI/VCI). Multiple FR-SSCS connections can be associated with one common part CS (CPCS).

The principal job of FR-SSCS is to emulate the FR UNI. In so doing, it supports frame relay forward and backward congestion notification (FECN, BECN), as well as the discard eligibility (DE) bit.

The CPCS is responsible for the following operations:

- Support of message mode (fixed-length blocks) or streaming mode (variable-length blocks) operations
- Assured operations: CPCS is responsible for traffic integrity (retransmission of lost or corrupted PDUs)
- Nonassured operations: CPCS is not responsible for traffic integrity

Figure 11–13 provides an example of the FRS operations. The interface between the frame relay entity and the AAL entity occurs through the frame relay core SAP (service access point) defined in the frame relay specifications. Therefore, the IWF must accommodate to the frame relay service definitions at this SAP. Ideally, the frame relay entity has no awareness of the AAL and ATM operations.

In accordance with the frame relay specifications, the service primitives contain up to five parameters: core user data, discard eligibility (DE), congestion encountered (CE) backward, congestion encountered (CE) forward, and connection endpoint identifier (CEI).

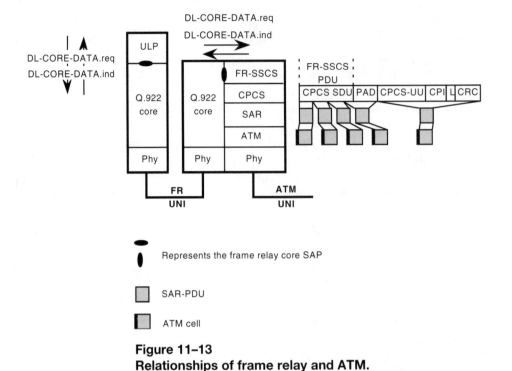

Figure 11–13
Relationships of frame relay and ATM.

The core user data parameter is used to convey data between the end-users in the frame relay service, and in Figure 11–13, it is represented by FR-SSCS PDU. The DE parameter is sent from the core service user to the service provider (FR-SSCS), and is mapped into the ATM CLP bit.

The two congestion parameters supply information about congestion that is encountered in the network. The congestion encountered forward parameter is used to indicate that congestion has occurred in transferring data to the receiving user. The congestion backward parameter indicates that the network has experienced congestion in transferring these units from the sending user.

The connection endpoint identifier (CEI) parameter is used to further identify a connection endpoint. For example, this parameter would allow a DLCI to be used by more than one user, and each user would be identified with a connection endpoint identifier value.

The AAL 5 PDU introduced in Chapter 7 (see Figure 7–25) is used to support frame relay and ATM interworking. As before, the CPI field is not yet defined. The CPCS-UU field is passed transparently by the ATM network. The length field is check for oversized or undersized PDUs.

CRC violations are noted, and a reassembly timer can be invoked at the terminating endpoint.

Traffic characterization at the B-ICI. Appendix A of the ATM Forum B-ICI specification provides guidelines on how to characterize frame relay traffic in terms of the ATM conformance parameters discussed in Chapter 9. The following parameters are described: (a) peak cell rate (PCR), (b) sustained cell rate (SCR), and (c) maximum burst size for CLP = 1 or 0. The reader is encouraged to read Appendix A of the ATM Specification, if more detailed information is needed.

SMDS Service

Figure 11–14 depicts the configuration and layers for the SMDS service offered by the B-ICI. The services offered by the IWF to SMDS are similar in concept to those described in the frame relay service (FRS): The IWF must transport SMDS traffic transparently through the ATM backbone network(s). It must map the SMDS PDUs into cells at the sending IWF and reassemble the cells into the SMDS PDUs at the terminating IWF. In addition, the IWF uses a specific, more detailed AAL 3/4 for its AAL operations. For this operation, AAL 3/4 invokes the common part convergence sublayer (CPCS), as well as the segmentation and reassembly sublayer (SAR). It uses the AAL 3/4 PDU described in Chapter 7. Therefore, this operation is not described again here, because it is

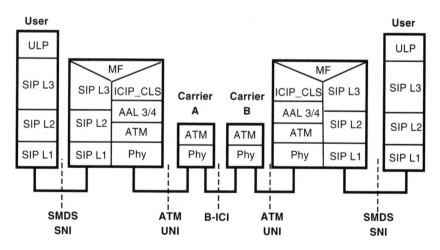

Figure 11–14
SMDS service layers and interfaces.

explained in the section titled "Type 3/4 Segmentation and Identification Operations" (specifically Figure 7–18 of Chapter 7).

Since SMDS is a connectionless service, the intercarrier interface protocol connectionless service (ICIP_CLS) layer maps the SMDS data units and the AAL PDUs. Its operations are consistent with the SMDS ICI specifications, as well as the ITU-T recommendations.

Figure 11–15 provides an example of the mapping between SMDS and ATM. This example shows the traffic flowing from the SMDS CPE to the ATM B-ICI. On the left side of the figure, the SMDS L3_PDU is processed by the SMDS interface protocol, layer 3 (SIP L3). Fields, such as BEtags, are discarded after all L2_PDUs have been reassembled into the L3_PDU.

Almost all the fields in the L3_PDU are simply mapped into the ICIP_CLS_PDU without alteration. In addition, these fields are also encapsulated into the ICIP_CLS_PDU user data field, as depicted by the dashed arrows in the figure.

The relationship of the SMDS L3_PDU fields and the

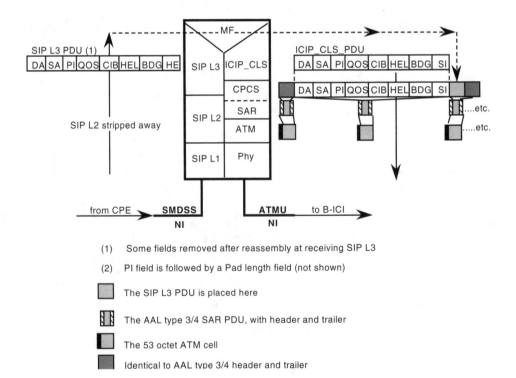

(1)   Some fields removed after reassembly at receiving SIP L3

(2)   PI field is followed by a Pad length field (not shown)

☐ The SIP L3 PDU is placed here

▥ The AAL type 3/4 SAR PDU, with header and trailer

■ The 53 octet ATM cell

■ Identical to AAL type 3/4 header and trailer

Figure 11–15
Relationships of SMDS and ATM.

ICIP_CLS_PDU fields are as follows. First, the destination address and source address are 8-octet fields. They each contain two subfields, the address type and the address. The address type field is 4 bits in length, the address is 60 bits in length. SMDS uses a 10-digit address with a prefix of 1 before the address in accordance with the ITU-T E.164 and the North American Numbering Plan (NANP). The address type field is coded as 1100 for an individual address and 1110 for group addresses. The bits that follow the 1100 code contain a prefix of 1 and then 10 digits of binary coded decimal (BCD) values. The remaining bits are coded as 1s. The ATM mapping functions (MF) simply map these addresses, without alteration, into the address fields of the ICIP_CLS_PDU.

The protocol identifier (PI) identifies the ICIP user, and (for the ATM B-ICI) service can range from the decimal values of 48 to 63. The PAD length (PL) field indicates that the octets in the PDU are 32-bit aligned, but is set to 0 for this operation.

The quality of service (QOS) field is not used, and is present (and set to all 0s) to ensure alignment with SMDS—which includes it to ensure alignment with the metropolitan area network (MAN), which does not define how it is used . . . (I did not make this up). The CRC 32 indication bit (CIB) is used to indicate the absence or presence of the CRC32 field. For B-ICI, it is set to 0.

The header extension length (HEL) is a 3-bit field indicating the number of 32-bit words that exist in the header extension (HE) field. It is set to 011 to indicate a 12-octet header extension field.

The bridging (BDG) field is used to insure alignment with SMDS (and MAN). The HE field contains service specific information (SI), including the ICIP version (version is 1), as well as carrier and explicit selection subfields (which are not yet defined).

Finally, the information (I) field (not shown in figure) can contain ICIP-user data, which can range from 36-9288 octets.

The header and trailer shown at the common part convergence sublayer (CPCS) is identical to the AAL 3/4 header (see Figure 7–17, Chapter 7).

ATM BACKBONES FOR LANS

Some people see ATM as a viable option for a LAN hub, and believe it will compete successfully with FDDI backbones (this writer is included in this group). The costs of ATM switches and line cards must come down. In addition, Ethernet hubs are proving to be successful, and are relatively inexpensive, but a recent study conducted by the Yankee Group and published by the *Broadband Networking News* [BROW94] made a cost/performance comparison of some of the new technologies, as they applied to local area networks. The analysis and forecast was based on ten users per media segment, and the costs and speed associated with the technology.

As this Figure 11–16 shows, the Yankee group contends that for now, and in the future, ATM offers the "biggest bang for the buck." Of course, all prices will drop, but this study reveals that ATM will continue to give the best overall cost/performance value. Jennifer Pigg, of the Yankee Group, said the study was made on 500 users.

As of this writing, several vendors offer ATM products for LAN hubs. Most are based on running ATM over existing physical layer technology. This most common implementations are illustrated in Figure 11–17. Subsequent discussions in this section will explain several alter-

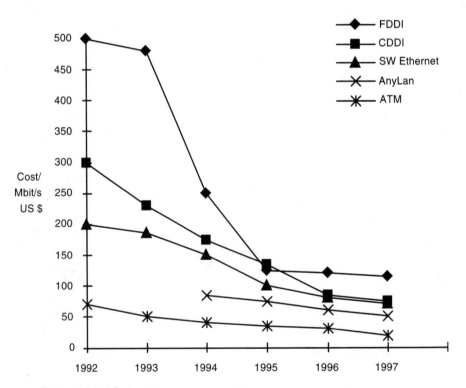

Figure 11–16
Forecast on cost/performance of new technologies (Based on 10 users per segment). [BROW94]

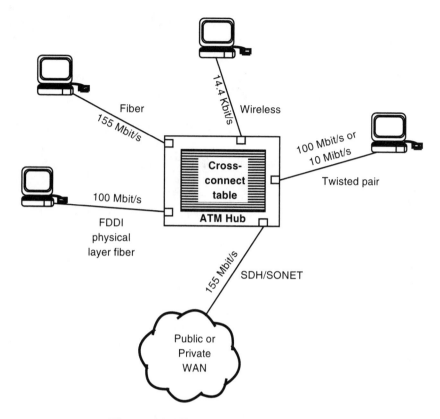

**Figure 11–17
ATM hub, examples of connections.**

natives for implementing the ATM hub. This discussion is based on my work with several hub and router vendors, RFC 1577, RFC 1483 [KING94] and [BELL94].

ATM LAN Emulation

As discussed in earlier chapters, ATM is a connection-oriented technology. It sets up virtual connections between two or more parties. The virtual connections are identified with virtual circuit IDs, known in ATM as virtual path identifiers and virtual channel identifiers.

Since LANs are connectionless and use media access control (MAC) addresses to identify communicating end stations (ES), some means must be provided to correlate MAC addresses with ATM identifiers. One approach is called LAN emulation. It is so named because an ATM backbone network operates between the LANs, and the LANs are unaware of this interface. The ATM network plays the role of a LAN. The approach is called LAN emulation, even though the ATM network may indeed be a LAN. But it does not use common LAN protocols, such as Ethernet.

As shown in Figure 11–18, the address resolution protocol (ARP) is used to translate and map the MAC addresses and ATM identifiers. A LAN emulation server (LES) provides the mapping service. When a LAN endstation sends a MAC frame to a router (which is called a LAN emulation client, or LEC), the router forms an ARP request with the destination MAC address in the target physical address of the ARP packet, and sends it to the LES. The LES retrieves the ATM id of the destination LES router, and returns it to the enquiring LES in an ARP response.

Next, this router sets up an ATM virtual connection with the desti-

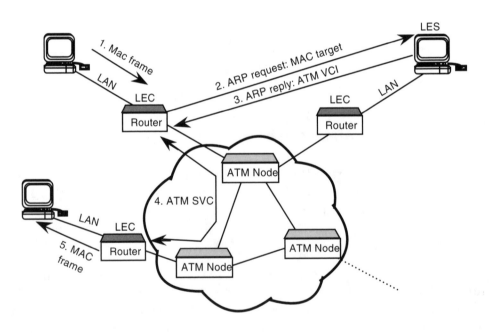

LES is LAN emulation server
LEC is LAN emulation client

Figure 11–18
ATM LAN emulation.

nation router through the ATM switched virtual call protocol, Q.2931. After the connection is established, traffic is placed into ATM cells and relayed to the destination router, which then strips away the ATM headers, reassembles the MAC traffic into a MAC frame, and delivers it to the destination ES.

ATM Edge Routers

The technique associated with the name edge routers is based on using network and/or subnetwork address (such as IP) to ATM VPI/VCIs. This work is part of RFCs 1577 and 1483, and is part of Netedge's architecture. It also uses the ATM multicasting operation with ARP to discover LANs that are connected to the ATM backbone. For example, a router sends an ARP with a target IP address. Those receiving routers that know about this address respond to the sending router with their ATM VPI/VCI. Thereafter, a Q.2931 operation is used to set up the virtual pipe for the transfer of the traffic. Of course, the connection can be left up if traffic warrants a nailed-up connection, which is likely the case for an ATM backbone through which LAN segments are connected.

The edge router approach is quite similar to LAN emulation, except by using network addresses instead of MAC addresses, the flexibility of subnetting can be employed. Subnetting allows an organization to divide an IP address from a relatively flat network and host structure to a more useful network and subnetwork and host structure. Thus, an organization can use only one IP-registered address, and assign the subnet address in a manner that is tailored to the organization's network topologies.

ATM Virtual Routers

Virtual routers are yet another variation for using ATM for LAN interconnections. This approach adds a special centralized route server to the LAN-ATM topology. It is a hardware-based device that assumes the responsibility for route discovery on the Internet, thus relieving the routers of this time-consuming task. When a relocated or new workstation issues a PDU from a LAN to a locally attached router, this router forwards the PDU to the route server. This server knows about the routes in the Internet, and it sends back to the router an ATM VPI/VCI through which a relevant destination router (and network) can be reached.

RFC 1483 AND RFC 1577

The Internet authorities have released two request for comments (RFCs) that describe how an ATM network is used to carry traffic of other protocols and networks. The ideas behind these RFCs are summarized in Figure 11–19. RFC 1483 describes two different methods for

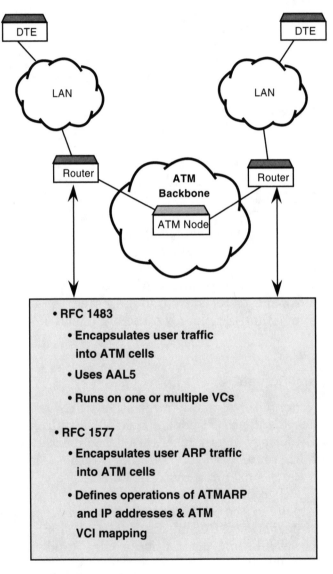

Figure 11–19
Major aspects of RFCs 1483 and 1577.

carrying connectionless network traffic over an ATM network. Para-phrasing, RFC 1483: the first method allows the multiplexing of multiple protocols over a single ATM virtual circuit. The protocol family of a transported PDU is identified by prefixing the PDU by an IEEE 802.2. logical link control (LLC) header. This method is called "LLC Encapsulation". The second method performs higher-layer protocol mul-tiplexing implicitly by ATM virtual circuits (VCs). It is called "VC Based Multiplexing".

RFC 1577 specifies how to carry IP datagrams and ATM address resolution protocol (ATM ARP) requests and replies over ATM adapta-tion layer type 5 (AAL 5). It also defines the role of an ATM ARP server, and the use of the ARP in resolving IP addresses and ATM virtual circuit IDs.

The ATM Data Exchange Interface (DXI)

The ATM data exchange interface (DXI) was developed to offload some of the more complex operations of ATM from a conventional cus-tomer CPE. This interface is abbreviated ATM DXI.

An additional piece of equipment the data circuit-terminating equipment for this operation is installed to support ATM DXI. It is usu-ally implemented with a data service unit (DSU) (see Figure 11–20). Once this equipment is installed, the CPE is relieved of the require-ments to support all the features of the ATM CS and the SAR. The CPE's principal job is to perform AAL 3/4, or AAL 5 CPCS encapsulation. Its only other requirement is to encapsulate this PDU into an ATM DXI frame. These operations are rather modest and do not require any signif-icant "refitting" of the CPE. The DSU performs the SAR operations and acts as the interface to the ATM network at the ATM UNI.

DXI Modes

DXI operates with three modes: Mode 1a is used only for AAL 5, mode 1b operates with AAL 3/4 and AAL 5, and mode 2 operates with AAL 3/4 and AAL 5.

The principal differences between these modes lie in how many vir-tual connections are allowed across the interface and the size of the user payload (SDU) that is permitted. Additionally, each mode defines slightly different headers and trailers that are created by the DTE and/or DCE at the CPCS sublayer. Table 11–2 summarizes the major features of the three DXI modes (not all modes are described in this section).

Figure 11–21 shows the relationship of the DTE layers and the DCE/SDU layers for AAL 5 traffic. The DTE DXI data link layer is

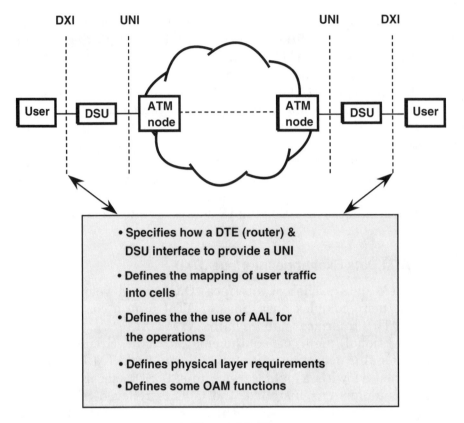

• Specifies how a DTE (router) &
  DSU interface to provide a UNI

• Defines the mapping of user traffic
  into cells

• Defines the the use of AAL for
  the operations

• Defines physical layer requirements

• Defines some OAM functions

Figure 11–20
ATM DXI.

closely related to an HDLC interface. Indeed, the use of HDLC-type frames eases the task of the DTE, because HDLC is well known and implemented in many products. The task of the DTE, is a relatively simple one to create a header that will provide enough information for the DCE to create a virtual circuit in the ATM network. In essence, the DXI header contains a DXI frame address (DFA), which is used to convey the VPI and VCI values between the DTE and DCE. The DFA is 10 bits in length for modes 1a and 1b, and 24 bits long in mode 2.

Figure 11–22 shows the activities for the support of AAL 5 in modes 1a and 1b. The basic idea is to convey the DTE SDU across the ATM DXI to the DCE. The SDU is nothing more than the I field of the particular AAL protocol. This figure shows that the DTE encapsulates the DTE SDU into the DXI frame. The headers and trailers of this frame are then used by the DCE to receive the traffic and establish the virtual connec-

Table 11–2   ATM Data Exchange Interface (DXI)

- *Mode 1a*
  Up to 1023 virtual connections
  AAL 5 only
  Up to 9232 octets in DTE SDU
  16-bit FCS between DTE and DCE

- *Mode 1b*
  Up to 1023 virtual connections
  AAL 3/4 for at least one virtual connection
  AAL 5 for others
  Up to 9232 octets in DTE SDU for AAL 5
  Up to 9224 octets in DTE SDU for AAL 3/4
  16-bit FCS between DTE and DCE

- *Mode 2*
  Up to 16,777,215 virtual connections
  AAL 5 and AAL 3/4 (2^{24-1}): one per virtual connection
  Up to 65,535 (2^{16-1}) octets in DTE SDU
  32-bit FCS between DTE and DCE

tion. The DCE is required to perform the ATM adaptation layer 5 common part convergence sublayer (AAL 5 CPCS) as well as AAL segmentation and reassembly operations (AAL 5 SAR). The DCE also contains the ATM layer, which is responsible for the management of the cell header.

This specification does not define the operations of the service specific convergence sublayer, which is defined in ITU-T recommendation I.363.

Figure 11–23 shows examples of several of the frames transported across the DXI. Figure 11–23(a) illustrates modes 1a and 1b for AAL 5. Figure 11–23(b) illustrates mode 1b with AAL 3/4. The intent of the operations in Figures 11–23(a) and (b) is to emulate frame relay encapsulation, which, once again, requires few changes to the installed DTE de-

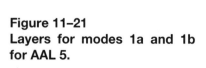

**Figure 11–21
Layers for modes 1a and 1b
for AAL 5.**

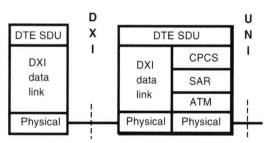

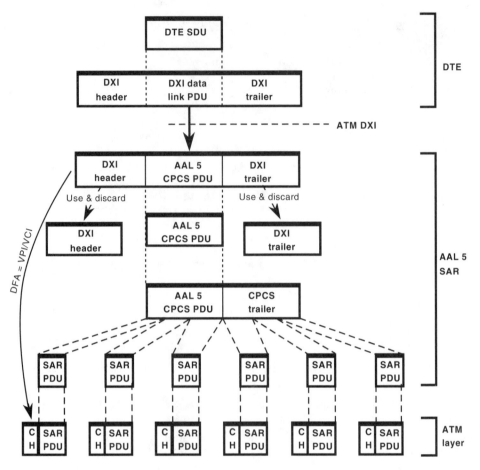

Figure 11–22
Modes 1a and 1b for AAL 5.

vices in the industry. Finally, Figure 11–23(c) shows the contents of the mode 2 data link frame.

The DXI header and trailer are variations of the HDLC/LAPD header and trailer (see Figure 11–24). The leading and trailing flags and the FCS fields are used in accordance with conventional HDLC operations. The DXI frame address (DFA) carries the bits for the VPI and VCI. Bits 6 through 3 of octet 1 represent the four least significant bits (LSBs) of the VPI. Bits 8 and 7 of octet 1 and bits 8 through 5 of octet 2 represent the six least significant bits (LSBs) of the VCI.

The four most significant bits (MSBs) of the VPI are set to 0 by the DCE on sending and ignored on receiving. Obviously, they are not coded

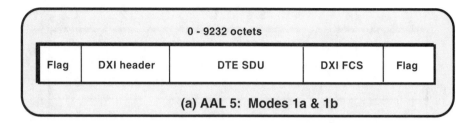

(a) AAL 5: Modes 1a & 1b

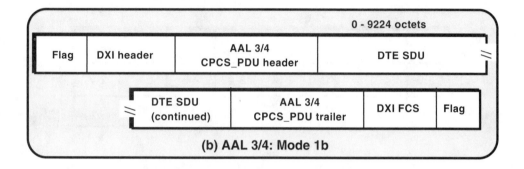

(b) AAL 3/4: Mode 1b

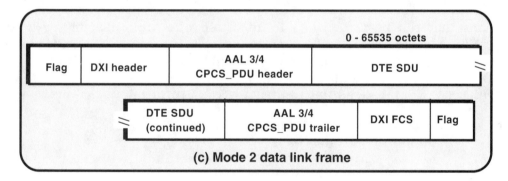

(c) Mode 2 data link frame

Figure 11–23
ATM DXI frames.

in the DFA field. The ten MSBs of the VCI are set to 0 by the DCE on sending and ignored on receiving; they are not coded in the DFA field, either.

The congestion notification (CN) bit is used by the DCE if the last ATM cell that composes the DXI frame has the payload type identification (PTI) field set to 01x. The cell loss priority (CLP) bit is copied from the CLP bit sent from the DTE into the ATM cell header. The DCE does not see this bit when traffic is sent from the DCE to the DTE.

Since DXI modes 1a and 1b restrict the number of virtual connec-

Bit	8	7	6	5	4	3	2	1	Octet
Flag	0	1	1	1	1	1	1	0	0
DXI Header	DFA						RSVD	0	1
	DFA				CN	RSVD	CLP	1	2

	8	7	6	5	4	3	2	1	Octet
DXI Trailer	2^8	2^9	2^{10}	2^{11}	2^{12}	2^{13}	2^{14}	2^{15}	n-1
(FCS)	2^0	2^1	2^2	2^3	2^4	2^5	2^6	2^7	n
Flag	0	1	1	1	1	1	1	0	n+1

Figure 11–24
DXI header and trailer for AAL 5.

tions that can be established to 1023, ten bits are sufficient for the VPI/VCI labels (2^{10-1} = 1023). And, since mode 2 permits 16,777,215 virtual connections, twenty-four bits are sufficient for the VPI/VCI (2^{24-1} = 16,777,215). Table 11–3 shows the mappings of the modes 1a and 1b 10-bit DFA and the mode 2 24-bit DFA to the VPI/VCI mappings.

DXI Support for Frame Relay

The following requirements must be met at the DXI for frame relay:

Frame relay QOS will remain intact from end-to-end

The frame relay user shall not be aware of the ATM operations

The frame relay DLCI must be mapped to the ATM VPI/VCI and vice versa

The frame relay DE bit must be mapped to the ATM CLP bit

QOS remains intact end-to-end

Order of frames will remain intact end-to-end

Congestion and flow control operations must be consistent end-to-end

Table 11–3   DXI DFA Mappings to ATM VPI/VCI

Address Mapping	DFA Octet	DFA Bit	VPI Octet	VPI Bit	VCI Octet	VCI Bit
MODEs 1A and 1B	1	6	2	8		
	1	5	2	7		
	1	4	2	6		
	1	3	2	5		
	1	8			3	2
	1	7			3	1
	2	8			4	8
	2	7			4	7
	2	6			4	6
	2	5			4	5
MODE 2	1	8	1	4		
	1	7	1	3		
	1	6	1	2		
	1	5	1	1		
	1	4	2	8		
	1	3	2	7		
	2	6	2	6		
	2	5	2	5		
	2	8			2	4
	2	7			2	3
	3	8			2	2
	3	7			2	1
	3	6			3	8
	3	5			3	7
	3	4			3	6
	3	3			3	5
	3	2			3	4
	4	8			3	3
	4	7			3	2
	4	6			3	1
	4	5			4	8
	4	4			4	7
	4	3			4	6
	4	2			4	5

SUMMARY

ATM is viewed as a transport mechanism for user multiapplication traffic as well as traffic from other networks. Generally, ATM internetworking entails encapsulating user-network PDUs into the ATM cell through the invocation of AAL 1, 3/4, and 5 modes.

The ATM DXI was published by the ATM Forum to provide a means of off-loading some of the more complex AAL and ATM functions from a user DCE.

Synchronous Optical Network (SONET)

INTRODUCTION

This chapter introduces the synchronous optical network (SONET), also known as the synchronous digital hierarchy (SDH). From the B-ISDN perspective, SONET and SDH provide the physical layer for ATM networks. For simplicity, the term SONET is used, instead of SONET/SDH.

This chapter is a review of the SONET material introduced in the flagship book for this series, *Emerging Communications Technologies*. The reader familiar with SONET can skip this chapter, and proceed to Chapters 13 and 14, which explain the OAM relationships of ATM and SONET, as well as other physical layer protocols and interfaces that are used by ATM. The reader should be familiar with the subject of networks and synchronization, discussed in Chapter 2, in the section entitled "Timing and Synchronization in Digital Networks."

PURPOSE OF SONET

SONET is an optical-based carrier (transport) network utilizing synchronous operations between the network components. The term SONET is used in North America, while the term SDH is used in Europe. SONET is:

- A carrier transport technology that provides high availability with self-healing ring topologies
- A multivendor approach allowing multivendor connections without conversions between the vendors' systems (with some exceptions)
- A network that uses synchronous operations with powerful, yet simple, multiplexing and demultiplexing capabilities
- A system that allows the direct access to low-rate multiplexed signals
- A network that is scalable to higher capacity as technologies improve
- A system that provides extensive OAM services to the network user and administrator

SONET provides a number of attractive features when compared with current technology. First, it is an integrated network standard on which all types of traffic can be transported. Second, the SONET standard is based on the optical fiber technology that provides superior performance vis-à-vis the older microwave or cable systems. Third, because SONET is a worldwide standard, it is now possible for different venders to interface their equipment without conversion operations (with some exceptions—depending on how the optional headers in the SONET frame are implemented).

Fourth, SONET efficiently combines, consolidates, and segregates traffic from different locations through one facility. This concept, known as grooming, eliminates back hauling and other inefficient techniques currently being used in carrier networks. Back hauling is a technique in which user payload (say, from user A) is carried past a switch with a line to A and sent to another endpoint (say, user B). Then, the traffic for B is dropped, and user A's payload is sent back to the switch and relayed back to A. In present carrier network configurations, grooming can eliminate back hauling, but it requires expensive configurations (such as back-to-back multiplexers connected with cables, panels, or electronic cross-connect equipment).

Fifth, SONET eliminates back-to-back multiplexing overhead by using new techniques in the grooming process. These techniques are implemented in a new type of equipment, called an add-drop multiplexer (ADM).

Sixth, the synchronous aspect of SONET makes for more stable network operations. Later sections in this chapter explain how synchronous networks experience fewer errors than the older asynchronous networks, and provide much better techniques for multiplexing and grooming payloads.

Seventh, SONET has notably improved OAM features relative to current technology. Approximately 5 percent of the bandwidth is devoted to OAM.

Eighth, SONET employs digital transmission schemes. Thus, the traffic is relatively immune to noise and other impairments on the communications channel, and the system can use the efficient time division multiplexing (TDM) operations.

PRESENT TRANSPORT SYSTEMS AND SONET

The present transport carrier system varies in the different geographical regions of the world. The structure is different in Japan than in North America, which is different than the structure in Europe. This disparate approach is complex and expensive, and makes the interworking of the systems difficult. Moreover, companies that build hardware and software for carrier systems must implement multiple commercial platforms for what is essentially one technology.

While SONET does not ensure equipment compatibility, it does provide a basis for vendors to build worldwide standards. Moreover, as shown in Figure 12–1, SONET is backwards compatible, in that it supports the current transport carriers' asynchronous systems in North America, Europe, and Japan. This feature is quite important because it allows different digital signals and hierarchies to operate with a common transport system, which is SONET.

FOUNDATIONS FOR SONET

SONET did not just appear suddenly on the scene. Extensive research work has been underway for over a decade on many of the features that are found in SONET. One of these projects was Metrobus, an optical communications system developed at AT&T's Bell Labs in the early 1980s. Its name was derived from its purpose: to be placed in a metropolitan area to serve as a high-speed optical transport network.

Metrobus demonstrated the feasibility of effectively using several new techniques that found their way into SONET. Among the more notable were: (1) single-step multiplexing, (2) synchronous timing, (3) ex-

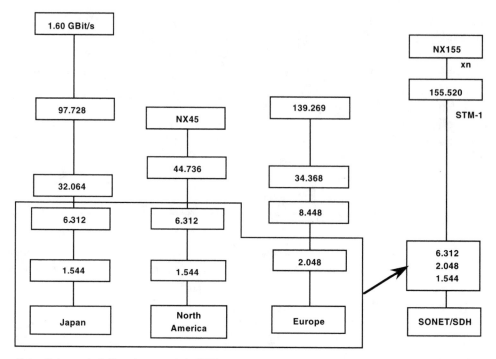

Note: Unless noted otherwise, speeds in Mbit/s

Figure 12–1
SONET support for current technologies.

tensive overhead octets, (4) accessing low-level signals directly, (5) point-to-multipoint multiplexing, and (6) the employment of 150 Mbit/s (146.432) media as the network transmission capacity. This latter decision, along with the ensuing research and testing, was important, because this signal rate can accommodate voice, video, and data signals, compressed HDTV, as well as exploit CMOS technology. Moreover, it permitted the use of relatively inexpensive graded-index, multimode fibers, instead of the more expensive single-mode fibers [LEE93], although single-mode fiber is now the media-of-choice for SONET.

SONET was developed in the early 1980s, and was submitted to the T1 Committee during this period. This initial proposal had a bit rate of 50.688 Mbit/s, a 125 μs signal, and a frame format of 3 rows by 265 columns (264 octets * 3 rows * 8 bits per octet * 8000 = 50,688,000). It did not arouse much interest until the Metrobus activity became recognized.

Later, using the innovative features of Metrobus, the SONET designers made modifications to the original SONET T1 proposal, principally in the size of the frame and the manner in which DS0, DS1, and DS3 signals were mapped into the SONET frame.

From 1984 to 1986, various alternatives were considered by the T1 Committee, which settled on the STS-1 rate as a base standard. During this time, the ITU-T had rejected the STS-1 rate as a base rate in favor of an STM-1 rate of 155.520 Mbit/s base rate. For a while, it appeared that the North American and European approaches might not converge, but the SONET frame syntax and structure were altered one more time to a rate of 51.84 Mbit/s, which permitted the rate to be multiplexed (concatenated) by an integer of three to the European preference of 155.52 Mbit/s. This work has resulted in almost complete compatibility between the North American and European approaches.

SYNCHRONOUS NETWORKS

Most digital networks in operation today have been designed to work as asynchronous systems. With this approach, each terminal (device) in the network runs with its own clock. These clocks are not synchronized from a central reference point.

The purpose of the terminal clock is to locate the digital 1s and 0s in the incoming data stream—a very important operation in a digital network. Obviously, if bits are lost in certain payloads, such as data, the traffic may be unintelligible to the receiver. What is more important, the loss of bits or the inability to locate them accurately can cause further synchronization problems. When this happens, the receiver usually does not deliver the traffic to the user, because it is simpler to discard the traffic than to initiate resynchronization efforts.

Because each clock runs independently of others, large variations can occur between the terminal's clock and the rate at which the data is received by the terminal. For example, experience has demonstrated that a DS3 signal may experience a variation of up to 1789 bit/s for a 44.736 Mbit/s signal.

Moreover, signals such as DS1s are multiplexed in stages up to DS2, DS3, and so on, and extra bits are added to the stream of data (bit stuffing) to account for timing variations in each stream. The lower level signals, such as DS1, are not accessible nor visible at the higher rates. Consequently, the original stream of traffic must be demultiplexed if these signals are to be accessed.

SONET is based on synchronous transmission, meaning the average frequency of all the clocks in the network are the same (synchronous) or nearly the same (plesiochronous). As a result of this approach, the clocks are referenced to a stable reference point; therefore, the need to align the data streams or synchronize clocks is less necessary, because the synchronous signals, such as DS1/CEPT1, are accessible, and demultiplexing is not needed to access the bit streams. Also, the synchronous signals can be stacked together without bit stuffing. For those situations in which reference frequencies may vary, SONET uses pointers to allow the streams to "float" within the payload envelope. Indeed, synchronous clocking is the key to pointers; it allows a flexible allocation and alignment of the payload within the transmission envelope.

This concept of a synchronous system is elegantly simple. By holding specific bits in a silicon memory buffer for a defined and predictable period of time, it is possible to move information from one part of a PDU (a payload envelope) to another part. It also allows a system to know where the bits are located at all times. Of course, this idea is "old hat" to software engineers, but it is a different way of thinking for other designers. As one AT&T engineer put it, "Since the bits are lined up in time, we now know where they are in both time *and* space. So, in a sense, we can now move information in four dimensions, instead of the usual three."

The U.S. implementation of SONET uses a central clocking source—for example, from a end office. This central office must use a highly accurate clocking source known as stratum 3. Stratum 3 clocking requires an accuracy of 1.6 parts in 1 billion elements. Chapter 2 provides more detailed explanations of synchronization, and clocking operations, and the accuracy levels of the stratum 1-4n clocks.

OPTICAL FIBER—THE BEDROCK FOR SONET

It is likely that the reader has at least a general understanding and appreciation of the advantages of using optical fiber as the transmission medium for a telecommunications system. This section will summarize the major aspects of optical fiber, with a few thoughts.

- Optical transmission has a very large information capacity. Gigabit/s rates are easily obtainable in today's systems.
- Optical fibers have electrically nonconducting photons instead of the electrons found in metallic cables such as wires or coaxial ca-

bles. This characteristic is attractive for applications in which the transmission path traverses hostile environments. For example, optical cables are not subject to electrical sparks or interference from electrical components in a building or computer machine room.

- Optical fibers suffer less loss of signal strength than copper wire or coaxial cables. The strength of a light signal is reduced only slightly after propagation through several miles of cable.
- Optical fibers are more secure than copper cable transmission methods. Transmission of light does not yield residual intelligence that is found in electrical transmission.
- Optical cables are very small (roughly the size of a hair) and weigh very little. For example, 900 copper wire pairs pulled through 1000 feet in a building would weigh approximately 4800 pounds. Two optical fibers, with protective covers pulled the same distance, weigh only 80 pounds and yet yield greater capacity.
- Optical fibers are relatively easy to install, and operate in high and low temperatures.
- Due to the low signal loss, the error rate for optical fibers is very low—a point made earlier in Chapter 6 in the discussion on the rationale for the size of an ATM cell

Without further ado, we now examine how SONET exploits the performance of optical fiber.

PERTINENT STANDARDS

The SONET architecture is based on standards developed by the American National Standards Institute (ANSI), and the Exchange Carriers Standards Association (ECSA). In addition, Bellcore has been instrumental in the development of these standards. Although SONET has been designed to accommodate the North American DS3 (45 Mbit/s) signal, the ITU-T used SONET for the development and publication of the Synchronous Digital Hierarchy (SDH).

Due to the complexity of implementing a system such as SONET, the SONET implementation in the United States is divided into three phases. Phase 1 is divided into the implementation of the basic transfer rates, multiplexing scheme, and testing of the frame formats. Phase 2 consists of a number of mapping operations into the optical envelope from other tributaries such as FDDI and ATM. Phase 3 deals with more

Table 12–1 SONET/SDH Standards

SONET Add-Drop Multiplex Equipment (SONET ADM) Generic Criteria, TR-TSY-000496, Issue 2 (Bellcore, September 1989).

Integrated Digital Loop Carrier System Generic Requirements, Objectives, and Interface, TR-TSY-000303, Issue 1 (Bellcore, September 1986) plus Revisions and Supplements.

Digital Synchronization Network Plan, TA-NPL-000436, Issue 1 (Bellcore, November 1986).

Synchronous Optical Network (SONET) Transport Systems: Common Generic Criteria, TR-TSY-000253, Issue 1 (Bellcore, September 1989). (A module of TSGR, FR-NWT-0000440.)

Transport Systems Generic Requirements (TSGR): Common Requirements, TR-TSY-000499, Issue 3 (Bellcore, December 1989). (A module of TSGR, FR-NWT-000440.)

Synchronous Optical Network (SONET) Transport Systems: Common Generic Criteria, TA-NWT-000253, Issue 6 (Bellcore, September 1990), plus Bulletin No. 1, August 1991.

Generic Reliability Assurance Requirements for Fiber Optic Transport Systems, TA-NWT-000418, Issue 3 (Bellcore, to be issued).

ANSIT1.101 Synchronization Interface Standards for Digital Networks.

ANSIT1.106, Digital Hierarchy-Optical Interface Specifications (Single-mode).

ANSIT1.102, Digital Hierarchy-Electrical Interfaces.

G.700 Framework of the Series G.700, G.800, and G.900 Recommendations.

G.701 Vocabulary of Digital Transmission and Multiplexing, and Pulse Code Modulation (PCM) terms.

G.702 Digital Hierarchy Bit Rates.

G.703 Physical/Electrical Characteristics of Hierarchical Digital Interfaces.

G.704 Synchronous Frame Structures Used at Primary and Secondary Hierarchical Levels.

G.705 Characteristics Required to Terminate Digital Links on a Digital Exchange.

G.706 Frame Alignment and Cyclic Redundancy Check (CRC) Procedures Relating to Basic Frame Structures Defined in Recommendation G.704.

G.707 Synchronous Digital Hierarchy Bit Rates.

G.708 Network Node Interface for the Synchronous Digital Hierarchy.

G.709 Synchronous Multiplexing Structure.

elaborate implementations to support operations, administration, maintenance, and provisioning (OAM).

The SONET standard has been incorporated into a synchronous digital hierarchy standard published by the ITU-T. In addition, Bellcore supports this standard on behalf of the United States Regional Bell Operating Companies (RBOCs). The relevant documents for SONET/SDH are listed in Table 12–1.

TYPICAL SONET TOPOLOGY

Figure 12–2 shows a typical topology for a SONET network. End-user devices operating on LANs (FDDI, 802.3, 802.5, etc.) and digital transport systems (such as DS1, E1, etc.) are attached to the network through a SONET service adapter. This service adapter is also called an access node, a terminal, or a terminal multiplexer. This machine is responsible for supporting the end-user interface by sending and receiving traffic from LANs, DS1, DS3, E1, ATM nodes, and others. It is really a concentrator at the sending site, because it consolidates multiple user traffic into a payload envelope for transport onto the SONET network. It performs a complementary, yet opposite, service at the receiving site.

The user signals, whatever they are, T1, E1, ATM cells, and the like, are converted (mapped) into a standard format called the synchronous transport signal (STS), which is the basic building block of the SONET multiplexing hierarchy. The STS signal is an electrical signal, and the notation in Figure 12–2 of "STS-n" means that the service adapter can multiplex the STS signal into higher integer multiples of the base rate. The base rate is 51.84 Mbit/s in North America and 155.520 Mbit/s in Europe. Therefore, from the perspective of a SONET terminal, the SDH base rate in Europe is an STS-3 multiplexed signal (51.84 * 3 = 155.520 Mbit/s).

The terminal/service adapter (access node) shown in Figure 12–2 is implemented as the end-user interface machine, or as an add-drop multiplexer. The latter implementation multiplexes various STS-n input streams onto optical fiber channels, which now is called the optical carrier signal, and designated with the notation OC-n, where n represents the multiplexing integer. OC-n streams can also be multiplexed and demultiplexed with this machine. The term "add-drop" means that the machine can add payload or drop payload onto one of the two channels. Remaining traffic passes straight through the multiplexer without additional processing.

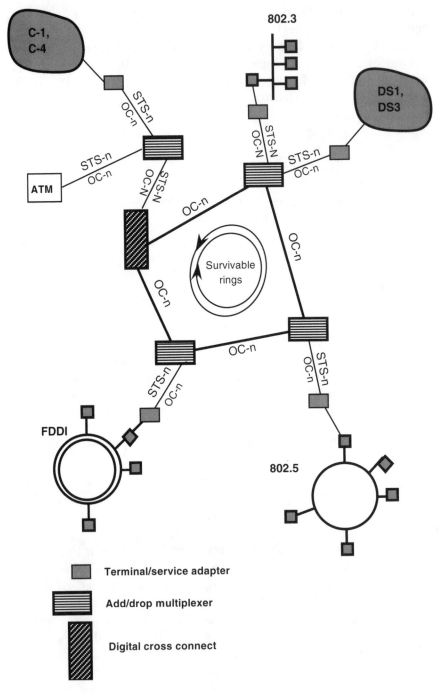

Figure 12–2
SONET topology.

The digital cross-connect (DCS) machine usually acts as a hub in the SONET network. It can not only add and drop payload, but it can also operate with different carrier rates, such as DS1, OC-n, and CEPT1, as well as make two-way cross-connections between them. It consolidates and separates different types of traffic. The DCS is designed to eliminate devices called back-to-back multiplexers. As we learned earlier, these devices contain a plethora of cables, jumpers, and intermediate distribution frames. SONET does not need all these physical components because cross-connection operations are performed by hardware and software.

The topology can be set up as either a ring or a point-to-point system. In most networks, the ring is a dual ring, operating with two optical fibers. The structure of the dual ring topology permits the network to recover automatically from failures on the channels and in the channel/machine interfaces. This is known as a self-healing ring and is explained later in this chapter.

While SONET establishes no strict requirements on how ATM operations relate to these SONET components, and, because implementations are vendor-specific, the ATM layer could reside at a SONET service adapter, an add-drop multiplexer, or a DCS. Later discussions in this chapter and in Chapters 13 and 14 explain the ATM and SONET relationships.

Figure 12–3 shows another example of a SONET topology and its multiplexing schemes. Service adapters can accept any signal ranging from DS1/CEPT1 to B-ISDN, as well as ATM cells. Additionally, sub-DS1 rates (such as DS0) are supported. The purpose of the service adapter is to map these signals into STS-1 envelopes or multiples thereof. As explained earlier, in North America all traffic is initially converted to a synchronous STS-1 signal (51.84 Mbit/s or higher). In Europe, the service adapters convert the payload to an STS-3 signal (155.520 Mbit/s).

Lower-speed signals (such as DS1 and CEPT1) are first multiplexed into virtual tributaries (VTs, a North American term) or virtual containers (VCs, an European term), which are sub-STS-1 payloads. Then, several STS-1s are multiplexed together to form an STS-n signal. These signals are sent to an electrical/optical (E/O) converter where a conversion is made to a OC-n optical signal.

SONET Configuration

Figure 12–4 shows a simplified diagram of a SONET configuration. Three types of equipment are employed in a SONET system: (1) path terminating equipment, (2) line terminating equipment, and (3) section ter-

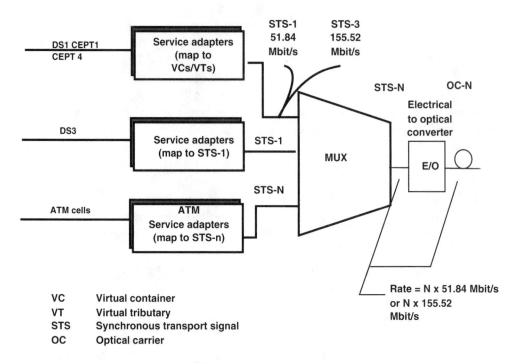

VC	Virtual container
VT	Virtual tributary
STS	Synchronous transport signal
OC	Optical carrier

Figure 12–3
SONET multiplexing.

minating equipment (regenerator). These components are introduced in this section and described in more detail later in the chapter.

The path terminating equipment is a terminal or multiplexer, and is responsible for mapping the user payload (DS1, CEPT4, FDDI, etc.) into a SONET format. It must extend to the network elements that assemble and disassemble the payload for the user CPE. The line terminating equipment is a hub. It provides services to the path terminating equipment, notably multiplexing, synchronization, and automatic protection switching. It does not extend to the CPE, but operates between network elements. The section terminating equipment is a regenerator. It also performs functions similar to HDLC-type protocols: frame alignment, scrambling, as well as error detection and monitoring. It is responsible for signal reception and signal regeneration. The section terminating equipment may be part of the line terminating equipment.

OAM at the three components.   Each of these components utilize substantial OAM information (overhead). Path level overhead is inserted at the SONET terminal and carried end-to-end to the receiving terminal.

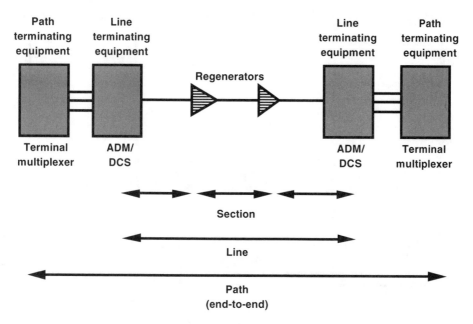

Figure 12–4
SONET configuration.

The overhead is added to DS1 signals when they are mapped into virtual tributaries.

Line overhead is used for STS-n signals. This information is created by line terminating equipment such as STS-n multiplexers. The SONET line concept is important to network robustness, because a line span is protected in case of line or equipment failure, or a deterioration of conditions. Functions operate at the line level to provide for alternate paths— an operation called protection switching. Part of the line overhead is used for protection switching.

The section overhead is used between adjacent network elements such as the regenerators. It contains fields for the framing of the traffic, the identification of the STS payload, error detection, order wires, and a large variety of network-specific functions.

SONET LAYERS

ATM has been designated by the ITU-T to operate with SONET. Figure 12–5 shows the relationship of the ATM layers and the layers associated with SONET. The virtual channel and virtual path layers of ATM run on top of the SONET physical layer.

The physical layer is modeled on three major entities: transmission

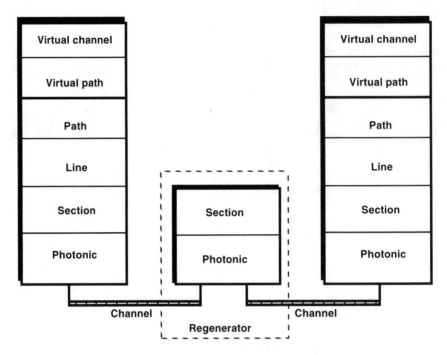

Note: Layer stacks may vary at multiplexers, switches and other line terminating equipment

Figure 12–5
A SONET/ATM layer configuration.

path, digital line, and the regenerator section. These layers correspond to the SONET section, line, and path operations that were introduced in the previous section.

The section and photonic layers comprise the SONET regenerators. The photonic layer is responsible for converting the electrical signal to an optical signal and then regenerating the optical signal as it is carried through the network. This stack may vary in different implementations. For example, at an ATM switch, the SONET path layer might not be accessed because it is intended as an end-to-end operation. The manner in which the layers are executed depends on the actual design of the equipment.

AUTOMATIC PROTECTION SWITCHING (APS)

One of the more interesting aspects of SONET is the provision for automatic protection switching or APS. This feature permits the network to react to failed optical lines and/or interfaces by switching to an alternate facility (as illustrated in Figure 12–6). Protection switching operations are initiated for a number of reasons. As an example, the network manager may issue a command to switch the working facility operations to the protection facility for purposes of maintenance or testing. Or, more commonly, APS operations are initiated because of the loss of a connection or the deterioration in the quality of the signal.

APS can be provisioned for a 1:1 or a 1:n facility. With the 1:1 option, each working facility (fiber) is backed up by a protection facility (fiber). With a 1:n option, one protection facility may service from one to a maximum of fourteen facilities.

As a general practice, the 1:1 operation entails the transmission of traffic on both the working and protection facilities. Both signals are monitored at the receiving end (the tail end) for failures or degradation of signal quality. Based on this analysis, the working or protection facility can be selected, and switching operations can be sent back to the sender (headend) to discern which facility is being employed for the transmission of the traffic.

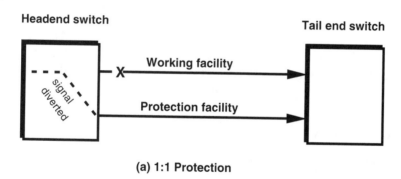

(a) 1:1 Protection

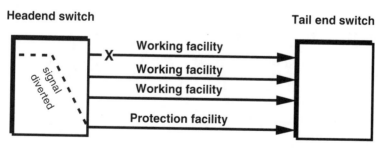

(b) 1:n Protection

Figure 12–6
Protection switching.

For the 1:n APS, the switching is reverted. That is to say, the traffic is sent across the working facilities and the protection facility is only employed upon the detection of a failure. So the protection facility is not employed until a working facility fails.

PAYLOADS AND ENVELOPES

SONET is designed to support a wide variety of payloads. Table 12–2 summarizes some typical payloads of existing technologies. The SONET multiplexer accepts these payloads as sub-STS-1 signals (or VTs).

Table 12–3 shows the relationships of the OC, and STS levels. The synchronous transport signal-level 1 forms the basis for the optical carrier-level 1 signal. OC-1 is the foundation for the synchronous optical signal hierarchy. The higher-level signals are derived by the multiplexing of the lower-level signals. As stated earlier, the high-level signals are designated as STS-n and OC-n, where n is an integer number.

As illustrated in Table 12–3, OC transmission systems are multiplexed by the n values of 1, 3, 9, 12, 18, 24, 36, 48, and 192. In the future, multiplexing integrals greater than 192 will be incorporated into the standard. Presently, signal levels OC-3, OC-12, and OC-48 are the most widely supported multiples of OC-1.

Envelopes

The basic transmission unit for SONET is the STS-1 synchronous payload envelope (SPE or frame). SDH starts at the STS-3 level. All levels are comprised of 8-bit octets transmitted serially on the optical fiber.

Table 12–2 Typical SONET Payloads

Type	Digital Bit Rate	Voice Circuits	T1	DS3
DS1	1.544 Mbit/s	24	1	—
CEPT1	2.048 Mbit/s	30	—	—
DS1C	3.154 Mbit/s	48	2	—
DS2	6.312 Mbit/s	96	4	—
DS3	44.736 Mbit/s	672	28	1

Table 12–3   SONET Signal Hierarchy

OC Level	STS Level	Line Rate (Mbits/s)
OC-1*	STS-1	51.840
OC-3*	STS-3	155.520
OC-9	STS-9	466.560
OC-12*	STS-12	622.080
OC-18	STS-18	933.120
OC-24	STS-24	1244.160
OC-36	STS-36	1866.230
OC-48*	STS-48	2488.32
OC-96	STS-96	4876.64
OC-192	STS-19	9953.280

*Currently, the more popular implementations
(Note: certain levels are not used in Europe, North
America, and Japan)

For ease of documentation, the payload is depicted as a 2-dimensional map (see Figure 12–7). The map is comprised of N rows and M columns. Each entry in this map represents the individual octets of a SPE. (The "F" is a flag and is placed in front of the envelope to identify where the envelope begins.)

The octets are transmitted in sequential order, beginning in the top lefthand corner through the first row, and then through the second row, until the last octet is transmitted—to the last row and last column (0_n).

The envelopes are sent contiguously and without interruption, and the payload is inserted into the envelope under stringent timing rules. Notwithstanding, a user payload may be inserted into more than one envelope, which means the payload need not be inserted at the exact beginning of the part of the envelope reserved for this traffic. It can be placed in any part of this area, and a pointer is created to indicate where it begins. This approach allows the network to operate synchronously, yet accept asynchronous traffic.

Figure 12–8 depicts the SONET STS-1 envelope. It consists of 90 columns and 9 rows of 12-bit octets, and carries 810 octets or 6480 bits. SONET transmits at 8000 frames/second. Therefore, the frame length is 125 microseconds (μs). This approach translates into a transfer rate of 51.840 Mbit/s ($6480 \times 8000 = 51,840,000$).

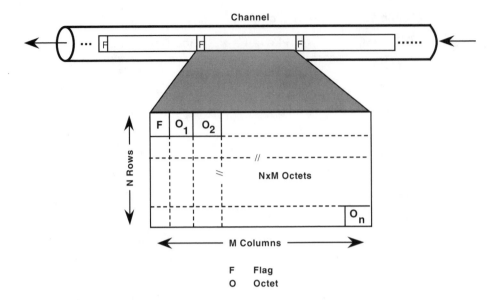

Figure 12–7
The synchronous payload envelope (SPE).

The first three columns of the frame contain transport overhead, which is divided into 27 octets, with 9 octets allocated for section overhead and 18 octets allocated for line overhead. The other 87 columns comprise the payload or STS-1 SPE (although the first column of the envelope capacity is reserved for STS path overhead). The section overhead in this envelope is also known as region overhead in certain parts of the world, and the line overhead is also known as the multiplex section. The frame consists of two distinct parts: the user SPE part and the transport part.

Since the user payload consists of 86 columns or 774 octets, it operates at 49.536 Mbit/s (774 * 8 bits per octet * 8000 = 49,536,000). Therefore, the user payload can support VTs up to the DS3 rate (44.736 Mbit/s).

The SDH envelope begins at STS-3. As shown in Figure 12–9, it consists of three STS-1 envelopes, and operates at a bit rate of 155.52 Mbit/s (51.840 × 3 = 155.52 Mbit/s). The STS-3 SPE has sufficient capacity to carry a broadband ISDN H4 channel.

The original SONET standard published by Bellcore had no provision for the European rate of 140 Mbit/s. Moreover, it was inefficient in how it dealt with the European 2.048 Mbit/s system. Bellcore and the T1 committee accommodated European requests and accepted the basic rate for SDH at 155.52 Mbit/s; other higher multiplexing rates were also ap-

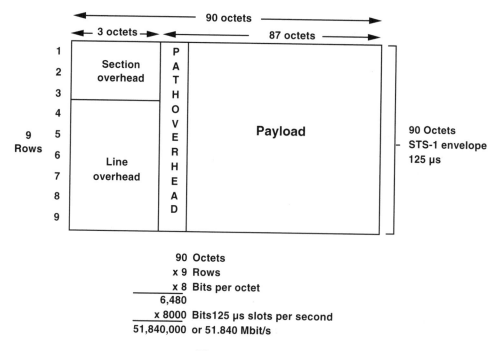

90 Octets
x 9 Rows
x 8 Bits per octet
_____
6,480
x 8000 Bits125 µs slots per second
_____
51,840,000 or 51.840 Mbit/s

**Figure 12–8
STS-1 envelope.**

proved. All parties worked closely to accommodate the different needs of the various administrations and countries, which resulted in a worldwide multiplexing structure that operates with North American, European, and Japanese carrier systems.

Mapping ATM Cells into the SONET Envelope

Figure 12–9 shows that ATM cells can be mapped into the SONET envelope. The SONET header contains a byte called the H4 byte. It is used to point to the beginning of the first ATM cell in the payload. Since a 155.52 signal does not accommodate exactly an even multiple of 53 byte cells, ATM cells can run over an STS boundary. The H4 byte contains the position of the initial ATM cell. The position can vary from 0 to 52. In addition to the pointer operation for locating cells, an ATM receiver can also find the cells by checking any 5-octet sequence and determining if the fifth octet computes on the ATM header error control (HEC). The receiver continues to check 5-octet sequences until it computes on a valid HEC octet. This means the receiver has now found a

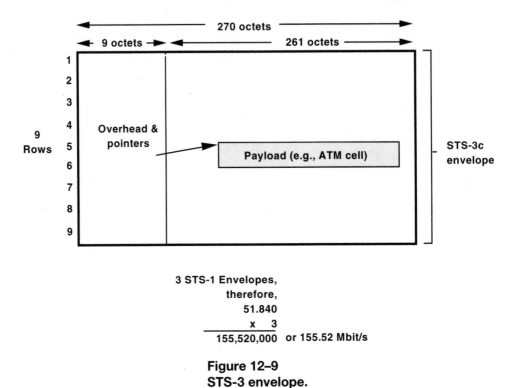

Figure 12–9
STS-3 envelope.

cell, and after several other checks, the receiver achieves synchronization on the cells.

PAYLOAD POINTERS

SONET uses a new concept called pointers to deal with timing variations in a network. The purpose of pointers is to allow the payload to
"float" within the envelope area. As Figure 12–10 shows, the SPE can occupy more than one frame. The pointer is an offset value (a variable)
that shows the relative position of the first octet of the payload. During
the transmission across the network, if any variations occur in the timing, the pointer is increased or decreased to compensate for the variation. While SONET is designed to be a synchronous network, different
networks may operate with different clocks at slightly different rates. So,
the pointers and the floating payload allow the network to make adjustments to these variations. In effect, payload pointers allow the existence
of asynchronous operations within a synchronous network.

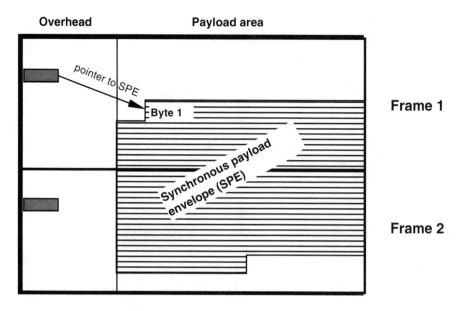

Overhead   **Payload area**

pointer to SPE

Byte 1

Synchronous payload envelope (SPE)

Frame 1

Frame 2

Figure 12–10
Floating payloads.

Traffic must be synchronized in the SONET network equipment before it is multiplexed. For example, as individual transport signals arrive at a multiplexer, they may be misaligned due to timing and bit rate differences. The bit rate variation could occur because of asynchronous operations between other equipment. The SONET equipment will synchronize the traffic such that: (1) the individual transport overhead octets are aligned and (2) payload pointers have been changed to adjust the user payload within the envelope. Therefore, two types of timing adjustments take place. One timing adjustment takes place within the SPE with pointers, and the other takes place with buffer adjustments at the receiver.

SONET makes pointer adjustments on a full octet (8 bits). Therefore, this large compensation requires complex and precise operations. The problem leads to jitter and has not yet been solved satisfactorily. Chapters 13 and 14 discuss this issue further.

MAPPING AND MULTIPLEXING OPERATIONS

This section expands the explanations in the previous sections, and shows more examples of the SONET mapping and multiplexing functions. One idea should be kept in mind when reading this section: A principal function of these operations is to create a payload format and syntax that is the same for any input (DS1, CEPT1, etc.) after the initial multiplexing and pointer processing is complete. Therefore, the T1 and CEPT1 rates of 1.544 Mbit/s and 2.048 Mbit/s respectively are mapped and multiplexed into a 6.912 Mbit/s frame. Then, these signals are multiplexed further into higher levels.

This section does not show all the mapping and multiplexing possibilities, but concentrates on the VT 1.5 group (1.544 Mbit/s) and the VC-12 group (2.048 Mbit/s). Figure 12–11 shows the VT 1.5, which multiplexes four DS1 systems. First, the bipolar code (BI) is converted to unipolar code (UNI). Each 1.544 Mbit/s DS1 signal is converted to a 1.728 Mbit/s virtual tributary. The additional bits are created to provide flags, buffering bits, conversion bits, and VT headers.

Even though bit stuffing is usually associated with asynchronous systems in which the bits compensate for speed differences between the input and output, SONET also uses the technique. The intent is to create constant output stream of 6.912 Mbit/s, which requires insertion of the stuffed bits.

The four DS1s are multiplexed to equal a 6.912 Mbit/s VT 1.5 output. Then the 6.912 Mbit/s output is input into additional multiplexing functions in which each VT has path, line, and section overhead bits added. In addition, pointer bits are added to align the VT payload in the SONET envelope. The result of all these operations is a 51.840 Mbit/s STS-1 signal.

The European CEPT1 is converted to a VT 2.0 (called VC-12 in Europe) signal of 6.912 Mbit/s (see Figure 12–12). It can be seen that the approach of the multiplexing scheme is to provide a preliminary payload output of 6.912 Mbit/s for all input streams.

For the CEPT1 conversion, 3 CEPT transmissions of 2.048 Mbit/s are input into the SONET conversion operation. The operation adds flags, buffering bits, and VT overhead bits, which equal 256 kbit/s. Therefore, each CEPT signal is converted to a 2.304 Mbit/s signal. 3 CEPT1 signals at 2.304 equal the desired 6.912 Mbit/s output stream. This stream is called the transmission unit group 2 (TUG-2) in the SDH standards.

Figure 12–13 shows how 28 DS1s are mapped into the DS1 payload, and how a DS3 transmission is mapped into the STS-1 payload. The two mappings in Figure 12–13 are taken from two separate operations on two separate input streams. They are shown together to illustrate how both input streams are mapped first to 48.384 Mbit/s, second to 50.112 Mbit/s, and finally to 51.840 Mbit/s.

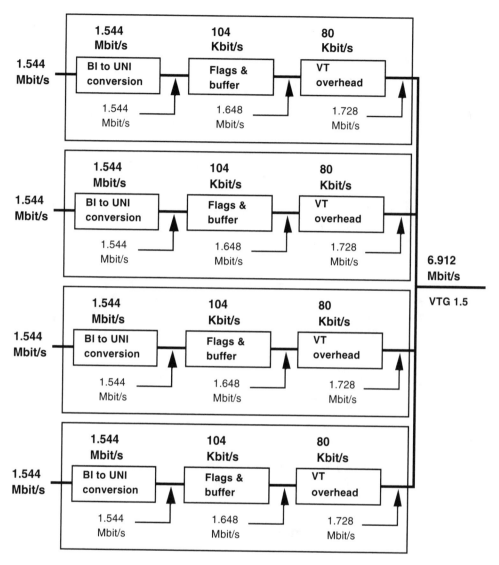

Figure 12–11
Virtual tributary (VT) 1.5.

The purpose of the initial multiplexing and mapping is to create an intermediate stream of 48.384 Mbit/s; thereafter, both DS1, CEPT, and DS3 transmissions are treated the same. All these transmissions have path, line, and section overhead bits added as well as the STS-1 pointer. The result is shown on the righthand side of the figure as the 51.840 Mbit/s STS-1 envelope.

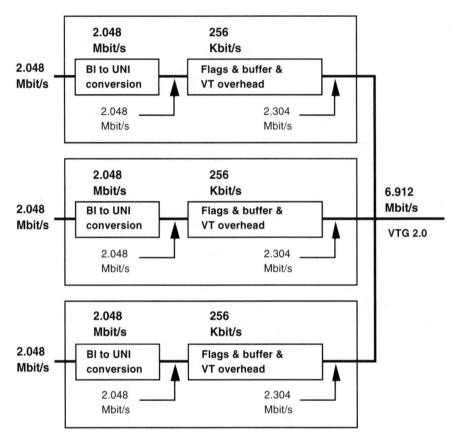

Figure 12–12
Virtual tributary 2 (VT 2.0) or tributary unit group 2 (TUG-2).

The Control Headers and Fields

Figure 12–14 provides a general view of the control fields used by the SONET equipment for control and signaling purposes. The section overhead and the line overhead make up the transport overhead that consumes nine rows of the first three columns of each STS-1 payload. This equals 27 octets allocated to the transport overhead. Nine octets are allocated for the section overhead and 18 octets are allocated for the line overhead. These fields are explained in the next chapter. On a more general note, headers are used to provide OAM functions such as signaling control, alarms, equipment type, framing operations, and error checking operations.

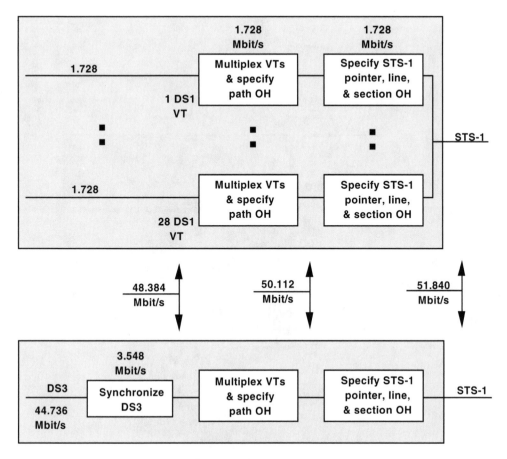

Figure 12–13
The STS-1 payload.

SONET EQUIPMENT

The next set of figures show the major equipment that is used in SONET networks. The terminal multiplexer, ADM, and building integrated timing system (BITS) are shown in Figure 12–15. The terminal multiplexer is used to package incoming T1, E1, and other signals into STS payloads for network use. The architecture of the terminal multiplexer consists of a controller, which is software driven; a transceiver, which is used to provide access for lower-speed channels; and a time slot interchanger (TSI), which feeds signals into higher-speed interfaces.

The add drop multiplexer (ADM) replaces the conventional back-to-back M13 devices in DS1 cross-connections. ADM is actually a synchro-

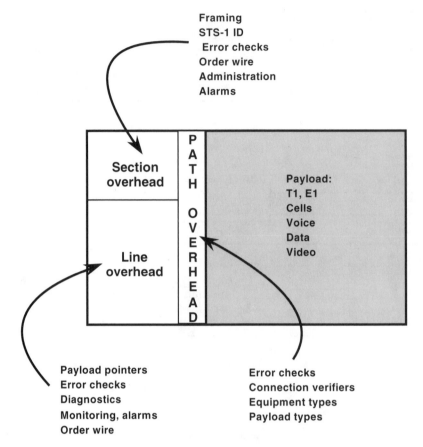

Framing
STS-1 ID
 Error checks
Order wire
Administration
Alarms

Section
overhead

P
A
T
H

O
V
E
R
H
E
A
D

Line
overhead

Payload:
T1, E1
Cells
Voice
Data
Video

Payload pointers
Error checks
Diagnostics
Monitoring, alarms
Order wire

Error checks
Connection verifiers
Equipment types
Payload types

Figure 12–14
SONET control fields.

nous multiplexer used to add and drop DS1 signals onto the SONET ring. The ADM is also used for ring healing in the event of a failure in one of the rings. The ADM can be reconfigured for continuous operations.

The ADM must terminate both OC-n connections as well as conventional electrical connections. The ADM can accept traffic from incoming OC-n and insert it into an outgoing OC-n. ADMs can also provide groom and fill operations, although this capability is not defined in the current Bellcore standards manuals.

The ADM multiplexers are required to convey the DS-n signals as are they are—without alteration. They operate bidirectionally, which means they can add-drop DS1, E1, and other signals from either direction. The ADM uses both electrical and optical interfaces, which are specified in great detail in the ITU-T and ANSI/Bellcore documents.

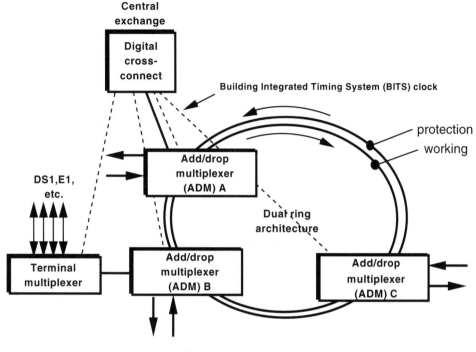

Figure 12–15
SONET equipment.

Timing is distributed to the network elements with the building integrated timing system (BITS), which is used at these elements to synchronize the output onto the lines.

It is conceivable that ADMs will become protocol converters as the technology matures. This means that instead of only providing simple multiplexing and bridging functions, they may also perform protocol conversion functions by internetworking SONET with LANs, SMDS, frame relay, and others.

The topology for the ring can take several forms. Figure 12–16 shows a simple arrangement, known as a unidirectional self-healing ring (USHR). Two fibers are used in this example; one is a working fiber, and the other is a protection fiber. In the event of a failure on a fiber or at an interface to a node, the ring will take corrective action (self-heal) and cut out the problem area. An example of this operation is provided shortly.

Although not shown in Figure 12–16, the topology can also be established to include four fibers and operate with a second arrangement, known as bidirectional SHR (BSHR), in which case traffic shares the

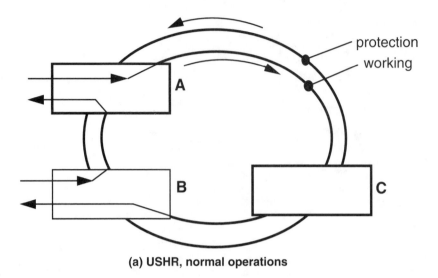

(a) USHR, normal operations

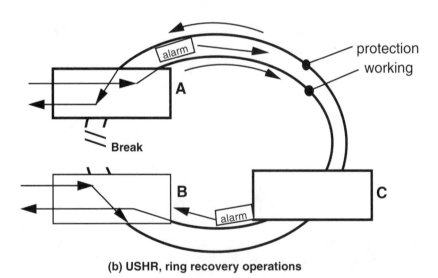

(b) USHR, ring recovery operations

Figure 12–16
Normal operations and ring recovery operations.

working and protection fibers between two nodes and traffic is routed over the shortest path between nodes.

Path protection switching (PPS) is achieved by using fields in the overhead headers. During normal operations (Figure 12–16[a]), STS-1 signals are placed on both fibers, so the protection fiber carries a duplicate copy of the payload, but in a different direction, and as long as the signals are received at each node on these fibers, it is assumed all is well. When a problem occurs, such as a fiber cut between nodes A and B, the network changes from a ring (loopback) network to a linear network (no loopbacks). In this example, node A detects a break in the fiber, and sends an alarm to the other nodes on the working fiber. The effect of the signal is to notify node B of the problem. Since node B is not receiving traffic on the protection fiber from node A, it diverts its traffic onto the fiber, as shown in Figure 12–16(b).

The digital cross-connects (DCSs) systems are used to cross-connect VTs, see Figure 12–17. One of their principal jobs is to process certain of the transport and path overhead signals and map various types of tributaries to others. In essence, they provide a central point for grooming and consolidation of user payload. The DCS is also tasked with trouble isolation, loopback testing, and diagnostic requirements. It must respond to alarms and failure notifications. The DCS performs switching at the VT level, and the tributaries are accessible without demultiplexing. It can segregate high bandwidth traffic from low bandwidth traffic and send them out to different ports.

Figure 12–18 shows the traffic on one ring (the outer ring of the two

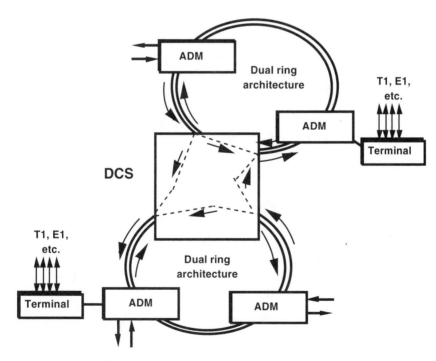

Figure 12–17
Digital cross-connects (DCS) systems.

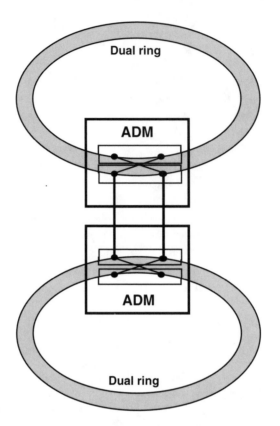

Figure 12–18
Multiple rings.

dual rings). Some traffic is relayed around the same ring and other traffic is diverted and cross-connected to the other ring.

For some applications, it may be necessary to provide extra capacity
in the system. For others, it may be necessary to ensure survivability of
the network in the event of problems. In either case, path protection
switching (PPS), and self-healing rings (SHRs) are employed, and in
some instances multiple PPS rings may be employed. An SHR is a collection of nodes joined together by a duplex channel. This arrangement is
quite flexible. The rings are connected together, but they are independent of each other, and can operate at different speeds. The rings can be
expanded by adding other ADMs, DCSs, and PPS rings to the existing
topology. The ADMs are called serving nodes. Any traffic that is passed
between the rings is protected from a failure in either of the serving
nodes. The small boxes within the ADM in Figure 12–18 depict selectors
that can pass the signals on to the same ring, or to the other ring.

Figure 12–19 shows one example of how SONET is being deployed.
Figure 12–19(a) is a typical non-SONET access network using the cur-

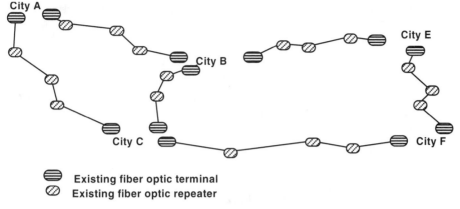

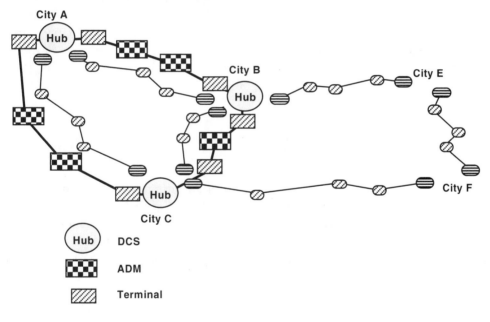

Existing fiber optic terminal
Existing fiber optic repeater

(a) Typical structure of the network

Hub   DCS

ADM

Terminal

(b) Overlaying the network

Figure 12–19
SONET development.

rent optical fiber technology. Most of the connections are point-to-point between high-density metropolitan areas that employ optical fiber terminals at each end, and, if necessary, repeaters on the line. Figure 12–19(b) shows how SONET is being used to improve and modernize the network. SONET is deployed between cities A, B, and C. This deployment occurs for a number of reasons: (1) growth of the subscriber base between these cities, (2) exhaustion of the current network's capacity, or (3) the desire to modernize the current T1/E1 system. Eventually, a SONET network could connect cities E and F.

PROGRESS IN SONET PENETRATION

SONET and SDH installations are used mostly for new or expanding systems. It is expected that older carrier systems will be rewired and replaced with SONET systems. Nonetheless, most estimates are that T1 and E1 will still be quite prevalent through the end of this century. Only time will tell, but recent announcements and deployments of SONET technology (as well as the drop in prices) lead this writer to think that most of the older technology will be replaced by SONET by the year 2000.

SUMMARY

Modern telecommunications and applications need increased carrier capacity for wide area transport service. Broadband WANs provide the answer, and SONET is being positioned to provide this high-speed transport service. From the perspective of the ITU-T and other standards groups, ATM will provide the switching operations for a B-ISDN with the underlying physical operations of the ATM traffic supported by the SONET operations.

Signaling: Operations, Administration, and Maintenance (OAM)

This chapter describes the network management operations for ATM, generally known as operations, administration, and maintenance (OAM) or in some installations, simply signaling. Since ATM and SONET are interrelated, the ATM and SONET OAM information flows F1-F5 are examined, as well as the section, line, and path overhead octets. The SONET alarm surveillance operations, including yellow signals and red alarms, are explained. The interim local management interface (ILMI) and the ATM MIB are also included in this chapter.

A brief note is in order about two terms used in this chapter. The term far-end receive failure (FERF) means the same as a newer term, remote detect indicator (RDI). I shall continue to use the term FERF because this term is used in more installations and specifications at this time.

THE NETWORK MANAGEMENT MODEL

Work is underway on many aspects of the ATM network management standards. Currently, five areas have been defined for an ATM network management model, and are illustrated in Figure 13–1. They are labeled M1 through M5 and are focused on the following activities:

M1 Management of ATM end devices

M2 Management of private ATM networks

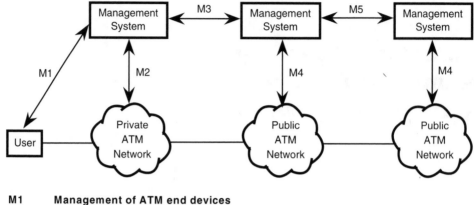

M1 Management of ATM end devices
M2 Management of private ATM networks
M3 Management of links between public and private networks
M4 Management of public ATM networks
M5 Management of links between public networks

Figure 13–1
ATM network management model.

M3 Management of links between public and private networks

M4 Management of public ATM networks

M5 Management of links between public networks

This figure shows the placement of these operations in the context of the ATM interfaces.

Be aware that these standards are not complete. It is anticipated that most of the work will be complete in 1995.

OPERATION AND MAINTENANCE (OAM) OPERATIONS

The OAM functions are associated with the hierarchical layered design of SONET/SDH and ATM. Figure 13–2 shows the five levels of the corresponding OAM operations, which are labeled F1, F2, F3, F4, and F5. F1, F2 and F3 functions reside at the physical layer; F4 and F5 functions reside at the ATM layer.

The Fn tags depict where the OAM information flows between two points. This numbering scheme is part of the B-ISDN architecture defined by the ITU-T I.610, and is a convenient tool to readily identify the

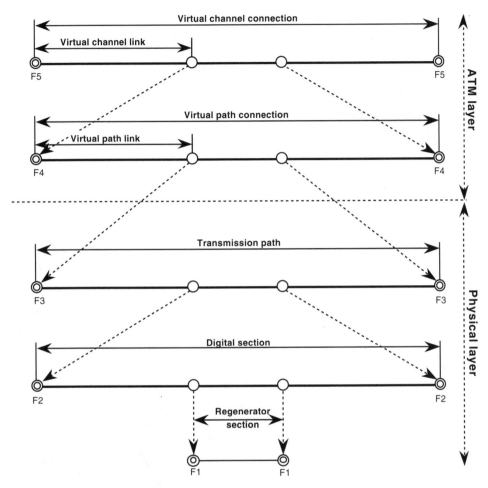

Figure 13–2
The hierarchical relationship. [I.311]

originating and terminating endpoint of an OAM message. The five OAM
flows occur as follows (see also Figure 13–3):

F5   OAM information flows between network elements (NEs) per-
       forming VC functions. From the perspective of a B-ISDN
       configuration, F5 OAM operations are conducted between
       B-NT2/B-NT1 endpoints. F5 deals with degraded VC perfor-
       mance, such as late arriving cells, lost cells, and cell insertion
       problems.

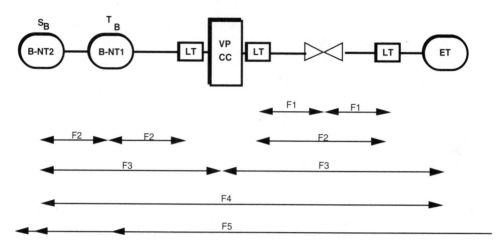

Figure 13–3
Information flows in the B-ISDN.

F4 OAM information flows between NEs performing VP functions. From the perspective of a B-ISDN configuration, F4 OAM flows between B-NT2 and exchange termination (ET. F4) OAM reports on an unavailable path or a virtual path (VP) that cannot be guaranteed.

F3 OAM information flows between elements that perform the assembling and disassembling of payload, header, and control (HEC) operations and cell delineation. From the perspective of a B-ISDN configuration, F3 OAM flows between B-NT2 and VP cross-connect and ET.

F2 OAM information flows between elements that terminate section endpoints. It detects and reports on loss of frame synchronization and degraded error performance. From the perspective of a B-ISDN configuration, F2 OAM flows between B-NT2, B-NT1, and LT, as well as from LT to LT.

F1 OAM information flows between regenerator sections. It detects and reports on loss of frame and degraded error performance. From the perspective of a B-ISDN, F1 OAM flows between LT and regenerators.

Figure 13–4 shows the SONET and ATM OAM flows from the context of their layers. F1, F2, and F3 OAM flows pertain to the SONET section, line and path layers respectively. ATM does not distinguish be-

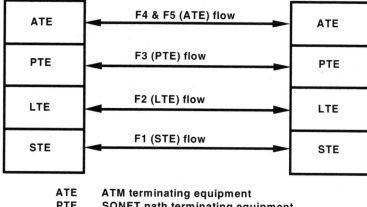

ATE   ATM terminating equipment
PTE   SONET path terminating equipment
LTE   SONET line terminating equipment
STE   SONET section terminating equipment

Figure 13–4
SONET and ATM OAM flows.

tween a VP and VC "layer," but F4 and F5 still describe the OAM flows between a VP and VC respectively.

ATM FUNCTIONS AT THE U- AND M-PLANES

The ATM layer management functions occur at the user plane (U-plane) and the management plane (M-plane) in the B-ISDN reference model.

U-Plane Operations

U-plane operations are discussed in several parts of this book. This section concentrates on management operations for the U-plane.

The U-plane provides several UNI support services. The information for these services are conveyed in the ATM cell header. The contents of this header are explained in Table 13–1. The reader should study the footnotes of this figure to obtain a more detailed understanding of these UNI operations. Many of the code points are somewhat generic, and their specific use is defined in other specifications or left to a user-specific implementation.

The ATM header is predefined for these operations. Metasignaling

Table 13–1 Predefined Header Field Values

Use	Octet 1	Octet 2	Octet 3	Octet 4
		Value[1,2,3,4]		
Unassigned cell indication	00000000	00000000	00000000	0000xxx0
Metasignaling (default)[5,7]	00000000	00000000	00000000	00010a0c
Metasignalling[6,7]	0000yyyy	yyyy0000	00000000	00010a0c
General broadcast signaling (default)[5]	00000000	00000000	00000000	00100aac
General broadcast signaling[6]	0000yyyy	yyyy0000	00000000	00100aac
Point-to-point signaling (default)[5]	00000000	00000000	00000000	01010aac
Point-to-point signaling[6]	0000yyyy	yyyy0000	00000000	01010aac
Invalid pattern	xxxx0000	00000000	00000000	0000xxx1
Segment OAM F4 flow cell[7]	0000aaaa	aaaa0000	00000000	00110a0a
End-to-end OAM F4 flow cell[7]	0000aaaa	aaaa0000	00000000	01000a0a

[1]"a" indicates that the bit is available for use by the appropriate ATM layer function (for example, ILMI).
[2]"x" indicates "don't care" bits.
[3]"y" indicates any VPI value other than 00000000.
[4]"c" indicates that the originating signaling entity shall set the CLP bit to 0. The network may change the value of the CLP bit.
[5]Reserved for user signaling with the local exchange.
[6]Reserved for signaling with other signaling entities (e.g., other users or remote networks).
[7]The transmitting ATM entity shall set bit 2 of octet 4 to zero. The receiving ATM entity shall ignore bit 2 of octet 4.
[8]"0" in VPI/VCI fields means VPI/VCI values can be present.

is used by a metasignaling protocol for the establishment and releasing of virtual channel connections. For PVCs, metasignaling is not used.

General broadcast signaling, as its name implies, is used to send broadcast information. How it is employed is network-dependent. It is not used in PVC operations. The F4 information flow is for OAM operations, discussed earlier.

The three bits in the cell header to identify the payload type is called the payload type identifier (PTI) (see Table 13–2). As the name

Table 13–2   Payload Type Indicator (PTI) Encoding

PTI Coding (MSB first)	Interpretation
000	User data cell, congestion not experienced, SDU-type = 0
001	User data cell, congestion not experienced, SDU-type = 1
010	User data cell, congestion experienced, SDU-type = 0
011	User data cell, congestion experienced, SDU-type = 1
100	Segment OAM F5 flow related cell
101	End-to-end OAM F5 flow related cell
110	Reserved for future traffic control and resource management
111	Reserved for future functions

Note: PTI values of 000–011 indicate user information
      PTI values of 100–111 indicate management information or are reserved

suggests, the main function of the PTI is to identify the type of information residing in the payload of the cell. It also is used for congestion notification and OAM operations. Code points 0-3 identify user cells, and the other code points identify OAM cells, and indications if congestion has or has not been experienced. Interestingly, the generic flow control field of the ATM cell header does not contain the congestion notifications, which are coded in the PTI field.

M-Plane Operations

M-plane operations are divided into three major categories for OAM services and are supported with the parameters in the cell header as shown in Table 13–3. This section will explain each of these services.

Fault management cells are sent to indicate a problem, such as a loss of a connection, a failed interface, or a failed component. Fault management cells are also used to provide loopback tests.

Performance management cells are used to monitor and report on the performance of connections. Statistics—such as errored cells, lost cells, or severely damaged cells—are reported with performance management operations.

The activation/deactivation function performs performance monitoring and continuity check of connections. It allows the activating and deactivating of cells for VPC/VCC management.

Table 13–3 OAM Services in the ATM Cell

Function	Services
Fault	Alarm surveillance with AIS (alarm indication signal)
Fault	Alarm surveillance with FERF (far-end receive failure)
Fault	Loopback
Fault	Continuity check
Performance	Forward monitoring
Performance	Backward reporting
Performance	Monitoring/reporting
Activation/deactivation	Performance monitoring (activation/deactivation)
Activation/deactivation	Continuity check

End-to-End and Segment Flows

Figure 13–5 shows the manner in which the OAM layer management traffic flows between a user device, a public ATM switch, and/or a private ATM switch. The flows are called F4 and F5 in accordance with the B-ISDN standards. The F4 flow is used for segment or end-to-end VP termination management, whereas the F5 flow is used for segment or end-to-end VC termination management. F4 is identified with VCI values 3 and 4; and F5 is identified by using the payload type identifier (PTI) code points of 4 and 5 (in Table 13–2).

The distinction between end-to-end and segment flow is defined in ITU-T I.610. Segment flow is considered one in which a single VP or VC link is identified, or a group of VPs or VCs are identified that fall within administration of a single network provider. So, an end user may or may not see any aspect of segment flows, since they are managed independently by the network provider.

The OAM layer management information flows may occur end-to-end, between private and public switches, or between the private switch and the user terminal/router.

The F4 and F5 operations. The F4 and F5 OAM information cell formats are illustrated in Figure 13–6. They are quite similar, and the basic differences pertain to the values in the VPI/VCI and PTI fields.

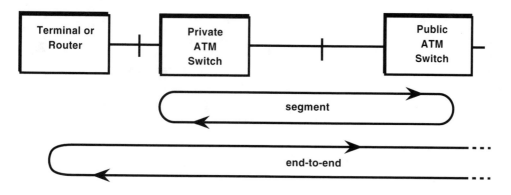

Notes:

Segment flow can take other forms: eg, within networks, etc.
F4 flow is for VPs
F5 flow is for VCs

Figure 13–5
OAM traffic flows.

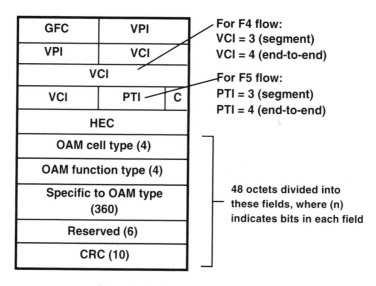

Figure 13–6
F4 and F5 information flows.

The F4 OAM cell format uses the VPI value that is the same as the user's cells, and identifies the F4 information flow as segment flow with VCI = 3, or end-to-end flow with VCI = 4. For the latter, this value identifies the connection between two end-to-end ATM layer management entities (LMEs).

For the F5 flow, both the VPI and VCI values are the same as the user cells, and the payload type (PT) field identifies the flow as segment flow (PT = 100), or end-to-end flow (PT = 101).

The OAM cell type is identified as fault management (0001) for both information flows. The function specific fields are coded in accordance with ITU-T recommendation I.610. Table 13–4 shows the coding for the function type field and the associated OAM type field.

The 360 bits are coded to provide more information about the specific OAM message. As of this writing, the ITU-T had not defined all the variations for this field. Later discussions provide examples of how this field is coded. The reserved field is not defined at this time, and is filled with zeroes. The 10-bit cyclic redundancy check (CRC) field detects an error in the 48-octet cell SDU. The receiving ATM entity will not process any corrupted OAM data units.

Table 13–4   Coding for Function Field

Function (cell type)	Value	Operation	Value
Fault management	0001	Alarm surveillance with alarm indication signal (AIS)	0000
Fault management	0001	Alarm surveillance with far end receive failures (FERF)*	0001
Fault management	0001	Cell loopback for connectivity verification	0010
Fault management	0001	Continuity check	0100
Performance management	0010	Forward monitoring	0000
Performance management	0010	Backward reporting	0001
Performance management	0010	Monitoring/reporting	0010
Activation/deactivation	1000	Performance monitoring	0000
Activation/deactivation	1000	Continuity check	0001

*Also called remote defect indicator (RDI) in some specifications

THE SONET OAM FUNCTIONS

Before proceeding further with the ATM F4 and F5 OAM flows, it is necessary to examine the OAM flows provided by the physical layer. This section introduces the SONET OAM operations and the F1, F2, and F3 operations. After this discussion, the F4 and F5 flows are examined in more detail.

Maintenance and Alarm Surveillance

SONET maintenance functions include trouble detection, repair, and restoration. To support these functions, SONET is designed with a number of alarm surveillance operations to detect a problem, or a potential problem. Before the surveillance operations are explained, the terms state, indication, and condition must be defined.

The term state describes an occurrence in the network that must be detected. A network element (NE) enters a state when the occurrence is detected and leaves the state when the occurrence is no longer detected. The detection of an occurrence may lead to an alarm being emitted by the NE, which is called an indication. An indication represents the presence of a condition.

Indications sometimes are not reported, but are available for later retrieval by an operating system (OS). Others may be reported immediately, as an alarm or a non-alarm indication.

Failure States

Several failure states are monitored by SONET NEs:

- *Loss of signal (LOS):* The LOS state is entered when a signal loss is detected. State is exited when two valid frame alignment flags are detected. Flags are introduced in Chapter 12.
- *Loss of frame (LOF):* The LOF state is entered when a NE detects four consecutive framing errors and is exited when alignment is detected for 3 ms.
- *Loss of pointer (LOP):* The LOP state is entered when a NE cannot interpret an STS or floating VT pointer in eight consecutive frames of VT super frames, or if eight consecutive new data flags are detected. The state is exited when a valid pointer with a correct new data flag is detected.
- *Equipment failures:* Equipment failures are vendor-specific, and include conditions such as CPU failure, and power failure.

- *Loss of synchronization:* Loss of synchronization is reported to OS upon detection of the loss of a primary or secondary reference.

Alarm Indication Signals (AIS), FERF, and Yellow Signals

The purpose of alarm indication signals (AIS) is to alert downstream equipment that a problem at an upstream NE has been detected. Different types of AISs are reported for the various layers. Figure 13–7 shows the relationships between the layers and AIS.

This figure shows two aspects of OAM. To address the first aspect, on the left of the figure are vertical (↑) arrows and their associated OAM indications. Their purpose is to inform the downstream entity of a failure. The position of the vertical arrows is meant to convey the following events (note that the AIS OAM flow is upstream to downstream):

1. An upstream section terminating equipment (STE) informs a downstream line terminating equipment (LTE) of a failure (a line AIS)
2. An upstream STE informs a downstream path terminating equipment (PTE) of a failure (an STS path AIS)
3. Upon detection of a failure, a line AIS, an STS path AIS, or an upstream STS PTE informs a downstream STS DTE of the fail-

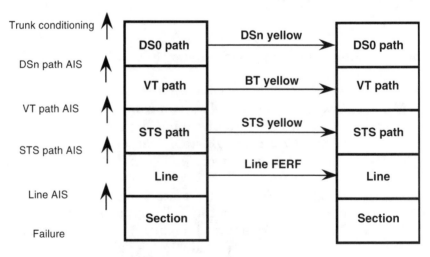

Figure 13–7
Maintenance signals and layers.

ure (a VT path AIS, DS3 AIS, or DS0 AIS, depending on the specific STS-SPE)

4. If DSn signals are being transported, a NE informs a downstream NE of the failure, or a termination of the DSn path (DSn AIS)

To address the second aspect, line far-end receive failure (FERF) is a SONET line-layer maintenance signal, and yellow signals are STS and VT path-layer signals. Yellow signals can be used for trunk conditioning, and are used by a downstream terminal to report an upstream terminal's failure to initiate trunk conditioning on the failed circuit. These signals are used for troubleshooting and trouble sectionalization [BELL89a].

The position of the horizontal arrows ($\rightarrow$) in Figure 13–7 is meant to convey the following events (note this OAM flow is the opposite AIS OAM flow; it is downstream to upstream):

1. A downstream LTE informs an upstream LTE of a failure along the downstream line (line FERF)
2. A downstream PTE informs an upstream PTE that a downstream failure indication has been declared along the STS path (STS path yellow)
3. A downstream VT PTE informs an upstream VT PTE that a failure indication has been detected along the downstream BT path (VT path yellow)
4. DSn yellow signals are generated from for failures or for DSn paths that are terminated (DSn yellow)

A number of factors lead to the use of DSn yellow signals, which is beyond our general descriptions for this chapter. The interested reader should consult Bellcore TR-TSY-000499 for more information.

Examples of Remedial Actions upon Entering a Failure State

Figure 13–8 provides an example of how NEs react to a failure. This example shows only a few actions among a wide array of possible actions. Obviously, the various types of AIS, FERF, and yellow signals sent between the NEs will vary, depending upon the nature of the failure.

Two parts of Figure 13–8 have not been explained—the red alarm and performance monitoring parameters. The red alarm is generated if an NE detects a failure state that persists for 2.5 seconds, or if the NE is subject to continuous, intermittent failures. The collection of per-

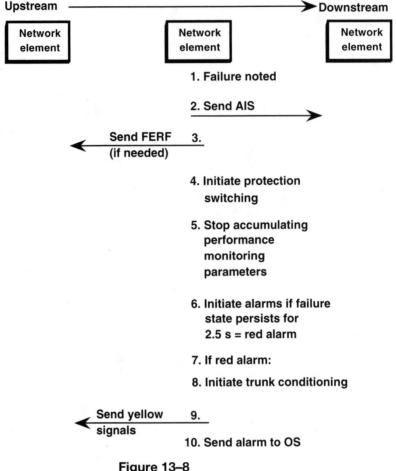

Figure 13–8
Example of OAM actions.

formance monitoring parameters is suspended during the handling of a failure state—after all, there is no meaningful performance on which to report.

THE OAM HEADERS

With a few exceptions, the alarm surveillance signals and other OAM signals are conveyed in the SONET headers. Figure 13–9 illustrates the three headers for a SONET frame. Each box in this figure is one octet of information.

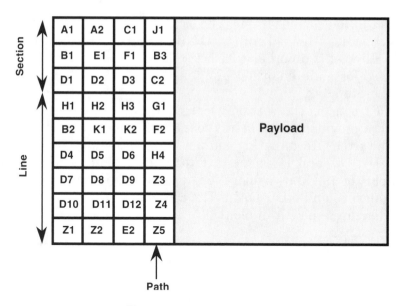

A1	A2	C1	J1
B1	E1	F1	B3
D1	D2	D3	C2
H1	H2	H3	G1
B2	K1	K2	F2
D4	D5	D6	H4
D7	D8	D9	Z3
D10	D11	D12	Z4
Z1	Z2	E2	Z5

Section

Line

Payload

Path

Figure 13–9
SONET overhead octets.

Section Overhead

The A1 and A2 octets are the framing octets. They are provided with all STS-1 and STS-n signals. The bit pattern is always 1111011000101000 in binary, or F628 in hexadecimal. The purpose of these octets is to identify the beginning of each STS-1 frame. The receiver initially operates in a search mode and examines bits until the candidate A1 and A2 pattern is detected. Afterwards, the receiver changes to the maintenance mode, which correlates the received A1 and A2 values with the expected values. If this mode detects the loss of synchronization, the search mode is then executed to once again detect the framing bits.

The C1 bit is used for STS-1 identification. It is a unique number that is assigned to each STS-1 of an STS-n signal. The C1 octet in the STS-1 is set to a number that corresponds to its order in the STS-n frame. The C1 value is assigned to each STS-1 signal before the signal is byte-interleaved into an STS-n frame. The C1 octet is simply incremented from zero through n to indicate the first, second, third, through n STS-1 signals to appear in the STS-n signal. The identifying number does not change in the STS-1 signal until byte-deinterleaving occurs.

The B1 octet is the bit interleaved parity (BIP-8) byte. SONET/SDH performs a parity check on the previously sent STS-1 frame and places the answer in the current frame. The octet checks for transmission errors over a section. It is defined only for the first STS-1 of the STS-n signal.

The E1 octet is an order wire octet. It is a 64 kbits/s voice path that can be used for maintenance communications between terminals, hubs, and regenerators.

The F1 octet is the section-user channel octet, and is set aside for the network provider to use in any manner deemed appropriate, but it is used at the section terminating equipment within a line.

The D1, D2, and D3 octets are for data communications channels and are part of 192 kbits/s operations used for signaling control, administrative alarms, and other OAM. The contents of these octets are left to the manufacturer-specific implementation.

Line Overhead

The line overhead occupies the bottom six octets of the first three columns in the SONET/SDH frame (shown in Figure 13–9). It is processed by all equipment except for the regenerators. The first two octets (labeled H1 and H2) are pointers that indicate the offset in octets between the pointer and the first octet of the synchronous payload envelope (SPE). This pointer allows the SPE to be allocated anywhere within the SONET/SDH envelope, as long as capacity is available. These octets also are coded to indicate if any new data are residing in the envelope.

The pointer action (H3) octet is used to frequency justify the SPE. It is used only if negative justification is performed. The B2 octet is a BIP-8 parity code that is calculated for all bits of the line overhead.

Octets K1 and K2 are the automatic protection switching (APS) octets. They are used for detecting problems with line terminating equipment (LTE) for bidirectional traffic and for alarms and signaling failures. They are used for network recovery as well.

All the data communications channel octets (D4-D12) are used for line communication and are part of a 576 kbits/s message to be used for maintenance control, monitoring, alarms, and so on.

The Z1 and Z2 octets had been reserved for further growth, and are now partially defined. The Z2 octet is now defined to support a line layer for n block error operation on a broad band ISDN UNI. Finally, the E2 octet is an order wire octet.

STS Path Overhead (STS POH)

The path overhead remains with the payload until the payload is demultiplexed finally at the end MUX (the STS-1 terminating equipment). Path overhead appears once in the first STS-1 of the STS-Nc. The path overhead octets are processed at all points of the SONET/SDH system. SONET/SDH defines four classes provided by path overhead:

Class A Payload independent functions (required)

Class B Mapping dependent functions (not required for all payload types)

Class C User specific overhead functions

Class D Future use functions

All path terminating equipment must process class A functions. Specific and appropriate equipment also processes class B and class C functions.

For class A functions, the path trace octet (J1) is used to repetitively transmit a 64-octet fixed-length string in order for the recipient path terminating equipment to verify a connection to the sending device.

The BIP-8 (B3) is also a class A field. Its function is the same as that of the line and section BIP-8 fields, to perform a BIP-8 parity check calculated on all bits in the path overhead.

The path signal label (C2) is used to indicate the construction of the STS payload envelope (SPE). The path signal label can be used to inform the network that different types of systems are being used, such as SMDS or FDDI—something like a protocol identifier for upper-layer protocols. For ATM traffic that is loaded into the frame C2 is set to 00010011. It is also coded to indicate if path-terminating equipment is not sending traffic; that is to say, that the originating equipment is intentionally not sending traffic. This signal prevents the receiving equipment from generating alarms.

The path status octet (G1) carries maintenance and diagnostic signals such as an indication for block errors, for class A functions. For class B functions, a multiframe indicator octet (H4) allows certain payloads to be identified within the frame. It is used, for example, for VTs to signal the beginning of frames. It also can be used to show a DS0 signaling bit, or as a pointer to an ATM cell.

G1 is used when cells are transported over DS3 facilities. It serves to inform a receiving upstream node that a failure indication has been detected by a downstream node on the DS3 path.

For class B functions, the multiframe indicator octet (H4) is used for certain payloads to indicate the phase of the STS SPE in different length super frames. It can be coded to indicate up to forty-eight 125 ms phase boundaries.

For class C functions, the one F2 octet is used for the network provider. For class D functions, the growth octets of Z3 through Z5 are available.

ATM Use of the OAM Octets

It is evident from these discussions that the physical layer OAM is quite important to ATM. To reinforce this thought, Figure 13–10 shows an example of several OAM flows in relation to an ATM interface. These octets perform the following services:

J1   Verifies a continued connection between the two ATM switches (contents = user defined)

G1   Indicates an STS yellow signal (contents = the value 1 in bit 5)

B3   A BIP-8 calculation results on the previous STS SPE (contents = even parity calculation)

B2   A BIP-8 calculation results on the previous line overhead and STS-1 envelope (contents = even parity calculation)

Z2   Conveys back to the originator (as an FEBE, far-end block error) the error counts from the B2 calculations (contents = count in the Z2 octet of third STS-1)

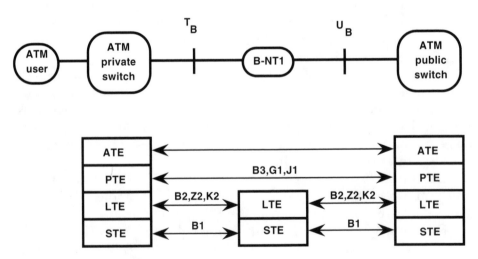

Figure 13–10
Example of OAM flow at the physical layer.

K2   Indicates a line FERF (far-end receive failure), and that the LTE is entering a LOS or LOF state (contents = 100 in bits 6, 7, and 8)

B1   A BIP-8 calculation results on all bits of the previous STS-N frame (contents = even parity calculation)

Using Payload Pointers for Troubleshooting Timing Problems

Chapter 2 describes how timing inconsistencies can create clocking variations in the network components, and Chapter 12 also introduces the SONET pointers, which are used to compensate for the variations. Chapter 14 explains how the pointers keep track of the payload. If problems occur, the network manager looks for two possible sources—an NE or the timing feed. As depicted in Figure 13–11, tests can be conducted with test sets to determine where pointer adjustments are being made. By working back toward the upstream NEs (test 1, test 2, test 3), the tests reveal a point where pointer adjustments are not being made; the NE will exhibit pointer adjustments on the output side, but not at the input side (test 2 and test 3). The next task is to determine if clock

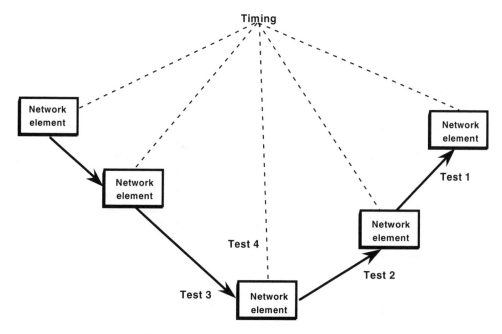

Figure 13–11
Troubleshooting timing problems.

recovery board in the NE is faulty, or if the BITS timing has been isolated from the NE (test 4).

OAM AT THE ATM LAYER

We now return to OAM at the ATM layer. This section shows some examples of ATM OAM operations. The examples are not exhaustive, but will give the reader an idea of how ATM OAM is implemented. Figures 13–4 and 13–5 provide useful references for our examination of ATM-layer OAM operations. The reader should review Tables 13–3 and 13–4 as well.

Fault Management

AIS and FERF. The physical layer OAM alarms can trigger ATM layer alarms. This relationship can be demonstrated by reviewing Figure 13–7, which is redrawn in Figure 13–12. The physical layer informs the ATM layer about a problem, which permits ATM to issue AIS/FERF cells. In this situation, the ATM alarms would identify a physical problem.

Figure 13–13 shows the relationships of the physical, VP, and VC AIS, and FERF operations. Be aware that this example represents only one combination of how these OAM operations are implemented. That is to say, physical-layer OAM actions do not necessarily have to invoke ATM-layer actions. Likewise, certain ATM actions can be generated in-

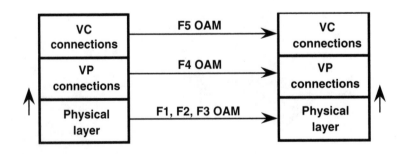

Figure 13–12
Relationship of physical and ATM layer OAM.

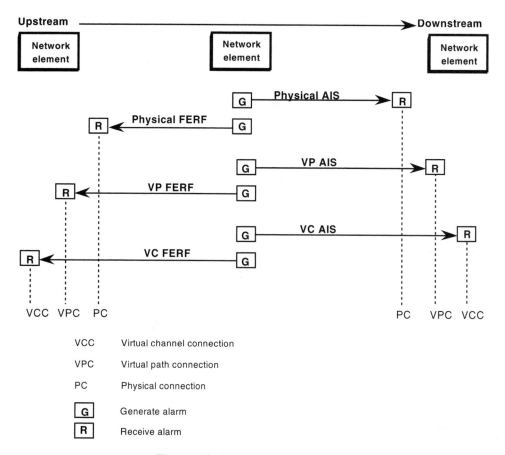

Figure 13–13
Relationship of the OAM alarms.

dependently of the physical-layer actions. For this example, ATM VPC and VCC AIS and FERF operations should generated due to the physical-layer defect.

Loopbacks. Figure 13–14 shows how ATM OAM loopbacks are performed. A network element generates the OAM cells and forwards them to another network element, which is responsible for returning them (the loopback) to the generating network element. The cells are used to isolate faults on channels and network elements, and to make certain the path is fully connected. They are used to perform a variety of tests, both for preservice and after the service has been initiated.

Each loopback cell contains the id of the generating network element and the ID of the network element that is to loop the cells back to

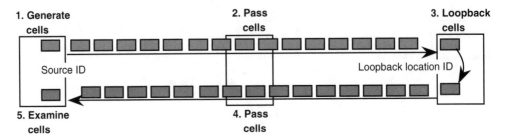

Figure 13–14
Loopback testing.

the originator. Any intermediate site must pass the cells on to the loop-back site (as cells go forward), and the generating site (as cells are returned). Each cell contains an identifier that is used to correlate related OAM cells, in case multiple loopbacks are occurring on the same connection.

Figure 13–15 shows the format for an OAM loopback cell. The OAM cell type is coded as 0001; the OAM function type is coded as 0010. The 360 bits specific to the OAM type are divided into the following fields:

- *Loopback indication:* A bit that is set to 1 before the cell is looped back. The loopback node sets the bit to 0, indicating it has been looped back.
- *Correlation tag:* Used to identify (correlate) related OAM cells within the same connection.
- *Loopback location ID:* An optional field that identifies the site that is to loop back the cell.
- *Source ID:* An optional field that identifies the site generating the cell.

Performance Management

Performance management entails the periodic evaluation of an ATM equipment and software. The goal is to assess the ATM system in a systematic way in order to determine how the network is performing, if components are deteriorating, and if error conditions are acceptable. VPC and VCC monitoring can be performed end-to-end or on VPC/VCC segments. Recall that a segment represents one part of a connection, such as one network provider (say, out of several that are part of the virtual circuit).

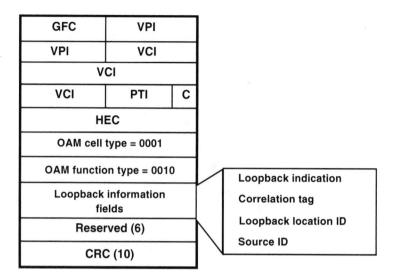

Figure 13–15
The OAM loopback cell.

Performance management consists of:

- *Forward monitoring:* Generating cells from one network element to a receiving network element
- *Backward monitoring:* At the receiving network element, checking the cells and reporting back to the generating network element
- *Monitoring/reporting:* Storing the results of the monitoring activities based on filtering selected parameters and thresholds

Figure 13–16 depicts the performance monitoring operations. A block of cells on one connection are sent to an endpoint. These cells are bounded by OAM cells, which are not part of the block. Each user cell in the block has a BIP-16 calculation performed on the user payload. An OAM cell (a forward monitoring cell), which contains the same VPC/VCC as the user cells, is inserted behind the block of cells containing the result of the BIP-16 calculation, as well as other information (explained shortly). In addition, the OAM cell contains a count of the number of user cells in the block. The blocks can vary in size, and an OAM cell can be inserted at times that do not interfere with ongoing operations.

The receiving network element receives the user and OAM cells and

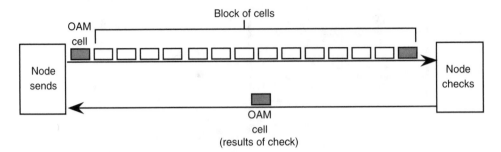

Figure 13–16
Performance monitoring.

compares the BIP-16 value in the forward monitoring OAM cell to a BIP-16 calculation it executed over the user cells. It also counts the number of cells in the block and compares this count with the count in the OAM header to determine if any cells have been lost or if extra cells have been inserted. This information is stored, and later sent back to the originator in the form of a backward reporting OAM cell.

These operations may occur in both directions, if the performance management system has been so configured.

Figure 13–17 shows the format for an OAM performance monitoring cell. The OAM cell type is coded as 0010; the OAM function type is coded as 0000, 0001, or 0010 in accordance with Table 13–4. The 360 bits specific to the OAM type are divided into the following fields:

- *Monitoring sequence number:* A sequence number in forward monitoring cells to detect missing of inserted cells
- *Total user cell number:* Number of user cells in the block sent before this OAM cell
- *BIP-16 value:* Value of the BIP-16 calculation on the user cells that have been sent since the last OAM cell
- *Timestamp:* An optional field to indicate when the OAM cell was inserted
- *Unused:* Not used, and coded to all 6A hex
- *Block error result:* Used in backward reporting cell to indicate how many errored parity bits were received in the forward monitoring OAM cell
- *Lost or inserted cells:* Used in backward reporting to indicate how many cells were lost or inserted

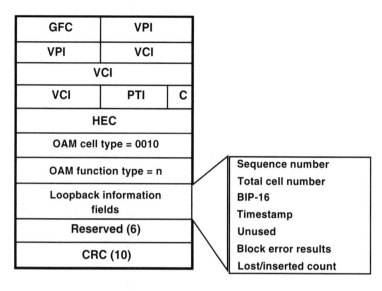

n = 0000, 0001, or 0010

Figure 13–17
The OAM performance monitoring cell.

Activation/Deactivation

Before the ATM VP/VC connections can be monitored, an end user or a network management system must initiate the OAM operations with a handshake (an activation). After the OAM operations are complete, another handshake is required to terminate these operations (a deactivation). The monitoring begins when one party (user, network management) sends an activate PDU. This party is called A. The responding party is called B. If this PDU is ACKed by B, the parties can execute the OAM described in the previous sections. If it is NAKed, no OAM can take place.

Figure 13–18 shows the format for an OAM performance monitoring cell. The OAM cell type is coded as 1000; the OAM function type is coded as 0000 or 0001 in accordance with Table 13–4. The 360 bits specific to the OAM type are divided into the following fields:

- *Message ID:* Identifies the type of message, coded as shown in Figure 13–18.
- *Directions of action:* Identifies the A-B, B-A, or two-way direction for the activation/deactivation

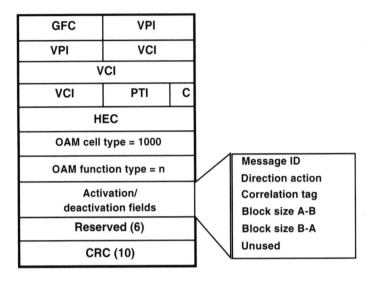

n = 0000 or 0001

Figure 13–18
Activation/deactivation cell.

- *Correlation tag:* Value to correlate requests and responses
- *PM block sizes A-B:* Indicates the size of the performance monitoring block; can be set to indicate block sizes of 128, 256, 512, or 1024 cells
- *PM block sizes B-A:* Same as above, except for the B-A direction
- *Unused:* Not defined

THE ATM MANAGEMENT INFORMATION BASES (MIBs)

The ATM network management activities have focused on the efforts of the ITU-T and the ATM Forum. The ITU-T has published several specifications on operations, administration, and maintenance (OAM) that deals with alarms, and performance monitoring.

Since the ITU-T work has not been completed, the ATM Forum has published several documents that deal with network management at the UNI and the NNI.

Theoretically, the ATM Forum specifications are "interim", in that they will go-away when formal international standards are in place. Realistically, once interim standards are in place, it is difficult to dislodge them.

The management information base (MIB) is one of the most important parts of a network management system. The MIB identifies the network elements (managed objects) that are to be managed. It also contains the unambiguous names that are to be associated with each managed object.

Network management protocols (such as CMIP and SNMP) rely on the MIB to define the managed objects in the network. The MIB defines the contents of the information carried with the network management protocols. It also contains information describing each network management user's ability to access elements of the MIB. For example, user A might have read-only capabilities to a MIB, while another user may have read/write capabilities.

Two MIBs have been defined for ATM network elements. They are examined and compared in the following sections.

THE INTERIM LOCAL MANAGEMENT INTERFACE (ILMI)

While ATM OAM specifies a number of management operations, it is not complete, and does not provide enough diagnostic, monitoring, and configuration services at the UNI. Therefore, the ATM Forum has published an interim local management interface, known as the ILMI. It uses the Simple Network Management Protocol (SNMP), and a management information base (MIB).

As depicted in Figure 13–19, the operations revolve around a UNI management entity (UME), which resides at each device that supports the ILMI. The UME accesses the ATM MIB through SNMP. SNMP runs on a well-known VPI/VCI value. The ILMI does not use IP addressing.

Each UME contains an SNMP agent and perhaps a management application. Adjacent UMEs must contain the same MIB. The MIB is specified in the Internet's registration tree. It is prefixed by 1.3.6.1.4.1.353.

The ATM management information at the UNI is represented in the MIB. Figure 13–20 shows the tree structure of the ATM UNI ILMI MIB. It is organized into seven major categories. The physical-layer category contains objects common to all VPCs and VCCs, as well as objects that are unique to VPCs and VCCs. The bottom part of the figure shows the values used to identify each major grouping.

As a general statement, the tree structure corresponds to one physical interface. If a machine has more than one interface, an interface index value is used to identify each interface. Thus, the use of the "Interface Index" value shown at the bottom of this figure.

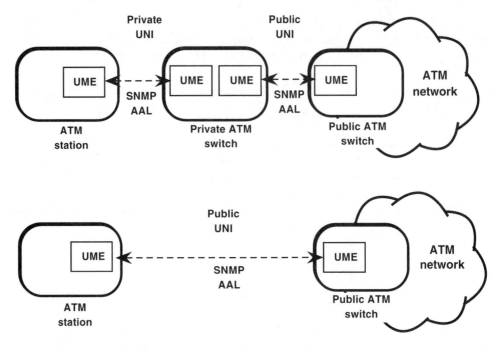

Figure 13–19
Interim local management interface (ILMI).

SNMP is used to manipulate the information in the MIB with Get, Get-Next, Set, and Trap operations. This part of the ILMI operates in accordance with Request for Comments (RFC) 1157.

The ILMI MIB Groups

Physical group. Each physical link (port) at the UNI has a MIB entry defined in the atmfPortTable. This table contains:

- A unique value for each port
- An address for the port
- The type of port (DS3, SONET, etc.)
- The media type (coaxial cable, fiber, etc.)
- Status of port (in service , out of service, etc.)
- Other information specific to the port

ATM layer group. This group includes objects pertaining to the ATM layer of a UNI interface. The atmfAtmLayerTable contains information about the UNI's physical interface. The table contains:

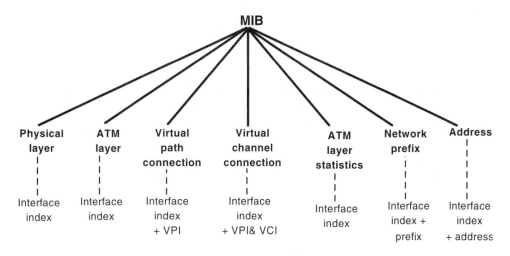

Figure 13–20
The ATM UNI ILMI MIB.

- The port ID (in MIB terms, the "Index"), which is a unique number to identify the port
- The maximum number of VCCs and VPCs supported and configured on this UNI
- The number of active VCI/VPI bits on the UNI (the number of bits in the header that can be used)
- An object to identify if the UNI port is public or private

Layer stastics group. The ATM stats group defines the atmfAtmStatsTable, which contains traffic statistics about the ATM layer at the UNI physical interface. The table contains:

- The port ID (index) that unambiguously identifies the physical interface
- Number of cells received and not dropped
- Number of cells received and dropped
- Number of cells transmitted across this interface

VPC and VCC groups. The virtual path and virtual channel groups define the atmfVpcTable and atmfVccTable respectively. These tables contain the following (similar) entries for the VPCs and VCCs on the UNI:

- The port ID (index) that unambiguously identifies the physical interface
- The VPI or VCI values for each connection
- The operational status (up, down, etc.) of the VPC/VCC
- Traffic descriptor parameters for the connection (both send and receive)
- QOS (send and receive) that this is applicable to the VPI or VCI.

Network prefix and address groups. Finally, these groups contain administrative and configuration information on addresses and interfaces.

ATM MIB (RFC 1695)

The IETF AToM MIB Working Group's efforts have been published as the ATM MIB in RFC 1695. Its purpose is to define a virtual store for ATM objects. This section provides an overview of the ATM MIB (it is almost a book unto itself, running 73 pages in length). Our focus is to gain a general understanding of RFC 1695; you can then study the RFC if more detailed information is needed. Figure 13–21 shows the structure of this MIB in relation to its object groups. Other objects are defined in the MIB, and will be explained shortly.

The ATM MIB Groups

Interface configuration group. The interface configuration group contains ATM layer information on local interfaces. The atmInterface-

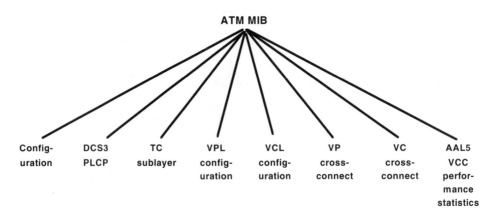

Figure 13–21
The ATM MIB object groups.

ConfTable contains this information, with one entry in the table per physical interface port. In this table are (as examples):

- The maximum number of VCCs/VPCs supported at each interface
- The number of active VCC/VPI bits in the cell header
- The values of VCI and VPI supporting the ILMI at each interface
- The type of address used at the interface (private, E.164, etc.)
- The IP address and textual name of the neighbor (the far-end node on this interface)

DS3 PLCP group.   The DS3 PLCP group contains DS3 PLCP configuration and state variable for ATM interfaces running over DS3. The atmInterfaceDs3PlcpTable contains this information, with one entry per port. In this table are:

- The number of DS3 PLCP severely errored framing seconds (SEFS)
- Indication if an alarm is present for the interface (yellow signal, loss of frame, none)
- The number of unavailable seconds encountered by the PLCP

TC sublayer group.   The TC sublayer group contains TC sublayer configuration and state variable for ATM interfaces using the TC sublayer over SONET or DS3. The atmInterfaceTC Table contains this information, with one entry per port. In this table are:

- The number of times the out of cell delineation events occur
- Indication if an alarm is present for the TC sublayer

The VPL and VCL groups.   The virtual path link group contains configuration and state information on each bidirectional virtual path link (VPL) at an ATM node. Likewise, the virtual channel link group contains similar information of virtual channel links (VCL). In this situation, a link is a segment of a VPC or a VCC. The concatenation of the VPLs or VCLs collectively form a VPC or VCC respectively. This idea is shown in Figure 13–22.

Each VPC/VCC is bidirectional. A virtual path and virtual channel identifier are used to identify the incoming and outgoing cells on each connection at the ATM device. Figure 13–23 shows this idea. As just explained, the associated VPLs for a connection form a VPC. The ATM

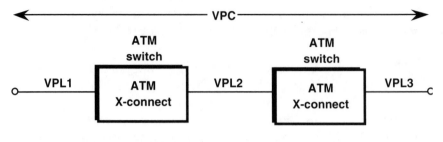

(a) VPC and associated VPLs

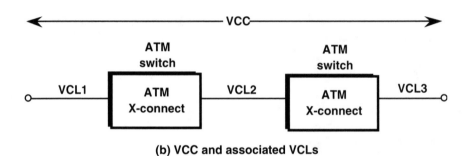

(b) VCC and associated VCLs

Figure 13–22
Associations of connections and links.

switch must map the VPI from an incoming port to an associated VPI on the outgoing port. This concept was explained in Chapter 8 (see Figure 8–5).

The VPL and VCL groups are defined by tables, with the OBJECT IDENTIFIERS of atmVplTable and atmVclTable respectively. They contain information on VPI and VCIs, as well as the values of the VPIs and VCIs.

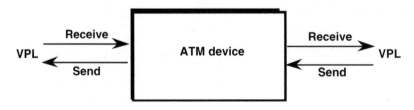

Figure 13–23
Bidirectional associations.

In addition, another table is used in conjunction with these tables. It is the traffic descriptor table, and is identified as atmTrafficDexcr-ParamTable. It contains information on traffic parameters and QOS classes for the receive and transmit directions for each ATM virtual link.

Figure 13–24 shows a general example of the traffic descriptor table and the VPL table. Be aware that this figure shows only parts of these tables, and "readable" names have been substituted for OBJECT IDEN-TIFIERS. The tables are referenced to each other with index pointers. The attractive aspect of this arrangement is that traffic parameters and QOS values need not be stored for each connection. The VPL (and VCL, not shown) have an index value that points to the relevant row of the traffic descriptor table. With this arrangement, traffic descriptor values can be changed easily and are not hard-coded to each connection.

In addition, each VPL and VCL can have different values for each direction of traffic flow (asymmetrical traffic flow). These directions are noted in Figure 13–23 as the Receive descriptor index and the Transmit cescriptor index. The traffic descriptor table also contains the traffic de-

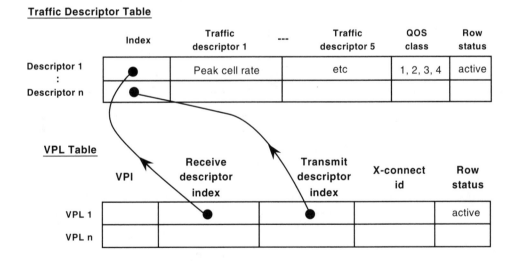

Traffic Descriptor Table

	Index	Traffic descriptor 1	---	Traffic descriptor 5	QOS class	Row status
Descriptor 1 :	●	Peak cell rate		etc	1, 2, 3, 4	active
Descriptor n	●					

VPL Table

	VPI	Receive descriptor index	Transmit descriptor index	X-connect id	Row status
VPL 1		●	●		active
VPL n					

Notes:

Column names are "readable" forms of OBJECT IDENTIFIERS in the MIB

Row entries are instances of the objects

Only selected parts of tables are shown

Figure 13–24
Example of tables in the ATM MIB.

scriptors for the connection, such as peak cell rate and sustained rate, as well as the QOS classes of 1, 2, 3, 4, which map to the AAL classes of A, B, C, D respectively. The row status column indicates if the connection is active, in a set up condition, and so on. For the VPL table, the column labeled X-connect ID is a value implemented only for a VPL that is cross-connected to other VPLs that belong to the same VPC.

The VP and VC cross-connect groups. The VP cross-connect group contains information on all VP cross-connects. It is used to cross-connect VPLs together in the ATM node. A unique value named atmVPCross-Connect Index is used to associate all related VPIs that are cross-connected. This table reflects three types of cross connects: (1) point-to-point; (2) point-to-multipoint, and (3) multipoint-to-multipoint.

Figure 13–25 shows an abbreviated, general view of the VP cross-connect table, which is named atmVpCrossConnectTable. Be aware that an identical table exists for VCs. As with the previous example, I have shown only part of this table, and "readable" names have been substituted for their OBJECT IDENTIFIERS. The terms low and high are used to represent the numerical values of the physical interfaces associ-

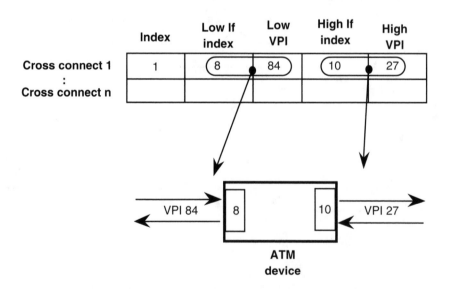

Note: Column names are "readable" forms of OBJECT IDENTIFIERS in the MIB

Figure 13–25
Example of the ATM cross-connect table.

ated with the VPC cross connect (the IfIndex in this figure). VPI 84 is associated with IfIndex 8, and VPI 27 is associated with IfIndex 10. Other parts of this table (not shown) are used with these entries to provide directional information. For example, the object atmVp-CrossConnectL2HOperStatus applies to the low-to-high direction, and the atmVpCrossConnectH2LOperStatus applies to the high-to-low status.

An entry to the cross-connect table is generated by a manager when a new connection is created at the ATM node. The row or rows in the table in Figure 13–24 are created, and a row status column is set to "create and wait." An agent then checks the requested ATM traffic parameters, QOS classes, and requested topology to ascertain if they are all consistent. As an example, the parameters for 8.84 receive direction must be equal to the parameters for 10.27 send direction. If all checks are satisfactory, the manager will set the row status column to "active." Then, an adminStatus column in set to "up" for all rows, which allows traffic flow to commence. Similar procedures are followed for setting up the VC cross connect table.

The AAL5 connection performance statistics group. The ATM MIB also contains objects pertaining to the performance statistics of a VCC at the interface associated with an AAL 5 entity. The aal5VccTable contains:

- The VPI value associated with the AAL 5 VCC
- The VCI value associated with the AAL 5 VCC
- Number of CRC-32 errors
- Number of discarded AAL 5 CPCS PDUs that were discarded because they were not fully reassembled during a required time
- Number of discarded AAL 5 CPCS PDUs that were discarded because the AAL 5 SDUs were too large

THE ILMI MIB AND THE ATM MIB

The ILMI MIB is intended for use at the UNI and not between the ATM switches. The ATM MIB is intended for use between ATM switches, and also contains LMI objects. Both MIBs contain many entries that are the same, even though the objects have different OBJECT IDENTIFIERS. The major differences is that the ILMI MIB does not have objects

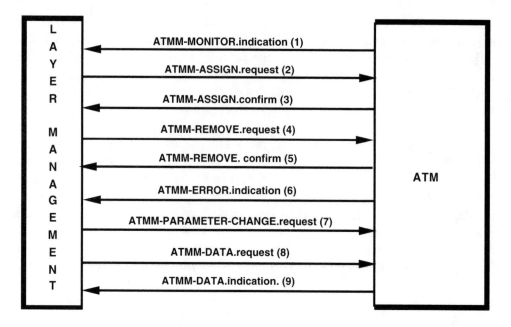

1. Issued by an ATM layer management entity (LME) to deliver the content of an ATM_PDU, to facilitate an OAM function

2. Issued by an ATM LME to request the establishment of an ATM link

3. Issued by an ATM to confirm the establishment of an ATM link

4. Issued by an ATM LME to request the release of an ATM link

5. Issued by an ATM to confirm the release of an ATM link

6. Issued by an ATM to indicate an error even and invoke appropriate management actions

7. Issued by an ATM LME to request a change in a parameter of the ATM link

8. Issued by an ATM LME to request transfer of a management ATM_SDU

9. Issued to an ATM to indicate the arrival of a management ATM_SDU

Figure 13–26
Layer management and ATM primitives.

pertaining to: (1) VP/VC cross connect configurations, (2) VCC AAL 5 CPCS layer performance, and (3) AAL 5 entity performance and configuration parameters.

THE LAYER MANAGEMENT/ATM PRIMITIVES

Earlier discussions in this book have explained the concepts of B-ISDN layer management (specifically, Chapter 5, Figure 5–2). The layer management service definitions are implemented with nine primitives. These primitives define the interactions between the ATM management entity and the ATM entity. The text below Figure 13–26 describes the functions of each of the primitives, so we shall not need to explain further.

TYPES OF SIGNALING

During the development of the ATM specifications, three types of signaling were considered: (1) packet signaling, (2) clear channel signaling, and (3) common channel signaling. These specifications pertain to SVCS and OAM. The latter was selected for the reasons stated below.

With packet signaling, each cell would contain both user plane and management plane information about that cell. This approach was not chosen because of its associated overhead, and the fact that not all cells need to be so identified. With clear channel signaling, a separate channel would be reserved for the management plane. This approach was not chosen, based on the experience with the ISDN D channel, which is used only a fraction of the time.

Status of Common Channel Signaling Standards

The common channel signaling has been chosen as a long-range solution, and as of this writing the pertinent documents are being developed by the ITU-T SG 13. It is based on many of the concepts of SS7, which uses a separate channel for signaling. Much of the work is complete, but no commercial implementations are available at this time. The reader can obtain this information from the ITU-T, by requesting the following documents: Q.73, Q.2100, Q.2110, Q.2130, Q.2140, Q.2120,

Q.2761-2764, Q.2951, Q.2953, Q.2957, Q.2731, Q.2733, Q.2737, and Q.2650.

SUMMARY

ATM networks implement extensive network management services, generally known as operations, administration, and maintenance (OAM). The ATM and SONET F1-F5 information flows provide a formal model for OAM messages.

The section, line, and path overhead octets of the SONET frame are used for alarm surveillance operations, as well as yellow signals and red alarms. The interim local management interface (ILMI) and the ATM MIB are published by the ATM Forum.

Physical Layer Services for ATM

INTRODUCTION

This chapter examines the B-ISDN concept of using SONET at the physical layer to support the ATM operations. In addition, the ATM Forum has defined three other physical layer operations to act as service providers to ATM. They are DS-3 for 44.736 Mbit/s operations, FDDI for 100 Mbit/s operations, and a private 155.52 Mbit/s UNI on twisted pair. This chapter examines each of these physical layer operations. The analysis begins with a look at the primitives that are passed between ATM and the physical layer. The chapter also shows and explains several examples of payload mappings.

Several of the operations described in this chapter make use of the OAM features supported in the SONET headers. We shall explain their contents briefly here, because they were covered in more detail in Chapter 13.

PHYSICAL LAYER OPTIONS FOR ATM

SONET/SDH is not the only physical layer that ATM can use. Indeed, it is likely that shielded twisted pair, unshielded twisted pair, and the FDDI physical (PHY) sublayer and physical media dependent (PMD) sublayer will used more than SONET/SDH. Figure 14–1 shows the choices that are emerging in the marketplace for an ATM physical layer.

The ATM Forum has released specifications on all these physical

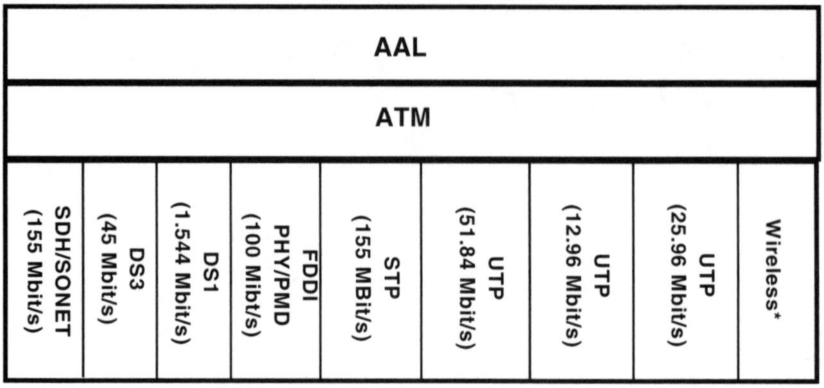

AAL								
ATM								
SDH/SONET (155 Mbit/s)	DS3 (45 Mbit/s)	DS1 (1.544 Mbit/s)	FDDI PHY/PMD (100 Mibt/s)	STP (155 MBit/s)	UTP (51.84 Mbit/s)	UTP (12.96 Mbit/s)	UTP (25.96 Mbit/s)	Wireless*

*Not yet developed as a standard

FDDI	Fiber distributed data interface
PHY	Physical sublayer
PMD	Physical media dependent sublayer
STP	Shielded twisted pair
UTP	Unshielded twisted pair

Figure 14–1
Physical layer options.

layer interfaces and protocols, with the exception of the wireless medium. Some vendors will run ATM over current wireless systems. For example, SONET radio interfaces will support ATM traffic.

THE ATM/PHYSICAL LAYER PRIMITIVES

As the reader might expect, physical layer primitives (service definitions) for ATM are part of the B-ISDN architecture. However, the physical layer might be non-B-ISDN systems, such as DS3, FDDI, or others. So, be aware that this section reflects the view of B-ISDN, and may or may not be found in other physical-layer operations.

Figure 14–2 shows the primitives operating between ATM and the physical layer. Chapter 3 explained that an OSI-type protocol entity can send and receive four types of primitives: (1) request, (2) indication, (3) response, and (4) confirm. The ATM/B-ISDN uses two of them, the request and indication primitives. The interface is quite simple, and as the

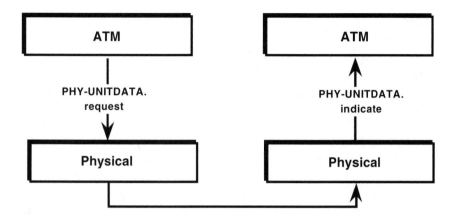

The ATM-entity passes one cell per PHY-UNITDATA.request and accepts one cell per PHY-UNITDATA.indicate.

**Figure 14–2
ATM—physical-layer primitives.**

figure shows, a request primitive results in one cell being passed from the ATM layer to the physical layer; an indication primitive results in one cell being passed from the physical layer to the ATM layer.

ATM MAPPING INTO SONET STS-3c

Chapter 13 introduced SONET payloads and STS-3c. This section continues this discussion, and covers both a public and private UNI. The focus is on the physical-layer operations for the U-plane. The M-plane operations are covered in Chapter 13.

Operations are supported through two sublayers of the U-plane model: the physical media dependent (PMD) sublayer, and the transmission convergence (TC) sublayer. As expected, the PMD is responsible for bit timing and line coding. The TC is responsible for HEC operations, identification of the cells in the payload, cell delineation within the payload, pointer processing, cell scrambling/unscrambling (if necessary), frequency justification, and multiplexing.

The 155.52 Mbit/s frame supports a transfer rate of 149.760 Mbit/s for the actual cells in the payload. The other bits in the frame are overhead. The cells do not compute to an even integer multiple of the cell length, so a cell can cross into another SPE frame.

The format for the ATM payload in STS-3c is shown in Figure 14–3. Since the functions of these fields were explained in Chapter 13, this discussion shall only describe any special considerations for their use for cell payloads.

The boxes with Xs denote that the STS-3c field is not defined. The C2 octet is used to indicate that the payload is loaded with ATM cells when it is set to 00010011.

The A1 and A2 octets are the conventional framing octets. The C1 octets are also used in the conventional manner, and are set to 00000001-00000010-00000011 respectively in the three C1 octets. Likewise, the B1 and B2 octets perform BIP-8 operations for section and line monitoring, respectively. The H octets support the pointer and concatenation functions, and the remainer of the octets are used for diagnostics, alarms, and so on.

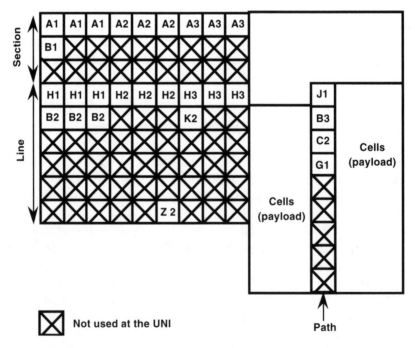

Figure 14–3
Payload mapping of cells in SONET STS-3c at the UNI.

The G1 octet is used to alert an upstream node of an out-of-cell delineation (OCD) using the HEC operations. The exact method for use of G1 is under study.

ATM MAPPING INTO DS3

Because of widespread use, the DS3 carrier system is emerging as the preferred transport mechanism for ATM traffic. In order for this feature to be implemented, a physical layer convergence protocol (PLCP) quite similar to the PLCP in IEEE 802.6 and the SMDS specifications has been defined.

ATM cells are carried in the DS3 frame by mapping 53-byte ATM cells into a DS3 PLCP payload. The PLCP is then further mapped into the DS3 information payload. This concept is illustrated in Figure 14–4, which depicts a DS3 PLCP transmission stream. As the reader might expect, it consists of a 125 µs frame running within a DS3 payload. The frame consists of twelve rows of ATM cells with each cell preceded by four octets of overhead. The overhead is used for framing, error checking, bit stuffing (if necessary), alarm conditions, path overhead identifiers, and reserved octets. These fields are described shortly. Cell delineation is accomplished in a simple manner by placing the cells in predetermined locations within the PLCP.

As Figure 14–4 shows, the following PLCP overhead octets are used for the UNI operation. The framing octets (A1, A2) use the conventional framing pattern employed in SONET and SDH. The bit interleaved parity-8 field (B1) is also used in the conventional manner to support the monitoring of path errors. The BIP-8 field is calculated over the entire envelope structure, including the path overhead and the associated 648 octets of the ATM cells of a previous PLCP frame.

The cycle/stuff counter (C1) provides the minimal nibble stuffing cycle and length indicator for the PCLP frame. Its purpose is to frequently justify the 125 µs PLCP frame. This operation is implemented for every third frame of a 375 µs stuffing. Bit stuffing is not used in this scheme. Either 13 or 14 nibbles (4 bits) are inserted into the third frame.

The PLCP path status field (G1) is used to indicate a far-end block error (FEBE), based on the contents of BIP-8 in the previous frame. It can be coded to indicate how many BIP-8 errors were detected in that frame during its traversing the path from the source node. This field con-

PLCP framing		POI	POH	PLCP payload	
A1	A2	P11	Z6	First ATM cell	
A1	A2	P10	Z5	ATM cell	
A1	A2	P9	Z4	ATM cell	
A1	A2	P8	Z3	ATM cell	
A1	A2	P7	Z2	ATM cell	
A1	A2	P6	Z1	ATM cell	
A1	A2	P5	X	ATM cell	
A1	A2	P4	B1	ATM cell	
A1	A2	P3	G1	ATM cell	
A1	A2	P2	X	ATM cell	
A1	A2	P1	X	ATM cell	
A1	A2	P0	C1	Twelfth ATM cell	Trailer
1 octet	1 octet	1 octet	1 octet	53 octets	13 or 14 nibbles

Object of BIP-8
calculation

POI   Path overhead indicator

POH   Path overhead

BIP-8   Bit interleaved parity—8

X   Unassigned—Receiver required to ignore

Note: Overhead of PLCP yields a cell transport rate of 40.704 Mbit/s:
424 bits per cell x 12 cells per frame x 8000 = 40,704,000 bit/s,
with 96k cells per second in throughout (8000 x 12 = 96,000)

**Figure 14–4
Running ATM over DS3.**

tains one bit for signaling that a failure indication has been declared along the DS3 path.

The path overhead identifier (P0-P11) is used to index the adjacent path overhead octet of the DS3 PLCP. The specification provides rules for the coding of the POI with the associated POH. For example, P11 is coded as 00101100 to identify an associated POH of Z6. The growth octets (Z1-Z6), as their name suggests, are reserved for future use. Finally, the nibbles were explained earlier.

Figure 14–5 provides a example of the order of byte transmission of the PLCP frame. The order is, in relation to Figure 14–4, left to right, and top to bottom with the most significant bits (MSB) on the left and the least significant bits (LSB) on the right. .

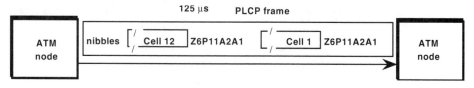

Figure 14–5
Order of byte transmission of the PLCP frame.

Other Aspects of the DS3 Scheme

Scrambling may be performed to compensate for bit patterns that create problems for equipment. If performed, the operation is based on ITU-T I.432. The PLCP frame must have its timing traced to a primary reference source (PRS). Cell delineation using HEC is not necessary, because the cells are placed in fixed locations in the PLCP. HEC operations must still be performed in accordance with ITU-T 1.432.

ATM MAPPING INTO THE 100 MBIT/S MULTIMODE FIBER INTERFACE

The ATM Forum UNI also specifies the interface for an ATM/FDDI configuration across the U-plane. This interface is not a full FDDI operation. Only the physical layer of FDDI is used, and the interface is on a private UNI. It does not have (or need) the elaborate OAM schemes for long-distance public communications lines, such as SONET. Therefore, OAM is provided by the interim local management interface (ILMI) (see Chapter 13). The media access control (MAC) layer of FDDI is not used in this implementation. This interface is shown in Figure 14–6.

This physical layer adheres to the FDDI physical media dependent (PMD) specification (ISO DIS 9314-3). The network interface unit (NUI) must provide the functions for AAL 3/4 traffic.

Functions of the U-Plane Physical Layer

The functions of this interface are grouped into two sublayers: the physical media dependent (PMD) sublayer and the transmission convergence (TC) sublayer. The TC is responsible for cell delineation through the use of FDDI control codes and header error control (HEC) generation and verification. HEC is calculated for the four octets of the cell header and the results are inserted in the HEC field.

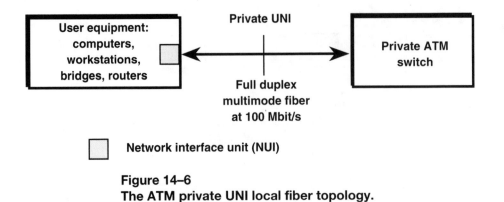

Figure 14–6
The ATM private UNI local fiber topology.

The PMD is responsible for the actual timing of the bits and the coding of these bits onto the physical medium. The physical media sublayer operates at 100 Mbit/s with a 125 Mbaud rate, which is the same rate used on conventional FDDI networks.

PMD sublayer. This sublayer uses 62.5 micron multimode fiber at 100 Mbits/s with the 125 Mbaud 4B/5B encoding scheme (ANSI X3T9.5) (FDDI). The FDDI control codes are used in a limited manner. The mnemonic JK is used to signal an idle line and the mnemonic TT is used to signify the beginning of a cell. That is to say, TT is used for cell delineation. The cell octets then follow contiguously on the channel, and the cell and its start of cell code (TT) must also be contiguous to each other on the channel. Other mnemonics shown in Table 14–1 are either reserved or not recommended for usage. The only other FDDI mnemonic is QQ, which is used to code a loss of signal indication.

TC sublayer. These sublayer operations are independent of the PMD, and thus not concerned with the characteristics of the medium. Their principal job is the generation and receiving of the control codes and the cells. The TC operations are depicted in Figure 14–7.

TC generates the TT code and the cell. It uses the JK code for synchronization purposes. In the event of the loss of synchronization, the JK code is used to regain octet alignment. Therefore, a least one JK code is inserted between each cell, which ensures that only one cell will be lost in the event of a synchronization problem. Otherwise, this interface follows the pertinent ISO and ANSI specifications.

Table 14–1   Control Codes for a 100 Mbit/s Link

Mnemonic	Definition
JK (sync)	Idle
II	Reserved
TT	Start of cell
TS	Reserved
IH	Not recommended
TR	Reserved
SR	Reserved
SS	Unused
HH	Not recommended
HI	Not recommended
HQ	Not recommended
RR	Unused
RS	Reserved
QH	Not recommended
QI	Not recommended
QQ	Loss of signal

Figure 14–7
Example of cell transmission of the fiber link.

ATM MAPPING INTO THE 155.52 MBIT/S PRIVATE UNI

ATM mapping is designed to allow the ATM switch to act as a hub in a local area network (LAN) environment. Two options are available for this interface: optical fiber and shielded twisted pair.

Multimode Fiber Interface

This interface is a point-to-point multimode fiber, and operates full duplex between an ATM switch and a host. The fiber is 62.5/125 micron, graded index, multimode fiber (using a wavelength of 1300 nm), with an option of 50 micron core fiber available. At 62.5, the distance between the switch and the host is up to 2 km.

This interface uses the conventional STS-3c coding and mapping schemes that were described earlier in this chapter and in Chapter 13.

Shielded Twisted Pair Interface

This interface is a point-to-point shielded twisted pair (STP), and operates full duplex between an ATM switch and a host. The cable is a 150Ω connection, as specified in EIA/TIA 568, 1991. The maximum distance between the STP interfaces is 110 m, using either Type 1 or Type 2 cable in accordance with ANSI/IEEE 802.5 (Type 6 cable can be used for short patches). The physical connector is shown in Figure 14–8 and is based on ANSI/IEEE 802.5 standard.

Figure 14–9 shows how the cells are organized for transport across the STP interface. A set of 26 cells is preceded by an OAM cell, which is also 53 octets in length. The first five octets in the OAM cell are coded to provide octet and frame synchronization. Most of the octets in the remainder of the OAM cell are not defined. The sixth octet contains three bits used for OAM (discussed in Chapter 13) for far-end receive failure (FERF), errored frame indicator (EFI), and alarm indication signal (AIS).

PRIVATE UNI FOR 51.84 MBIT/S AND SUBRATES

The ATM Forum has also published specifications for running ATM over Category 3 unshielded twisted pair cabling for the following rates [ATM94b]: (1) 51.84 Mbit/s, (2) 25.92 Mbit/s, and (3) 12.96 Mbit/s. In ad-

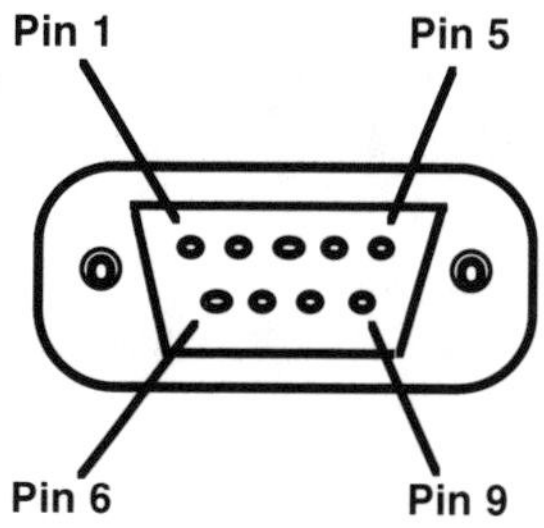

	Pin #	Signal
	1	Transmit +
	2	Not used
	3	Not used
	4	Not used
	5	Receive +
	6	Transmit −
	7	Not used
	8	Not used
	9	Receive −
	Shell	Chassis

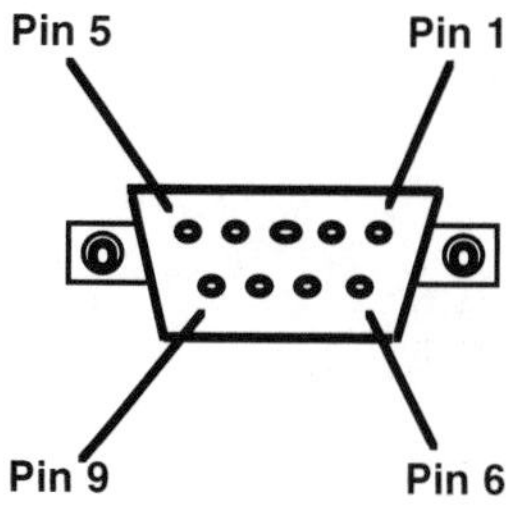

	Pin #	Signal
	1	Receive +
	2	Not used
	3	Not used
	4	Not used
	5	Transmit +
	6	Receive −
	7	Not used
	8	Not used
	9	Transmit −
	Shell	Chassis

Figure 14–8
Plug and jack pin assignments for shielded twisted pair interface.

dition, alternative cable types may be used. Table 14–2 summarizes the permissable rates and distances for Categories 3 and 5 cable.

The bit rate of 51.84 Mbit/s is the SONET STS-1 rate as defined in ANSI T1.105. The physical medium dependent (PMD) sublayer uses a carrierless amplitude modulation/phase modulation (CAP) for bit trans-

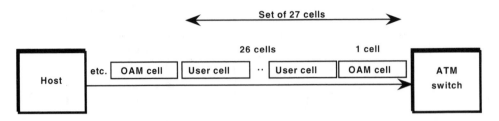

Figure 14–9
Example of cell transmission on shielded twisted pair.

mission and timing. This technique is used in many high speed modems, and the constellation map is almost identical to V.22 bis, a widely used modem in personal computers. Of course, the symbol rate for V.22 bis is only 1200 baud. The symbol rate for the 51.84 Mbit/s interface is 12.96 Mbaud, and 4 data bits are mapped into a 16-CAP constellation diagram, as shown in Figure 14–10. The lower rates of 25.92 Mbit/s and 12.96 Mbit/s use a 4-CAP code and 2-CAP code respectively. For more information on these three interfaces, refer to [ATM94b], part II.

MAPPING DS1, DS3, AND CEPT PAYLOADS INTO SONET FRAMES

This section provides the reader with examples of how several user payloads are mapped into the SONET SPE. The focus of this section is carrier payloads such as DS1, DS3, and CEPT1. During this discussion, keep in mind that SONET can carry today's carrier payloads. However, the reverse case is not true; today's carriers cannot always carry SONET payloads.

SONET is designed to be "backward compatible" with the carrier technologies in Europe, North America, and Japan. Therefore, the DSn and CEPTn payloads are supported and carried in the SONET envelope.

Table 14–2   Cable Lengths and Bit Rates for Categories 3 and 5 Cable

Cable Type	Bit Rates		
	51.84 Mbit/s	25.92 Mbit/s	12.96 Mbit/s
3	100m	170m	200m
5	160m	270m	320m

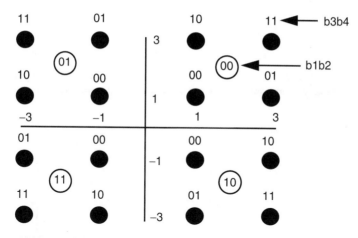

Figure 14–10
Constellation map for 51.84 Mbit/s twisted pair inter-face.

These payloads range from the basic DS0/CEPT0 of 64 kbit/s up to the higher speed rates of DS4 and CEPT5.

In addition, cells are also carried in the SONET envelope, which results in the technology being both backward compatible (supporting current technology) and forward compatible (supporting cell technology).

The VT/VC Structure

SONET supports a concept called virtual tributaries (VT) or virtual containers (VC)—the former phrase is used in SONET, and the latter phrase is used in SDH (see Figure 14–11).

Through the use of pointers and offset values, VTs/VCs, such as DS1, DS3, and CEPT1, can be carried in the SONET envelope. The standard provides strict and concise rules on how various VTs/VCs are mapped into the SONET envelope.

VT/VCs are used to support sub-STS-1 levels, which are lower-speed signals. To support different mixes of VTs/VCs, the STS-1 SPE can be divided into seven groups. As seen in Figure 14–12, each group occupies columns and rows of the SPE and may actually contain 4, 3, 2, or 1 VTs/VCs. For example, a VT group may contain one VT 6, two VT 3s, three VT 2s, or four VT 1.5s. Each VT/VC group must contain one size of VTs/VCs, but different groups can be mixed in one STS-1 SPE.

The four sizes of the VT supported by SONET are: VT 1.5 = 1.728 Mbit/s, VT 2 = 2.304 Mbit/s, VT 3 = 3.456 Mbit/s, and VT 6 = 6.912

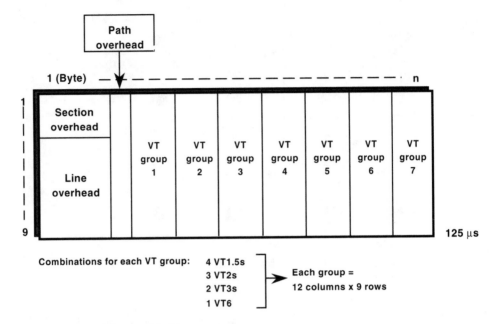

Figure 14–11
Virtual containers (VCs)/virtual tributaries (VTs).

Mbit/s. If the reader adds the number of columns that should exist in Figure 14–11, the total number of columns shown is only 88, not the 90 columns explained earlier. Shortly, we will see that two more columns are added to compensate for the differences between the bandwidth required in the payloads and the bandwidth available in the STS-1 envelope.

VT1.5 is called VC1-11 in Europe and it accommodates the T1 rate. VT2 is called VC-12 in Europe. It accommodates the Europe CEPT1 rate of 2.048 Mbit/s. VT3 is not employed in Europe. It is used in North America to optimize multiplexing DS1c transport signals. VT6 is called VC-2 in Europe and it accommodates the 6.912 Mbit/s rate from all three regions.

The various administrations and standards groups from Japan, North America, and Europe worked closely together to accommodate the three different regional signaling standards. The initial SONET standards published in the United States in 1984 were reviewed by Japan and the European PTTs to see if these requirements would meet their needs. During this time, the ANSI T1 committee had become involved with Bellcore in the development of SONET.

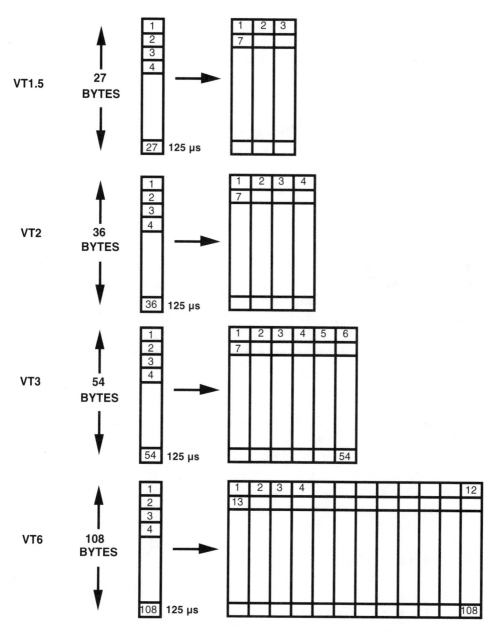

Figure 14–12
The tributaries and containers to accommodate regional multiplexing schemes.

Discussions continued through the European Telecommunications Standard Institute (ETSI), and agreement was reached on a subset of the multiplexing schemes of the three regions. ETSI stressed the importance of the intermediate rates of 8 and 34 Mbit/s in contrast to the ease of doing international networking. Reason prevailed, compromises were reached, and the importance of international internetworking came to the fore with multiplexing schemes based on 1.5, 2.48, and 6.312 Mbit/s capabilities.

Floating and Locked VT Mode

Two options dictate how the VT payload is mapped into the frame. One option is called the floating mode, for obvious reasons. Floating mode provides a convenient means to cross-connect transport signals in a network. Floating mode allows each VT SPE to float with respect to the complete envelope. This approach also obviates the use of slip buffers, which have been used in the past to phase-align the individual multiplexed signals as required. While the use of the slip buffers allows the system to repeat or delete a frame to correct for frequency variations: They should be avoided, if possible, because they impose additional complexity and may further impair the system. Payload pointers eliminate the need for slip buffers.

Another option is called the locked mode. With this approach, the pointers are not used and the payload is fixed within the frame. It cannot float. Locked mode is simpler, but it requires that timing be maintained throughout the network. Because all signals have a common orientation, the processing of the traffic is performed efficiently. However, slip buffers must be employed to adjust to any timing and synchronization differences that may be present in the system.

Figure 14–13 shows how ATM cells are mapped into a SONET or SDH payload envelope. The payload pointers can be used to locate the beginning of the first cell. Additionally, cell delineation is achieved by the receiver locking onto the 5 bytes that satisfy the HEC operations. In this manner, the receiver knows where a cell is positioned in the envelope. The receiver also is able to detect an empty cell.

It is unlikely that cells would be positioned at the first byte of the payload. If they are, an STS-3c system can carry 44 cells, and bytes 1-8 of the 45th cell. The remainder of the 45th cell is placed in the next SONET frame.

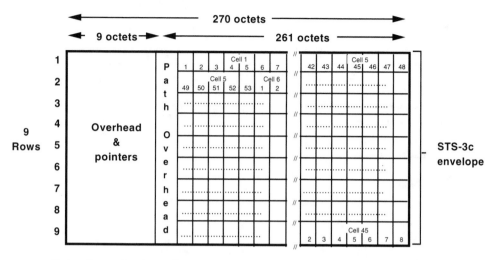

Note: Example shows first cell aligned exactly in beginning of payload area.
May be positioned anywhere in the payload.

Figure 14–13
Running ATM in SONET envelopes.

INTERWORKING ATM AND SONET

The specific implementations and topologies for interfaces between SONET and ATM are not defined in the international standards. Vendors are free to build their architecture based on their own design preferences. Notwithstanding, a possible scheme is depicted in Figure 14–14. As discussed in earlier parts of this book, an add-drop multiplexer (ADM) is used to add and drop payload at various locations in a network. Therefore, an ADM must be able not only to extract ATM cells from incoming SONET frames and drop off to a local node, but also to add ATM cells at this same node for transmission downstream. This example shows the reception and transmission of a SONET OC-48 envelope.

The first task is to receive the SONET envelope, examine the SONET overhead, act upon it, and then remove it. Thereafter, the payload, consisting of ATM cells, is examined to determine if the cells are to be dropped at this site or forwarded to the next site.

The ADM is responsible for checking the cell header (VPI and per-

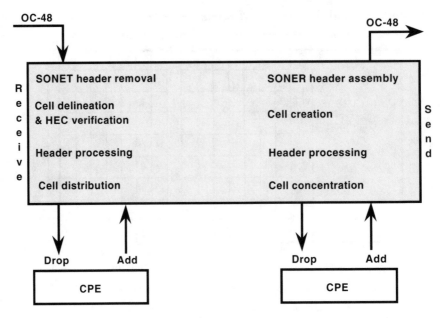

Figure 14–14
ATM and SONET interworking.

haps VCI) and making decisions as to the processing of the traffic. It
may drop the cell at this node or relay the cell to another node.

The architecture is based on four major operations. The first operation converts the STS-3c payload to an ATM stream at the input and
performs a complementary function at the output. The second operation
locates the cells within the payload for an incoming transmission, and
places the cells inside the SONET envelope for an outgoing transmission. The third operation examines the label in the ATM cell header (the
VPI and perhaps VCI). The fourth operation distributes the cells to the
outlets at this node or passes the cells to an outlet at this node. In its
simplest form, these operations make decisions on whether traffic is
passed or dropped at this node.

SUMMARY

The B-ISDN concept uses SONET at the physical layer to support
the ATM operations. The ATM Forum has defined three other physical
layer operations that act as service providers to the ATM layer. They are

DS3 for 44.736 Mbit/s operations, FDDI for 100 Mbit/s operations, and a private twisted pair UNI. Cells are mapped into these systems, based on the use of special line codes to identify the position of the cells on the media.

The SONET SPE can be used in a wide variety of ways to support various combinations of DSn virtual tributaries (VTs) and CEPTn virtual containers (VCs).

The ATM Market

INTRODUCTION

This chapter discusses how ATM is being deployed, and describes some of the vendors' ATM products. Obviously, with a dynamic environment such as ATM, the ATM environment will have changed by the time this book comes to print. Therefore, this chapter represents a snapshot of the happenings and announcements about ATM technology and the ATM marketplace. It is by no means exhaustive.

Forecasts on the Use of ATM

Surveys are appearing that predict the use (or nonuse) of frame relay, SMDS, and ATM. Some of these surveys project the usage out to 2003 (ambitious, to be sure). Figure 15–1 illustrates one of the surveys, which was published in the May 23, 1994 issue of *Telephony* magazine.

As this chart suggests, frame relay is slated for early success. The last few months of 1994 support this prediction, in that frame relay is beginning to grow in usage. The survey also predicts that SMDS will grow substantially in the next four years and take away some of the frame relay market. The same prediction is made for ATM. The soothsayer that made up this survey looked into the next decade and saw a cessation of the use of frame relay and SMDS, and the dominance of ATM.

Other technologies are not shown in this chart. For example, the survey discussed B-ISDN as a separate technology, and predicts that it

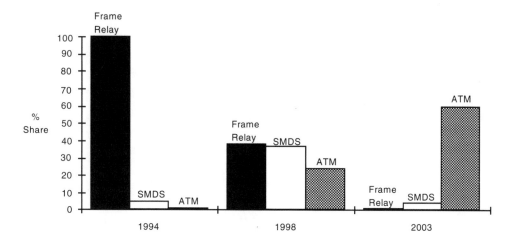

Figure 15–1
Relative position of frame relay, SMDS, ATM.

shall have a significant marketshare by 2003. This writer did not include this part of the survey, since the survey did not distinguish what part of B-ISDN was ATM.

My personal experience, and the views of my clients, note the relative positions of ATM, frame relay, and SMDS somewhat differently. First, if frame relay continues its present growth trend, it will not have diminished in use to the extent that this study shows by 1998. Once a technology grabs a share of the market, it takes a long time for vendors and customers to shed it (X.25 is a prime example—its use is still growing). However, I do agree that ATM will have a significant part of the market by 1998.

Another study conducted by the Yankee Group predicts a relatively modest growth in the ATM switch market between the years 1993 and 1994, but a dramatic growth thereafter (see Figure 15–2). The Yankee Group predicts growth principally in switches designed for individual enterprises, although sales will be significant in central office switches and backbone switches for networks.

Studies, like the ones cited in these past few illustrations, are conducted by many marketing firms and research organizations. Their techniques for collecting this information vary greatly, and generally consist of conducting surveys among vendor and user groups.

Of course, no one can predict accurately what these markets will be. But it is clear to most of the people in this industry that while these

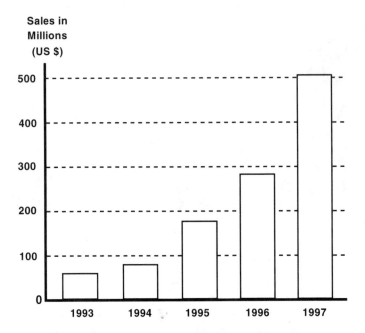

Source: The Yankee Group and *Broadband Networking News,* August 25, 1993

Figure 15–2
Forecast on the ATM switch market.

studies may not be completely accurate, there is enough activity among vendors to be assured that there is indeed substance to these studies.

ATM OVER T1/E1

It was only a matter of time before ATM offerings appeared that used T1/E1 facilities. One of the earliest was from ADC Kentrox. This company has an ATM CBR module that fits into its ATM Access Multiplexer. As Figure 15–3 shows, the system accepts a serial video (or voice) stream across a V.35 or RS-449 interface. The stream is given to the ATM module that runs AAL 1 operations.

The system allocates the bandwidth for the video session (video conference, etc.) whenever the video equipment is turned on. When the session is over and the equipment is turned off, the bandwidth is made available to other applications operating on the system. Additionally, the

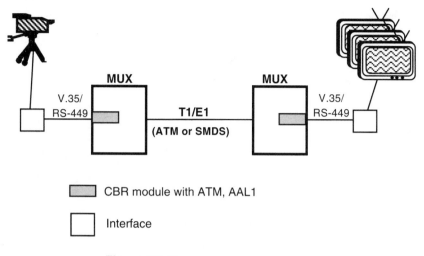

CBR module with ATM, AAL1

Interface

Figure 15–3
ATM or SMDS for T1/E1 Speeds.

module operates with StrataCom's user-to-network interface (UNI) on its IPX switches.

It was also only a matter of time before the costs of ATM hardware would come down. As with almost all new technologies, the initial prices are high. The initial offerings of V.32 modems, for example, were priced at several thousand dollars. This modem can be purchased now for about $100 US.

The same situation holds true for ATM interface cards, as Figure 15–4 shows. According to Connectware, this company will start shipping (in early 1995) Unix workstation cards that operate at 100 Mbit/s. By the time this book is printed, the costs for ATM interface cards will be even lower than these prices.

TRIALS AND TEST BEDS

A wide variety of ATM-based broadband implementations and tests are taking place in the United States. Some of the more notable ones are:

- Time Warner Interactive Video Trial: ATM to the home
- NREN test beds: Federal government is funding several test beds
- California Research and Education Network (CREN): Using ATM for connecting various state, business and telephone facilities

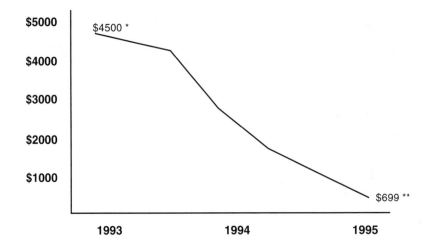

* from Fore Systems, Inc. first quarter of 1993

** from Connectware, Inc. first quarter of 1995

Figure 15–4
Workstation ATM adapter card.

- North Carolina Broadband Superhighway: First statewide public ATM and SONET-based network
- Viacom interactive TV: Rival to the Time Warner system
- SNET/Rochester Telephone: Video dial tone trail is underway
- US West: COMPASS system, starting with ISDN, SMDS and moving to ATM

The Time Warner Cable company is testing ATM through a central office switch in Florida to support a variety of television applications. Additionally, it intends that the ATM switch (based on AT&T equipment) will be able to handle voice, video, and data. Time Warner has named this network the Full Service Network (FSN).

The installation provides approximately 4000 residential customers in the Orlando area with on-demand video, which encompasses not only movies but famous/well received sports happenings, and other notable presentations/events. Also, the Time Warner plan is to provide subscribers with access to telephone networks, shopping services, and other consumer-based applications.

Time Warner has opted to use the AT&T GCNS-2000 switch for its backbone network. This AT&T switch supports up to 20 Gbits/s rates and will accommodate the well accepted rates of DS3 and SONET 155 Mbits/s. The homes targeted for this technology will have fiber run to the local box. The homes then will be wired with coaxial cable. In fact, many of the homes are already wired with coaxial cable, so the installation from the home to the box should be relatively easy.

The announcement should not be taken lightly, because it encompasses a tacit acceptance of the ATM technology (as well as the AT&T switch) with the potential to utilize this type of application across approximately 7 million Time Warner subscribers in 36 states. If a nationwide network were to be implemented with this technology, Time Warner would require several hundred ATM switches.

ATM VENDORS

ATM is, without question, the most "hyped" technology currently in the industry. However, unlike some of the emerging technologies, which are entering the market more slowly than anticipated, ATM products are not just being announced, but they are also being implemented.

The newer ATM products are intended for two purposes. Some of the ATM switches are used for carrier transport systems and interfaces principally because of the marketing philosophy of the vendor or because of their capacity. As examples, Northern Telecom's Passport products from the Magellan family, AT&T's GNS-2000, Fujitsu's Fetex-150, and StrataCom's PBX are targeted for the CPE market.

Table 15–1 provides a comparison of these offerings, which were sourced from the Business Communications Review, October, 1993 [GASM93].

Traditional router, hub, and hub vendors have developed ATM interfaces for implementation across LANs within user installations. As examples, Ascom Timeplex, Cisco, DEC, IBM, Redex, and Wellfleet are offering ATM-based products for LAN and workstation interconnectivity.

Another set of products is used as interfaces (typically between routers and hubs). These devices have been designed around DSU architecture. Most of the router and hub offerings use these DSUs as their initial product to the public. Eventually, the hubs and routers will incorporate this interface into the product itself. Table 15–2 provides examples of these vendors.

Table 15–1   Examples of ATM Vendors [GASM93]

Vendor	Product	Interfaces	Services	Pricing
Alcatel Data Networks	1100 HSS	ATM at 34/45 Mbit/s, 100 Mbit/s and 155 Mbit/s, Frame relay and HDLC/SDLC at 64 kbit/s to 2 Mbit/s, SMDS access at 2 Mbit/s and 16 Mbit/s	ATM, frame relay, HDLC, and SMDs	N/A
Cascade Communications	B-STDX-9000	X.21, V.35, RS-449, EIA-530/A, HSSI, ATM DXI	Frame relay, SMDS, ATM	$30,000 for base unit $160,000 for typical fully redundant DS3 configuration
DSC	Megahub iBSS	ATM UNI at DS3/E3 and OC-3	Frame relay SMDS, ATM	
Fore Systems	ASX-100 and ASX-100 SwitchCluster	Ethernet, FDDI TAXI, OC-3, DS3	High-speed work group applications	4-port ASX-100 priced at $27,95, 16-port switch at $47,930
General DataComm	APEX	Ethernet, ATM, frame relay and HDLC modules on LAN side, ATM ports operating at DS1, DS3, and OC-3 through OC-12	LAN hub or backbone router on a WAN switch	From $32,500 to $150,000
GTE Gov't. Systems	SPANet	T1, Ethernet, DS3, OC-3, and video	Video Ethernet	
Hughes Network Systems	Developing ATM matrix switches for its Strategy packet switch line	Frame relay, video, voice and ATM over DS3 and OC-3, T1/T3 and E1/E3 WAN	Frame relay video, voice ATM	N/A

Company	Product	Technologies/interfaces	Applications	Price
IBM	Transport Network Node (TNN)	HDLC, fiber channel, ISDN, frame relay and continuous-bit-rate (CBR) voice/video	HDLC fiber channel, ISDN frame relay, and CBR voice/video	N/A
LightStream	LightStream 2010	T3/E3, ATM UNI	Frame relay, X.25, HDLC	Prices start $25,000
NCR/AT&T	UniverCell	OC-1 to OC-12 and T1/E1	Various	N/A
N.E.T.	Adaptive ATMX	ATM at DS3, SONET, Ethernet and token ring	Enterprise-wide virtual LAN	$2,700–4,000 per port, SONET and DS3 at $3000 per port
Network Systems Corporation	Enterprise Router Switch	FDDI, token ring, Ethernet	ATM and Ethernet switching	N/A
Newbridge Networks	36150 Main Street	DS1/DS3, 100 Mbit/s, 140 Mbit/s 155 Mbit/s ATM, SONET OC-3/ OC-12, Ethernet, token ring, FDDI, video, T2 TDM	N/A token ring, FDDI, video	Ethernet
Newbridge Networks	Vivid ATM Hub	Ethernet, token ring, FDDI video, 100 Mbit/s, 140 Mbit/s, OC-3 and DS3 ATM	Local work group connectivity	N/A
Northern Telecom	Magellan Passport	T1/E1, T3/E3, OC-3, token ring, FDDI, Ethernet, frame relay	Frame relay, voice	N/A
StrataCom	BPX	ATM at T3/E3 and SONET/SDH up to OC-12, T1/E1	Frame relay, voice, video	$75,000 to $250,000
SynOptics	LattisCel	155 Mbit/s ports	High-speed work group applications	N/A
Telematics	AToM	DS1/E1, DS3/E3, SMDS, OC-3, frame relay, X.25 and ATM	Frame relay, SMDS, ATM	N/A

Table 15–2   ATM-Based Routers, Hubs, and Interfaces [GASM93]

Routers, Hubs, and Concentrators Vendor	Product
ADC	ACC-1, AAC-3, ATMosphere
Cabletron	ATM module for Multi Media Access Center (MMAC) hubs
Chipcom	ONline System Concentrator intelligent hub
Cisco Systems	ATM upgrade to Cisco 7000 router
DEC	DEC NIS 600 router/smart hub, Gigaswitch FDDI-to-FDDI matrix switches
Hughes LAN Systems	Enterprise Hub
IBM	8250 hubs
Network Systems Corporation	6400 and 6800 Series routers
Proteon	Corporate Network Exchange 400
Retix	RouterXchange 7000
3Com	LinkBuilder Multiservices Hub, NETBuilder II bridge/router, CellBuilder
Ungermann-Bass	Access/One hub
Wellfleet	Routers
Xyplex	Network 9000 Routing Hub

Interfaces Vendor	Product	Description
ADC Kentrox	DataSmart ADSU	T3/E3, ATM DSU, also supports SMDS
Digital Link	DL3200/ATMJ Digital Service Unit	DS3
Fore Systems	SBA-100 and SBA-200 S-bus adapters, GIA-100 GIO Bus Adapter, TCA-100 Turbochannel Adapter, ESA-200 EISA Bus, MCA-200 Microchannel Bus	SBA products for SUN workstations, GIA for Silicon Graphics workstations, TCA for DEC workstations
Hughes LAN Systems	Workstation cards	For workstations that plug into Hughes hub
IBM	Adapters	For Microchannel and EISA PCs and RISC workstations

Table 15–2   ATM-Based Routers, Hubs, and Interfaces (continued)

Interfaces Vendor	Product	Description
N.E.T.	ATMX Adapter Card	For attaching SUN 4 workstation to ATMX switch
Network Peripherals	Workstation interface	S-bus, EISA and Micro-channel interfaces
SynOptics	Workstation interface	S-bus interfaces

DEC AND IBM ATM EFFORTS

Digital Equipment Corp. (DEC) has announced a wide array of ATM-based products due to be released during the 1994–1995 period. Thus far, a total of thirteen products have been described to form a base for internetworking LAN users as well as for the use as a CPE for carriers. The ATM switches, currently under design, operate at 10.4 Gbit/s and 3.2 Gbit/s; they are focused on local, departmental LAN interconnections. In addition, DEC is developing workstation interfaces, line cards, and switching modules for its current line of hubs and routers.

Since DEC has a wide customer base using Ethernet technology, the plan is to provide scalability up to ATM bandwidth. It is anticipated that a portion of the DEC products will compete directly with IBM, Newbridge, and Northern Telecom offerings.

The initial announcements for the DEC ATM switch will support interfaces for DS3 and 155 Mbit/s channels. It will be designed to receive and send ATM cells to and from workstations, routers, other switches, and LAN hubs and, in turn, forward the ATM cells to wide area networks or other switches. Presently, this switch does not offer support for LAN interfaces, although DEC intends the interface to be provided through another DEC module, which at this time is called the DEC 900 MultiSwitch™ hub.

DEC also intends to provide some interesting flow control mechanisms for congestion management. One product, called Flow Master, is intended to control bursty LAN traffic based on a modified "leaky bucket" algorithm in which credits are used to determine how much traffic the user is allowed to send to the network node.

DEC also intends to support not only data, but voice, video, and other CBR traffic. Therefore, it has announced support for the currently published ATM Forum class of services, including a, c, d, and possibly b.

DEC also has an interesting feature for rerouting around failed circuits with a product called the Resilient Virtual Circuit. The idea is to provide for a number of physical circuits and allow the paths to be switched if one of the active physical circuits becomes inoperable.

DEC has also announced several products for late 1995 that will interface certain types of DEC hubs and routers with SONET's 622 Mbit/s interface.

In mid-1993, IBM announced a wide array of ATM-based products. They are slated to be introduced into the industry in late 1994 and early 1995. This figure shows the products and their relationship to ATM and frame relay networks. It is envisioned that ATM will evolve from some of IBM's current offerings, such as the 6611 bridge/router and the 3745-based frame relay interface.

IBM is currently working on a high-performance routing (HPR) system, which was formerly known as APPN+. The 6611 and an HPR gateway is being designed to SNA, APPN, TCP/IP, IPX, NETBIOS, and so on with an ATM network.

IBM also intends to provide frame relay across all of IBM's major platforms, including its AS/400s, 3172s, and 3174s.

In addition, the transport network node (TNN) will be designed to support both frame relay and ATM. The goal is to provide coexistence for a hybrid ATM and frame relay network. The TNN is slated to be available in late 1994 or early 1995. The IBM 8250 hub, also slated for arrival slightly earlier, is built on technology from Chipcom.

The IBM technology is VLSI-based, which permits speeds from 25 Mbit/s up to 155 Mbit/s over shielded or unshielded twisted pair.

ATM PROGRESS IN EUROPE

The ATM activity in North America is by no means unique. Europe is undergoing similar implementations. This section provides several examples of European ATM networks and applications that are using ATM.

United Kingdom

British Telecom (BT) has launched a effort to support UK universities' research on carrier-oriented technologies. BT is contributed £2.5 million to the effort. The Super Joint Academic Network (SuperJanet) will be used. SuperJanet uses ATM and connects fifty sites. The research consists of a consortium of six universities: Imperial College, London; Loughborough University of Technology; Oxford Brookes University; University College, London; University of Cambridge; and University of Lancaster.

The project will investigate issues such as security, configuration management, traffic monitoring, and multimedia conferencing.

On another front, BT is testing ATM switches from six manufacturers at a Birmingham site, but intends to introduce ATM in a careful manner. Some of its SMDS infrastructure will be converted to ATM during 1995.

ATM support of medical applications. In the UK, Leeds General Infirmary's (LGI) Minimal Invasive Therapy Group (MITG) will use ATM for remote training. Its site will connect to St. James' University Hospital, and use multimedia devices. The devices will be located at LGI will be linked to lecture halls in St. James through Torch Communications optical fiber links. Applications include training traffic, x-ray images, magnetic resonance imaging (MRI), and computer-aided tomography (CAT) images.

Under the second phase of the project, another eight hospitals (including Brafford, Sheffield, Manchester, Milllesborough, and Hull) will be connected to the system. These connections will use Mercury's switchband service and migrate to ATM.

Equipment will be the AVA-200, an ATM video adapter designed for point-to-multipoint operations. The AVA-200 will be used with cameras designed for minimal invasive therapy. The AVA-200 will be linked with Fore Systems' ATM switches.

An AVD-100 accepts video ATM cells from the AVA-200, decodes the cells, and displays them on standard TV monitors. It operates with the ATM Forum 100 Mbit/s optical specification, or on 155 Mbit/s SDH.

ATM and frame relay. The internetworking of frame relay and ATM is proceeding in Europe, As an example, Energis (UK's third long-distance carrier) plans to offer frame relay services over an ATM backbone. The intention is to use the system mainly for LAN interconnections. Energis (owned by National Grid Company) claims to have invested £250 million for a nationwide, fiber-based synchronous digital hierarchy (SDH) network.

Initially, frame relay will service as the access interface to the ATM backbone. Later ATM interfaces will be provided. Speeds of 64 kbit/s and up will be offered, and the frame relay CIR will be tailored to user requirements.

Examples of other Countries' ATM Efforts

Finland. In September 1994, Telecom Finland launched a nationwide ATM service, called DatNet. This service came about as a result of a 16-month trial between Tampere and Helsinki. By end of 1994, the service will reach ten major cities, and to Stockholm. By year end, access to SDH at 155 Mbit/s is planned, and 622 Mbit/s is slated for 1995.

At Stockholm, a new group of BT, Telel Danmark, Norwegian Telecom, and Telecom Finland will support this node.

Customer access rates range from 256 kbit/s to 32 Mbit/s. The service prices are (for examples) $4400 US a month for a 10 Mbit/s Ethernet connection of about 200 kilometers. Charges include CPE, maintenance, and single-mode fiber access. ATM equipment are APEX-DV2, and MAC ATM devices.

Poland. The Polish Research and Academic Networks organisation (NASK) is installing an ATM-based network, with the initial links connected through SDH. NASK has ordered 27 APEX-DV2 switches from General DataCom. The initial implementation is with partner Ericsson Schrack with six switches in Warsaw, and is called WARMAN. This Network will support voice, video, and LAN internetworking. WARMAN consists of over 500 different organizations, most of which are universities and R&D firms. The network will also serve government entities.

In 1995, another twenty-one switches will be deployed to other cities: Cracow, Poznan, Torun, Wroclaw, Dgansk, Lublin, Lodz, Szczecin, and Katowice. Also, plans are being made for connecting to other systems, notably, UK's SuperJanet and Finland's FUNET (Finnish University Network).

SOME FINAL THOUGHTS

In my ongoing work with ATM, I am struck by how fast the technology has surfaced from the research labs and entered into the mainstream of the telecommunications industry. Most of my clients were not aware of ATM as recently as 1992. Today, it is one of the foremost technologies on their minds. Why? The answer is really simple. These people are looking for two capabilities to enhance their information systems: (1)

A common platform to support voice, video, and data applications, and (2) a common platform to support local and wide area networks. ATM and the MAN are the only two prominent, standardized technologies that have been designed to meet these two critical functions.

As of this writing, much ado is made about the cost of the ATM technology. ATM interfaces are expensive, and many terminals and workstations do not need the bandwidth provided by ATM. This fact does not concern me. ATM interfaces will be inexpensive and affordable in the near future. How can we know this? Just look at the cost of a V.22 bis modem in 1984 (several hundred dollars), and the cost of a V.32 modem as late as 1989 (several *thousand* dollars). Today, these are available for less than $100.

However, for the immediate future, we shall see that ATM will be implemented in a gradual fashion. Organizations will bring in "islands of ATM" to solve specific bottleneck problems. We shall see the gradual integration of ATM into hubs, and routers, and eventually into large central office switches.

So, should you commit to ATM? If you are a switch, multiplexer, or router vendor, and you have not yet made a commitment to ATM in your products, good luck. If you are a potential customer, wait a short period; the ATM technology is maturing—mass production of ATM hardware and keen competition will surely make this technology cost-effective for most organizations.

In conclusion, I would like to thank you for allowing me to describe the ATM technology to you. Since ATM is changing so rapidly, you shall probably see a second edition of this book in the near future.

References

In addition to the formal standards for the systems described in this book, these references should prove useful to the reader. Many of them were used for the development of this material.

[AHMA93] Amhad, R., and Halsall, F. (1993). Interconnecting high-speed LANs and backbones, *IEEE Network*, September.

[AMOS79] Amos, J.E., Jr. (1979). Circuit switching: Unique architecture and applications. *IEEE Computer*, June.

[ARMT93] Armitage, G.J., and Adams, K.M.(1993). Packet reassembly during cell loss, *IEEE Network*, September.

[ATM92a] ATM Forum. (June 1, 1992). *ATM user-network interface specification, Version 2.0.*

[ATM93a] ATM Forum. (August 5, 1993). *ATM user-network interface specification, Version 3.0.*

[ATM94a] ATM Forum. (March, 1994). *Education and training work group*, ATM Forum Ambassador's Program.

[ATM94b] ATM Forum. (July 21, 1994). *ATM user-network interface specification, Version 3.1.*

[ATT89a] (January, 1989). Observations of error characteristics of fiber optic transmission systems, CCITT SGXVIII, San Diego, CA.

[BELL82] Bellamy, J. (1982). *Digital Telephony*, New York, NY: John Wiley and Sons.

[BELL90a] (May, 1993). Generic requirements for frame relay PVC exchange service, TR-TSV-001369, Issue 1.

[BELL89a]. (September, 1989). Synchronous optical network (SONET) transport systems: common generic criteria, TR-TSY-000253, Issue 1.

[BELL94] Bellman, R.B. (1994). Evolving traditional LANs to ATM, *Business Communications Review*, October.

[BLAC89] Black, U. (1989). *Data Networks, Concepts, Theory and Practice*, Prentice Hall.

[BLAC91] Black, U. (1991). *X.25 and related protocols*, IEEE Computer Society Press.

[BLAC93] Black, U. (1993). *Data link protocols*, Prentice Hall.

[BLAI88] Blair, C. (1988). SLIPs: Definitions, causes, and effects in T1 networks, *A Tautron Application Note, Issue 1*, September. (Note: my thanks to this author for a lucid explanation of slips.)

[BNR92a] Bell Northern Research. (1992). Global systems for mobile communications, *Telesis*, 92.

[BNR94a] Discussions held with Bell Northern Research (BNR) designers during 1993 and 1994.

[BROW94] Brown, P.D. (ed.). (1994). The price is right for ATM to become a serious competitor, *Broadband Networking News*, May.

[CCIT90a] (1990). Voice packetization-packetized voice protocols, CCITT Recommendation G.764, Geneva.

[CDPD93] (July 19, 1993). Cellular digital packet data system specification, *Release 1.0*.

[CHER92] Cherukuri, R. (August 26, 1992). Voice over frame relay networks, A technical paper issued as Frame Relay Forum, FRF 92.33.

[CHEU92] Cheung, N.K. (1992). The infrastructure of gigabit computer networks, *IEEE Communications Magazine*, April,.

[COMM94a] Korostoff, K. (April 18, 1994). Wide-area ATM undergoes trial by MAGIC, *Communications Week*.

[DAVI91] Davidson, R.P., and Muller, N.J. (1991). *The Guide to SONET*, Telecom Library, Inc.

[DELL92] Dell Computer, Intel, and University of Pennsylvania, A study compiled by Marty Baumann, *USA Today*, date not available.

[dePr91] dePrycker, M. (1991). *Asynchronous Transfer Mode*. Ellis Harwood Ltd.

[dePR92] de Prycker, M. (1992) ATM in Belgian Trial. *Communications International*, June.

[DUBO94] DuBois, D. Simnet Inc., Palo Alto, CA. A recommendation from a reviewer of *Emerging Communications Technologies*. (Thank you Mr. DuBois.)

[ECKB92] Eckberg, A.E. (1992). B-ISDN/ATM traffic and congestion control, *IEEE Network*, September.

[EMLI 63] Emling, J.W., and Mitchell, D. (1963). The effects of time delay and echoes on telephone conversations. *Bell Systems Technical Journal*, November.

[FORD93] Ford, P.S., Rekhter, Y., and Braun, H.-W. (1993). Improving the routing and addressing of IP. *IEEE Network*, May.

[FORU92] Frame Relay Forum Technical Committee. (May 7, 1992). "Frame relay network-to-network interface, phase 1 implementation agreement, Document Number FRF 92.08R1–Draft 1.4.

[GASM93] Gasman, L. (1993). ATM CPE—Who is providing what?, *Business Communications Review*, October.

[GOKE73] Goke, L.R., and Lipovski, G.J. (1973). Banyan networks for partitioning multiprocessor systems. First Annual Symposium on Computer Architecture.

[GRIL93] Grillo, D., MacNamee, R.J.G., and Rashidzadeh, B. (1993). Towards third generation mobile systems: A European possible transition path. *Computer Networks and ISDN Systems*, 25(8).

[GRON92] Gronert, E. (1992). MANS make their mark in Germany. *Data Communications International*, May.

[HAFN94] Hafner, K. (1994). Making sense of the internet. *Newsweek*, October 24.

[HALL92] Hall, M. (ed.). (1992). LAN-based ATM products ready to roll out. *LAN Technology*, September.

[HAND91] Handel, R., and Huber, M.N. (1991). *Integrated broadband networks: An introduction to ATM-based networks*. Addison-Wesley.

[HERM93] Herman, J., and Serjak C. (1993). ATM switches and hubs lead the way to a new era of switched internetworks. *Data Communications*, March.

[HEWL91] Hewlett Packard, Inc. (1991). Introduction to SONET, A tutorial.

[HEWL92] Hewlett Packard, Inc. (1992). Introduction to SONET networks and tests, An internal document.

[HEYW93] Heywood, P. (1993). PTTs gear up to offer high-speed services. *Data Communications*, August.

[HILL91] SONET, An overview. A paper prepared by Hill Associates, Inc., Winooski, VT, 05404.

[HUNT92] Hunter, P. (1992). What price progress?, *Communications International*, June.

[ITU93a] ITU-TS (1993). ITU-TS draft recommendation Q93.B "B-ISDN user-network interface layer 3 specification for basic call/bearer control. May.

[JAYA81] Jayant, N.S., and Christensen, S.W. (1981). Effects of packet losses on waveform-coded speech and improvements due to an odd-even interpolation procedure. *IEEE Transactions of Communications*, February.

[JOHN91] Johnson, J.T. (1991). Frame relay mux meets cell relay switch. *Data Communications*, October.

[JOHN92] Johnson, J.T. (1992). "Getting access to ATM. *Data Communications LAN Interconnect*, September 21.

[KING94] King, S.S. (1994). Switched virtual networks. *Data Communications*, September.

[KITA91] Kitawaki, N., and Itoh, K. (1991). Pure delay effects of speech quality in telecommunications. *IEEE Journal of Selected Areas in Communications*, May.

[LEE89] Lee, W.C.Y. (1989). *Mobile cellular telecommunications systems*. McGraw-Hill.

[LEE93] Lee, B.G., Kang, M., and Lee, J. (1993). *Broadband telecommunications technology*. Artech House.

[LISO91] Lisowski, B. (1991). Frame relay: what it is and how it works. *A Guide to Frame Relay, Supplement to Business Conmunications Review*, October.

[LIZZ94] Lizzio, J.R. (1994). Real-time RAID stokrage: the enabling technology for video-on-demand. *Telephony*, May 23.

[LYLE92] Lyles, J.B., and Swinehart, D.C. (1992). The emerging gigabit environment and the role of the local ATM. *IEEE Communications Magazine*, April.

[McCO94] McCoy, E. (1994). SONET, ATM and other broadband technologies. TRA Document # ATL72 16.9100, *Telecommunications Research Associates*, St. Marys, KS.

[MCQU91] McQuillan, J.M. (1991). Cell relay switching. *Data Communications*, September.

[MINO93] Minoli D. (1993). Proposed Cell Relay Bearer Service Stage 1 Description, T1S1.1/93-136 (Revision 1), ANSI Committee T1 (T1S1.1), June.

[MORE9] Moreney, J. (1994). ATM switch decision can wait, *Network World*, September 19.

[NOLL91] Nolle, T. (1991). Frame relay: Standards advance, *Business Communications Review*, October.

[NORT94] Northern Telecom. (1994). Consultant Bulletin 63020.16/02-94, Issue 1, February.

[[NYQU24] Nyquist, H. (1924). Certain factors affecting telegraph speed. *Transactions A.I.E.E.*

[PERL85] Perlman, R. (1985). An algorithm for distributed computation of spanning tree in an extended LAN. *Computer Communications Review, 15*(4) September.

[ROSE92] Rosenberry, W., Kenney D., and Fisher, G. (1992). *Understanding DCE.* O'Reilly & Associates.

[SALA92] Salamone, S. (1992). Sizing up the most critical issues. *Network World.*

[SAND94] Sandberg, J. (1994). Networking. *Wall Street Journal*, November 14.

[SHAN48] Shannon, C. (1948). Mathematical theory of communication, *Bell System Technical Journal, 27*, July and October.

[SRIR90a] Sriram, K. (1990a). Dynamic bandwidth allocation and congestion control schemes for voice and data integration in wideband packet technology, *Proc. IEEE. Supercomm/ICC '90, 3*, April.

[SRIR90b] Sriram, K. (1990b). Bandwidth allocation and congestion control scheme for an integrated voice and data network. *US Patent No. 4, 914650*, April 3.

[SRIR93a] Sriram, K. (1993). Methodologies for bandwidth allocation, transmission scheduling, and congestion avoidance in broadband ATM networks. *Computer Networks and ISDN Systems, 26*(1), September.

[SRIR93b] Sriram, K., and Lucantoni, D.M. (1993). Traffic smoothing effects of bit dropping in a packet voice multiplexer. *IEEE Transactions on Communications*, July.

[STEW92] Steward, S.P. (1992). The world report '92. *Cellular Business*, May.

[WADA89] Wada, M. (1989). Selective recovery of video packet loss using error concelment. *IEEE Journal of Selected Areas in Communications*, June.

[WALL91] Wallace, B. (1991). Citicorp goes SONET. *Network World*, November 18.

[WERK92] Wernik, M., Aboul-Magd, O., and Gilber, H. (1992). Traffic management for B-ISDN services. *IEEE Network*, September.

[WEST92] Westgate, J. (1992).*OSI Management*, NCC Blackwell.

[WILL92] Williamson, J. (1992). GSM bids for global recognition in a crowded cellular world. *Telephony*, April 6.

[WU93] Wu, T.-H. (1993). Cost-effective network evolution. *IEEE Communications Magazine*, September.

[YAP93] Yap, M.-T., and Hutchison (1993). An emulator for evaluating DQDB performance. *Computer Networks and ISDN Systems, 25*(11).

[YOKO93] Yokotani, T., Sato, H., and Nakatsuka, S. (1993). A study on a performance improvement algorithm in DQDB MAN. *Computer Networks and ISDN Systems, 25*(10).

Abbreviations

2 B+D: B, B and D channels
AA: Administrative authority
AAL CP: AAL common part
AAL: ATM adaptation layer
ADM: Add-drop multiplexer
ADPCM: Adaptive differential pulse code modulation
AFI: Authority Format Identifier
AIS: Alarm indication signals
ANSI: American National Standards Institute
AP DPCM: Adaptive Predictive DPCM
APS: Automatic protection switching
ATM: Asynchronous transfer mode
B-ICI: B-ISDN Intercarrier Interface
B-ISDN: Broadband-Integrated Services Digital Network B-ISDN
B_c Committed burst rate
B_e: Excess burst rate
BECN: Backward explicit congestion notification
BER: Basic encoding rules; Bit error rate
BI: Bipolar code
BIP-8: Bit interleaved parity 8 field
BITS: Building integrated timing system
BLER: Block error rate
BRI: Basic rate interface
BSHR: Bi-directional SHR
C: Cell loss priority
C-Plane: Control-plane
C/R: Command/response
C/S or C/SAR: Convergence services and segmentation and reassembly
CAC: Connection admission control
CBR: Constant bit rate
CDV: Cell delay variation
CEI: Connection endpoint identifier
CES: Circuit emulation service
CIR: Committed information rate
CLP: Cell loss priority
CMIP: Common Management Information Protocol
CPCS: Common part of convergence sublayer (aka Common part CS)
CPE: Customer premises equipment
CRBS: Cell relay bearer service
CRC: Cyclic redundancy check
CRS: Cell relay service
CS: Convergence sublayer
CSU: Channel service unit
DCC: Data country code

DCE: Data circuit-terminating equipment
DCS: Digital cross connect
DE: Discard eligibility
DFI: Domain format identifier
DLCI: Data link connection identifier
DPCM: Differential pulse code modulation
DQDB: Distributed queue dual bus
DSP: Domain specific part
DSU: Data service unit
DXI: Data exchange interface
E/O: Electrical/optical
EA: Address extension
ECSA: Exchange Carriers Standards Association
EFI: Errored frame indicator
EIM: External interface module
EIR: Excess information rate
ESF: T1 extended superframe
FECN: Forward explicit congestion notification
FERF: Far-end receive failure
FIFO: First-in, first-out
FRS: Frame relay service
GCRA: Generic cell rate algorithm
GFC: Generic flow control
HDLC: High level data link control
HEC: Header error control
ICD: International code designator
ICI: Intercarrier interface
ICIP: ICI protocol
ID: Identifier
IDI: Initial domain identifier
IDP: Initial Domain Part
IE: Information element
ILMI: Interim local management interface
ISDN: Integrated services digital network
ISO: International Standards Organization
ITU-T or ITU-TS: Formerly known as CCITT
IWF: Interworking functions
IWU: Interworking unit
IXC: Interexchange carrier
LAN: Local area network
LAPD: Link access procedure for the D channel
LATA: Local access and transport area
LCNs: Logical channel numbers
LI: Length indicator
LMEs: Layer management entities
LMI: Local management interface
LOF: Loss of frame

LOP: Loss of pointer
LOS: Loss of signal
LSB: Least significant bit
M bit: More data bit
M-plane: Management plane
MAN: Metropolitan Area Network
MIB: Management information base
MID: Message identification
ms: Millisecond ms
MSB: Most significant bit
NANP: North American Numbering Plan
NE: Network element
NNI: Network-to-network interface
NT: Network termination
NUI: Network interface unit
OAMP: Operation, administration, maintenance, and provisioning services
OAM or OAMP: Operation, administration, and maintenance services or Operation, administration, maintenance, and provisioning services
OC-n: Optical carrier signal
OC: Optical carrier
OS: Operating system
OSI: Open Systems Interconnection
OUI: Organization unique ID
PA: Pre-arbitrated access
PAM: Pulse amplitude modulation
PCI: Protocol control information
PCM: Pulse code modulation
PCR: Peak cell rate
PD: Propagation delay
PDH: Plesiochronous digital hierarchy
PDUs: Protocol data units
PL: Physical layer
PLCP: Physical layer convergence protocol
PM: Physical medium (sublayer)
PMD: Physical media dependent
PPS: Path protection switching
PRI: Primary rate interface
PTI: Payload type identifier
PTOs: Public Telecommunications Operators
PTTs: Postal Telephone and Telegraph Ministries
PVCs: Permanent virtual circuits
QA: Queued arbitrated access
QD: Queuing delay
QOS: Quality of service
RBOCs: Regional Bell Operating Companies
RTS: Return to send

SAAL: Signaling ATM adaptation layer
SAPs: Service access points
SAR: Segmentation and reassembly
SCR: Sustainable cell rate
SD: Switching delay
SDH: Synchronous Digital Hierarchy
SDU: Service data unit
SFM: Switch fabric module
SMDS: Switched Multi-megabit Data Services
SN: Sequence number
SNI: Subscriber-to-network
SNMP: Simple Network Management Protocol
SNP: Sequence number protection
SONET: Synchronous Optical Network
SPE: Synchronous payload envelope
SS7: Signaling system #7
SSCF: Service specific coordination function
SSCOP: Service specific connection-oriented part
SSCS: Service specific CS
STDM: Statistical time division multiplexer
STP: Shielded twisted pair
STS: Synchronous transport signal
SVC: Switched virtual calls
TA: Terminal adapter
TAT: Theoretical arrival time
TC: Transmission convergence
T_c: Time interval
TCP Transaction Control Protocol
TCP/IP Transaction Control Protocol/Internet Protocol
TDM: Time division multiplexing
TE: Terminal equipment
TEI: Terminal endpoint identifier
TMM: Transmission monitoring machine
TS: Timestamp
TSI: Time slot interchanger
U-plane: User plane
UDP: User datagram protocol
UME: UNI management entity
UNI: User-to-network interface
UPC: Usage parameter control
VBR: Variable bit rate
VC: Virtual channel
VC: Virtual container
VCC: Virtual channel connection
VCI: Virtual circuit identifier
VPC Virtual path connection
VPN: Virtual private network
VT: Virtual tributary
WAN: Wide area network

Index

Note to readers: Page numbers referring to a figure are marked with an italic *F*, page numbers referring to a table are marked with an italic *T*, and page numbers referring to a calculation are marked with an italic *C*.